TERRY SPINKS MBE

Life was a Roller-Coaster

Terry Spinks as a young amateur boxer wearing the black vest of West Ham.

TERRY SPINKS MBE

Life was a Roller-Coaster

Bob Lonkhurst

Published by BL Associates

Published by
BL Associates
6 Drayton Avenue
Potters Bar
Hertfordshire

First published 2012

Printed and Bound in Great Britain by
Berforts Information Press Ltd,
Stevenage, Hertfordshire

A catalogue record for this book is
available from the British Library

ISBN 978-0-9540271-6-2

CONTENTS

Also by Bob Lonkhurst

MAN OF COURAGE: *The Life and Career of Tommy Farr*

GENTLEMAN OF THE RING: *The Life and Career of Jack Petersen*

EAST END IDOL: *The Amazing Story of Terry Spinks MBE*

FEN TIGER: *The Success of Dave 'Boy' Green*

LIFE IS JUST A SCHEME: *Autobiography of Danny Clark*
(Charity Publication)

CHATTERIS THUNDERBOLT: *The Eric Boon Story*

DEDICATION

FOR

ROSEMARY

A special lady whose love, patience, caring and understanding ensured Terry overcame long periods of ill health to live a comfortable albeit restricted life in his later years.

.....but never forgetting the skill, professionalism and kindness of consultant neurosurgeon Mr Fary Afshar and neurologist Dr. John Jestico.

FOREWORD

Boxing is surely the most unique activity within the field of sport. Despite the demands and effects of combat, the respect between fighters of all levels is incredible. Consequently, many lifelong friendships have been formed following battles in the ring. The warmth which existed between Terry Spinks and Bobby Neill more than 40 years after their three incredible fights in London is a classic example. Their respect for one another was moving.

Terry also became friends with Derry Treanor and the late Billy Rafferty, both of whom defeated him. He made many trips to Scotland during the 1960's, stayed at their homes and went racing with them. It was as though they were old school chums. For many years he was close to the late Howard Winstone who took the British title from him in 1961, and wept openly when told of Howard's death.

To demonstrate the esteem in which Spinks was held, I have decided against a traditional foreword written by a household name. Instead, I invited a number of leading personalities from entertainment and boxing, as well as former opponents, to open this book with tributes of their own. It came as no surprise that nobody refused.

Terry's trip to the Melbourne Olympics in 1956 was due almost entirely to an exhaustive press campaign of which Reg Gutteridge OBE was a prime mover. It is therefore appropriate that his words head the sequence of tributes.

'This is a story of public acclaim from medals to misery; the constant fight to survive and win a battle of the booze and despondency. The chirpy cockney kid, introduced to royalty and a succession of mayors, modelled for Madam Tussauds, clowned with the Crazy Gang, was admired by the Russians and had a foreign postage stamp issued in his honour. He lost to only one Englishman, retired at 24, and as a Vice-President of the London ExBoxers Association, is still hailed and hoorayed while attending numerous charity events.

The author, with painstaking research and hours of interviewing, including some former opponents, has made Spinks as individual as a fingerprint. I was ringside for all his professional fights and the pink-faced little champion never failed to please nor pleaded excuses. His story is filled with success, but also sadness. It is remarkably revealing and gripping. You really couldn't make it up.'

Reg Gutteridge OBE
(International Broadcaster and Sports Writer).

* * *

'If Terry Spinks makes a come-back, he could still be champ. I don't mind if he hits me because he's bigger than me. I'm used to falling over! It's been a pleasure to watch him at work. I'll bet his book will be a knockout.'

Sir Norman Wisdom

* * *

'Terry Spinks was always a hero in our household. I was just a kid when he won gold in the Olympics, but like the rest of the country, we all cheered his wonderful achievement. It was when he turned professional, however, that I really began to take a long term interest in his career.

My father, the comedian Ted Ray, was a great boxing fan as old time fighters will know, and would always be seen at the big shows around London. He used to bring me home programmes of the tournaments, and I watched with interest as Terry Spinks crept up the bill until he was headlining the shows.

What a wonderful career he had, and what pleasure he gave to so many people. Terry has always been a gentleman inside and outside the ring, and I am honoured to call him my friend as I often see him at the London Ex-Boxers Association meetings.

I would like to join the long list of people who demand that Terry's wonderful achievement at the Olympic Games should be recognised in the Queen's Honours List.'

Andrew Ray
(Actor).

* * *

'I was lucky to be a reporter with *Boxing News* and then Terry's local newspaper the *Stratford Express* when the 'Golden Boy' was at his peak. Apart from remembering his wonderful boxing skill and a left jab that was forged in heaven, I have warm memories of him being a loveable rascal. He and the other two Terrys (Gill and Brown), were king leg-pullers who could make life very perplexing for a young newspaper reporter learning his trade. Many was the time they would feed me false information just to see if I would fall for it.

Those were the good old days when sports journalists could be trusted to protect their friends in the game, and I used to turn a blind eye to the 'Golden Boy's' shenanigans. Some would say I was being less than professional by not reporting his extra curricular activities, but I was of the opinion that what he did in private was his personal business.

I think his marvellous manager, Sammy (Smiler) McCarthy, would agree with me when I say that if Terry had been just that bit more dedicated as a professional he could have challenged for world honours, but he took the decision to enjoy life, and who can blame him for that?

He is a lovely boy (I still think of him as being the cherubic youngster I watched from his days of proudly wearing the West Ham black vest), and I would like to see a statue erected to him in east London while he is still alive so that he knows how much he was, and is loved and admired. Box on, Tel.'

Norman Giller
(Author and Journalist).

* * *

'When I was a lad I used to go to the library to find out as much as I could about great East End fighters. I knew a great deal about Berg, Lewis and many others, but to my mind Terry Spinks was always the greatest.

He is my hero, both as an amateur and professional, and as a young boxer I tried to model myself on him. I was proud and thrilled when I got to know him, and I still love him to this day.'

John H Stracey
(Former world welterweight champion).

* * *

'Terry was a terrific amateur, but lacked power as a professional. Consequently, he had to work hard for every minute of every round. He became champion because he had a tremendous heart and incredible determination.

I was a fighter who got really steamed-up before a fight except when I fought Terry. It was a strange thing, but I can only put it down to the fact that he was such a lovely guy.

We had three real battles, but there was never any hard feeling. I was so sorry when I heard how ill he was, especially when I realised how lucky I had been. I have always been very fond of Terry and still love meeting him.'

Bobby Neill
(Former British featherweight champion).

* * *

'I have known Terry since he was a young schoolboy, and he is the same now as he was then, polite, smart, with a wonderful personality and sense of humour.

As a boxer he had tremendous natural ability, and I honestly believe that if he had been more dedicated to training he could have become world champion.

We have stuck together through many highs and lows, but we are as close today as when Terry was boxing. He is my dearest friend.'

Sammy McCarthy
(Former British featherweight champion, manager and life-long friend of Spinks).

* * *

'My greatest victory was the night I beat Terry Spinks because of his greatness as a boxer. I was more elevated by that victory than any other in my entire career.'

Derry Treanor
(Former British featherweight title challenger who beat Spinks at Streatham Ice Rink on 1 September 1959).

* * *

'Terry was the kindest, best-hearted man I have ever known. I never heard him say a bad word about anyone. He couldn't walk past a tramp in the street without giving him a few quid. He must have given thousands away, but the trouble was he got taken advantage of because of his generosity.'

John Branch
(Former Army PTI, Boxing Trainer, and Terry's employer for more than a decade).

* * *

'You were the best when you won gold in a vest.'

Ken Buchanan MBE
(Former world lightweight champion).

* * *

'Nobody ever taught Terry, it was all natural ability with him. He never knew what he was going to do, it was all reaction.

If he had been a more vigorous trainer he would have been a world champion. He was totally undisciplined and would laugh if he could have one over on the trainer. Yet he had a tremendous heart which was demonstrated by the fact that each time he won a title he had to overcome men who had previously beaten him - Vladimir Stolnikov and Bobby Neill.'

Bob Paget
(Boxing trainer and life-long friend of Spinks).

* * *

'Terry was the best known sporting face in the country during the 1960's and '70's. Everywhere we went people knew him. Not just in London, but in Wales, Scotland, Ireland and the Midlands, it didn't matter. He was always the centre of attraction, and everyone wanted to be with him.

We've always had something special. When he trained me, we were like father and son, or even brothers. I love him to death, and that comes from the heart.'

Johnny Claydon
(Former amateur and professional boxer trained by Spinks. Was Southern Area lightweight champion and two-time British title challenger).

* * *

'Winning the gold medal as he did was an incredible achievement. He was only 18, just a wee boy, but he fought like a real man. He was exceptional, and can be compared with Muhammed Ali at the same age.

We have been friends for 45 years. I love him to bits and would travel to London at the drop of a hat to see him. Just hearing his name makes me get all the Melbourne memorabilia out.'

Dick McTaggart
(Olympic gold medallist 1956, British Empire & Commonwealth Games champion 1958, European gold medallist 1961, five-times ABA champion).

* * *

'The true boxing fans all admire and respect Terry. When he joined the London Ex-Boxers Association it was a two-way thing. He is good for us, and becoming a member got him back into boxing again. Since becoming a Vice-President he has represented the Association at many functions. He is a first class ambassador for us and the sport of boxing in general. By not being honoured for his Olympic achievement we felt he had been let down by the nation.'

Stephen Powell
(President of the London Ex-Boxers Association).

* * *

'Everyone looked up to Terry when he came back from the Olympics with a gold medal. He was always a very smart, go forward little gentleman who never got into any bother. We became close friends, and I still respect him today like I did when he was boxing. He has been a credit to the sport.'

Billy Walker
(Former ABA heavyweight champion, England international, and challenger for the British and European heavyweight titles).

* * *

'Everyone who knows anything about boxing knows who Terry Spinks is and what his achievements were. I first met Terry when I was a young amateur in the 1970's, and wanted to follow in his footsteps and win a gold medal. Alas, it wasn't to be.

Terry has remained a close friend ever since, and after my retirement from boxing has supported all my charity events. He is a diamond and a real East End hero. Above all, he is a man of honour.'

Charlie Magri
(Former World, British and European flyweight champion).

* * *

'When Terry won the gold medal at Melbourne in 1956, I was as excited as if I had won it myself.

There I was watching the Olympics on TV when I saw this little boy I had boxed in an exhibition on a Stable Lads show three years earlier. I hadn't even realised he won an ABA title because he looked too young to be a boxer.

From that point, I followed his career with interest, and my only regret is that we never met in the ring as professionals. It would have been an incredible contest of skill, and a wonderful advert for boxing.'

Dai Dower MBE
(Former European, British and British Empire flyweight champion).

* * *

'I owe my whole career to Terry Spinks. He introduced me to boxing which eventually got me into acting. Although he was the

'Golden Boy' who everyone wanted to be with, he was like a second dad to me, and first took me to football at West Ham when I was only nine. There were always long queues in those days, but if we couldn't get in he would bunk me through a back door.

I'll always remember how polite he was to people, he is a great ambassador for sport. I am proud and privileged to know him, and still have his gold dressing gown he gave me years ago.'

Glen Murphy
(Actor -London's Burning).

* * *

'Even before I won a boxing title, I used to think Terry Spinks was the finest amateur champion on earth. I still thought so when I was undisputed world middleweight champion. I was emotional about him, and had so much admiration and respect for him. He had won an Olympic gold medal, so it was an honour to be in his company. You couldn't meet a better person than Terry.'

Alan Minter
(Former undisputed world middleweight champion).

ACKNOWLEDGEMENTS

The books about Terry Spinks would never have been possible without the help of many people, not least my good friend the late Reg Gutteridge, OBE. Unable to make the commitment himself, Reg asked if the task interested me. The fact that he thought I was capable of it has to be the greatest compliment of my short journalistic career. I extend my gratitude to him and sincerely hope that the end products would have met with his professional approval.

Special thanks go to Sammy McCarthy for his invaluable contribution. A life-long friend of Spinks, he provided me with a succession of amusing stories as well as dealing with important aspects of their relationship in boxing.

I am extremely grateful to Jarvis Astaire, Johnny Claydon, Jackie Bowers, Terry Rees, Terry Gill, Terry Murphy, Johnny Thurgood and Bernie Dillon, all of whom were close to Spinks during his boxing days. Their contributions have been immense.

Former opponents, Bobby Neill, Derry Treanor and Terry Toole found time to provide great insight into their contests with Terry for whom all retain special affection. I thank them.

Terry's first wife Valerie and their son Jarvis provided valuable information concerning family life, while John Branch, Alfie Betts, Tony Rawlinson, Noel Boston, Nobby Clarke and Barry Noonan dealt with many matters unconnected with boxing. I was also assisted by Donnie Dirs, Raymond Lee and a host of other people to a lesser degree.

Many people volunteered tributes to Terry, and I make special mention of Sir Norman Wisdom, Dai Dower, John H Stracey, Billy Walker, Dick McTaggart, Bob Paget, Charlie Magri, Ken Buchanan, Alan Minter, Glen Murphy, Norman Giller, Andrew Ray and Stephen Powell. Their words confirm the esteem in which Terry was held, and I thank them for their time and consideration.

Claude Abrams, the former editor of *Boxing News*, kindly allowed me access to his photograph collection, while John Jarrett loaned cuttings of great significance.

I thank the staff of the National Newspaper Library at Colindale for their efficient and courteous service, the Public Records Office at Kew, and David Hamilton of the Court Service who gave particular help.

To ensure that this second book is as complete and accurate as possible I interviewed a number of people who were particularly close to Terry in the later years of his life. I mention in particular Terry Ellmore, Chris Carr, Richard Barber, Dave Porter and Lianne Jameson. I also thank Rob Strover who created the additional block of photographs.

I am particularly grateful to consultant neurosurgeon, Mr Fary Afshar and neurologist, Dr John Jestico, for affording me their valuable time for interviews. Their contributions enabled me to detail the extent of Terry's medical problems. It is also important to place on record that their skills and professionalism ensured that he survived several years longer than had been expected.

I extend sincere thanks to Lord Sebastian Coe for kindly allowing me to reproduce a moving message which he provided for an official brochure in 2006 to celebrate 50 years since Spinks and Dick McTaggart won their Olympic gold medals.

My special friend Sandie Ball patiently and professionally prepared the new chapters for this book and skilfully amended areas of the original one. I am also indebted to Nigel Wood, of Berforts Information Press Ltd, for his valuable assistance in fine tuning what was a difficult project.

Finally, I am indebted to Terry's cousin, Rosemary Ellmore, a remarkable lady who has worked tirelessly to assist me in preparing this and the original book. Apart from providing an abundance of documentation, she contacted many people on my behalf, made appointments and spent hours with me detailing difficult periods in Terry's life, particularly his illnesses. The books were her idea and she has been the driving-force and inspiration throughout. I hope I have not let her down.

INTRODUCTION

Fighters are unique people, in general representing a hard and often controversial sport with great dignity. At the end of gruelling and bloody contests, rarely do combatants fail to embrace one another with warmth and respect.

As a young fight fan my favourite venue was Shoreditch Town Hall where we queued to buy tickets for a card of six-rounders. Even without a championship contest the place was always packed, and the only security was a character named 'Sailor' on the door. The place buzzed with excitement, the atmosphere being like nowhere else I have ever been.

One of my early memories was of being amazed at the incredible support given to Terry Spinks, a young East End boxer who had just turned professional at the age of 19. I knew he had won a gold medal at the Melbourne Olympics the previous year, but thought he looked too young and frail to be fighting in the savage professional arena. Yet the more I watched him the more impressed I became. Never in my wildest dreams could I have imagined that more than 40 years later I would be asked to write his biography.

Terry's original biography, *East End Idol* was published in 2002 and completely sold out within months. Yet when he passed away in 2012 after a long illness, his story was far from complete because so much had happened during the ensuing 10 years. It was therefore decided to produce this second book incorporating all the new material with that contained in *East End Idol*. Suitable amendments and additions have been made to the original manuscript.

However, in view of the respect people had for Spinks I have used the tributes paid to him in the foreword of *East End Idol*.The opinions those individuals held for him a decade ago still apply today and it is therefore appropriate that they also form the beginning of this new book.

Four new chapters have also been written dealing with Terry's investiture at Buckingham Palace, relevant sporting and social events which he attended and the periods of poor health he endured, including a number of brain operations. An additional block of eight pages of black and white photographs have been added to illustrate the new material.

In order to write the books I spent many hours in Terry's company and was amazed at his popularity. Everywhere we went people recognised him. Whether it was at a social gathering or to meet an old opponent or friend, somebody would interrupt us wanting to shake his hand or have a chat. There were occasions when such interruptions were irritating or inconvenient, but Terry had time for everyone.

A chubby-faced, ever-smiling kid, Spinks grew up at Canning Town in the East End of London. He started boxing at the age of 10, but after winning a number of schoolboy honours, set his heart on becoming a jockey. He spent two years working at a Newmarket racing stable before weight problems brought his dream to an end.

Resuming his boxing career with the West Ham club, Terry won London and ABA flyweight championships in his first season as a senior, and boxed for England on five occasions. He was a star wherever he fought, being praised by local fans and critics in Warsaw and Berlin. He was cheered all the way to the dressing room in Moscow after losing a close decision at the Dynamo's Football Stadium.

Despite his considerable talent, the ABA selection committee considered Spinks too young and inexperienced to box in the forthcoming Olympic Games at Melbourne. This infuriated the press, and after a concerted campaign by experienced boxing writers for three London newspapers, he was a last minute choice. Just days beforehand he was emptying bins at the Albert Docks.

Undaunted by the task he faced, Terry beat five of the world's finest amateur boxers within a space of just eight days. His success made him the first British boxer to win a gold medal for 32 years. Prince Philip led the plaudits as he stood on the podium to receive it.

In April 1957, Spinks made the inevitable move into the professional ranks and won his first 19 contests. He had an incredible following and wherever he boxed there was a full house.

Always an immaculate dresser, he had a wardrobe full of stylish Italian suits, shirts and shoes. He bought a confectionery shop at Plaistow, ran a nice convertible car with personalised index plates, and owned a speedboat and caravan at Burnham-on-Crouch where he loved to spend time water-skiing. He had a wonderful sense of humour, and in one interview about his amateur career said, 'I have enough silverware to hold a banquet.'

Spinks was very high profile, and people wanted to be seen with him. The infamous Kray twins frequently invited him to charity functions they were hosting, prompting rumours regarding his association with them. Whenever they opened a club, Terry was invited to join other former East End boxers, show business personalities and people in public life, as a guest.

Respect, however is something of great importance in the East End, and that alone adequately sums up Terry's relationship with the Krays. Reggie in particular had great respect for him purely because he was a successful East End lad. In 1965, he invited Spinks to his wedding, and years later when he was ill in prison, always asked visitors how Terry Spinks was.

Regardless of what outsiders thought, Terry was never involved in any of the Krays' activities, and was never investigated or questioned by the authorities. They were former boxers themselves, they were fight fans and wanted to be seen with him. It was good for their image. In fact, Terry was not very street-wise and often asked one of their associates what line of business they were in. The gentleman in question always avoided the issue or changed the subject. Terry always maintained that he knew nothing of the Krays' affairs. 'I just knew them as honest businessmen,' he remarked.

In the ring, Spinks was being groomed as a future British champion, but three consecutive defeats during 1959 raised doubts as to whether he would make it. Stamina was his biggest problem, brought about by his love of the good life and a lack of discipline regarding his diet. Although he was a dedicated trainer, he had too greater liking for cream cakes, chocolate and bottles of pop.

Despite the set-backs, he battled back, and in September 1960 became British featherweight champion with a controversial stoppage victory over Bobby Neill. Two months later they met again in a winner takes all contest and Terry retained his title by a knockout in round 14.

Almost from the day he won the gold medal, Terry became something of a legend. His popularity continued to soar, his bank balance grew, but at a cost. His choirboy looks gradually began to show signs of his demanding trade. When he lost his title to the brilliant Howard Winstone in May 1961, it was clear that he was past his best.

Although he continued boxing for a further 18 months, Terry struggled against opponents who would have given him little trouble earlier in his career. When he retired from the ring in December 1962, he had the credible record of 41 victories and a draw from 49 contests.

Despite his massive popularity, life had not been a bed of roses for Terry. In fact it had been a massive roller-coaster ride. His addiction to gambling left him broke shortly after he retired from boxing, and in 1964 he was declared bankrupt, having paid insufficient income tax on his ring earnings. For several years he survived by doing contract cleaning, mini-cabbing and selling sporting goods.

In 1972 he got back into boxing when he was invited to train the South Korean boxing team for the Munich Olympics. Returning to Britain, he became a professional trainer for seven years before running two public houses in Kent and Sussex.

Fate then played its hand again. Two failed marriages followed by a serious illness resulting from excessive drinking, left him seriously ill in hospital for some time with brain damage. He was in a crisis situation. With his mother dead and his father in no position to look after him, he was facing the rest of his life in care.

At this point, however, Terry's story has a fairy-tale twist. Suddenly, his cousin Rosemary, with whom he spent school holidays as a boy, came to his aid. Although they had hardly seen each other for more than 20 years, she devoted her life to caring for him and bringing him back to good health.

When he was drinking heavily, Terry said he had nothing to live for. Without Rosemary, I am convinced that his life would have ended many years ago. She is a remarkable lady and a hero in her own right. Her love, patience caring and understanding gave the former gold medallist a life again and brought him back to respectability. One of the most respected British boxers, amateur or professional, his popularity had not waned one iota. At any big event, Terry Spinks was the man people wanted to meet.

Proof of his popularity was in his post bag, as almost daily letters arrived from all over the world. Fans requesting photographs and autographs sent good wishes along with moving comments about his career. The respect people had for Terry was never more evident to me than one night in February 2001 at Charlie Magri's pub at Mile End. He was one of many former champions attending a reunion event, and old opponent Bobby Neill pushed his way through the crowed bar to embrace him.

The same night, former world welterweight champion, John H Stracey, on hearing that I was writing Terry's biography, told of his fondness for the man and how he baby-sat his son. These were moving moments, but confirmed the esteem in which Spinks was held by former champions.

Terry is the only British boxer ever to have won a Schoolboys championship (1953), an ABA title (1956), Olympic gold medal (1956) and British professional title (1960). His achievements will never be forgotten, particularly in the East End, because he won his laurels at a time when competition was far greater than in modern times.

Winning the gold medal should have been officially recognised long ago. Sadly, those responsible for awarding New Year and Birthday honours continued to ignore Terry's nomination despite a determined campaign on his behalf for more than five years. This, however, only served to intensify the efforts of those seeking justice for the popular East End lad. People from all walks of life, including Members of Parliament and journalists, added their weight to a situation causing a great deal of frustration, anger and anguish.

The pressure and determination finally paid off, and towards the end of 2001 Terry was notified that he had been nominated for an MBE. When the official announcement was made, there was joy, excitement and tears from everyone who had worked so hard.

From a biographer's point of view, the timing was not good because plans were already in place to launch the original biography, *East End Idol*, on 28 February 2002, Terry's 64th birthday. The announcement of the honour meant that chunks of the manuscript had to be altered in double-quick time, leaving little opportunity for Christmas celebrations. Yet it was worth every minute of the extra work because celebrations of another kind loomed on the horizon.

Terry eventually received his MBE from Prince Charles at Buckingham Palace on 2 May 2002, which was Rosemary's birthday. This was followed by a massive party which the rejuvenated former boxer was well enough to thoroughly enjoy.

In 2005, however, there were signs that his health was deteriorating and over the next six years he underwent a series of brain operations. Although these were intermingled with spells of reasonable health, the strain was taking its toll. Eventually, in April 2012, his body gave up and he passed away peacefully at home with Rosemary at his side.

Researching Terry's life has been an absorbing and rewarding experience. It has also been demanding because so many people volunteered information. There are so many stories about him that one of the most difficult tasks was deciding what to leave out. He was absolutely idolised in the East End and that fact alone made selecting the title of his original biography so much easier. The title of this updated version is a statement of his incredible life.

I sincerely hope I have done Terry justice because his successes and misfortunes deserve to be chronicled. His story is amazing. It is one of success intermingled by failure, sadness tempered by humour, and not least of courage and emotion. He is part of East End folk-lore, and I consider myself extremely privileged to have known him and to have been given the opportunity to write his enthralling story.

Bob Lonkhurst
Potters Bar, 2012

1

BORN TO BE A FIGHTER

For more than a century the East End of London has been a hotbed for boxing. A densely populated area which stretches along the capital's docklands, it has always been one of the roughest and toughest parts of the United Kingdom.

Areas such as Stepney, Aldgate, Whitechapel, Bethnal Green, Bow, Mile End, Poplar, Canning Town and beyond have, for years, been the breeding grounds for fighters of all levels. Extensive damage sustained during two world wars, continuing high levels of unemployment, countless run-down properties and a large immigrant population are just a few of the factors which have contributed to making the region a haven for fighting.

Many great champions grew up and learned their trade amid poverty in the East End. In 1915, Ted 'Kid' Lewis from Aldgate won the world welterweight title; Teddy Baldock from Poplar was recognised as bantamweight champion of the world in 1927, and Jack 'Kid' Berg, affectionately known as 'The Whitechapel Whirlwind,' became junior lightweight champion in 1930. Many other boxers have won European, British and British Empire titles, yet all were seasoned professionals with years of experience behind them.

In 1956 a young amateur boxer from Canning Town joined the all-time greats from the East End when he travelled to the other side of the world to win an Olympic gold medal. Terry Spinks was just 18 years old when he became flyweight boxing champion in the Melbourne Olympics.

Terry's success made him the first Briton ever to win gold in the flyweight division, and the first man to win a boxing gold medal for his country in 32 years. It was an incredible achievement by a lad originally considered by the ABA selection committee to be too young and inexperienced to compete in such an important competition.

Undaunted by the task he faced, Spinks boxed with a maturity beyond his years to outpoint five of the world's finest amateur boxers within the space of just eight days. He was a real hero and an East End welcome awaited his return home.

* * *

Terry was born on 28 February 1938 at Plaistow Nursing Home, 26 Howards Road, London, E13. His parents lived at 115 Liverpool Road, Canning Town, but shortly after his birth moved to a small terraced house at 86 Morgan Street.

Adjacent to the Victoria Docks, Canning Town developed during the 1850's. It became a major industrial area and provided the work-force for the Thames Ironworks and Beckton Gasworks as well as the docks. There was, however, high unemployment during the early 1900's and the closure of the Thames Ironworks caused considerable distress and hardship to many families.

Much of the property in and around Canning Town was rented, but most was in poor condition. Money-grabbing landlords were reluctant to spend what was needed for proper maintenance, and there were insufficient laws to force them. During the 1930's hundreds of Victorian houses in the area had to be demolished because they were unfit for human habitation. Many others had to be shored up by huge blocks of timber while awaiting structural repairs.

Christened Terence George Spinks, Terry was an only child which, in some ways, proved to be an advantage. Despite being born during difficult times, he received tremendous love from both parents and wanted for nothing.

His father, George, affectionately known to everyone as 'Tich' because of his size, was a bookmaker, a trade he had been involved in all his life. Mum, Doris, a short blonde haired lady, was a tireless worker for everyone in her family and could turn her hand to a multitude of tasks.

Doris was an extremely homely person who loved cooking and housekeeping. She spent hours cleaning, and 86 Morgan Street was always immaculate. She was also exceptionally strong. Her father was a coal merchant, and from a young age Doris shovelled coal into sacks which she singled-handedly lifted up on to the cart. Her strength came in useful on several occasions when she became involved in disputes with both men and women.

Terry was just 18 months old when war broke out in 1939. His father joined the Royal Air Force, so with the East End under imminent threat of German bombs, Doris took Terry to Boughton, a village in Kent situated between Canterbury and Faversham. They rented a house opposite the village pub and were joined by Doris' sister-in-law Ethel and her daughter Shirley.

Nearby was a large army barracks where the Irish Regiment were based. Terry loved watching the soldiers, wearing their green berets with plumes at the front, marching on the parade ground. The movement of lorries and their equipment entertained him for hours.

Being too young to understand the dangers and implications of the war, Terry, like many other youngsters, saw it as one big adventure. Late evening was the most exciting time of the day as German planes flew overhead on bombing missions to London. There was tremendous excitement as soldiers from the Irish Regiment attacked them with anti-aircraft fire.

Terry loved the Kentish countryside and throughout the summer and autumn months accompanied his mother who worked on the land picking hops, fruit and potatoes. One of his most vivid memories was of seeing a dog-fight in the sky above Boughton. His mother was helping a farmer make bales of hay when they suddenly heard the screams of diving war planes. Several Spitfires were chasing a Messerschmidt which was eventually shot down.

The German pilot was seen to bail out and within minutes local British soldiers told everyone in the field to go to their houses and lock their doors. Doris took Terry straight home and put him to bed, but as soon as she had left the room he went to the window to see what was happening outside. About half an hour later a policeman called at the house saying everyone could go about their business. The German pilot had been captured and was detained in the guardroom at the barracks.

By this stage of his life Terry had seen very little of his father. As a Sergeant Flight Engineer in the Royal Air Force, Tich was stationed at RAF Cottesmore in Leicestershire working specifically on the Lancaster bombers. Incredibly, he remained there for the duration of the war, some sources claiming it was because he was the camp bookmaker.

Throughout the war, Tich got just two weeks holiday a year, and a weekend leave every two months. In order to see his wife and son he would sometimes travel to Kent, but his stay would be no more than 36 hours.

There were occasions when the family would meet at Morgan Street although this was rare because of the danger from bombing raids. On one occasion when Terry was about three years old, Doris took him home to see his father. Although their house was undamaged, they were horrified to find that three properties on the opposite side of the road had been demolished by bombs. In an adjoining street six more houses had been reduced to heaps of rubble. Fortunately, Terry was too young to understand the significance of what had occurred, and the horrific sight left no lasting memories.

The blitz was the most disastrous event in the history of the East End. Between September 1940 and April 1941, the entire area was battered and burned. Night after night, with the docks and City of London as their targets, droning German bombers filled the skies like locusts. The raids became so frequent that it was headline news whenever there was a lull. People were petrified as every night they huddled in air-raid shelters and the underground not knowing if they would see their homes again. Nights without sirens were an exception.

In West Ham there was total devastation. More than 1,100 people were killed and about 6,000 injured. The worst night was 19 March 1941 when 176 high explosive bombs and mines, and countless incendiary bombs were dropped on the Borough. Over 580 premises were hit in one single night of horror. By the last 'all-clear,' the toll of damage in West Ham alone read: 32 factories demolished, 68 schools destroyed and damaged, 110 churches hit, and eight hospitals put out of action.

At the age of five, Terry started school at Staple Street Primary at Boughton. Although he was taught basic arithmetic and reading, the only lesson he really liked was games. He was adventurous but lacked concentration, and all he wanted to do was go outside in the playground.

One day when he was about six he was running to school when he got knocked down by an army lorry. Without looking, he ran out of an alley into the road where the lorry struck him. He was rushed to Canterbury hospital where it was found that he had suffered nothing more serious than bruising and shock. After being detained for a few days a policeman collected him from the hospital and took him home.

Terry's favourite animals were horses. With his father being a bookmaker and his Uncle Johnny a jockey, much of the family conversation related to them. Whenever he went to a farm with his mother, the only animals he was interested in were horses.

During the war, his Uncle was a medic in the Royal Navy and stationed in Africa. He thought a great deal about Terry and often sent him parcels containing statues of race horses with jockeys on their backs. They were mounted on small boxes which he always filled with sweets.

'There you go son, your Uncle Johnny's written again,' the postman would say to Terry each time he delivered a parcel from Africa.

* * *

As soon as the war was over Terry and his mother returned home to Morgan Street, a property they rented from a private landlord. It was extremely compact with a living room at the front, a back room and scullery. Upstairs there were two bedrooms, the staircase to which was concealed behind what looked like a cupboard door.

There was no bathroom, and the toilet was a basic cubicle in the back yard. Nevertheless, hygiene was important and twice a week Doris stood a tin bath in the middle of the kitchen floor and filled it with three large saucepans of water which had been boiled on the gas stove. Jugs of cold water were added and Terry was always the first to be bathed. His mother and father followed, both using the same water. On other occasions when Terry needed a good wash, Doris put him in the kitchen butler sink and cleaned him up.

The Spinks family were extremely fortunate because despite Canning Town and neighbouring areas being the most heavily bombed, there was no damage to their house. All around them, war had completely demolished streets of houses along with factories and other types of property. Many of those left standing had structural damage or windows blown out from nearby blasts. Heaps of rubble and timber spilled across pavements into the roads making them impassable to traffic. It was a brutal contrast from the relative tranquillity which Terry had become accustomed to in the Kent countryside.

Many people were homeless, and food and soup were provided at public halls. Prefabricated houses known as Nissen Huts were erected in many streets as temporary accommodation. Yet East End folk have always been unique for the way they support one another in a crisis. They worked and socialised together, went to dances and sporting events determined to put the devastation of war behind them. Many houses were crowded as those fortunate enough to have avoided catastrophe cared for others whose homes had been destroyed.

As life slowly got back to normality, the characters of the East End went about their business. Every day cries could be heard from the chimney sweep, rag and bone man and toffee apple seller. Terry and his mates got to know them all, but his favourite was an elderly knife-sharpener who rode the streets on a tricycle fitted with a large circular stone.

Terry was a well brought up boy, his parents having taught him good manners from a very young age. He treated all adults with great respect, and those he didn't know well he addressed as Mr or Mrs. Adults closer to him were called Aunt or Uncle. He would never dream of answering back, but whenever he did misbehave, his mother was quick to give him a good clout.

Despite the devastation and disruption caused by war, Terry didn't suffer as badly as many other youngsters in the poverty stricken East End. His father being a bookmaker, made good money, and other people in the family were also quite well off. Consequently, they saw to it that he didn't go without anything. His mother ensured that he had three meals a day, one of which was always hot. Sunday was special because Doris prepared a big roast with all the trimmings.

Terry spent a lot of time with Grandpa Jordan, his mum's father, who was a coal merchant. He had stables at nearby Freemasons Road and most evenings Terry went there with him to feed the horses. It was a real thrill for him whenever he was lifted up into the back of one of the big carts.

Grandpa Jordan also had a lorry, and during the summer and autumn months made frequent trips to Kent where he bought large quantities of fresh fruit at wholesale prices. It was a profitable sideline to his coal business, and at weekends he set up a stall outside his house and did a roaring trade. Large queues of people formed all day because after the bleak years of war fresh fruit was a real luxury in the East End.

Every summer, Terry, his mother, Aunt Ethel and cousin Shirley returned to Kent for the hop-picking season. It was an annual event for London families, and for many a working holiday. Each family had their own hut in the hop fields where the women did the cooking. Doris always took Terry on the train while Grandpa Jordan took all the bedding and heavy belongings needed for a four week stay, in his lorry.

* * *

It was not until after he returned to Canning Town that Terry really got to know his father. War had deprived them of precious years together, but once he was discharged from the Royal Air Force, Tich became the perfect dad. He set aside at least one evening a week which he devoted entirely to Terry who longed for him to come home from work in the evenings. Being an only child he got extra love and attention. They idolised each other and built a close father and son relationship which would last for life.

As soon as he was back in civilian life, Tich resumed his street bookmaking activities. He was clever with figures, having received a good education. When he was 18 he started work as a clerk for well-known East End bookmaker, Bert Tatman, at an office in Hermit Road, Canning Town. He packed it up when he joined the RAF, but after the war decided to set up business on his own.

As it was a full-time occupation, Tich had a telephone installed in the back room of 86 Morgan Street which he used as his office. An old-fashioned object with a handle at the side, it was mounted on a wooden box on a cupboard. Local people wanting a bet knew all they had to do was call Albert Dock 2865.

As a street bookmaker, Tich had a number of people working for him as 'runners'. Most mornings they would stand at known locations on the streets, collect cash and betting slips from punters and take them to Tich at Morgan Street before the racing began. Saturday was the busiest day of the week, and at tea-time Tich and his cronies would sit around the kitchen table doing up the bets and counting their profit. Eight hundred pounds for a week's hard graft was not uncommon and represented a huge amount of money in the late 1940's.

Most bets taken were of just a few shillings win or each-way. A pound or more was a big bet as most of the punters were ordinary working-class folk, or often the unemployed gambling their dole money.

Big races such as the Grand National and Derby attracted a huge number of bets. As street betting was illegal, Tich was always uneasy on big race days. The continuous stream of 'runners' calling at his house with bundles of betting slips and pockets full of cash was always likely to attract the attention of the law. Everyone involved therefore had to be constantly on their guard, taking different routes to Morgan Street or going round the block a few times to see if they were being followed.

Whilst some police officers were prepared to turn a blind eye to the activities in exchange for certain considerations, they did have to show some arrests. Nevertheless, many a pound passed from bookmaker to copper in order that street betting could flourish.

It was general knowledge that street bookmakers were not arrested very often. Most of the time, the police were content to feel the collars of 'ringers' on a charge of obstruction. Invariably, the allegation was that the individual arrested had shouted a warning thereby allowing the bookie to escape arrest. Usually the offender had no previous convictions meaning that when he appeared at court he was ordered to pay a small fine. This was paid by the bookmaker who, meanwhile, continued to go about his business.

There were a few occasions when Tich got arrested, but often by prior arrangement with the police. It was good business sense because he knew most of the local officers and liked to keep them sweet. This way, they got arrests and he was allowed certain freedom to work. He always pleaded guilty because he knew the likely penalty would be a fine. After the magistrate had given him a formal seven days to pay he went back to his patch and carried on as before. Within a few hours he usually had enough ready cash to pay the fine.

This was the environment the young Terry Spinks grew up in. At a very young age he knew all the dodges that were worked and nothing was kept from him. It was a way of life. He also knew that many of the local coppers liked a bet so he never had any fears of anything terrible happening to his dad.

Despite his tender age, Terry picked up on everything and was soon trying to copy his father. 'I get my kicks through playing the horses,' he told a Sunday newspaper reporter many years later. 'I have done since I was an eight year-old who ran a book among our street gang, and fluttered a bob when I could raise it.'

* * *

After settling back at Canning Town, Terry went to St Lukes Junior School and it was there that he learned the basics of the noble art. One day a teacher asked if any boys in the class wanted to join the school boxing club. 'To tell you the truth, I wasn't that keen on school and didn't go much on most of the lessons either,' Terry recalled years later. So, thinking it might help him miss some lessons, he put up his hand.

The club was run by the headmaster, Mr. Iceon, who soon realised that Terry had natural ability. He took a personal interest in him and apart from sessions in the club, stayed behind after school on other occasions to give him personal tuition. 'He was a smashing schoolmaster,' said Terry. 'Due to him I got really hooked on boxing and I am ever thankful to him.'

Most kids in the East End were taught to defend themselves at an early age, but Terry already knew quite a bit about boxing. His father often told him about the days when he boxed as a boy at Star Lane Secondary School. Terry also loved listening to stories about his great uncle, Sid Butler, a professional middleweight from Canning Town who had been a sparring partner to Len Harvey.

Sid was a real crowd pleaser who often boxed over 15 rounds. Between 1925 and 1931 he had 52 fights of which he won 20, lost 23 and drew nine. He boxed at a number of London venues including Premierland, the Ring at Blackfriars and the National Sporting Club. He also travelled as far afield as Belfast, Plymouth, Leicester and Birmingham.

The first real fight Terry was ever involved in was when he was just seven. One afternoon he was walking home from school minding his own business when he was suddenly set upon by a bigger boy. Luckily, he was just outside his front door, so he called for his dad to hold his football boots. Without further ado, or any fear, he clouted the other boy and bloodied his nose. They had quite a set-to before Tich broke it up and gave them each half a crown.

'So you are going to be a boxer are you?' enquired Tich as Terry walked indoors.

'Yes dad,' he replied. 'I'm going in for boxing at school.'

As his love of boxing grew Terry joined the Lyle Amateur Boxing Club at Plaistow Wharf. Most large companies and factories in the East End had a boxing club and competition between them was keen. The gym of the Lyle was up several flights of stairs at the top of the factory.

Terry's first trainer was Billy 'Kid' Brookes, a former professional who had boxed out of Stratford. With his natural ability, Spinks progressed quickly and developed into a well schooled young boxer. His tiny frame and cherubic face were deceiving because he had a quick left jab and lightening footwork to match.

Despite standing only three feet ten inches tall and weighing under four stones, he had his first official contest within a few months of joining the Lyle club. He was in fact so small that he had some difficulty climbing through the ropes.

Terry could box rings round most of his school mates, prompting Tich to tell everyone his son had the makings of a champion. At first few people took much notice because many fathers tended to describe their sons' abilities in exaggerated terms. It was not long, however, before Terry proved his father's judgement to be sound.

Terry stayed at the Lyle Club for about a year before joining West Ham. By this time he had moved to Ashburton Road Secondary

School, and in his first term was entered for the West Ham Schools boxing championships. These were staged at Holbrooke Road School where four rings were erected in the school hall and teachers acted as the judges. After beating a number of boys to reach the final of the Minor B class, Terry won his first medal at the age of 11 in his first competition. His father was so proud that in the later years of his life he carried the medal with him attached to his watch-chain.

The following year Terry was not so successful, being outpointed in the final by one of his mates, Jackie Bowers. The defeat was by no means a disgrace because Jackie would go on to become a National Schoolboy champion in 1952, a successful senior amateur and eventually a professional. They boxed again the following year on a Festival of Britain show and Bowers, now a successful trainer at the Peacock gymnasium in Canning Town, was disqualified for persistent holding.

* * *

For many lads in the East End boxing became a way of life. Boys as young as eight had for years crammed into gyms in the roughest and most run down areas. Their sole purpose was learning how to box because it was a way by which they could express themselves and release their frustrations. For many it was boxing or a life of crime.

The West Ham Boys & Amateur Boxing Club, which is a registered charity, was formed in 1922 by Captain David Myers, a local man from Forest Gate. Affiliated to the ABA, London Federation of Boys clubs, and also the London Football Association, the club's present day patron is His Royal Highness, Prince Michael of Kent. Since formation it has been privileged to have the support of many prominent people. Life Vice-Presidents include a number of judges and high ranking army officers.

In 1947, on an official trip to the East End, His Royal Highness, Prince Philip, met young boxers at the Dockland Settlement. He also paid a visit to West Ham boxing club.

The club was originally based in an army hut before moving to a room above a pub. In March 1950 a new gymnasium was opened in the old bottling room at the rear of the Black Lion public house at Plaistow High Street. It provided the club with the best training facilities in the country and in the early 1950's had about 250 active boxers.

The gym was a wooden building with a solid stone floor and

was originally built as a stable. Two large punch-bags hung from a heavy wooden beam, and thick padded mats were laid across the ring floor as protection for boxers against a fall. West Ham was a thriving club buzzing with activity. Every evening as many as 40 youngsters packed into the gym and there was always a wonderful spirit. At times so many were there that sessions on the bags had to be cut from three rounds to one so that everybody got a turn.

Once Terry started training at West Ham he couldn't get enough of it. He went to the gym every Monday, Wednesday and Friday evening and worked with great enthusiasm. Each session lasted an hour and included stints of skipping, shadow-boxing, sparring and punching the bag.

Terry's first trainer at the club was Jackie Gubbins, an ex-professional boxer considered by many critics to be the best amateur coach in the country. They got on really well together and Spinks progressed rapidly under the man whom he had tremendous respect for. The defeat by Jackie Bowers proved to be only a temporary set-back and he went on to win a total of four West Ham Schoolboy championships.

'Mr. Gubbins taught me so much as a youngster,' recalled Terry in later life. 'He was a great trainer and I owe him a great deal for helping me to become a future champion.'

Although he was only 12 when he first went to West Ham, Terry quickly made friends with a number of boys, some of whom were slightly older than him and top class boxers. Terry Gill won a schoolboys championship in 1951 and was a Junior ABA champion in 1952 and 1953; Ron Redrup was a schoolboy champion in 1950 and Junior ABA winner in 1952; Dave Enifer won schoolboy titles in 1952 and 1953 followed by Junior ABA honours in 1954 and 1955. Their success spurred him on and he was determined that one day he too would become a champion like them.

Terry also had tremendous respect for the Hinson brothers, Ron and Dennis, who were much older and more mature. Ron won the ABA lightweight championship in 1951, and Dennis the same championship in 1953 whilst serving in the Army. The club was packed with talent, and Spinks learned from those boys a bit older than himself. Although he was extremely small and baby-faced, they recognised his skill and ability, and spent plenty of time giving him advice.

As they progressed, Terry and his mates, Roy and Danny Enifer, Terry Gill, Terry Brown and Jackie Bowers were boxing on a regular basis, both for their schools and club. With many boxing clubs in the East End there were inter-club and open competitions most Saturday's of the season. Terry's dad always went out with his pals on a Saturday night, but if the boys were boxing he always said he would give a pound to those who won. It became quite expensive because he often got home late to find as many as six lads sitting in his living room waiting to be paid.

Apart from strong inter-club competition there was also plenty between the lads within their clubs. 'There were so many of us boxing in those days that you always got fights,' said Terry. 'There was great incentive to win and keep moving up the ladder, because you knew that if you lost there were plenty of others to take your place.'

* * *

During the last weekend of January 1953, a large area of the East End was flooded when the wall of the River Thames collapsed close to the side of the Thames Ironworks. West Ham and Canning Town were among the worst hit areas. The new Keir Hardie Estate was a sea of water throughout Sunday night, and on the Monday everywhere was covered by thick mud.

Thousands of people were effected, with hundreds marooned for up to 15 hours in upper floors of houses until the floods subsided the following day. Some were rescued by Salvation Army workers who borrowed pleasure boats from Barking Park lake. RAF dinghies and rowing boats were brought from Poplar as every possible effort was made to help people in difficulty.

Inside some houses the water reached a height of two feet, and police toured the worst effected areas telling everyone to stay upstairs. When the water eventually subsided, everything was covered with a thick layer of sludge. The situation was so bad that relief funds were set up. To help dry out ground floors the local council delivered one hundredweight of coal free to the worst effected houses in Canning Town, including those at Morgan Street.

Bus routes were disorganised and cars stranded in lakes of water. Schools were unable to re-open, and Terry's old primary school, St Lukes at Canning Town, suffered extensive damage. A well-known landmark, it stood in the middle of a lake of water like a castle ringed by a huge moat. The pressure of water caused part of its surrounding wall to collapse.

On the Sunday morning, Terry was awoken at 4.30am by his father who had gone downstairs and found the water seeping under the front door. Grandpa Harry Jordan arrived with his coal lorry and told Terry to jump out of the bedroom window into the back. Immediately after he had done so, however, he insisted on going back to get his best suit.

* * *

Although Spinks won most of his schoolboy and junior contests, it was during the 1952-53 season that people really began to sit up and take notice of him. After winning the West Ham Schools Junior 'A' championship he went on to become Essex Schoolboy champion, the finals taking place at Warley Barracks, Brentwood. Victory took him into the National Schoolboy quarter-finals in the 5 stone 11 division.

At this stage of the competition contests were between boys from different regions. Having become an Essex champion, Terry boxed for Region Two, comprising of boys who had qualified from Essex and Suffolk. On 14 February 1953, at Camberwell Baths, he faced R. Nelson from Region One, which was London. Spinks won comfortably and two weeks later boxed in the national semi-finals, staged over two days at Wolverhampton. It turned out to be a real adventure, and being a long way from home the Essex and London lads, their families and friends, all joined forces. They had a great time and many, including Terry, returned home victorious.

Despite his success there were moments of concern for Spinks and his followers. Before the official weigh-in, he had to lose two pounds otherwise he would not have been allowed to box. Although he made the 5 stone 11 limit just in time, it was a monumental struggle for the lad who had not yet reached 15.

During the contest his right eye was closed midway through the opening round after being caught by his opponents head. Despite the handicap, Terry boxed brilliantly to take a unanimous decision.

The finals of the National Schoolboy championships, sponsored by the *London Evening Star*, were at Wembley Arena on 20 March and attracted a crowd of 8,000. Always a popular event, one newspaper estimated that the original entry for the championships was more than 30,000 boys from all parts of the United Kingdom.

Spinks was the first of four West Ham schoolboys to contest the finals. Despite the importance of the event he showed no nerves as he calmly went about his task. Against Brian Jones from Priory School, Pinner, Middlesex, he punched hard and with great accuracy. Urged on by more than 400 friends, family and schoolmates from the East End, he always had the edge over his opponent. He never gave Jones the chance to settle and gained a fairly easy victory. When he was presented with the coveted shield, he received a real east London cheer.

The success of Spinks was later matched by his mate Danny Enifer, already a national schoolboy champion in 1952. By winning his second title he became the first ever double champion from the borough of West Ham. Apart from Spinks and Enifer every other winner in the Junior 'B' class came from London, thus demonstrating the strength of schoolboy boxing in the capital. Club mate Laurence Florino also won a title in the Senior 'A' class, and all three boys later received personal congratulations from the mayor.

Recalling his achievement years later Terry said: 'I was really thrilled to win the schoolboys title and I was in great company that year. Freddie King, Danny Enifer and Bernard Hart all won titles there as well, and we are still all good friends.'

* * *

As a boy Terry spent most of his school holidays with his grandmother, whom he called Nanny Spinks. She was separated from her husband, a Petty Officer in the Royal Navy, and rented a large double-fronted house at Goodmayes in Essex. It was also home to several other members of the family; Terry's Uncle John, Aunt Olive and their two children; Aunt Iris who was also separated from her husband, and her daughter Rosemary.

The family were extremely poor and to help make ends meet Nanny Spinks worked as a bar-maid at a nearby pub. One of her few treats was going to the pub in the evening, but not having much money all she could afford was a cheap bottle of stout. Terry always had money in his pockets, so when he was staying with her he often gave her half-a-crown so that she could treat herself.

Terry loved holiday times at Goodmayes and always looked forward to the end of each school term. Being only 10 when he first went there, Tich took him, but as he got older he travelled alone by bus or on his bicycle.

Although he knew some local boys of his own age, Terry spent most of the time with his cousin Rosemary who, like him, was an only child. They had similar childhoods and gained tremendous comfort by discussing things which worried them. In particular, both experienced great loneliness from having to stand outside pubs during the evenings whilst their parents were in the bar having a drink.

Terry and Rosemary became like brother and sister. In the

evenings she would sit on his knee while he read her a bedtime story, and despite her being seven years the younger, they went everywhere together. They sat beside the railway line collecting train numbers, and often went to Goodmayes Park for the day. They also loved going fishing at Matchstick Island, Dagenham. On a Saturday morning, Terry frequently took Rosemary to the Odeon cinema at Green Lanes, Dagenham, especially if a cowboy film was showing.

Often during holiday times, a travelling fair visited the locality. It had a freak show and a boxing booth, and they spent many afternoons absorbing the action. Terry loved watching the booth fighters as they took on a stream of all-comers desperate to win a pound. Although only a boy, he closely watched their defensive skills and later, in the privacy of his bedroom, practised some of the moves he had seen.

One day when Terry and Rosemary told Nanny Spinks they were going to the fair, she said, 'Try and win me a set of saucepans.' As soon as they reached the fairground, Terry tried his hand at the side-stalls. Within no time he had won a set of saucepans. They were so excited that they ran all the way to the pub where Nanny worked. 'Look Nan, I've got your saucepans,' shouted Terry through the bar door.

Even as a youngster, Terry had a very generous nature and paid for everything he and Rosemary did. Yet despite their closeness, it wasn't all peace and tranquillity. One day, Nanny Spinks told Terry to take Rosemary to the pictures, because she had never been before. Being very young, she began to cry when the lights went out and became so upset that he had to take her home. Annoyed at not being able to see the film, he thumped her all the way back to the house. The next day, however, all was forgotten, and they were pals again. It was the start of what would become a very special friendship, and although she was his cousin, Rosemary would become Terry's dearest friend.

2

LIFE AS A STABLE LAD

When he was not at school or involved with boxing, Terry spent his leisure time at St Lukes Church Club. Situated next to the school, it was formed to give youngsters the opportunity to play billiards, table tennis and darts, and more importantly, keep them off the streets. Terry loved playing football, and as a boy tried most games, but as time passed by, boxing was the only sport to which he would become totally dedicated.

As a youngster he was never short of money, much to the envy of many of his school mates. By having their own businesses, his father and grandfather were quite well off and both gave him plenty of pocket money so he could enjoy himself.

As he grew older, Terry earned extra money by selling newspapers for one of his father's friends. They had a stand outside the Imperial Picture Palace at Canning Town, and he often earned up to 15 shillings a week. Although he tried to save some of it, he quite often went and placed bets on horses.

With his father being a bookmaker, Terry lived in a racing environment from the moment he returned to the East End. Although he loved reading comics, he also became fascinated by the racing pages of national newspapers. He soon understood how to read a race-card and by the age of eight ran a book at school.

At least once a week he and a group of mates all took half a pound of sweets to school. At break-times they huddled behind the bike-sheds or in a corner of the playground with the racing pages of a newspaper. With Terry acting as the bookmaker, they selected their fancies and he gave them the odds.

'If a lad picked a 3/1 winner, I'd have to give him four sweets,' said Spinks. 'When they picked a loser, they gave me sweets. That was in the days of rationing, and some kids lost their whole week's supply on one horse.'

Terry soon became obsessed with gambling and it wasn't long before pocket money was used instead of sweets for playground bets. 'I did pretty well,' said Spinks, 'because even when I was a lad my dad sometimes gave me a tip.'

When Terry was about 12, his father and Uncle Harry took him to the races for the first time. He already had the urge to become a jockey, but after savouring the atmosphere in real life, talked of nothing else.

Tich had plenty of contacts and when Terry was 14, took him to meet Epsom trainer, Herbert Smythe. Despite his enthusiasm, he still had another year to do at school so Smythe invited him to return after he had left.

Terry also loved going greyhound racing, and although he was still a boy, his father didn't discourage him from having a bet. Tich had a number of dogs including a top class one called Rock Street Queen, which he raced regularly at West Ham, Hackney, Romford and Walthamstow.

Terry was still determined to become a jockey and when he was about to leave school at the age of 15, had a stroke of good fortune. He and his father knew a man who delivered hay to the Newmarket stable of Marcus Marsh, well known from having trained Derby winners, Windsor Lad and Tulyar. After a word in the right place, Terry was taken on as a stable lad immediately after he left school in July 1953.

Leaving home came as a real shock to the youngster. His lodgings at the Temperance Hotel in Newmarket were very different to Morgan Street where everything was always warm and immaculately clean. Instead, he shared a dingy basement room with eight other stable lads. Beds were laid side by side on the floor, and the room had only one window with heavy metal bars across it. Because it wouldn't shut properly, the room was damp and cold as wind and rain blew through the gap.

Terry hated living there, but stuck it for three months before asking the stable to move him to new accommodation. Whilst his new lodgings were an improvement, the youngster was still unhappy. He slept in a room which contained two beds, and because of his early start each day he usually went to bed early. Most mornings he awoke to find a different person in the bed beside him. He eventually discovered that the landlady let the other bed out to lorry drivers who usually arrived late in the evening.

Although Terry loved his job, the living conditions made him unhappy and he dreaded leaving work at the end of the day. After a couple of months he told another stable lad of his plight. The lad knew a lovely couple, Mr and Mrs Bill Parkinson, who lived at All Saints Road and occasionally took in lodgers. Terry was introduced to them and it was agreed that he could stay for a trial period. They got on so well that he lodged with them for the next two years.

Mr and Mrs Parkinson treated Terry like a son and he regarded their house as his second home. Their friendship was so strong that even after he left Newmarket, he continued to visit them whenever he could, and always took a present.

Life as a stable lad came as a real shock to Terry because he hadn't known what to expect. In order to be at the stables by 6.45 am, he had to be out of bed by six o'clock. He had two horses to look after, Passion and Canabair, and a strict daily routine had to be followed.

On arriving at the stables the first thing he did every morning was tie up the first horse and then brush and groom it. The saddle and reins were put on and the horse was then led out of the yard for a gallop over Newmarket Heath. Terry loved riding and this was the highlight of his day. After a gallop of one and a half hours, the horse was taken back to the stables, groomed again and covered with a blanket.

After a break of half an hour for breakfast, Terry went through the same routine with the other horse. He usually finished at about 12.30 pm, returned to his lodgings for a change of clothes, and quite often spent the afternoon in a betting shop. At 4.30 pm he returned to the stables where he and other lads would muck-out, then sweep and hose down the entire yard. He then groomed both of his horses again and did not leave work until after Marcus Marsh had carried out a full inspection at about 6.00pm.

The job was demanding, but in his first year Terry's weekly wage was just six shillings. It was not without some dangers and on two occasions horses fell on him, but luckily he escaped serious injury each time. He worked seven days a week with only a Sunday off every third week.

Badly in need of a break he always went home on his day off. It was worth it because his mum always prepared a special Sunday lunch and made a fuss of him. If his dad or Uncle Johnny had earned good money they would spoil him and he often returned to Newmarket on the Sunday evening with as much as £15 in his pocket.

The other lads soon got to hear of Terry's riches and somebody was always at the station to meet him off the train. 'Did you have a good weekend?' they would ask. Terry's problem was that he was too generous and accepted all the offers to go out for a drink in the week. More often than not he finished up paying and by the following Friday was usually broke.

Although he sometimes went to the cinema, Terry spent a lot of his spare time during the evenings and weekends at an institute in Newmarket town centre. It provided leisure facilities specifically for apprentice jockeys and stable lads, and had two snooker tables, table tennis, darts and a bar selling soft drinks and light refreshments.

While Terry was living at Newmarket, Teddy Boy clothes became the fashion, and whenever he went home all his mates were wearing them. Hating to be the odd one out he persuaded his mother to buy him an outfit. He was so proud that he wore it when he returned to Newmarket one Sunday evening.

That night he went straight to the stables, but was seen by Marcus Marsh who was horrified because the fashion hadn't reached Newmarket. 'What on earth do you think you look like?' he shouted. 'Get those clothes off and don't wear them here again. I'm not having Teddy Boys in my stables.'

With more than 15 stables in Newmarket, Spinks got to know hundreds of people involved in racing. He was a likeable and popular young man and made a lot of good friends. His stable jockeys, Charlie Smirke and Tony Gosling, and on occasions, Doug Smith, all liked him and treated him well. He also became close friends with Manny Mercer, brother of top jockey Joe.

On Saturday evenings Terry and a group of mates often went to a dance at the Town Hall. He loved music and dancing, but whenever he took a girl home it was often a long walk back to his lodgings because there were no late night buses.

While he was at Newmarket Terry first got the taste for beer. He was friendly with Barry Hills, at the time a head lad at a neighbouring stable, who would later become a top trainer. Sometimes on a Saturday evening they would meet up with a local blacksmith and go to a pub for a game of darts. Feeling out of place drinking orange juice, Spinks tried a few glasses of light ale. 'I found I enjoyed it and never looked back,' he recalled with a cheeky smile.

Terry was never happier than when he was riding a horse. Marcus Marsh recognised that he was very talented and on one occasion took out a jockey club licence for him to ride as an apprentice in a race at Warwick. In the days leading up to the race, his mount, Wedding Gift, was heavily backed. This became a concern to Marsh, so the ride was taken from Spinks and given to Bill Rickaby, the top jockey for the nearby stable of Jack Jarvis.

* * *

Despite the demands of his job Terry did not abandon his boxing which was extremely popular amongst the racing fraternity. He had only been at Newmarket for a few weeks when applications were invited for a boxing tournament organised to raise funds for Newmarket Town Football Club. Many of the contests were between stable lads and amateurs from local boxing clubs. Not having boxed competitively for some months, he was anxious to get back into action, so he put his name down.

Terry entered the open class and outpointed D. Buttress of Chatteris YABC over three rounds in what was described by the Newmarket Journal as 'undoubtedly the best fight of the evening.' The report added:

> The contest had plenty of action, and what so many other contests lacked, a fair amount of skill. Spinks in particular impressed onlookers and it was no surprise when at the end of the evening he was awarded the Jack Solomons cup for the best boxer.

Sammy McCarthy was there to present the prizes, and other prominent figures from professional boxing were Sam Russell, Jack King, Snowy Buckingham, and Jack Solomons who was guest of honour. 'That was a fine performance son,' said Jack in presenting Terry with his award. 'I reckon we will see a lot more of you in the future.'

A few months later Terry entered the 6 stone 4 open class of an annual Stable Lads competition to be held at Newmarket. Lads boxing was extremely popular and attracted tremendous betting. Many lads were entered for the various competitions by their stables even though they were poor boxers. Refusal to take part could mean the sack.

Within a few days of putting his name down for the competition Terry was approached by stable jockey Charlie Smirke, a very influential figure. 'Charlie came up to me and whispered that he'd heard I won a schoolboy title,' recalled Spinks. 'When I told him it was true, he asked me to keep quiet about it.'

Marcus Marsh knew about Terry's involvement in boxing when he employed him, and was particularly impressed when he discovered he had won a National Schoolboys championship. A good boxer was good for the prestige of the stable, so he rigged up a gymnasium in a loft above a garage at the stables, so that Spinks and other lads could train properly. Terry was joined by former Stable Lads champion, Charlie Leggett, and Doug Butters who trained them.

The championships were held over two days at King Edward VII Memorial Hall at Newmarket. Wally Swinburn, Jock Gaston, Geoff Lewis, Tony Rawlinson and many other star apprentices were also entered. In the programme Spinks was described as being the winner of his last 40 contests and was considered unbeatable locally.

Boxing brilliantly, Terry won three contests in the 6 stone 4 class, all on points, to win a Lads championship at his first attempt. His prize was the Charlie Smirke cup, and the famous jockey was there to present it in person. Smirke was a real boxing fanatic who encouraged stable lads and apprentice jockeys to take up boxing. He had been a good fighter and although he was getting on in years, could still handle himself. He was always willing to pass on tips to lads and often sparred with Terry and others at the stable. He was also a generous man and if they ever needed anything they only had to ask him.

After Terry won the championship at Newmarket he and Charlie became good friends. 'I knew what was going on,' remarked Spinks. 'I reckon Charlie must have won a packet on me that night.'

Smirke attended all of Terry's stable lads contests and became one of his greatest fans. He once told him to forget about riding and concentrate on a career in boxing.

Winning his first championship was the start of a successful two years for Terry. A few weeks later he won the Epsom Grandstand Association 6 stone 7 open competition. He trained regularly, running one afternoon and working out in the gym the next.

Boxing regularly, he won a host of cups and trophies and the only stable lad to beat him was his friend Tony Rawlinson, who was two years his senior. Rawlinson, from the Dick Perryman stable, had won four Liverpool Schoolboy titles before becoming a stable lad. He and Spinks often sparred together, but in 1954 found that they were to meet in a preliminary contest of a competition at the Memorial Hall.

Tony won on points, but before the contest was advised to stay at home because he had no chance. There was always heavy betting at Lad's competitions, and he was a 7/1 outsider, an indication of how highly Terry was regarded.

In 1954 Spinks won an annual Stable Lads Championship at

Marlborough and was presented with a handsome trophy by his boss Marcus Marsh. Later that year he won the Lads Boxing Championship of Cambridge and received a silver cup from top jockey Eath Smith.

The 1955 annual Stable Lads Championships were organised by Sir Gordon Richards and staged at Marlborough in March. Spinks had grown considerably by this time and competed in the 7 stone 7 class. As in most competitions he entered, he was too fast and punched too hard and accurately for his opponents. In the semi-final he stopped R. Rowan from the A.E. Waugh Stable in the second round. In the final he went one better stopping W. Murphy (Captain Hastings-Bass Stable) in the opening round. Murphy was outclassed and the 17 year old from east London stood out as a lad with a great future in the ring.

Terry's success earned him a unique, beautifully designed silver table set, which had been donated by the *London Evening Star* newspaper. Salt, pepper and mustard containers were created in the form of a jockey's boot, whip, spurs and saddle. In making the presentation, Sir Gordon Richards told Terry: 'You have won this wonderful prize which really has everything. Well done!' Spinks also received a cup for being the most stylish boxer in the championships.

Among the crowded audience were European, British and British Empire flyweight champion, Dai Dower, and Joe Beckett the former British heavyweight champion. Both stated that they were very impressed by the performance of Spinks. The press were equally complimentary and one newspaper included the comment; 'This youngster who shapes up like a pro…'

Terry's run of success continued, and later in 1955 he won a Cambridge Racing Lads competition staged in the open air at Newmarket Football Ground. His prize was the Willie Snaith Cup, and to his delight it was presented to him by his boyhood idol, Sammy McCarthy, who was accompanied by his trainer, Snowy Buckingham. Spinks and McCarthy had known each other for some while in the East End, but when he shook hands with Sammy, Terry said: 'One day I think I'll be turning professional and I'd like you with me Sammy, and you to train me Mr Snowy.'

McCarthy had a high regard for Terry and went to watch him box on another Stable Lads show. 'I was so impressed with him because those he boxed, although called stable lads, were men,' he recalled. 'They looked so strong as opposed to Terry because he was so boyish. Yet from the first bell he was class. He outboxed them all and won the championship.'

Later that year Terry was at a Stable Lads show at the Cambridge Corn Exchange which had been organised by Royston trainer, Mr W. Stephenson. When his opponent pulled out at the last minute he was left without a contest. Instead he boxed a three two minute rounds exhibition with Dai Dower, a great supporter of Stable Lads boxing. The bout was the highlight of a great evening where the guests were professional promoter, Jack Solomons and Dower's manager, Nat Sellar. The contests were refereed by personalities from the professional game, Sam Russell, Jack Hart and Ted Broadribb.

Dower, an ABA champion in 1952 and Olympic flyweight quarter-finalist at Helsinki the same year, was more than half a stone heavier than Spinks, who attacked as though it was for real. Dai, however, showed amazing footwork and body movement, and Terry found it difficult to lay a glove on him.

Whilst it was a wonderful exhibition of boxing, there were some hilarious moments. The first was when Dower played an old gag by indicating to Spinks that his boot-lace was undone. As Terry lost concentration, the Welshman poked him with a couple of light playful punches to the head.

The London boy, however, had the last laugh as they shook hands for the final round. Primed by Nat Sellar, Terry had retained some drinking water in his mouth, and as the bell sounded he squirted it into Dower's face. People screamed with laughter but nobody more than Dai.

* * *

Despite his dreams of becoming a jockey, Terry didn't make it. Like so many other lads weight problems brought his boyhood ambition to an end. Although he was terribly disappointed to leave Newmarket it had been a wonderful experience and he had made a host of friends. Apart from the riding, he had continued to develop as a boxer and won every possible honour in Stable Lads events.

Terry's passion for working with horses was so great that he hadn't contemplated any other job. After moving back to Canning Town he had little motivation and drifted between jobs which he took purely to earn some money. For a few months he worked for a company at Aldgate which bottled whiskey and gin. He then moved to Smithfield meat market where he was a salesman, starting at 4.30 am each morning, Monday to Friday. He stuck that job for about six months before eventually finding work he really liked.

His Uncle Fred worked for a large disposal company with a contract to clear refuse from the docks and got Terry a job with him. They both had huge green metal bins and their task was to remove rubbish from ships after they docked. They worked at the Royal Albert, Victoria and Poplar docks, and Terry loved it. No two days were the same as boats carrying a variety of cargos arrived from all over the world. His wages of £10 a week was the best he had ever earned. With the job being local it meant he could go to the gym in the evenings for boxing training. More importantly, the work was hard and demanding, and helped toughen him up for what would prove to be the most important year of his boxing career.

3

THE ROAD TO STARDOM

Good judges of boxing were quick to recognise the skill and natural ability of Terry Spinks at a very young age. Even while he was still working at Newmarket, three professional managers tried to persuade him to leave the amateurs, but each time his answer was the same. 'I'm not interested,' he told them. 'I want to be a jockey.'

Even after returning to Canning Town, Terry still hoped that one day his dream would come true. He had tremendous love for horses and thought about riding all the time. He returned to Newmarket at every opportunity, not only to see his friends but to saviour the atmosphere as well.

Boxing, however, was Terry's second love, and by 1955 he had won 15 major cups and trophies, and it was claimed that he had lost only four of 180 contests. The only competition he hadn't entered as a junior was the National Federation of Boys Clubs championships. Although West Ham strongly supported the championships, Terry didn't qualify for entry because he was working at Newmarket during the seasons when he was eligible.

Once he was back in the East End, Spinks wasted no time in re-joining West Ham. He trained hard under senior coach Billy Walker, a meat-market worker from Chadwell Heath, who had been a good professional featherweight during the early war years. They got on well together and Terry was one of the most regular attenders at the gym. He progressed well, but being a very modest young man was always quick to express gratitude to his coach. 'Since Mr. Walker became my coach I am four times better than I ever was,' he told a local newspaper reporter.

Before he could box competitively again for West Ham, Terry had to seek reinstatement by the ABA. With his record, and the backing of the club, this proved to be a formality. He couldn't wait to get back into action and his first fight after re-joining West Ham was at Briggs Social Club, Dagenham, on 9 December 1955. He boxed brilliantly to outpoint G. Rix (Barking Amateur Boxing Club) over three two minute rounds.

Because of his age, Spinks had to move up to senior level for the 1955-56 season, so he made the ABA championships his target. The first hurdle was the North East London Divisional championships at York Hall, Bethnal Green, on 15 and 16 March 1956. Victories over P. Pestaille (knockout in the first round) and John Holt of Repton (points) were the perfect preparation.

Full of confidence, Terry boxed brilliantly to beat Bernie Dillon (Stepney Institute) who was disqualified in round two of the flyweight semi-final for persistent holding. The following night, he beat old opponent John Holt on points to win a senior title at his first attempt.

Amateur boxing was, at that time, in a very healthy state, and the London ABA boasted that they had 9,000 registered senior members in the 10 recognised weight divisions, with thousands of juniors and schoolboys preparing to graduate later on.

Terry's victory in the North East Divs took him to the London championships at the Royal Albert Hall on 9 April. They were always special occasions with the semi's commencing at 4.00pm and the finals at 8.00pm. There was a tremendous demand for tickets and all 7,000 seats were sold weeks in advance.

Having boxed in front of a larger crowd at Wembley Arena three years earlier, the occasion didn't get to the 18 years old Spinks. He was cool and controlled as he boxed beautifully to stop Ron Rice (Downham) in the second round of the flyweight semi-final. Later in the evening he punched hard and accurately to outpoint the aggressive Eric Secombe of St Pancras in the final. *'Boxing News'* described Terry as 'the most pleasing winner who gave delightful performances.'

As London champion, Terry had booked his place in the ABA finals to be staged at Wembley Arena on 27 April. Few critics gave him much chance of success, especially when he was drawn against Alex Ambrose of the Army in the semi-final. In a preview of the championships, *Boxing News* predicted: 'Spinks has the skill but may be too frail.'

Ambrose was fancied by many critics to win the ABA flyweight title, but Spinks once again boxed with a maturity beyond his years. He astonished everyone by the workmanlike way he went about his task to secure a points victory. It was an incredible result because Ambrose had lost just two of 15 contests that season, both due to cut eyes. He was Imperial Services champion and already being chased by several professional managers, yet he was dazzled and out-sped by the brilliance of the young Londoner.

Spinks was the first boxer to reach the final, and after his victory, Reg Gutteridge writing in the late edition of the *London Evening Standard*, predicted: 'He could well be the shock of the championships.' Few other critics, however, gave Terry a chance in the final against the experienced Scot, Peter Walsh, of the Royal Northern Club.

Aged 26, Walsh took boxing so seriously that he had to beat his twin brother John, to win the Army Egyptian final seven years earlier. He had been trying for six years to get to Wembley, having faced such men as John Smillie, Chick Brogan, Dick Currie, Frankie Jones and Jimmy Quinn, all of whom went on to become successful professionals.

Dominating the fight from the start, Spinks took Walsh out of his stride. Using his left hand to great effect, he boxed brilliantly throughout the three rounds to gain a comfortable points victory. The 18 year old East End lad had confounded the critics by beating two of the outstanding flyweights in Britain to become ABA flyweight champion at his first attempt.

Despite his wonderful achievement, Terry was more concerned about his friend and club mate, Ron Redrup, who was boxing Bernard Foster in the middleweight final. Showered and smartly dressed he sat at ringside and cheered non-stop throughout the fight. At the end he appeared more excited about Redrup's victory than his own.

Before leaving the ringside, he was asked by a national newspaper reporter what it felt like to be an ABA champion. 'I don't know,' replied Spinks, 'I still can't believe it.'

Most papers reported his victory, and there were comments that he had boxed like Sammy McCarthy when he became British featherweight champion a few years earlier. Few people knew, however, that Sammy was Terry's idol and they had already become good friends.

Terry's success brought almost immediate reward because when Derek Lloyd went down with tonsillitis, he was drafted into the ABA team for a two match trip to Poland. West Ham club mates Terry Gill and Terry Collins were also in the squad.

Spinks' first contest was just nine days after winning the ABA title and he was considered extremely unlucky to suffer his first defeat at senior level. His opponent, Henryk Kukier, was a vastly experienced boxer, having won the European flyweight title at

Warsaw in 1953. Although it was his first international, Spinks gave a delightful display in a cat and mouse contest, only to lose by a majority decision, (60-57, 60-56, 57-59). In a steamy Turkish-bath atmosphere beneath the glass topped roof of the Gwardia Stadium at Warsaw, he was the hero in England's 8-2 defeat by the Poles.

Terry's tight defence, moving and jabbing with his left hand, pleased the Polish crowd but failed to impress two of the judges. He jabbed and hooked at will, stood up to his opponent when the going got tough, and was never slow to throw intelligent counter punches.

It wasn't until the final round that Kukier managed to get on top, but even then he almost went to the floor as Spinks nailed him with a thunderous straight left. The decision in favour of the Polish boxer was extremely unpopular with the home supporters who mobbed Terry as he left the ring. Their reaction was a clear indication of how well he had performed. In fact, he received more punishment from slaps on the back as he made his way back to the dressing room than he did during three rounds in the ring.

Terry was unconcerned about the result because he knew he had performed well. 'Do you think they will let me box against Russia?' he asked George Whiting of the *London Evening Standard* once everything had calmed down.

After the contest, the Polish national coach, Felix Stamm, said he believed Spinks was the best British amateur since Dai Dower. He said he had the ability to do well at the forthcoming Olympics at Melbourne if selected.

The second match of the Polish tour was two days later, on 8 May, at Gdansk. The ABA were beaten 5-4, but again Spinks performed admirably. Using his fantastic speed and boxing skill, he outpointed Janusz Litke, who took a real hiding and was floored in round two as well as being injured around both eyes. Terry received another wonderful ovation as he left the ring.

All Spinks had to show for his tremendous displays in the two Polish internationals was a porcelain statue of a woman. 'What do I want this rubbish for?' he remarked when he got home and showed it to his parents. He promptly threw it in the dustbin, but when he was not looking Tich retrieved it and treasured it throughout his life.

The trip to Poland was memorable for a number of reasons, not least the poor structural state in many areas. A typical iron curtain country, it was still suffering from the effects of war more than a decade earlier. Many buildings were still boarded up and the people were poorly dressed. Few had any money, and it was commonplace to see groups of women dressed in dungarees doing heavy dirty manual work. It reminded Terry of the East End during the late 1940's, although he couldn't understand why the country was still in such a poor state of repair.

As soon as they arrived in Poland the British boxers were advised to stay closely together for security reasons. Shortly after checking into their hotel at Warsaw, they were confronted by a huge Russian man who was violently drunk on vodka. He was a frightening sight as he staggered around the foyer screaming abuse at everyone, punching doors and kicking furniture. 'I got quite worried at one stage,' recalled Terry, 'because he was so big and completely out of his head.'

Terry shared a room in the hotel with West Ham club-mate Terry Gill. In the middle of the night Gill was awoken by Spinks screaming, 'wake up Tel, wake up, that bloody Russian's in here.' It transpired that he had woken up, and through the bedroom curtains, seen the shadows of trees outside moving across the window.

By his brilliant performances in Poland, Spinks had made a highly successful start at international level and the ABA selectors had no hesitation in picking him for a forthcoming trip to Russia and Finland where three matches were scheduled in nine days. Terry had already been selected to box for London against the Imperial Services at the Royal Albert Hall on 29 May, when he was due to face old foe, Alex Ambrose. The Russian trip, however, was the first ever by a British boxing team, so rather than risk injury he pulled out of the Imperial Services match.

The good performances of Spinks and Collins in Poland prompted rumours that both were about to turn professional. This was emphatically denied by Captain David Myers, secretary of West Ham. 'There has not even been an approach from professional people,' he told the *Stratford Express*. 'I don't know how these rumours started.'

The British team were given the red carpet treatment as they arrived in Moscow. It was a prestigious occasion and the Soviets treated it with the importance it deserved. Officials carrying armfuls of flowers greeted the team as they stepped from the plane at the airport. Spinks cockney humour soon clicked into gear as he remarked, 'Blimey, aren't they going to bury us first.' The baby of the team had no nerves and as soon as he was on the tarmac he turned to Reg Gutteridge and asked where the nearest bookie was.

Terry has vivid memories of the trip and found the Russian people so different to those back home. They appeared miserable, with no sense of urgency about what they were doing. In the evenings, the hosts insisted on showing the British boxers films of activities which had taken place during the last world war. They seemed anxious that visitors to their country knew just how much they had suffered. Terry found this difficult to understand because folk back in the east end of London had put the horrors of war behind them. They had grafted together, were cheerful and anxious to move on rather than dwell on the past.

Despite the confidence gained from his fights in Poland, Terry faced a mammoth task in Russia. His first contest on 20 June was against the 22 year old USSR champion, Vladimir Stolnikov. Despite battling hard, Spinks took a bit of a beating, although he never looked in danger of being stopped. The Russian took a unanimous decision and set his team on the way to an 8-3 victory over the ABA.

Three days later, Terry faced Viktor Bystrov, and before the fight was told that Bystrov was the Russian word for 'quick.' 'If that's the case,' quipped the Londoner, 'tell them Spinks is English for "run like hell"!'

Spinks was first into the ring and when the Russian arrived he presented him with a bouquet of flowers. It was the hottest Moscow summer for 30 years and all the British boxers lost weight. Terry was down to 7 stone 12½, but had lost none of his strength. The lively Londoner did most of the attacking and often rocked Bystrov with heavy accurate punches. The Russian countered well on the retreat and although Spinks had a great last round, the Soviet took a unanimous decision. It was not received favourably by the local fans who booed and cat-called loudly.

Nicknamed 'Babydoll' by the Muscovites, Spinks was cheered all the way to the dressing room by the 20,000 crowd who were convinced he had been robbed of victory. Like the match two days earlier, it was held in the open air at the Dynamo Football Stadium. With the Russians leading 2-0, the match had to be abandoned as storms and torrential rain hit Moscow causing flooding.

Although he lost decisions in two demanding contests in Moscow within the space of three days, Terry suffered no ill effects. He was extremely strong and fit, and five days later in Helsinki, boxed brilliantly to outpoint Ossi Palvalin in the ABA's 6-4 victory over Finland.

Aside from the boxing, the trip to Helsinki turned out to be quite eventful for Spinks. The day before the international match he and other members of the ABA team were out jogging in order to keep themselves loose. As they approached a fairground the main group were some 30 yards in front of Terry who was on his own. Johnny Thurgood was some distance further back. Suddenly a gang of Finnish youths came running towards them, and as they reached Spinks one of them lashed out at him, knocking him to the ground. Thurgood clouted the yob as he ran off, but was unable to hold on to him.

Spinks was furious and started to run after them. 'I'm going to kill him,' he yelled as the other boxers held him back. They calmed him down because with the international match taking place the following day, the last thing they wanted was for him to get involved in a fight outside the ring.

The following evening whilst Terry was taking part in his contest, Johnny Thurgood sat in the arena gloved up. All of a sudden he spotted the youths involved in the altercation the previous day. When they saw him they started shouting abuse and one walked up and punched Johnny on the ear before running away pursued by a security man. The incident had no ill-effect on Thurgood who, like Spinks, boxed his way to a fine points victory. Terry was awarded the Helsinki Fair Play trophy for the best boxer of the match. Although he was only in his first season as a senior, he had already become one of Britain's most popular amateur boxers. The baby-faced tot endeared himself to fans wherever he went, and they loved his cockney humour.

Since being called up for international duty, Terry didn't box on any club shows. After a short break he was on his travels again, this time as a member of the London ABA team for matches in Germany. On 31 August he battered Waldemar Stephanie almost at will to take a wide points decision in Berlin. A huge contingent of British soldiers stationed in the Berlin zone were among the 4,000 crowd. They cheered wildly as Spinks hammered the German to bring blood streaming from his nose and mouth in the second round. The home fans were amazed at the way their man was outfought, and yelled for the contest to be stopped.

Writing in the *Daily Express*, Sydney Hulls insisted that on this form Spinks must be picked for the Olympic Games in Melbourne. 'Rarely have I seen any boxer, amateur or professional, take command of a bout so completely as Spinks did,' he wrote.

Two days later Terry put on an even more decisive performance when outpointing Rudolph Waletzko in Hanover. The 18 year old German was a late substitute and having had only eight contests, was no match for the talented Londoner. Spinks was in fact very comfortable in both contests because he had the benefit of club coach Billy Walker in his corner.

* * *

With the Olympic Games due to commence in Melbourne in November, the English, Scottish and Welsh Amateur Boxing Associations had the responsibility of selecting a team of six boxers to represent Great Britain. Serious problems arose, however, when the Scottish and Welsh representatives broke away from the English body following a disagreement over the make-up of the selection committee. A further disagreement arose over whether Terry Spinks should be included in the team.

It was unanimously agreed that five boxers – Tommy Nicholls (featherweight), Dick McTaggart (light), Nicky Gargano (welter), John McCormack (light-middle) and Ron Redrup (middleweight) would go to Melbourne. The breakaway committee, however, preferred that the sixth place went to ABA bantamweight champion Owen Reilly with Spinks as a reserve. They contended that Terry was too young and inexperienced to compete in a tournament of such importance. The committee clearly failed to recognise or consider the maturity of his performances at international level during the preceding four months.

The English ABA were adamant that Spinks should be selected instead of Reilly an opinion shared by a number of prominent London boxing journalists. Reg Gutteridge of the *Evening News* had tremendous admiration for Spinks. With the support of Walter Bartleman of the *Star* and Sydney Hulls of the *Daily Express*, he started a campaign in support of Terry's nomination. Almost daily, something was written in one of the papers urging his selection.

In the East End feelings ran high regarding his non-selection. Some people knocked at Terry's door, while others stopped him in the street, all saying what a crazy situation it was. Tich was so angry that he couldn't keep his mind on his work, a damaging situation for a bookmaker. He and a group of pals even offered to put up the £1,500 for Terry's fare, but the ABA wouldn't hear of it.

Eventually the ABA bowed to the pressure from the press and Spinks was drafted into the British squad at the end of September 1956. His selection was unanimously approved at a meeting of the British Olympic Association presided over by the Marquess of Exeter. Owen Reilly was made a reserve, but was eventually added to the team when a Scottish businessman offered to pay his expenses.

Terry had never given up hope of being selected and remained in constant training. When the call eventually came through, he was actually training at the West Ham gym. 'Pack your bags,' said Captain Myers excitedly, 'they've changed their minds.'

Before being selected Spinks gave the selectors a firm reminder of his capabilities when he boxed for West Ham in Basle on 14 September against a combined Swiss and German team. Boxing brilliantly, he soundly outpointed R. Haas of Basle giving yet another demonstration of his maturity and a clear indication that boxing abroad held no fears for him.

When it came to packing, the first things Terry put into his suitcase were swimming trunks and suntan oil. 'I was going to enjoy those Australian beaches,' he recalled later. 'I wasn't going out there to be a hero.'

In order to keep in shape for the Olympics, Spinks agreed to take three contests in October before leaving for Australia. The first was against Frank Spenser of Cannock St Lukes on the Austin Motors Club show against West Ham at Longbridge. It was his first contest over four three minute rounds, but there was a bizarre situation at the end of the third.

Assuming the fight was over, somebody switched on all the lights. Spenser clearly thought it was over as well because he walked slowly to his corner only to hear his second shout, 'Hurry up Frank,' before pushing him on to his stool. Spenser then got up, walked to referee, Martin Curley, who waved him away.

The bell sounded for round four which Spenser didn't know existed. The fight was very close at this point, but the Birmingham boxer, having paced himself for three rounds, tired badly, allowing Spinks to forge ahead and take the decision. It was a dangerous fight for Terry to take because he gave away weight to a bantamweight. Defeat during the build-up to the Olympics would have been extremely embarrassing.

Ten days later Spinks boxed for London against Rome at the Royal Albert Hall and was the victim of the most terrible decision. Showing wonderful skill and speed he appeared to have coasted to victory against Salvatore Manca, only to find himself on the wrong end of a split decision. The two Italian judges scored in favour of Manca, whilst the other official from London voted for Spinks.

It took some time for the crowd to realise what had happened, but once it registered they exploded into a noisy demonstration. Terry just smiled through the booing, cat-calls, slow hand clapping and stamping of feet. Even members of the large Italian contingent joined in, and the announcement of the next contest was completely drowned.

The Italian officials were both members of the international panel of referees and judges, and therefore men of great experience. Veteran boxing writer, Walter Bartleman, was just one journalist mystified by their decision. 'I am at a complete loss to understand their assessment which resulted in a storm of booing,' he wrote in the *London Evening Star.* Bartleman did, however, draw comfort from the result because Spinks, having won the first two rounds by punching Manca around the ring with good shots to head and body, eased up in the third. The journalist was therefore of the opinion:

> His defeat means little, but he has learned much that will stand him in good stead when he boxes for Britain in the Olympics. In particular, he knows there must be no easing up in the third round even though victory seems assured.

Tom Phillips writing in the *Daily Herald* was equally disgusted by the decision in favour of the Italian:

> One of the worst decisions I have seen ruined what promised to be one of the greatest boxing events of the season . . . Spinks had won by a street with brilliant high-speed boxing. In every round he had punched Manca all over the target area and all around the ring.

Terry had been first into the ring at the start of the match and the decision angered team-mates Ron Redrup and Nicky Gargano. Consequently, their performances were below their normal standard. Recalling the fight years later, Terry's cockney humour was predictably evident. 'The geezer never laid a glove on me throughout the contest,' he said. 'I'll never forget it and I don't think the Italian restaurants up west were very popular that night either.'

Terry knew it was a shocking decision, but soon put it out of his mind. Six days later he had a final tune-up for the Olympics on a Fitzroy Lodge club show at Manor Place Baths. He gave a delightful performance by clearly outpointing former spar-mate Eric Secombe, who volunteered to face him over four rounds.

Satisfied with his performance over the longer distance, Spinks knew he was in good shape for the biggest test in his life. His first fight in the Olympic Games was just five weeks away.

4

OLYMPIC CHAMPION

The attitude of the ABA towards the British Olympic team left a great deal to be desired. With only a few weeks to go before they left for Melbourne, no arrangements had been made for special training. Incredibly, the ABA appeared content to leave such an important matter in the hands of individual clubs or trainers.

Even before the British team had been picked, West Ham Amateur Boxing Club offered the use of their training headquarters. The club could boast one of the most expensively equipped gymnasiums in the country, and their eminent list of vice-presidents included the Marquess of Queensbury. Even after Terry Spinks and Ron Redrup were selected to go to Melbourne, the ABA showed no interest in the offer.

Spinks' fights against Frank Spenser and Eric Secombe were arranged by his club secretary, David Myers, in order to keep him sharp. Fitzroy Lodge also offered to help, but got no response from the ABA. Ron Redrup was, in fact, so disgusted with the ABA that he threatened to pull out of the team unless he got proper sparring.

In the weeks leading up to the Olympics, Terry was working in the docks with his Uncle for Deards during the day, and training at West Ham in the evenings. About three weeks before he was due to fly to Melbourne, the company allowed him time off to make his final preparations.

With nothing organised by the ABA, Terry was left very much to his own devices, but he received tremendous support from everyone at West Ham, especially Billy Walker. Most mornings, he was up at 6.00am and running on the Beckton Road. On other occasions, he and Ron Redrup ran around the outside of Victoria Park, a distance of three miles.

Spinks and Redrup trained at 'The Black Lion' gym three

evenings a week and their intense programme included sparring, shadow-boxing, bag work and floor exercises.

The selection of Spinks and Redrup delighted members of West Ham County Borough Council who invited them to attend a meeting at the Town Hall on 30 October 1956. Introducing them to Council members, the Mayor, Alderman Michael Sullivan, congratulated them on their selection and conveyed the good wishes of everyone present for their success at the Games.

With the exception of Redrup, Terry didn't meet any of his fellow team members until 5 November when they gathered at Heathrow Airport for the flight to Melbourne. In a preview of his prospects, *Boxing News* predicted that Spinks was in good shape but would have to tighten his defence to have any real chance of success.

The flight to Australia took five days with stops at Dublin, New York, Honolulu, Singapore and Sydney, before finally reaching Melbourne. With the exception of Dublin the stops were of several hours, enabling the boxers to leave the plane and do some light training. In Honolulu Spinks found some shops close to the airport and bought an outrageously bright red shirt emblazoned with yellow flowers.

Shortly after arriving at Melbourne Terry had a brush with the team manager, Flt. Lieut. McInnes-Sharpe. As the bus, which had collected the British team from the airport, stopped at the Olympic Village, all the boys charged off to share rooms with their mates. Everyone was laughing and in high spirits, but as Terry led the pack he suddenly heard a shout of, 'Come back, come back at once.'

'I thought that perhaps we were dashing into the women's section or something which seemed like a very good reason for not taking any notice,' recalled Spinks. 'So we kept running.'

Shortly afterwards all the boxers were called to an official meeting regarding a matter of discipline. 'I have been sent here to manage you,' snapped McInnes-Sharpe, much to the annoyance of Spinks and his team mates. 'You left the bus without my permission. I did not tell you to leave, and in future you will do as you are told. Has anybody anything to say?'

'Yes I have,' retorted Spinks. 'I'm not in the RAF. I'm used to looking after myself and don't need your help.'

The team manager was completely taken aback by Terry's response, and after a few moments of eerie silence, brought the meeting to a close.

The team received a warm welcome when they arrived at Melbourne. At the Olympic Village they had a house to themselves in which Terry room-shared with Tommy Nicholls. They settled in

Terry aged 18 months with his mother.

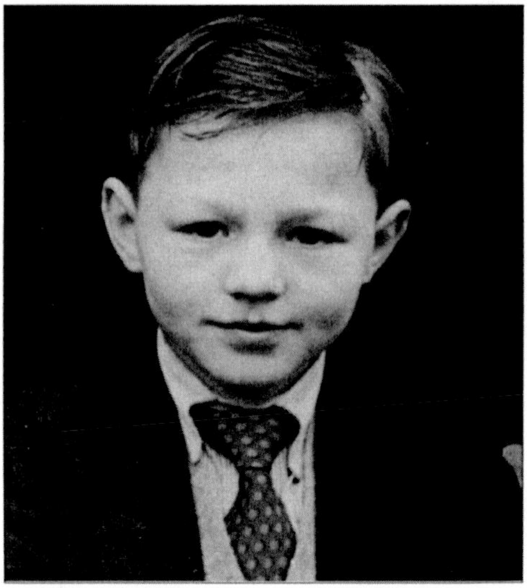

Terry aged seven - his first school photograph.

Terry (left) with friends at the Normandie Cafe, Cliftonville Lido near Margate, while on a family holiday.

Ashburton School Junior Boxing Team 1950. Spinks, aged 12, is seated second from right.

Spinks (right) with Danny and Roy Enifer in 1953 after winning a National Schoolboys Championship.

A lover of horses, Spinks admires Balfour Declaration at a Newmarket stable.

Spinks (front) and other stable lads, exercise horses at Marcus Marsh's stable, Newmarket in 1955.

With Mr and Mrs Bill Parkinson with whom he lodged for two years whilst a stable lad at Newmarket between 1953 and 1955.

Nat Sellar (far left) and Jack Solomons (centre) join British and European flyweight champion Dai Dower and Spinks, aged 15, as they shake hands after boxing an exhibition bout at Newmarket in 1953.

Terry proudly displays some of the trophies he won boxing in stable lads championships between 1953 and 1955.

Spinks (left) throws a left hook to the body of Janusz Litki whom he outpointed during an international match between England and Poland at Gdansk on 8 May 1956.

Spinks (right) attacks Ossi Palvalin during an international match between England and Finland at Helsinki on 28 June 1956.

Terry's beloved parents, Tich and Doris, raise their glasses at their Canning Town home on hearing of his Olympic success on 1 December 1956.

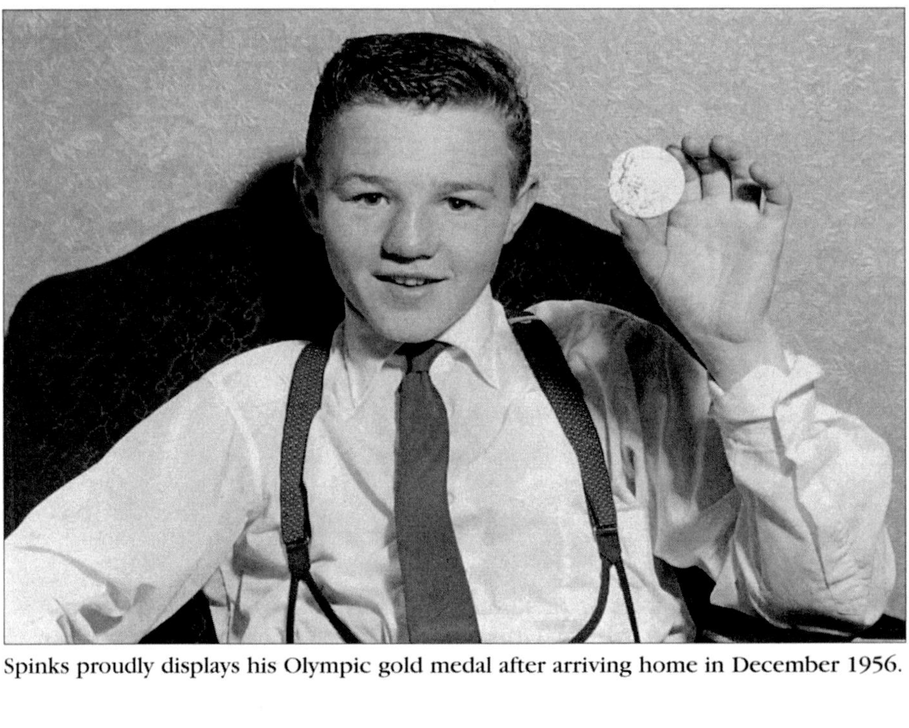

Spinks proudly displays his Olympic gold medal after arriving home in December 1956.

quickly, got on well together and soon made friends with other British athletes. They loved the food which Spinks described as being like home-cooking. Their preference was the Australian steaks, a favourite with many of the visiting athletes.

The weather in Melbourne was like an English spring and conditions suited the British boxers. Terry was fortunate that unlike some of his team-mates who arrived there suffering from travel sickness, he had no ill effects. He was therefore able to resume training without delay.

The daily routine was to be up at 6.00am, and after a quick cup of tea, everyone was out on six miles of roadwork. On returning, a good breakfast was followed by several hours of general loosening up and relaxation by playing table tennis or casual walking. After lunch there were a few hours of work-outs in the gym before having time to themselves during the evening.

Lack of sparring was a great concern to the team manager and coach, Flight Sergeant Jack 'Chiefy' Roy, both from the Royal Air Force. Roy decided to approach the Royal Naval authorities to seek permission for the British boxers to spar with sailors from ships anchored in Melbourne harbour. When no help was forthcoming the boxers were left with no alternative but to spar with each other in local gyms. Being the smallest member of the squad, Terry worked out with Owen Reilly (bantamweight), and Tommy Nicholls the featherweight.

Another concern to everyone was the quality of the Australian style boxing gloves borrowed from local police and military clubs for training. They had metal eyelet holes in the thumbs for ventilation and these caused some minor injuries. Spinks sustained a graze at the side of his nose and Dick McTaggart an abrasion on the top lip.

Apart from training there was not much for the boxers to do. Terry was fortunate in that he had plenty of cash with him. Before he left home his family had a whip round and gave him about £200 before he set off. He loved shopping and bought himself some nice clothes as well as presents to take home.

One evening he dressed himself up and went to a local cinema which was showing an 'X' rated film. As he reached the ticket desk the cashier took one look at him and said; 'You can't come in here, you're not 18.'

'Yes I am,' replied the baby-faced Londoner, 'Look I'm in the Olympics,' pointing proudly to his Olympic blazer badge. Even at 18 Terry endeared himself to people, particularly ladies, and after a bit of chat and some cockney humour he was allowed in free of charge. He loved the Australian people. 'They are certainly a friendly crowd,' he told an English reporter. 'They are doing everything they can to make us feel at home.'

* * *

Terry Spinks had reached the top in British amateur boxing by dedication, determination and an abundance of skill. His progress at senior level had been incredible, and the international matches he had boxed in abroad were a wonderful grounding for the task ahead. He loved foreign travel and felt at home as soon as he set foot in Australia.

Ever since he started boxing, Terry received tremendous support from his parents. They always made sure he had proper equipment and was smartly turned out. Although his mother worried whenever he was fighting, she used to launder his kit with loving care.

Terry was extremely proud about his appearance because he knew people looked at him and often remarked that he must come from a good home. Even at a very young age, this was important to him and did his confidence the world of good.

He never forgot the tremendous support given to him by his father, who spent more than £300 on his kit and training for the Olympics. 'It was worth it,' Tich proudly told a national newspaper reporter. 'He's no trouble, his only vice is clothes. He's got a cupboard full of suits, but what's wrong with that? It's better than smoking or chasing girls.'

* * *

The Olympic boxing competitions got underway on 24 November, and Spinks was the only British boxer in action on the opening night. His opponent, 22 year old Sammy Harris from Karachi, Pakistan, was much taller than the Londoner, but did not present any problems. Terry won a unanimous decision after three one-sided rounds in which Harris was completely out-boxed. He was in trouble several times in rounds two and three as the determined young Londoner caught him with solid punches. At the final bell, he was pinned against the ropes as Spinks pounded him with shots from both hands.

After the fight, Terry said that the only time he felt uneasy was when his 14 stone cornerman, Jack Roy, threatened to clip him round the ears if he didn't win.

'I wish all my opponents came from Pakistan,' said Spinks

cheerfully after sharing a shower with his beaten opponent. 'A workout like this was better than getting a bye.'

Despite the ease of his victory, Terry had to have heat treatment for bruising on his knuckles. Fortunately, the damage was minimal because two days later he was in action again against Abel Laudonio, a farm worker from Argentina. It was all Spinks in the opening round and he gave no indication of his hand problems as he pounded left jabs into the Argentinian's face. He threw plenty of rights as well, and one looping shot sent his opponent to the canvas.

In round two, Laudonio attacked head down, pumping hooks into Spinks body. The British boy moved well, kept out of danger, and ended the contest with a brilliant spell of fast moving boxing. It was enough to take a majority decision, but he left the ring limping having bruised his left leg in the final round.

In the quarter-final, Terry faced Vladimir Stolnikov of Russia, who had soundly beaten him in an international in Moscow five months earlier. Many critics thought this would be the end of the road for him and believed defeat was already in his mind. The night before the fight he had a nightmare and fell out of bed.

Spinks knew the Russian was progressing well in the competition and was on his mind more than he realised. In his dream, he and Stolnikov were standing toe-to-toe slugging away. When he awoke on the floor his team-mate Tommy Nicholls was standing over him. He told Terry that he had been thrashing about in bed yelling 'I'll get him, I'll get him.'

'When Tommy picked me up and found I was alright, I couldn't stop laughing for half an hour,' admitted the loveable cockney lad.

What was not generally known was that once Terry knew he had to face Stolnikov again, he became extremely perturbed. His team-mates became very concerned when they realised his anxiety, so they started a whispering campaign. They said the Russian was overweight, was frequenting steambaths, and had been seen wearing an overcoat to sweat away unwanted ounces on the roads of the Olympic Village at Heidelberg.

They convinced Terry that Stolnikov would be in no condition to stand up to a fast pace. Believing everything he was told, he went into the ring intent on setting a rapid pace. The ploy paid off, because although the Russian did most of the attacking, Spinks caught him with solid accurate shots as he pushed forward.

Using his superior speed and boxing skill, the Londoner began well and was soon piling up the points with left jabs. The grim-faced Russian, however, was always dangerous, and launched a series of powerful attacks. Towards the end of the opening round Spinks absorbed a number of stamina-sapping blows to the body and did well to weather the storm.

Terry came back well in round two and worried Stolnikov with well-timed left hooks and uppercuts. He also showed plenty of courage as the Russian kept boring in trying to land his powerful right hand.

The left jab was the essential weapon in Spinks' armoury, and he pumped it out to good effect throughout the final round. Refusing to be hustled out of it, his controlled boxing kept Stolnikov at bay. Then as the Russian tired towards the end, he used every ounce of energy to pump left after left to the face until the final bell. There was precious little in it, but Terry's better boxing earned him the decision and a place in the semi-finals.

'This was one fight I wanted to win,' said Spinks afterwards. 'I am delighted with the result.'

The semi-final stage of the competition proved extremely successful with three members of the British squad reaching the finals. Spinks, Tommy Nicholls and Dick McTaggart all won their contests by keeping cool heads against aggressive opponents.

Facing Rene Libeer of France, Terry again showed incredible maturity for his age. After a difficult opening round when he was shaken by several solid left hooks to the ribs, he was off his stool in determined fashion at the bell for the start of the second. Looking more assured, he snapped out his rapier-like left jab with tremendous accuracy. He took control of the fight and moved away from the Frenchman's dangerous hooks. On two occasions, short rights to the jaw shook Libeer who had no answer to the Londoner's incredible speed.

The third was a closer round as Rene rushed at Spinks forcing him back around the ring. Terry, however, never panicked and keeping a cool head, made persistent use of his accurate left jab as he retreated. They were perfect tactics and enough to earn him a close decision. There were, however, some heart-stopping moments after the final bell. The fight was so close that the score-cards of the referee and fourth judge were called for, and it was more than two minutes before the verdict was announced. 'It seemed like two hours,' remarked Spinks.

Some years later when he recounted his preparation for the semi-final, there was a hint of bitterness about Terry. 'What I needed was rest but what I got was gym work and routine training sessions,' he remarked. 'By my reckoning a fight was worth nine rounds of sparring, yet the night before I fought in the semi-final I had to do eight rounds in the gym. That decision could have cost us a medal.'

The time at Melbourne was not without moments of amusement and relaxation. Shortly after arriving there, Nicky Gargano met up with an old friend who worked in the town as an Estate Agent. He took Nicky, Terry and Ron Redrup on a tour of the Olympic Village, harbour, shopping centres and night spots so that they got a good feel of the place. They met a lot of local people who wished them luck and made them feel at home.

In the Olympic Village, a number of cars were parked for the convenience of the athletes, and drivers were available to chauffeur them around. One day after training, Spinks, Gargano and a couple of other boxers fancied going for a ride. Although no drivers were available, Terry suddenly found a car with the keys in the ignition. 'Come on,' he shouted, 'we don't need a chauffeur, I'll drive.'

Believing he could drive, the others all got into the car, but within a short distance he hit a number of other parked vehicles before stalling the engine. Without anyone noticing they managed to push the car back to where they found it, and all ran off laughing. To Terry it was just a prank.

* * *

The night that Spinks boxed Rene Libeer, the West Ham Amateur Boxing Club held their annual dinner at the Savoy Hotel in London. Loud cheers broke out when trustee, Lord Mancroft, read a telegram from club Chairman, Lt. Colonel Rudyard Russell, who was with the Olympic team in Melbourne:

> Best wishes from your Olympic representatives Redrup and Spinks.

Lord Mancroft was replying to a toast *'the club'* proposed by His Honour, Judge Carl Aavold, who said that when he went to the club to meet Spinks and Redrup, he found them delightful and modest outside the ring. 'I am sure that both of these young men are as proud of the club as the club are of them,' remarked the Judge.

Sir Isaac Wolfson, Life Vice-President of the club said, 'We are proud that Terry and Ron were chosen to box in the Olympics. Win or lose, we know they will be worthy bearers of the traditions with which this club tries to uphold.'

He added that it must be gratifying to all east Londoners present at the dinner to know that the three English boxers in the Olympic team were all from the East End.

* * *

An Olympic final is the dream of every athlete, but to reach one at the age of 18 is an incredible achievement. Spinks had done it in an era when boxers from Eastern European countries never turned professional. The top men invariably had the experience of more than 200 contests and represented their countries on many occasions. In reality, an 18 year old British lad was not in the same league as these men.

Despite having reached the final against incredible odds, Terry came very close to not being allowed to box. When he got up on the morning of the fight and stepped onto the scales for the customary check-weigh, he was found to be one and a half pounds over the flyweight limit of eight stones. The problem had arisen because the previous day he had been out relaxing in the scorching heat and became very thirsty. Without thinking of the possible consequences, he bought a couple of bottles of Coca-Cola and drank them.

There was pandemonium in the British camp because there was less than two hours before the official weigh-in at 10.00am. In a desperate effort to get the weight off him, coach Jack Roy lit a fire in the lounge of the team house. The windows and doors were shut tight and the curtains drawn to keep in the heat. The settees were pulled back and Terry skipped non-stop for more than half an hour in temperatures exceeding 100 degrees.

'The sweat rolled off me and the pounds disappeared,' he recalled, 'but I was so weak that Tommy Nicholls reckoned I would never come up for the second round in the final.'

Terry's opponent in the Olympic flyweight final was 26 year old Mircia Dobrescu, a tough Rumanian who had beaten Ireland's Johnny Caldwell, a future professional world bantamweight champion, in the semi-finals. Dobrescu, a strong favourite to win the gold medal, had a bye in the first round, and was thought to be the fresher of the two. Vastly more experienced than Spinks, he had reached the semi-finals of the 1952 Olympics at Helsinki, won a gold medal in the 1954 World University Games, and been narrowly beaten in the final of the 1955 European championships in Berlin.

Described as a 'Pocket Marciano,' Dobrescu was a muscular, barrel-chested little man, and although he stood just five feet tall he was built like a tank. In comparison Spinks looked pale and lean, his choirboy looks giving the impression of an enthusiastic schoolboy facing a man.

Appearances and reputations, however, held no fear for Terry because having grown up on the streets of the East End he had his own brand of toughness. Places don't come much tougher than Canning Town where he was getting into scraps with other youngsters soon after starting school. He didn't know the meaning of fear, and when he faced Dobrescu at the opening bell he was calm and focused on the task ahead.

The Rumanian started the fight aggressively and looked dangerous as he hurled a stream of punches from all angles. At close quarters, he pounded away at Terry's body, but the Briton remained calm. He was very focused, moved well and countered with sharp punches from both hands.

Dobrescu's weaving style earned him a caution in the opening round for ducking too low as he tried to bore in. He attempted to swamp Terry with wild rushes, but the determined 18 year old stood his ground and hit back with solid lefts and rights. Dobrescu was rocked back on his heels and when the bell ended the round there was an air of satisfaction about Spinks as he went to his corner.

Although the second round was quieter, Dobrescu pressed forward throwing his dangerous right hooks over Terry's left shoulder, putting him under continual pressure. The British fans had a scare when he slipped to the floor midway through the round, but he was up without a count and the referee ruled it a slip. There was no panic about Spinks, and with great maturity he continued to move and jab to pick up the points.

Spinks was really pumped up as he stood in his corner awaiting the bell to start the last round of what was the first final of the evening. Some 10 minutes earlier, as he waited to be called to the ring, the whole British team had screamed encouragement to him. 'Go out there and show 'em Tel,' yelled lightweight finalist Dick McTaggart as the 18 year old started his historic walk.

Dobrescu, who never stopped trying to force the fight, went straight on the attack, but was warned for holding when Terry caught him with some good shots. That final round brought one long roar from the huge crowd as the British boxer moved elusively, side-stepping the bobbing, weaving attack of Dobrescu. It was a thrilling contest and although he had to weather a number of stormy sessions, all the good boxing came from Spinks.

The crucial moment came when Terry was hurt for the first time by a right which drove him to the ropes. As Dobrescu moved in to follow up his advantage, the referee halted the action and warned Spinks for slapping. It was all the respite Terry needed and he was immediately back into his rhythm with left jabs and good combinations to head and body which made the Rumanian shake his head in despair.

The fight ended in spectacular fashion with both men fighting hard to secure victory. The accuracy of Spinks' punches was decisive and caught the judges eyes to win him a majority decision. There was tremendous cheering as his arm was raised because the vast majority of people had taken the 18 year old with the face of a choirboy to their hearts. Before the fight few critics believed he could beat a man of Dobrescu's experience, but he had done it in style.

It was a well earned victory because Terry adopted perfect tactics throughout the contest and boxed strictly according to a plan designed by team coach Jack Roy. His speed bewildered Dobrescu, yet when the going got tough he showed he could take a good punch without flinching. His superb ringcraft and more accurate punching made him a true world amateur champion. It would have been a cruel injustice if the referee and fourth judge had not swung the balance in his favour.

As the flyweight final was the first of the evening it meant that Terry became the first British boxer to win an Olympic gold medal for 32 years. The last were in Paris in 1924 when Harry Malin won the middleweight final and Harry Mitchell the light-heavyweight. Spinks was also the first Briton ever to win gold in the flyweight division.

Still looking fresh, Terry stepped on to the podium which had been placed in the ring. It was the proudest moment of his life as he was presented with the gold medal by the Marquess of Exeter, Vice-President of the International Olympic Committee Executive Board. Watching the presentation was the Duke of Edinburgh who had been among the 3,000 crowd to see the London boy's brilliant display.

The fans had really taken Terry into their hearts and the arena burst into thunderous cheering as he stood arms aloft clutching his medal. To his right stood John Caldwell of Ireland who won a bronze.

It was a highly successful Olympics for the British boxers, with Dick McTaggart winning gold in the lightweight division. Tommy Nicholls won a silver, while Nicky Gargano and John McCormack took bronze. Irish boxers Tony Byrne and Freddie Gilroy also picked up bronze medals. McTaggart was voted the most stylish boxer of the Games and was presented with the Val Barker trophy. Spinks was in third place.

The Scot was Terry's greatest admirer and had followed closely behind him to the ring. His hands already taped, and clad in his dressing gown, he sat behind the youngster's corner and urged him through every second of the enthralling final. 'His display gave me an incredible boost,' confessed McTaggart. 'When it was my turn, I was more determined than ever to win gold.'

Later that night a party was organised in honour of Spinks, McTaggart and the other medal winners. The celebration, however, did nothing for Terry who hated being the centre of attention. Once it was in full swing he quietly slipped away and went to bed to read his favourite comics.

Back in London, Reg Gutteridge was said to have been so excited when he heard the news of Terry's success that he danced on the tables at the *Evening News* offices in Fleet Street. Reg, who lost the lower part of his left leg in the D-Day Landings at Normandy in 1944, had campaigned relentlessly to get the ABA to send Spinks to Melbourne. His faith in the youngster was fully justified.

The following day Terry was relaxed and full of fun. Before the boxing competition started he insisted that if he won a medal he would ride a horse through the Olympic Village wearing the outrageous shirt he had bought in Honolulu. The shirt had been the subject of many jibes from his team-mates, but he was unperturbed. Up early, he went to a nearby riding-school and sweet-talked the proprietor into lending him a horse. Then, true to his word, he rode around the village, much to the amusement of everyone who saw him.

To win an Olympic gold medal is the greatest moment in any athletes career. For Terry it was particularly satisfying because not one newspaper tipped him to win an ABA title yet alone an Olympic medal. It was also the perfect response to those ABA selectors who considered him too inexperienced.

Terry never once doubted his own ability and remained full of confidence from the moment he was selected. 'I promised my parents I would bring home a medal,' he said shortly after beating Dobrescu. 'Well, I've kept my promise.'

He revealed that throughout the Olympic competition he had worn what he described as his lucky vest which had a number seven on the back. He had worn it in Poland and Russia, and when he took it off decided that when he got home he would donate it to the West Ham club together with the gloves he wore in the final. It was his way of saying 'thank you' for the tremendous support he had received from the club.

Throughout his life Terry always maintained that his victory was due largely to the efforts of his West Ham coach Billy Walker. 'He taught me everything,' he insisted. 'Before I went to Melbourne I was in tip top condition, thanks to him.'

In the days following Terry's success, stories of his life and achievements were splashed all over the newspapers. Many magazines did special feature articles about him, yet a year earlier he was practically unknown outside east London. Although he had reached the peak in world amateur boxing, he never stopped wishing he could become a jockey. The ultimate prize in sport for him would be to ride a Derby winner.

* * *

Back in Canning Town the news of Terry's success caused real excitement. To many people it was the best news they had heard since the declaration of peace more than 11 years earlier. Morgan Street had never seen anything like it and as the news spread, neighbours and friends began to troop to number 86 to congratulate Tich and Doris.

Everyone was invited in and there were celebration drinks until the early hours. Then at 4.00am a surprise visitor arrived. Eamonn Andrews, working for BBC television, arrived with a crew seeking an interview with Tich and Doris.

Even though the neighbours left, the little terraced house was still packed with back-up staff and equipment. Suddenly there was chaos when a cameraman caused a blackout by blowing all the fuses. The BBC, however, soon got things back to normal by sending an electrician to restore the lighting.

Tich and Doris were so overjoyed that once the interviews were over they invited the whole street back for a proper celebration drink. Their house was besieged as more and more reporters, photographers and newsreel cameramen arrived.

'If Terry were here now he would run out of the house,' said Doris.' 'He couldn't stand all the fuss.'

Tich revealed that from the moment his son was selected for the Olympics, he carried the first medal he ever won on his watch chain as a lucky emblem.

Later in the day dozens of reporters gathered at West Ham Conservative Club, where Tich had been a member for many years. When he and Doris arrived for a press conference they had tremendous difficulty getting inside because of the huge numbers of well-wishers. Inside, a Police Inspector from nearby Plaistow Police Station told them that as it was a very special occasion, a blind eye would be turned to the licensing laws. The Inspector stayed until the end and finished up very much the worse from drink.

All over Canning Town the pubs were packed as the whole neighbourhood appeared anxious to celebrate the occasion. For miles around the toast was *'Terry Spinks.'*

That evening the Spinks family threw a party for relatives, neighbours and friends at the nearby Abbey Arms in Barking Road. Terry was the toast. 'We expect him home sometime next week,' said his proud and jubilant father. 'We'll have some sort of welcome home party for him then.'

Over the next few days, letters and telegrams poured into the Spinks household, including one from Terry's idol, Sammy McCarthy. The volume was so great that a special delivery was needed from the local sorting office.

Within hours of him winning the gold medal, requests for Terry's services were received by his parents and the West Ham Boxing Club. 'If only a quarter of the requests could be met, Terry would get little rest,' Captain David Myers told the *London Evening Star* on 3 December. He said it was planned for him to box on the club show on 10 January at West Ham Baths against Derek Lloyd whom he succeeded as ABA champion.

Captain Myers said that he hoped Spinks would resist the obvious offers to turn professional and instead pursue the European championships in Prague the following May. 'Not many people realise that Spinks at 18, has achieved his great triumph in only his second senior season,' added Captain Myers. 'His father agrees with me that he has plenty of time, especially as it will be nearly three years before he could think in terms of a British professional title.'

At a meeting of West Ham Council the following day, the Mayor referred to the great pleasure with which he learned of Terry's success in Melbourne. He advised members that he had telegraphed congratulations to him. He promised that consideration would be given to the question of appropriately marking his outstanding achievement.

* * *

Back in Melbourne all medal winners were invited to a civic reception hosted by the Duke of Edinburgh. It didn't appeal to Terry who, as an ordinary lad, had no idea what was expected of him as an Olympic champion. Not wanting to be in the spotlight, he convinced his East End colleague Ron Redrup that the Duke wouldn't mind if he was absent. Instead they went and watched some horse racing.

The boxers remained in Melbourne for several days after the finals. Terry was always out sight-seeing, and together with other members of the squad was even taken aboard the Royal Yacht Brittania which was moored in Melbourne Harbour. Spinks and McTaggart created such a good impression with the Australian people that houses in the Olympic Village were later named after them.

The journey home became rather frightening when the plane developed engine trouble and had to make an emergency landing at Istanbul. After a couple of hours everybody was transferred to a larger Japanese aeroplane to continue the flight to London. Being inquisitive, Terry went for a walk and found his way into the upper area of the plane where there was a free bar. Tremendously excited by his discovery, he ran back to where Dick McTaggart and the other boxers were sitting. 'Hey Jock,' he shouted. 'Come quick, there's a bar up here, and it's free.'

Heathrow Airport was packed with friends and families of the athletes, newspaper reporters and photographers. There were wonderful scenes as excited people cheered and waved flags when the plane touched down.

Tich almost missed greeting Terry because earlier, when it was announced that the plane had been delayed, two newspaper reporters had taken him to a bar for a few beers and a bite to eat. As the plane was about to land he tried to make his way to the front of the crowd and join his wife, but it was packed tight. By this time Tich was slightly under the influence of drink, but desperate to see his son emerge from the plane, he tugged at the sleeve of a policeman on crowd control.

'Excuse me mate,' he said with slurred speech. 'I'm Terry Spinks' dad. Any chance of getting to the front?'

The copper took one look at him, smelt his breath and snapped, 'You're drunk, go away.'

When Tich persisted the officer became annoyed. 'Look, I've met about 30 blokes today who reckon they are Spinks' old man. Now clear off or you're nicked,' he said sternly.

Fortunately, another policeman standing nearby heard the commotion. He recognised Tich and persuaded his colleague to let him through. He joined Doris just in time to see the plane touch down.

After the aeroplane door opened, Terry followed Dick McTaggart down the steps. Tich and Doris were on the tarmac to greet him and there were hugs and tears all round. Having flown to Melbourne a month earlier, it was the longest period he had ever been away from home, and his parents were delighted to have him back. He had some jewellery for his mother and a woollen jumper for Tich. The £200 he took with him had all been spent.

At the press conference which followed, Spinks and the other boxers were put under tremendous pressure. They were bombarded with questions from excited reporters and barely given time to answer. Eventually, team coach Jack Roy called a halt. He explained that they were extremely tired after the long flight, but would be happy to answer more questions on another occasion.

It was about 1.00am before Terry and his parents arrived home to an incredible welcome. Canning Town was ablaze with Union Jacks of all sizes while flags and bunting hung from windows all along Morgan Street. Cheering crowds filled the street to greet him, and as he stepped from his car, excited neighbours lifted him on to their shoulders and carried him up and down the street.

Inside the house every member of the family had gathered to greet him, but Terry found it difficult to get excited. He was shattered, and after a short chat politely excused himself and went to bed.

When he awoke the next morning, Terry was amazed to find crowds of people outside his front door, wanting to see his gold medal. 'I wondered what all the fuss was about,' he recalled, 'but they were lovely people, so I had to keep them sweet.'

As it was almost Christmas some local children were given the day off school to celebrate Terry's success. When he saw them in the street outside his house he took the gold medal out to show them. He loved children and he was their hero. They were enthralled listening to his stories about the trip to Melbourne and would have stayed chatting all day if he hadn't told them he had other things to do.

Later that day, Spinks walked along Morgan Street to Rathbone Street market which had also been decorated with flags and bunting. It was a typical East End street market which bustled until well after 10.00pm on a Saturday evening. Despite most of the street being demolished during the war, the market still thrived well into the 1950's.

Many of the traders were local people who had known Terry all his life. They were thrilled about his success, and cuddled him and slapped him on the back as they offered congratulations. The market was packed with shoppers, many of whom had never seen him before, but they too stopped and made a great fuss of him.

Although he was never a great scholar, Spinks had fond memories of his days at Ashburton School. That afternoon, he therefore took his gold medal to the school to show the staff and pupils.

Terry had a good relationship with members of the press. In particular, he had great affection for Reg Gutteridge because of the tremendous support he had given him resulting in his eventual selection for the Olympics. 'If it hadn't been for Reg and a few others, I wouldn't have gone,' said Terry gratefully.

The London Evening Star also gave Spinks tremendous support, and at a special televised celebration on 17 December presented him with an illuminated address. The organisers, however, had a tremendous struggle getting him to appear. The shy and modest youngster didn't want any fuss and had to be coaxed to go along.

The actual presentation was made by 65 year old former police sergeant, Harry Malin, the last British boxer to have won an Olympic gold medal. Also present were Harry Mitchell who also won gold in 1924, Fred Grace aged 72 and Richard Gunn (85), who won gold medals at the 1908 London Olympics at light and featherweight respectively.

The illuminated address was an impressive item, and was endorsed:

> 'Presented to Terry Spinks by *The Star* on his return from his triumph in Melbourne 1956.'

The scroll bore the signatures of Malin, Mitchell, Grace and Gunn, and a list of other outstanding achievements in the ring by Terry, starting with his National Schoolboys championship in 1953 for which *The Star* had previously presented him with a framed certificate. In the years to come the two awards, dated three years apart, hung side-by-side on the parlour wall of Terry's home at Morgan Street.

Over the next few weeks Spinks gave countless interviews for newspapers and magazines, many of whom weren't normally interested in boxing. So much of his time was taken up that plans for him to box at West Ham Baths on 10 January were abandoned.

'Requests for personal appearances have come from all kinds of organisations,' said Captain Myers. 'Although he could accept only a small percentage, it would be impossible for him to train at the same time.'

A gold medal winner is high profile and television producers clamoured for Terry to be a guest on their shows. *Sports Desk*, *Top of the Pops* and *Six-Five Special* were just a few of the programmes he appeared on. Before each show a chauffeur-driven car collected him from Morgan Street, took him to the Studios and then home again afterwards.

Terry was bewildered by all the publicity and interest that was being shown in him. He was inundated with letters from boxing fans all over the world wanting autographs and photos. He even found that he had been elected President of a cycling club, but failed to understand why.

In the many discussions he has had over the ensuing years about winning the gold medal, he has always maintained that the worst part was all the fuss afterwards. Being just an East End lad he naively expected things to be exactly the same as when he left for Melbourne. Years later he was still amused by some of the things written about him in the newspapers.

The significance of what Terry had achieved was highlighted when he and his family were the recipients of a case of champagne sent to their home by the Duke of Edinburgh. They were shocked, but delighted, and the rarity of the moment made it even more precious.

The excitement of Terry's homecoming lasted for days. The Union Jacks and bunting still decorated the streets of Canning Town, and crowds continued to gather outside his house in the hope of seeing him. There was an endless stream of reporters and photographers, which eventually became tiresome. Terry, however, was very easy going, and one afternoon whilst drinking lemonade, he politely answered questions from selected press representatives in the quiet of his living room.

'I really felt on top of the world when I won that gold medal,' he told them. Before anyone could ask to see the medal he whipped it out of his pocket and opened the case.

Asked about his toughest fight, Terry smiled broadly as he remarked that they were all tough. 'But that Frenchman, Rene Libeer, who I met in the semi-final, he was a strong clever fighter.'

Terry was asked what he was going to do about his job. 'I dunno' he replied, but did reveal that Billy Butlin had offered him a position as a Physical Training Instructor at one of his holiday camps. 'I'm not certain about the future,' he continued, but insisted he would wear the vest of the West Ham club again. He carefully avoided giving a direct answer to the next question; 'Will you turn professional?'

Terry got some respite from the questioning when a group of schoolboys rang the door bell. Politely excusing himself from the reporters, he went out to show them the gold medal and didn't return.

Everybody at the West Ham Boxing Club were extremely proud of Terry's achievement. At the club show at West Ham Baths on 10 January, Vice-President, Lord Carnegie, a cousin of the Queen, presented him with a pair of gold cuff-links as a personal appreciation of his success. They had been specially designed and handmade. Each bore the Olympic five circle emblem and were inscribed *'West Ham A.B.C. 1956.'* On the back was engraved *'Gold medal winner – T. Spinks.'* At a club reception a few days later, Colonel John Courage presented Spinks with a personal gift of a gold tie-pin in the shape of a cockerel.

Terry was also presented with a gold watch on behalf of the club, as was team-mate Ron Redrup. He received a diamond ring from other admirers together with a number of other fabulous gifts.

At a special ceremony in the gymnasium at The Black Lion, Spinks donated the gloves he wore in the Olympic final to the West Ham Club. Today they are still displayed in a glass case on the wall of the gym with a photo of him as a youngster. On the opposite wall his Olympic vest and trunks are displayed in another glass case.

* * *

Top class sporting achievements invariably prompt requests for personal appearances, and Terry received many, particularly in the East End. For the purpose of publicity he was photographed exercising top greyhounds, Roeside Charm, Doon Marshal and Blue Sand at West Ham Stadium Dog Track. All were due to run in the December Stakes, and he was invited to present the trophy to the winning owner.

On 15 December he was invited to attend a function at Stratford Gaumont cinema and hang a present on the Christmas tree in the foyer. Before going on stage he hung his own personal gifts of a doll and pair of boxing gloves on the tree.

During the course of events on stage the Olympic Gold Medallist was too shy to speak. Instead, Captain David Myers, Secretary of West Ham Boxing Club, told the packed audience what he wanted to say. 'Terry is very glad to be here and is very proud for east London.' The teenager stood uncomfortably beside him with a nervous grin on his face as the audience yelled their appreciation at his attendance. He later went to the manager's office where he presented courtesy and long service awards to members of the cinema staff.

Terry's popularity was incredible, and just before Christmas he was sent a 30lb turkey by an admirer. Even at that age he had an exceptionally generous nature and decided to donate it to Queen Mary's hospital. 'It's yours,' he told the matron when he visited her. 'I would like the hospital to have it for Christmas.' He also hung an autographed pair of boxing gloves on a Christmas tree.

Apart from his native Canning Town, there was nowhere in Britain where Terry was greeted with more affection and enthusiasm than Newmarket. Although he had spent only two years there, local people regarded him as one of their own. He looked upon the town as his second home, and whenever possible returned to see Mr and Mrs Parkinson, with whom he had lived happily whilst he was a stable lad.

Soon after he became Olympic champion he was invited to appear at the Doric cinema in a show called *'Shilling a Second.'* It gave him the chance to spend the weekend with the Parkinsons and show them the gold medal. News that he was in town travelled fast, and reporters from local papers soon cornered him for interviews. Terry told them that Newmarket badly needed a properly equipped gymnasium. There were a number of stable lads in the town who, if handled correctly, could become successful in amateur boxing.

Just as he was preparing to spend a second day with the Parkinsons, Terry found he had to pay the price for fame. A baby giraffe born at London zoo had been named after him and the media were giving it maximum coverage. He was asked to return to London urgently for a television shoot with the animal. The next day a number of newspapers carried pictures of Spinks feeding the young animal which, despite being only two weeks old, stood six feet tall.

Invitations were received to a host of prestigious events. On 27 December, Terry met the Crazy Gang who were performing in their hit show *'These Foolish Kings'* at the Victoria Palace Theatre. During their act, Bud Flanaghan and Chesney Allen called him on to the stage and he received an incredible reception. After the show, he was invited back-stage where a crown was placed on his head by actress, Sonya Cordeau, to commemorate his Olympic success.

Since returning from Melbourne, Terry found himself on a real celebration circuit which included joining other Olympic medal winners at a special presentation ceremony at Buckingham Palace.

Early in the New Year, Spinks and Dick McTaggart were guests on the Billy Cotton Band Show at the London Palladium. Both wore their Olympic boxing kit as they gave a demonstration of skipping.

At one point, Cotton, a wonderful character, suddenly left the stage. When he re-appeared a few minutes later, he was wearing a pair of boxing shorts and carrying a skipping rope. He then positioned himself between the two gold medal winners and light-heartedly joined in their act.

At a function organised by the ABA at the Cafe Royal in London, Spinks and McTaggart were presented with gold watches by the National Sporting Club. At a separate event at the same venue a few days later, Terry and international footballer, Stanley Matthews, were guests of the NSC. When they were introduced by Donald Campbell, the ovation for Spinks lasted for two minutes.

Later in the month, Terry attended a Variety Club of Britain luncheon at the Savoy Hotel in the Strand. He was again joint Guest of Honour with Matthews who had been awarded a CBE in the New Year's honours list. Other guests included Judy Grinham and Margaret Edwards who had won gold and bronze respectively at Melbourne. When introduced to the packed gathering, Spinks had to stand on a chair to acknowledge the cheers.

Despite all the functions he attended, Terry still hated being in the limelight. He couldn't get used to it and whenever television cameras focused on him, he tried to hide. When the Dundee Corporation organised a dinner in honour of Dick McTaggart, he made an excuse not to attend. He was not being disrespectful to Dick who he adored, just avoiding another event where he was likely to be the centre of attention.

Meanwhile, letters poured into the offices of East End newspapers with suggestions as to how Terry could be honoured. One writer believed that the Borough of West Ham had a great opportunity, in the year of the Keir Hardie celebrations, to show it's appreciation for Spinks as the first West Hammer to win an Olympic boxing championship. It was suggested that the next new block of flats to be built in the borough be named after him. Alternatively, Morgan Street should be re-named Terry Spinks Avenue.

It was not long before Spinks became a target for Madam Tussauds. On 11 January 1957 he visited the famous waxworks where he was measured by Bernard Tussaud as a preliminary to the making of his effigy in wax. Once completed it was exhibited beside other immortals in sport including Gordon Richards, Freddie Mills and Sammy McCarthy.

On 1 February, West Ham Council unanimously agreed to adopt the proposals of a sub-committee set up to discuss how best to honour Terry. At a meeting with Councillors he expressed, with characteristic modesty, a desire for nothing elaborate. He asked that the ceremony be as simple and informal as possible. The Council, however, wanted the occasion to be special and arranged for a ceremony to take place at Stratford Town Hall on 19 February at 8.00pm. A notice was placed in local newspapers and the Spinks family advised that a chauffeur-driven car would collect them from Morgan Street.

It was all too much for Terry, and early in the evening of the event he told Tich he was going to the pictures instead. 'Don't be a little bastard,' said his father angrily. 'You have got to go.' Tich was particularly annoyed because in organising the event, the Council had permitted them to invite up to 20 guests. Shortly before the car was due to arrive, however, Terry disappeared from the house and hot-footed it to the Boleyn cinema at Upton Park.

Crowds of local people, photographers and reporters gathered outside the Town Hall waiting for Spinks to arrive. It was extremely embarrassing for Tich and Doris having to explain where he was. Determined that the show must go on, a Council official immediately contacted the local police station and arranged for Terry to be collected from the cinema. As he sat happily watching the film, a message was flashed on to the screen asking him to go to the foyer. Oblivious to the situation he left his seat and came face to face with a friendly policeman.

After a few words of reassurance, he agreed to accompany the officer to the Town Hall. Because he arrived in a police car, some sceptics thought he'd been up to mischief and a number of rumours began circulating amongst the onlookers. When it transpired what had really happened everyone, including the Council officials, found it thoroughly amusing.

At the reception Terry was presented with an illuminated address, framed and adorned with the seal of the borough, and signed by the Mayor and Town Clerk. In making the presentation, Alderman Michael Sullivan, JP, said he was very proud of West Ham boys, particularly Spinks and team-mate Ron Redrup. Congratulations and good wishes were extended by other members of the Council. A small presentation was also made to Redrup.

Councillor John Crowe said of Terry: 'Without boasting, he can say he has beaten the world at his weight. To have won an Olympic gold medal is a crowning glory for him and West Ham.'

The reception at Stratford Town Hall was small in comparison to a function Terry attended seven days later. He accepted an invitation to attend a luncheon at the Mansion House at the request of the Corporation of London to honour a visit to the City of

London by His Royal Highness, the Duke of Edinburgh. It was a massive event attended by the Lord Mayor and Lady Mayoress, the Sheriffs and their ladies, and other distinguished guests.

Pikeman of the Honourable Artillery Company were on duty, and the reception of guests commenced in the Salon at 12.15 pm. His Royal Highness arrived at 12.55 pm and was escorted by the Lord Mayor and Lady Mayoress by way of the Salon to the Egyptian Hall where the luncheon was being staged.

Terry was seated on a table which included Dick McTaggart, Judy Grinham and Gillian Sheen, all fellow gold medallists from Melbourne. A number of other medal winners were amongst the guests.

DOMINE DIRIGE NOS

Visit to the City

of

His Royal Highness The Duke of Edinburgh, K.G.

The Corporation of London

requests the honour of the Company of

Terence Spinks, Esq.

at a Luncheon at the Mansion House

on Tuesday the 26th February, 1957 at One o'clock, p.m.

The favour of an immediate answer, addressed to The Town Clerk, 55-61 Moorgate, London, E.C.2, is requested.

DRESS:—MORNING DRESS
OFFICERS—CEREMONIAL DAY DRESS

THIS CARD WILL NOT ADMIT.

Corporation of London luncheon invitation to Spinks - 26 February 1957

Although Terry wasn't aware of it at the time, all the attention he received was to have long-term consequences. Most nights brought a celebration dinner or gathering where he was guest of honour, and afterwards came the inevitable invitation: 'Come to a club – it's too early to go home yet.'

As an impressible 18 year old Terry didn't need asking twice. He was a lad who loved the bright lights and the attention he received wherever he went. The Astor Club, the Stork and the Pigalle – he knew all the best places in London's west end. At about five o'clock in the morning he would return to Canning Town for a rest before getting ready for another session that night.

'Cinderella would have looked like a witch in a week if she'd tried to keep up with me,' he once quipped when recalling his glory days. 'By the time I was 19 I'd drunk so much whisky I spoke cockney with a Scots accent.'

Apart from the celebrity events, Terry also loved going out with his mates, particularly fellow boxers Terry Gill, Terry Brown, Terry Murphy and a number of others from the Canning Town area. Since returning from Newmarket, most weekends were spent socialising.

At 5.00pm every Saturday, a dozen or more lads would meet at Whitechapel Waste and go for a few drinks at the Grave Morris pub next to Whitechapel Station. It was generally a quiet pub with no atmosphere, but at weekends they livened things up and it became a place where young people enjoyed visiting. They also used the Blind Beggar, a more trendy pub where there were plenty of girls. Most Saturday nights finished with a party at somebody's house until the early hours of Sunday morning.

On Sunday afternoons the same crowd often went to the Lyceum, a popular Mecca dance hall in the Strand. In the evenings they went for a meal followed by a cinema in the West End. By this time, Spinks usually had an attractive young lady on his arm.

The Ilford Palais was another of Terry's regular haunts. One night after his success at the Olympics, his presence was announced. Quite by chance and unbeknown to him, his cousin Rosemary had gone there with some friends and immediately went looking for him. The last thing the gold medallist wanted was to be seen with a group of 12 year olds, so he gave them a crisp white £5 note to get some drinks, and gave strict instructions not to return.

One of the doormen at the Palais at the time was Billy Walker, a big blond 18 year old lad from West Ham. He got to know Spinks well and had great respect for him. 'Everyone looked up to Terry,' remarked Billy years later. 'He was always a very smart, go forward little gentleman who never got into any trouble.'

One night, Billy had some bother at the Palais and knew he needed to get fit. Spinks suggested he went to the West Ham Boxing Club and even made an opening for him. Once Billy took up boxing, Terry followed his career closely and went to many of his amateur fights. They became very close friends, often going to Butlins Holiday Camp at Clacton at weekends. They never paid because Spinks knew all the dodges. They always climbed over a wall hoping to meet up with some girls with a key to a chalet.

Winning the gold medal heaped tremendous pressure on Terry, even when he was having a night out with his mates. Shortly after returning from Melbourne, a group of them went to the Sea-Span Club which was situated above a pub at St Osyth Beach, Clacton. As soon as word got around that Spinks was there, hundreds of people poured in off the street wanting autographs. It was so hectic that he didn't have time to socialise with his mates.

When the landlord rang the bell at closing time, Terry still hadn't had a drink. When he went to the bar to order one, the landlord said, 'You're too late, we are closed.'

'What do you mean?' snapped Spinks. 'I've just filled your pub and earned you a lot of money tonight. Now you are refusing to let me have a drink?'

'That's right,' said the landlord. 'I told you, we're closed.'

It was the one time that the normally placid youngster lost his cool. Turning away, he picked up a stool and threw it across the bar in frustration, smashing a few glasses in the process.

'Okay, okay,' shouted the landlord. 'I'm out of order. You're welcome to stay for a drink.'

Once everyone else was out of the bar, Terry and his mates settled down and were happily drinking until about 5.00am.

Spinks and his friends loved Chinese food, and often after a few drinks on a Friday or Saturday night, paid a visit to Chings, a Chinese Restaurant at Pennyfields in Limehouse. Like many other East End lads they were always up for a laugh and a bit of mischief. After a good feed and a few more drinks, they thought nothing of running out without paying. Although the restaurant owner chased them they were soon out of sight.

They considered the restaurant fair game and what they did was little more than boyhood pranks. Quite often they would go back a week or so later and pay. Then it would happen again before too long.

Another restaurant to fall foul of 'The Terry Boys' was Simons, an Indian restaurant also at Pennyfields. One night after a meal and a few drinks, the lads went, one by one, to the toilet in the back yard. As they started to make their escape over the back wall, one of them fell into a waste bin full of left-overs and chicken parts. His suit was ruined and as he climbed to his feet, Spinks shouted, 'Serves you right for trying to run off without paying.' He and the others then disappeared over the wall leaving their poor mate to find his own way out.

5

FIGHTING FOR PAY

Turning professional was a natural progression for Spinks because he had gone as far as possible with the amateurs. Whilst he always avoided the issue when it was raised by reporters, West Ham club secretary David Myers often said he believed that Terry would become a professional some time during 1957.

Although the newspapers confidently predicted that Spinks would never box as an amateur again, he and Ron Redrup both wanted one more contest in a West Ham vest. They were extremely grateful for the support they had received from the club which had been a big part of their lives for a long time. They therefore agreed to make their farewell appearances on a club show at West Ham Baths on 28 February 1957.

Spinks was originally matched with Peter Walsh, whom he beat in the ABA final, but he sustained a badly cut eye whilst defending his Scottish title. Determined that the Olympic champion should have a credible opponent, the organisers brought in new Scottish champion Laurie McKay as a replacement.

Anxious to do his part to ensure the show was a sell-out, Terry took 100 tickets and a huge number of posters to distribute. On the night, West Ham Baths was packed to capacity with fans wanting to see the Olympic gold medallist in action. It was his first public appearance in the boxing environment since returning from Melbourne and the welcome he received as he walked to the ring was deafening.

Although he boxed brilliantly, Terry had to pull out all the stops and use all his experience against a youngster who was not overawed by facing the Olympic champion on his own patch. McKay gave Spinks no respect and might easily have caused an upset. He was really up for the biggest occasion in his life and attacked from the opening bell. Counter-punching strongly he brought gasps from the crowd when he floored Spinks with a right to the head in the first round.

Honours were even in the second, but there was no doubt that the Londoner was finding McKay a real handful. When Terry went to the floor again in round three, his fans were becoming anxious. The referee, however, ruled it a slip. Spinks stepped up the pace as the round progressed and the huge local crowd got right behind him. Lightening left jabs followed by thundering rights to the body put him in command at the bell, and at last he was showing some of the form which won him the gold medal.

The plucky McKay tired badly in the fourth and Terry pressed home his advantage to make sure of victory. He received a wonderful ovation as his arm was raised, and it was the perfect present on what was his 19th birthday. After the fight, McKay went to Terry's dressing room and shook him warmly by the hand. 'The right man went to the Olympics,' he said. 'I'm glad you did so well.'

The following morning, Tich Spinks, who did not watch his son box, told local reporters what most people suspected. 'He can go no further as an amateur. He will now take a rest before making his professional debut.'

* * *

Since returning from Melbourne Terry had received many offers to turn professional. One came from Arthur Boggis, manager of British lightweight contender Dave Charnley. After a meeting with Terry and his father, Boggis invited them to join him at a show at the National Sporting Club. He even sent a chauffeur-driven car to Canning Town to collect them.

During the evening, Terry was called into the ring to take a bow. As he did so, the Master of Ceremonies told the dinner-jacketed audience that he would be turning professional under Boggis' management. 'No I'm not,' shouted Spinks who promptly left the ring. He went straight up to Boggis and told him that he still had other offers he wished to consider.

Spinks had long been an admirer of former British featherweight champion Sammy McCarthy from Stepney. Whenever his thoughts turned to pursuing a professional career it was always in his mind that he would love Sammy to be his manager. What had originally been a boyhood dream, however, suddenly became a reality. Having lost to Frenchman, Guy Gracia, at the Royal Albert Hall on 22 January, McCarthy realised he was well past his best.

Four days after Spinks had his final amateur contest, the BBC featured Sammy in a *'This Is Your Life'* programme. McCarthy shocked the world of boxing by announcing his retirement from the ring. He had made up his mind a few weeks earlier, but decided that the programme would be the perfect setting to make it official.

Terry was one of the special guests introduced by compere Eamonn Andrews. He said he was turning professional and told Sammy he wanted him to become his manager. Although they had spoken briefly about it a few weeks earlier, Sammy was delighted. The situation was ideal for the producers because it became an outstanding feature of the programme.

Terry's admiration for McCarthy, however, began long before that day. As an amateur boxer Sammy had a tremendous following in the East End. He even had his own fan club and whenever he fought, a dozen coaches loaded with his supporters left the 'Hope & Anchor' pub in Stepney to support him. Billboards throughout the East End would advertise: 'McCarthy Fights Tonight – Fare 2/6d.'

Injury prevented Sammy pursuing ABA titles in 1949 and 1950, and then in 1951 he was narrowly beaten in the North East London Divs by the talented West Ham boxer, Ron Hinson. Despite not winning a major amateur title, Sammy boxed for England on four occasions and secured three victories. He had an impressive amateur record of just seven defeats from more than 90 contests.

McCarthy was aged 19 when he turned professional under the management of Jack King with Snowy Buckingham as his trainer. By March 1953 he had notched up an unbeaten run of 25 fights, one of his victims being British featherweight champion Ronnie Clayton whom he outpointed in a non-title contest.

By this time Spinks was an established schoolboy boxer. He had followed Sammy's career closely and desperately wanted to meet him. One day the previous year, he got on a bus at Canning Town and travelled to Sammy's house in Commercial Road near to Arbour Square, because he wanted a photograph of him to put on his bedroom wall. With not a tinge of nerves, he knocked on the door, but walked away dejected having been told that Sammy was not at home.

Terry never gave up and eventually his luck changed. His Uncle Albert knew McCarthy's father quite well and arranged to take him to Commercial Road so that he could meet Sammy.

Having just won the national 5 stone 11 Schoolboy championship, it was a real treat for the youngster and an ideal moment to meet his idol for the first time. Sammy was very receptive and they spent over an hour talking about boxing and asking questions about each others career. It was the start of a friendship which would last for life.

Sammy's first impression of Spinks was that he looked so unlike a boxer. 'He looked so young and innocent,' recalled Sammy years later. 'I was very impressed with him because he was so polite and respectful when he was a young boy.'

As their friendship developed, Terry frequently called at Sammy's house just to say 'Hello.' If Sammy was out he would sometimes wait. Describing Terry's admiration for him, one reporter wrote:

> He admired him so much that it is said that to gain admission to Sammy's house in Commercial Road one would have to step over Spinks who was frequently sitting on the doorstep.

The first time Sammy actually saw Terry box was in the Stable Lads championships at Newmarket in 1953 when he was there to present the prizes. He was so impressed by his performance that he went back again especially to watch him. 'I could tell even then that he was very special,' said Sammy. 'He was very quick and had wonderful natural skill.'

The contact between them continued and when Terry returned to Canning Town to live with his parents, Sammy sometimes went to visit him. Terry used to go to Sammy's house as well.

In March 1955, McCarthy and his pal Alfie Betts, who drove him everywhere, went to York Hall, Bethnal Green, to watch the finals of the North East London Divs. Although Alfie was an ardent boxing fan he thought some of the contests in the ABA championships were unfair. As they were waiting for the flyweight final to get underway, he turned to Sammy and said, 'You see this little boy getting into the ring now, he's facing a mature man. It's so unfair.'

Sammy smiled and told him not to worry. 'Just watch carefully because my money is on the little boy.' It was Terry Spinks, who went on to win the fight comfortably with a fine display of boxing. McCarthy continued to follow Terry's progress and was absolutely thrilled when he won a gold medal.

They met a couple of times after Spinks returned from Melbourne and there were preliminary discussions about Terry eventually turning professional. Tich was present and liked the idea of Sammy becoming involved.

* * *

Once McCarthy agreed to become Terry's manager, he suggested they try to get Jarvis Astaire involved. Jarvis, an astute businessman, was heavily involved in boxing, and had given Sammy support throughout his career. Sammy trusted and respected him and believed he would be a great asset to Spinks. Discussions took place and Astaire agreed to become Terry's joint manager. His role would be to make arrangements for Terry's fights, deal with promoters and handle all business aspects, while Sammy would be responsible for training and fitness.

TERRY SPINKS

FORM No. 4

British Boxing Board of Control (1929)

RAMILLIES BUILDINGS, HILLS PLACE, LONDON, W.1

(Official Use only)
Application Record

Received -6 MAR 1957
Photos -6 MAR 1957
Medical Forms Rec'd -6 MAR 57
Passed by A. M. O. 13 MAR 1957
Recommended by
No. 4 Area Council
Date of Meeting -6 MAR 1957
Sig. of Secretary
Date of Issue 1.3.57
Granted by Board 13.3.57
Head Office Record
Licence No. 69854
Reg. No. B.17034
Entered

BOXER

APPLICATION FOR LICENCE

Fee: £1 per Annum

Received by Area Council Sec. -6 MAR 1957
Banked by Head Office: 7 MAR 1957
Head Office Receipt sent

Name in full — Professional: Terry George Spinks — Private:
Address: 26 Morgan St Canning Town London E16

Age 18 Date of Birth 28.2.38 Place of Birth E16 Nationality British

Exact Boxing Weight at the time of application for Licence: 8 stone

Number of Contests taken part in — Amateur: [illegible] — Professional: Nil

Name of Proposed Manager

I hereby apply for a Licence as a Boxer, and if this Licence is granted me I declare to adhere strictly to the Rules of The British Boxing Board of Control (1929) as printed, and abide by any further Rules or alteration to existing Rules as may be passed. I agree to pay the Fee in accordance with the above.

Date March 5th Signed Terry Spinks

Witness

Address

(Two Passport Photographs, full face without a hat, must accompany this application)

MUST BE WRITTEN IN INK

Terry Spinks' application for a professional boxing licence

Once everything was in place, promoters clamoured to stage Terry's first fight. The top promoter in London at the time was Jack Solomons, although it was rumoured that his close rival Harry Levene would stage Terry's professional debut. Jack, however, was a great wheeler-dealer and eventually succeeded in getting the former Olympic champion's signature.

Terry agreed to a purse of £250 to face Jim Loughrey from Derry at Harringay on 9 April. It was the biggest amount ever paid to a flyweight for his first professional contest. Top of the bill was a British lightweight championship contest between Joe Lucy and Dave Charnley, both of whom were former opponents of Sammy McCarthy. Ron Redrup and Terry Downes were also scheduled to make their professional debuts on the same bill.

Spinks was unique in that he was the first British Olympic gold medalist to turn professional. He sold his share of tickets and within a few days all 6,000 seats priced at ten shillings and one guinea had been sold.

Under the guidance of Sammy McCarthy, Terry became a full time professional from the start, unlike most young boxers who also had other jobs. He started full training at the Thomas A' Beckett gymnasium in the Old Kent Road in south London on 11 March. Initially, Sammy was his main sparring partner, but as the Beckett was the finest gym in London, used by most of the top fighters, there were always plenty of good men to spar with.

At first Terry found the transition from the amateur ranks quite daunting, but with hard work and dedication he soon settled down. In order to build up his stamina he did five or six miles on the road every morning. There were training sessions every day except Sundays, unlike his days as an amateur when he had been accustomed to three evenings a week in the gym and runs of just two miles.

Terry became very popular and loved working at the Beckett, a thriving gym used by most of the top boxers of the time. Henry Cooper and all of Jim Wicks' stable trained there, and men like Dave Charnley and Peter Waterman were always keen to give him advice and encouragement.

Jim Loughrey was a sensible choice of opponent. In his last fight he was narrowly outpointed by Dave Moore for the Northern Ireland flyweight title in a thrilling 12 rounder in Belfast. He was described as being a real tearaway who adopted a head-down, boring-in style of fighting. With a reputation for toughness, he was expected to expose any weakness Terry might have.

The weigh-in took place at Jack Solomons gym in Great

HARRINGAY ARENA Green Lanes, N.4.

Doors open 6.30
Commence 7.30

Jack Solomons presents

TUESDAY APRIL 9

NEW STARS ON PARADE ! YOUTH TAKES A BOW!

Lightweight Championship of Great Britain. 15 (3-min.) Rounds at 9st. 9lb.

THE FIGHTING PUBLICANS !

JOE LUCY v DAVE CHARNLEY

(Champion) (Challenger)

THE MATCH ALL FIGHT FANS HAVE BEEN WAITING FOR !

Featherweight Contest. 10 (3-min.) Rounds at 9st. 2lb.

BOBBY NEILL v VICTOR PEPEDER

(Paddington) Boxing's "Golden Boy"

(France) Undefeated in 1955—lost only one fight in 1956

THESE BOYS HAVE IDENTICAL RECORDS.

Flyweight Contest. 6 (3-min.) Rounds at 8st. 2lb.

TERRY SPINKS v JIMMY (Ginger) LOUGHREY

(Canning Town) Olympic Gold Medallist. First Pro Contest

(Belfast) The All-Action Irish Flyweight Terror—fought for the N. Irish title on February 2 . . lost on points.

Middleweight Contest. 6 (3-min.) Rounds at 11st. 4lb.

TERRY DOWNES v PETER LONGO

(Paddington) Ex-American Marine Champion, regarded in U.S. as outstanding amateur of 1956.

(Covent Garden) The former A.B.A. Middleweight Champion.

Welterweight Contest. 10 (3-min.) Rounds at 10st. 9lb.

TOMMY MOLLOY v LES MORGAN

(Birkenhead) Undefeated ! (Welterweight Champion of Wales)

Middleweight Contest. 8 (3-min.) Rounds at 11st. 10lb.

LEW LAZAR v PADDY DELARGY (Galway)

(Aldgate) Can he stop the Irish Tearaway?

The Fightin' Terror. The Hungry Fighter !

(Cohens v. Kellys) ?

Bantamweight Contest. 8 (3-min.) Rounds at 8st. 8lb.

GRAHAM VAN DER WALT v GEORGE DORMER

(Bantamweight Champion, South Africa)

(East Ham) Former A.B.A. Bantamweight Champion)

Light-Heavyweight Contest. 6 (3-min.) Rounds at 12st. 7lb.

RON REDRUP (West Ham) v ABE STANLEY

A.B.A. Middleweight Champion '56. First Pro Contest !

(Bournemouth) Eleven Bouts Undefeated

PRICES (inc. Tax): 10/-, 21/-, 42/-, 63/- and 105/-
(All Sold)

Tickets obtainable at Jack Solomons, 41 Gt. Windmill Street, London, W.1, (GERrard 9195/6) and at Harringay Arena, Green Lanes, N.4 (STAmford Hill 8221) and at Harringay Box Office, 62a Piccadilly, W 1, (HYDe Park 2891) and Agencies

Poster advertising Terry Spinks' first professional contest

Windmill Street at noon on the day of the fight. The place was packed, as was the entrance and narrow street outside, with many fans there just to get a glimpse of the former gold medallist.

That evening Harringay Arena was full to capacity for what promised to be an enthralling programme of boxing. Thousands of fans travelled the short distance from the East End, not only to support Spinks, but also Joe Lucy of Mile End, Lew Lazar (Aldgate) and George Dormer (East Ham) who were also on the bill.

The first professional contest is without doubt the most nerve-racking experience in a boxers career. Spinks, however, showed not the slightest sign of nerves as he climbed into the ring to massive cheers. He looked ice-cool as referee Pat Floyd issued his final instructions, and at the opening bell set about his task with grim determination. He moved well and Loughrey couldn't match him for speed, and all the scoring came from the Londoner's brilliant left jab.

Tremendous cheering greeted Spinks as he returned to his corner at the end of the opening round. He continued the good work in the second, during which Loughrey was warned for holding as Terry pounded him on the ropes. After coasting the third with good boxing, he really opened up in the fourth and sent the Irishman to the floor with a good right to the jaw. Although he was up at 'two' he was in further trouble when another hard right split his left eyebrow. Blood streamed down Loughrey's face and after a quick inspection referee Floyd called a halt.

Weighing 8 stone $1^1/_4$ to Loughrey's 8 stone, Spinks did a workmanlike job from the first bell and never left the issue in doubt. It was the perfect start to his professional career and it was to his benefit that he was in the ring long enough to get the feel of the pro arena. Boxing with great maturity, he did all that had been asked of him and he was cheered all the way back to his dressing room.

Three weeks later Terry was back in action, this time at the famous Manor Place Baths, Walworth in south London. His opponent, Jerry Parker from Beeston, was a good test having won 13 and drawn two of his 22 contests since turning professional 15 months earlier. A very busy fighter, this would be his 10th contest in 1957, and he had won the last five.

The promotion, staged by Jack Solomons, was his annual charity event on behalf of the Mayor of Southwark's Fund for the poor children, aged and needy of the Borough. With Terry Downes topping the bill and Ron Redrup making his delayed professional debut, it was a full house.

Spinks again had massive support and although he boxed well enough to take a points decision over six rounds, he sustained a cut over his left eye in the fourth. It was the first time for five years that he had sustained such an injury. Luckily it healed well, but there was some concern because he was already booked to box at Shoreditch two weeks later.

Shoreditch Town Hall was the real hot-bed for boxing in the East End. Regarded by many fans as the best small hall in the country, it had an incredible atmosphere. There was always a full house and fans queued to see a card of six rounders. Despite the roughness of the area there was rarely any trouble and the only security was a character called 'Sailor' on the door. Nobody messed with him and if they didn't have a ticket they didn't get in.

A square arena overlooked by a balcony, Shoreditch was always thick with cigarette and cigar smoke. Sometimes intimidating, it had all the background features of a crime movie. Betting was very much a part of the place with the main players seated close to the ring.

Wheeler-dealers and members of the criminal fraternity were also part of the fight game in the East End. They were always very much in evidence at Shoreditch, but rarely interfered. All were hard-core boxing fans who respected fighters because honour gained in the ring is generally respected in society. People looked up to fighters because coming from tough neighbourhoods everyone knew what they had done to achieve it.

His damaged eye healed, Spinks stepped into the ring at Shoreditch on 14 May to face Billy Kane of Belfast. With Terry Downes topping the bill against Dick Tiger of Nigeria, the place was packed to capacity and hundreds of fans were turned away.

Weighing 8 stone 1¾, Terry had his easiest victory so far as a professional. Dazzling his opponent with fast accurate punching and brilliant footwork, he punched the Irishman to a standstill. When referee Pat Floyd stepped in and called a halt in the second round, blood was streaming from Kane's nose.

Whilst the fans were thrilled with Terry's performance, there was great disappointment when his mate Terry Downes suffered his first pro defeat. In one of the best fights seen in London for years, the former United States marine was stopped in the sixth round.

Jack Solomons immediately signed Spinks for his big Eve of the Derby show at Harringay on 4 June and paired him against Jerry Parker in a return contest over six rounds. Parker gave a good account of himself five weeks earlier and felt that he left his effort too late. Fellow Eastenders Ron Redrup and Lew Lazar were also on the bill.

Although Spinks gained victory, it came about in unusual circumstances. Both he and Parker sustained badly cut eyes in the second round, but after a careful inspection referee Eddie Maguire allowed the fight to continue. During the interval both sets of cornermen worked to repair the damage, but early in round three both men were bleeding heavily again.

The referee stopped the action and ruled that neither man was in a condition to continue. As Terry was ahead on points at the time, he was awarded the decision which was recorded as a points victory over three rounds. Many people were baffled because such an ending is very rare, and it caused considerable debate in the press.

Being cut in his last two fights became a concern for Terry's fans and his handlers. In the amateur game his speed and boxing skill had kept him out of trouble, but the paid side was much different. Some critics believed that he didn't have the punching power to keep the more hardened pro fighters away.

Although trainer Snowy Buckingham was a good cuts man, he and Sammy McCarthy realised that a change of style was needed if Spinks was to avoid getting cut regularly. They therefore spent considerable time at the Thomas A' Beckett gym trying new tactics. They wanted to slow Terry down, which although tending to make him more vulnerable to punches, added considerably to his own punch power. It was a delicate process, but designed to change him from being a dancing boxer into an aggressive fighter, a style more suited to the professional ring.

To enable his cut eye to heal properly, Terry didn't box again for six weeks, but went to the gym most days. The change of tactics paid handsomely, and at Shoreditch Town Hall on 16 July he pounded out his most impressive victory to date. The critics who said he had no punch were made to eat their words as he hammered Scotsman, Pat Clancy, into retirement at the end of the third round.

Clancy was a credible opponent for the former Olympic champion, having outpointed Northern Ireland title holder Dave Moore in his last contest. Against Spinks, however, he had no answer to tremendous rights to the body which took all the steam out of him. Noticeably slower than usual, Terry placed his shots with precision and power rather than trying to swamp his opponent.

It was by no means one-way because Clancy used the ring well for a time and occasionally shook Spinks with good counter-shots. Early in round three, however, the Londoner's power began to tell. A vicious right uppercut to the chin sent the Scot sprawling for a count of 'eight.' A minute or so later a right cross to the jaw sent him to the floor for another 'eight' count. He looked shaky as he rose, and two more punches to the chin put him down again for 'four.' When the bell ended the round Clancy was draped over the ropes in Spinks' corner. Although he retired with a damaged lip, he avoided a certain knockout in the next round. It was his first defeat inside the distance, a tribute to the power that had recently been built into Terry's new fighting style.

Spinks was thrilled with his victory and the following day set off for Marcus Marsh's stable at Newmarket to relax. With the blessing of his manager, he had done this after all his fights since turning professional.

'I see no reason why Terry shouldn't get away from boxing for a few days now and again,' said Sammy McCarthy. 'He loves horses and finds the sport relaxing. The only reason he hopes to ride in races is for the excitement.'

Terry had seriously considered becoming a jockey and discussed the situation with Marsh when he was a stable lad. The trainer had great respect for him and told a national newspaper: 'He's a strong rider and has promise. I'll help him all I can, but it's going to be hard graft. Jockeys have to be nursed and brought along slowly, just like fighters.'

On returning to London, Terry spent a few days at the Thomas A' Beckett before accompanying British welterweight champion Peter Waterman and West Ham colleague Terry Gill to Bournemouth. Waterman, managed by Jarvis Astaire, and Gill by Sammy McCarthy, were due to box at Poole on 3 August, and set up their training camp at Harry Legge's Olympic gymnasium in Bournemouth. As Spinks was due to box at Southampton nine days later in his first contest outside London, Sammy thought it would be good experience for him to train in a different environment.

The three boxers were good friends. Spinks and Gill being mates outside boxing, had got to know Waterman from working at the Beckett. All trained by Snowy Buckingham, they ran together on the Bournemouth sands and worked alongside one another in the gym. At the Poole Football & Speedway Stadium, Waterman stopped Michel Francois of France in three rounds, and Gill maintained his unbeaten record with a points victory over Johnny Melfah of Ghana.

Spinks boxed a three-round exhibition with Teddy Peckham (Bournemouth), and was given a fantastic ovation by the 3,000 crowd when introduced. Displaying all his boxing skills, he delighted the fans throughout the three rounds, and was warmly applauded as he left the ring.

Southampton Ice Arena was packed on 12 August and hundreds had to be turned away. Promoter Stan Baker's show was the first in the town since 1939, and Spinks and Peter Waterman, having his second fight in nine days, were a tremendous attraction.

Facing old opponent Jerry Parker for the third time in 15 weeks, Terry boxed brilliantly from the first bell. He set a fast pace and floored Parker briefly with a short right to the jaw in the opening round. Good head punches rocked the Beeston man in the second, although Spinks appeared content to box rather than press for a stoppage. Whenever Parker attacked, Terry moved cleverly out of range rather than stand his ground and trade punches. It was a complete contrast from his fight with Pat Clancy.

Although Parker sustained a bad cut beneath his right eye in the fifth, he never gave up. He staged a grandstand rally in the final round, but it was not enough to snatch victory. Although some of the rounds were close, Spinks won convincingly. The Southampton fans loved Terry and cheered him all the way to the dressing room.

On the same bill, Peter Waterman scored his 38th victory in 41 bouts when he stopped Nick Moos of Holland in two rounds in the top of the bill contest.

Terry's progress in the paid ranks was recognised by the trade paper, *Boxing News*. Although he had only been a professional for four months he was made number four flyweight in Great Britain in their August ratings.

Spinks was back in action on 27 August, this time in his own backyard at Canning Town Public Hall. The place was packed for what was his first top of the bill contest, and all tickets were sold days in advance. His opponent was 24 year old George McDade from Glasgow who had won four of his five contests during 1957.

It was thrilling while it lasted because from the opening bell the stocky McDade bundled into Spinks trying to unnerve him with dangerous swings from both hands. Terry remained calm, and with clever footwork and sharp counter-punching, soon took control of the fight. Although both men scaled 8 stone 1½, Spinks towered above the Scot and had a good reach advantage. After a few anxious moments during the opening minute, his performance was faultless. His whole approach to the professional game looked much more assured.

Blood poured from McDade's nose in round two, and in the third Spinks sent him to the floor with a perfectly timed left hook to the chin followed by a short right. When the Scot rose he had a bad cut above his left eye and blood streamed from his nose. At the bell McDade looked in trouble and it came as no surprise when his cornerman, Tommy Gilmour, signalled his retirement.

Spinks had already been told that this was the last fight of his apprenticeship and in future he would be boxing eight rounds. 'I wish the fight had gone further, perhaps the full six rounds,' he said later in his dressing room. 'My next bout is my first eight rounder so I needed a longer contest for preparation.'

Terry's first fight over the longer distance was scheduled for Shoreditch Town Hall on 10 September against Irishman, Ivan McCready. Like Spinks he had had seven paid contests, winning six. His only defeat was in his fourth fight when he appeared to make a premature move up to eight rounds and was outpointed.

The top of the bill contest attracted great interest, but Terry caused a sensation when he revealed that he had been invited to ride two horses at Manchester just four days before the fight. Provided trainer Marcus Marsh agreed, he would be on *'Luing'* in the Cromwell Selling Handicap and *'Dominion'* in the Loom Handicap. Both horses were owned by the wife of boxing enthusiast, Mr Schmidt Bodner.

Newspaper cartoon of Terry as a jockey

Shoreditch promoter Harry Grossmith was furious because he couldn't bear the thought of a racing mishap ruining what he expected to be a sell-out show. Referring to a clause in the British Boxing Board of Control rule book dealing with the right of a

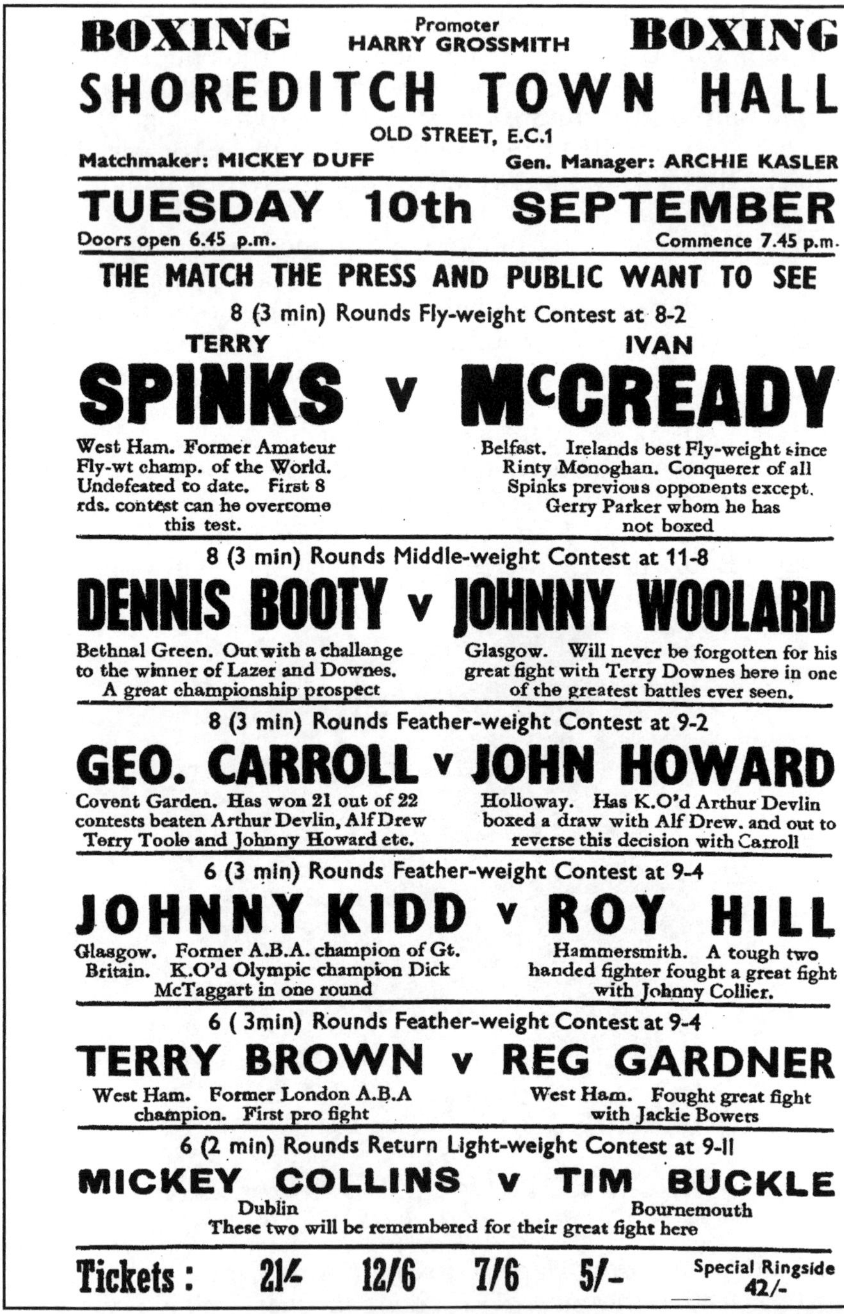

BOXING Promoter HARRY GROSSMITH BOXING

SHOREDITCH TOWN HALL

OLD STREET, E.C.1

Matchmaker: MICKEY DUFF Gen. Manager: ARCHIE KASLER

TUESDAY 10th SEPTEMBER

Doors open 6.45 p.m. Commence 7.45 p.m.

THE MATCH THE PRESS AND PUBLIC WANT TO SEE

8 (3 min) Rounds Fly-weight Contest at 8-2

TERRY SPINKS v IVAN McCREADY

West Ham. Former Amateur Fly-wt champ. of the World. Undefeated to date. First 8 rds. contest can he overcome this test.

Belfast. Irelands best Fly-weight since Rinty Monoghan. Conquerer of all Spinks previous opponents except. Gerry Parker whom he has not boxed

8 (3 min) Rounds Middle-weight Contest at 11-8

DENNIS BOOTY v JOHNNY WOOLARD

Bethnal Green. Out with a challange to the winner of Lazer and Downes. A great championship prospect

Glasgow. Will never be forgotten for his great fight with Terry Downes here in one of the greatest battles ever seen.

8 (3 min) Rounds Feather-weight Contest at 9-2

GEO. CARROLL v JOHN HOWARD

Covent Garden. Has won 21 out of 22 contests beaten Arthur Devlin, Alf Drew Terry Toole and Johnny Howard etc.

Holloway. Has K.O'd Arthur Devlin boxed a draw with Alf Drew. and out to reverse this decision with Carroll

6 (3 min) Rounds Feather-weight Contest at 9-4

JOHNNY KIDD v ROY HILL

Glasgow. Former A.B.A. champion of Gt. Britain. K.O'd Olympic champion Dick McTaggart in one round

Hammersmith. A tough two handed fighter fought a great fight with Johnny Collier.

6 (3min) Rounds Feather-weight Contest at 9-4

TERRY BROWN v REG GARDNER

West Ham. Former London A.B.A champion. First pro fight

West Ham. Fought great fight with Jackie Bowers

6 (2 min) Rounds Return Light-weight Contest at 9-11

MICKEY COLLINS v TIM BUCKLE

Dublin

Bournemouth

These two will be remembered for their great fight here

Tickets: 21/- 12/6 7/6 5/- Special Ringside 42/-

Poster advertising top of the bill contest between Terry Spinks and Ivan McCready

promoter to restrain a boxer from endangering himself and the box-office, the promoter threatened to take the matter to the Board if Spinks insisted on riding.

Sammy McCarthy had no problem about Terry riding and even offered Grossmith a three-figure sum as a guarantee of his boxers' appearance at Shoreditch on 10 September.

Spinks had recently put in a good deal of riding during a week-long stay at Newmarket and was excited at the prospect of riding in a race for the first time. 'The thought of having my first ride in public is more exciting than winning the gold medal in Melbourne,' he told interested reporters.

For some while Terry let it be known that he would love to become a jockey when he retired from boxing. His desire was not unique because Charlie Smirke, another cockney, made the switch some years earlier. He was a good boxer and some experts believed that had he not gone into racing he would have had a successful boxing career.

Having received no assurances that Terry would pull out of the races, Harry Grossmith referred the matter to the Board of Control. All parties were called to a meeting at the Board on 5 September, and after a lengthy discussion on a friendly basis, Spinks agreed to postpone his plans to ride until after the fight with McCready. There was no animosity and after the meeting Spinks, McCarthy and Grossmith shook hands for photographers in the street outside the Board offices.

In Ivan McCready, Terry faced a difficult task in his first contest over eight rounds. A former amateur international, he was described in some quarters as being Ireland's best flyweight since Rinty Monaghan. He had beaten all of Spinks' previous opponents with the exception of Jerry Parker, who he had not faced. In his last three contests he had beaten Billy Kane (ko.2), George McDade (points) and Jim Loughrey (rsc.6).

Shoreditch Town Hall was packed and the punters were not disappointed. Although it was Terry's toughest fight, he won it handsomely, despite being floored for the first time as a professional. He achieved success with aggressive fighting to match his superb boxing skills.

After steady thoughtful boxing for the first two rounds, Spinks was suddenly caught by a good right hook to the jaw at the end of the third. He went to the floor, but the bell sounded before the count was taken up. As he stared vacantly in the direction of his corner, Sammy McCarthy and Snowy Buckingham jumped into the ring and hauled him to his stool. Water was poured over his head and the ice bag held firmly at the back of his neck. The treatment quickly revived him and at the bell he was on his feet ready for the start of round four.

McCready attacked viciously, but Spinks stood and traded punches with him. 'Keep boxing, move around,' yelled McCarthy from the corner. Obeying orders, the Canning Town youngster stemmed Ivan's attacks with good left jabs and counter-punches, and kept away from further trouble. A number of critics recognised that he had developed a style very similar to that of McCarthy when he was at his peak.

Terry did exceptionally well over the longer distance and confirmed his strength and stamina as the fight developed. At the end, the powerful looking Irishman was hanging on.

McCready was disappointed to lose and immediately challenged Terry to a return. 'There's nothing Ivan would like better than another bundle with Spinks,' his manager Jackie Briers told *Boxing News*. 'We're not looking for any hometown decisions. Terry is certainly a good boy, but he lacks one thing Ivan has – a real punch. A re-match is a natural.'

There was no question of Spinks being given an easy ride in the professional ranks, and within a month he was in action again, this time at the Royal Albert Hall. His opponent, Indian-born Pancho Bhatachaji, a stocky aggressive 24 year old, had won 13 of his 15 professional contests during the past 18 months.

Although Spinks was rated as the number three flyweight in Britain behind champion Frankie Jones and Len 'Luggy' Reece of Wales, his handlers knew Bhatachaji would be a handful. Consequently, the training at the Thomas A' Beckett gym was intense as they concentrated on speed and movement.

Pancho set a blistering pace seeking to batter Spinks into an early defeat. The Indian was considerably stronger and his body shots made Terry back away at speed. Yet with the calm of a veteran he picked his punches with superb skill. Speed was essential because Bhatachaji never gave up attacking, but by the fifth round his eyes were puffed and his nose bleeding from the accuracy of Terry's left jab. Towards the end he was tiring badly, but Spinks didn't have the punch to end it and had to be content with a points victory.

Before the end of 1957, Terry had notched up two more victories within the space of eight days. Stanislas Sobolak of France was stopped in six rounds and Malcolm McLeod from Coventry outpointed over eight. His record of 11 consecutive wins in the space of just eight months was the best of any boxer in Britain during the year. It was a satisfactory transition to the professional ranks and a perfect base to build on.

At Leyton Baths on 2 December, Spinks was due to meet French-Algerian, Mohammed Mefta. Although he was not known in British rings, matchmaker Mickey Duff assured local reporters that he would give Spinks a good test. With all tickets sold, Mefta pulled out of the fight with just a couple of days to go and Sobolak replaced him.

At 8 stone 3½, Terry was giving away two pounds to his first overseas opponent. Although he pleased his army of fans with his performance, he failed to excite them. Boxing brilliantly he was a long way ahead on points when a horrible clash of heads brought the contest to an end. Blood poured from an ugly gash on the Frenchman's forehead leaving referee Tommy Little no alternative but to stop the fight.

Against the Dublin born McLeod on the Dick Richardson – Bob Baker bill at Harringay, Spinks was often under considerable pressure. The 24 year old Irishman put everything into a final onslaught in the last round and had Spinks reeling from heavy swinging punches to the head. Jabbing brilliantly, the Londoner rallied in the last minute to take the decision, but there was very little in it.

* * *

Still to reach the age of 20 and having been a professional fighter for only eight months, Terry had an exceptional standard of living. He was the proud owner of seven suits, 14 pairs of shoes and could afford to buy long-playing Frank Sinatra records whenever he liked.

At all the receptions he attended after returning from the Olympic Games, he was always immaculately dressed, looking more like a banker than a boxer. He spared no expense when it came to his appearance.

One day shortly after he returned from Melbourne, he was in the West End and took a fancy to a pair of brown crocodile-skin shoes displayed in a shop window. Although disappointed that there were none in his size, he had a pair made at a cost of £80.

Some years later he ruined the shoes by wearing them on a hop-picking weekend. It was something he and his friends had done for several years. They usually went to the Faversham area of Kent where they also went 'scrumping.' There were plenty of orchards in the area, and when they returned home they were laden with apples which were stored for Christmas.

Due largely to guidance from his father, Terry had by this stage of his life, always looked after his money. In September 1957, with an eye to the future, he gave his mother £1,000 as the deposit on a retail confectionery shop at New Barn Street, Plaistow. Although it was called 'Terry Spinks', and attracted a great deal of publicity, he took none of the profits. Doris managed the business which was held in trust for Terry.

Meanwhile, the former Olympic champion concentrated on his boxing. He knew that if he was to reach the top as a professional it would require tremendous determination and dedication. He had a strict daily routine, and whatever the weather, he was out running on the Beckton Road by 6.00am every morning. Then, after a good breakfast, he set off to the gym in south London for sparring at 12 noon.

The discipline and hard work soon brought rewards, and Terry's successes since becoming a professional earned him the Boxing Writers' Club *'Best Young Boxer of the Year'* award for 1957. Before the selection was made, however, his trainer, Snowy Buckingham told Tom Phillips of the *Daily Herald*, a founder member of the Boxing Writers' Club, not to vote for Spinks.

They had just finished a training session at the Thomas A' Beckett when Phillips remarked that Terry must be a candidate for the award. 'Don't vote for him Tom,' pleaded Buckingham. 'Please, please don't. That award is the kiss of death.'

Phillips was astonished at the trainer's outburst so he asked Terry what he thought. 'If Snowy says so, I don't want it,' replied the boxer.

'I mean it,' continued Buckingham. 'It is the poison ivy. Look what happened to all the others who got it. The unluck! I hope no boy I train ever gets it.'

Previous winners, including Sammy McCarthy in 1952, John Kelly (1953) and Dai Dower (1954), did not progress as had been expected. Dower was in fact knocked out by Young Martin of Spain only nine months after receiving the award.

The most unfortunate of winners was Bobby Neill who, in January 1957, had thrilled guests at the Annual Dinner with a wonderful speech. Three days later he was knocked out in eight rounds by Jimmy Brown in an eliminator for the British featherweight title in Belfast. Later that year Bobby was involved in a motor accident and sustained injuries so severe that his boxing career was thought to be over.

Buckingham had made his point, and whilst Phillips agreed to abide by his request, the majority of members of the Boxing Writers'

Club voted for Spinks. Voting was close, with Brian London, Dave Charnley, George Bowes and Tommy Molloy all being considered.

Terry was presented with the Geoffrey Simpson award together with a handsome engraved wrist watch at the Boxing Writers' Annual Dinner at the Criterion Restaurant, Piccadilly Circus in January 1958. Among the guests to congratulate him were Lord Derby, President of the ABA, and the Duke of Norfolk who, in a speech, warned against pushing youngsters too quickly in boxing.

Terry knew that he would be expected to make a short speech to acknowledge the award, but had no idea what to say. Before setting off from home, Tich wrote it out for him. When Terry addressed the gathering, however, everything he said was completely different. He later revealed that Eamonn Andrews wrote the speech for him.

By virtue of his victory over Malcolm McLeod in December, Spinks was considered the leading contender for the British flyweight title held by Frankie Jones. A British Boxing Board of Control rule, however, prevented him from fighting for the title until he was 21. During the course of the dinner, he confirmed to journalists that he had received an offer from Jack Solomons to meet Jones in a non-title fight at Harringay on 25 February 1958. After taking everything into account, however, the offer was rejected.

'What's the point of fighting him,' said Spinks to Chairman of the Boxing Writers' Club, Frank Butler. 'Even if I beat him, I can't fight for his title until I'm 21.'

Sammy McCarthy was quick to point out that newspaper reports saying they had signed a contract with Solomons were completely wrong. 'A match between them has not been seriously considered,' he added.

McCarthy also turned down an offer for Terry to box in South Africa, but they did agree to meet Ivan McCready in a return contest over eight rounds to be staged at the Empress Hall, Earls Court on 14 January 1958. When McCready subsequently pulled out through injury, he was replaced by Malcolm McLeod.

All boxers appearing on the Empress Hall bill were invited by the promoter, Harry Levene, to a luncheon at the fashionable Coq d'Or restaurant at Stratton Street, Mayfair on 3 January. The main event was a 10 rounds lightweight contest between world rated Cuban, Orlando Zulueta, and British Empire champion Willie Toweel from South Africa.

By this stage of his career Spinks visited a number of gyms in London in order to get the best possible sparring. One was Joe

Bloom's at Earlham Street, just off Cambridge Circus. While there, he got to know Toweel who trained at the gym for his fights in London.

Zulueta only arrived at Heathrow on the morning of the luncheon and was taken straight to the Coq d'Or. When he arrived he was introduced to Toweel who, at the time, was chatting to Spinks. The three boxers had a friendly conversation and the Cuban said he was privileged to meet the former Olympic champion.

In view of his good performance at Harringay a month earlier, a number of critics fancied McLeod to beat Terry. The Canning Town lad, however, learned a lot from that fight, and at the Empress Hall anticipated the Irishman's moves and avoided his big punches.

Although McLeod attacked furiously, Spinks countered well and shook him with right crosses to the head. His task was easier in this fight, and when the Irishman sustained a badly cut left eye in round three, he retired.

Spinks again went over old ground in his next contest, facing George McDade over eight rounds at Liverpool. Since their last meeting, however, McDade had won the Scottish flyweight title by outpointing Pat Clancy over 12 rounds. He had been promised that if he beat Spinks he would face Frankie Jones for the British title.

Despite his incentive, McDade could never match the London boy for skill. From the opening bell, Terry used his height and reach advantages well, and boxing with great confidence was never in any serious danger of losing. Time and again he cracked home good right crosses to the chin, and turned in his most decisive performance since turning professional.

Although McDade was always willing to stand and trade with Spinks, he was repeatedly picked off with left jabs. Terry in fact looked so far in front that the contest could have been stopped at any stage after the fifth round. Such an ending would have been a disappointment to the Merseyside fans who gave both men a great ovation at the end. It was a sporting contest in every sense and at the final bell McDade, without waiting for the referee, raised Terry's arm as a token of victory.

* * *

Although he had been a professional for less than a year, Terry was already finding it exceedingly difficult to make the flyweight limit. He even smoked quite heavily to try and keep his weight down, so it was decided that in future he would box at bantamweight.

'I know only too well the agonies of weight-making,' said his manager Sammy McCarthy. 'I could not let any boy in my charge go through what I had to. Terry is still growing and by the time he is fully matured he could even be a lightweight.'

Matchmaker Mickey Duff paired Spinks with 27 year old Attia Ben Aissa of Tunisia over eight rounds on Stan Baker's promotion at Streatham Ice Rink on 11 March. The match was made at 8 stone 8, giving Terry the opportunity to go into the ring at a weight at which he was comfortable.

In the meantime he celebrated his 20th birthday while training for the fight at the Thomas A' Beckett. Fellow professionals, Dave Charnley and Alex Buxton, presented him with a cake and Terry was made to blow out the candles. As a special treat to himself he bought his first motor car, a plush Ford Consul, even though he still hadn't taken his driving test.

The weigh-in for the fight with Aissa was at Toby's gym in Leroy Street, south east London. At 8 stone 5 and 14 ounces, Spinks had a weight advantage of more than a pound. He looked comfortable at the weight and told reporters that he felt much stronger. Aissa was known to be a tough competitor, having gone the distance with Italian champion Aristide Pozzali a year earlier. In a preview of the fight, *Boxing News* predicted that he would also go the distance with Spinks. The Londoner, however, was in explosive form and won by a knockout in round seven.

Throughout the fight, the Tunisian held his guard very high, so Spinks attacked the body. His shots were hard and Assia often looked in distress. He did well to survive until round seven when the end came in explosive fashion.

Driving his man around the ring, Terry worked him into a neutral corner where he let go with both hands. A beautifully timed short right hook crashed against the Tunisian's jaw sending him heavily to the floor where he laid on his back to be counted out. It was some time before he recovered, and only after a lengthy examination by a Board of Control appointed doctor, did he leave the ring.

Terry's next fight, against Alex Bollaert of Belgium at Leyton Baths on 31 March, nearly didn't take place. Five days beforehand he was crossing the road outside his confectioners shop at New Barn Street when he was hit by a motor cyclist. At first it was feared that he was badly hurt, but after examination at Poplar hospital it was found that he was only suffering from grazes to his left leg, so he was allowed home after treatment.

Over the preceding weeks Spinks had been taking driving lessons and was due to take his test the morning after the accident.

Although his parents suggested he postponed it, Terry insisted that he had fully recovered. Being a determined young man, he turned up at the Test Centre at Stratford full of confidence, and passed.

Before deciding if Terry was fit to box at Leyton Baths, Sammy McCarthy and Snowy Buckingham put him through some tests in the gym. He was made to stand against the ropes to see if there would be any danger of aggravating the grazes to his left leg. After movement and rough exchanges along the ropes, it was decided that he could go ahead with the fight.

Alex Bollaert, an Antwerp docker, was an ideal opponent for Spinks at this stage of his career. Although he had won less than half of his fights since 1952, he had met most of the leading continental bantamweights and lost close decisions to world champion Alphonso Halimi in Paris, Pierre Cossemyns, Mario D'Agata, and Italian champion Piero Rollo. In previous visits to Britain he had lasted the distance with Dai Dower, Vic Herman and George O'Neill.

His left leg heavily strapped, Spinks scored with good shots to the body in the opening round. From that point, the Belgian was concerned merely with survival and only when cornered did he throw any punches of significance. Despite this, Terry was very impressive and in the latter part of the contest landed a tremendous variety of shots.

The bell saved Bollaert at the end of round five after a left and right combination to the head had him reeling. He was on the floor for a count of 'seven' in the seventh from a straight right to the chin followed by a left and right to the head. The Belgian, however, proved his toughness by lasting the distance, although at the end his face was a mass of swelling and bruising. It was a devastating display by the young Londoner who, by flooring Bollaert, did something Halimi couldn't do over 10 rounds 13 months earlier.

Spinks had progressed well since turning professional, and by sensible match-making he boxed regularly. Two weeks after beating Bollaert he was in action again, this time at Harringay on the Dave Charnley – Peter Waterman bill on 15 April. His opponent was Eric Brett, a 20 year old miner from Retford, who had a reputation of knowing how to look after himself. Since turning professional in May 1956 he had lost only six of his 22 contests, and earlier in the year had pushed Dai Dower to the limit in a close fight.

In the April ratings, *Boxing News* put Spinks at number three in the bantamweight division behind British and Empire champion, Peter Keenan, and Freddie Gilroy. With Brett ranked joint fourth, their contest had the makings of a classic.

The two 20 year olds did not disappoint the packed house, and after eight rounds of brilliant boxing, Spinks got the decision, but only just. Although Brett took three rounds to get going, he earned his share of the credit for making it a memorable contest.

Spinks frequently threw rapid five and six punch combinations, and several times the Retford man was sent reeling across the ring from accurate left hooks and right crosses to the chin. Yet at no time was he overwhelmed and generally just grinned and went back into battle.

Most of the exchanges were even as Brett showed great defensive and countering skills. At the end, thunderous cheers rang out for both men who had provided the perfect prelude to the eagerly awaited main event between Charnley and Waterman.

The outcome of that fight was a great disappointment to Spinks because his close friend Waterman was given a real hiding by the British lightweight champion. The referee stopped the contest just before the end of the fifth round, and 12 hours later Peter announced his retirement from boxing. When Terry turned professional, Waterman was the star of the Thomas A' Beckett gym, yet they quickly became good mates. Being older and bigger, Peter looked after Terry and taught him a great deal.

'I felt terrible when he said he was retiring,' said Terry. 'I couldn't imagine what it would be like not having him around.'

Waterman left boxing as the undefeated British and European welterweight champion, with the fine record of 41 victories and two draws from 46 contests. Charnley was the only man ever to beat him inside the distance. When he passed away in 1986 at the age of 54, Terry Spinks was devastated.

6

STEP UP IN CLASS

Since moving up to bantamweight Terry had developed from a light-punching boxer into a two-fisted fighter with greater power. Although he was prone to cuts around the eyes, he was harder and more rugged. Part of his training for the Brett fight involved hour-long sessions hammering a horseshoe at a century-old forge at West Ham.

Away from boxing he received invitations to attend a variety of functions. He even became a member of a panel selected to judge an annual South London *'Miss Hair and Beauty'* competition. In May 1958, he was selected as reserve for the Boxers and Jockeys football team which played a Show-Biz Eleven in a charity match at Upton Park, the home of his beloved West Ham United.

Emerging unscathed from the fight with Eric Brett, Terry faced Henri Schmidt of France at Shoreditch Town Hall just two weeks later. Having faced Mario D'Agata in 1955, Pierre Cossemyns and a number of other continental champions, matchmaker Mickey Duff considered the Frenchman an ideal opponent for Spinks' development. His last contest had been for the French flyweight title. He last boxed in Britain in 1956 when he was outpointed by Dai Dower at Carmarthen.

When Schmidt arrived in Britain he only had a pair of white trunks with him. A British Boxing Board of Control ruling in force at the time, however, banned boxers from wearing white trunks in the ring. Before the fight, Spinks sportingly loaned the Frenchman his spare pair which were blue.

Despite Schmidt's considerable experience and his reputation of being a rough fighter, he appeared intent merely on survival. Spinks won every round with a faultless display of scientific boxing, and resisted the temptation to resort to two-fisted punching. The only moment of drama occurred in round six when the Londoner caught Schmidt off balance sending him sprawling through the ropes on to the time-keepers table.

After the fight, Terry's dressing room buzzed with speculation that he would soon be nominated as the official contender for Peter Keenan's British title. His sparkling victory over Schmidt had elevated him in the minds of his few remaining critics.

Although he claimed that Terry's punches never hurt him, the Frenchman was very complimentary when he spoke to members of the press. 'He seems stronger and better than Dower,' he remarked. 'He is fast and clever, but perhaps not yet ready for such experienced bantams as D'Agata.'

Spinks had done everything asked of him in his first year as a professional, and his victory over the Frenchman convinced most critics that he was ready to face a sterner test. Sammy McCarthy, as astute a manager as he was a boxer, carefully sifted through the many offers they received. He eventually decided that Pierre Cossemyns of Belgium was the man most likely to expose any weakness in his boxer.

Promoter, Stan Baker, staged the fight at the 10,000 capacity Empress Hall at Earls Court on 20 May. Despite there being a bus strike which seriously disrupted London for more than two weeks, there was a heavy demand for tickets for the big charity show in aid of the East London Aid Society. The top of the bill contest was to have featured Randolph Turpin against French light-heavyweight champion Charles Colin, but when the Leamington boxer withdrew at short notice, Ron Redrup took his place.

Pierre Cossemyns, an experienced 28 year old, had taken part in 53 contests in a professional career spanning eight years. He was reigning bantamweight champion of Belgium having first won the title back in 1952. He turned professional the previous year and remained undefeated in 29 contests until 1954.

Cossemyns held two victories over former Spinks' opponent Alex Bollaert with whom he had also drawn, and had also beaten Henri Schmidt twice. He had, however, lost his only two contests of 1958. A points defeat to world featherweight champion Hogan 'Kid' Bassey, whom he had beaten in 1952, was followed by a fourth round knockout to Freddie Gilroy in Belfast in March.

At the Empress Hall on 20 May, Cossemyns proved such a handful, that for the first time in his career Spinks was booed when he received a decision. After eight tremendous rounds a large section of the crowd thought the Belgian was robbed. Referee Bill Williams' decision in favour of the popular East End lad provoked one of the noisiest demonstrations seen at a London boxing arena for some years. A few of the more irresponsible hurled programmes and orange peel into the ring.

The crowd were so incensed that it was impossible to hear Master of Ceremonies, Johnny Best, announce the next contest. Bill Williams was subjected to vile abuse as he entered the ring to officiate another contest later in the evening. He was pelted with ice cream cartons, orange peel and torn programmes, and after the contest had to leave with a police escort.

The first two rounds of the contest were fairly even. Cossemyns attacked with swinging punches while Spinks, boxing on the retreat, jabbed him off with his left, making the Belgian look crude.

In the third, Terry became more confident and dropped his right hand as he tried to attack. Seeing the opening the experienced Belgian crashed a terrific left hook to the jaw which had Spinks wobbling. Another left hook sent him crashing to the floor for a count of 'nine.'

Sensing victory, Cossemyns gave the Londoner no chance to fiddle his way out of trouble, chasing him to the ropes where he landed a series of heavy left hooks. Spinks was in serious trouble and went to the floor for a count of 'seven.' He was still shaky when he rose, and before the end of the round was dropped again for a count of 'four.'

Realising he was in more danger of being beaten than in any of his previous 17 professional contests, Terry boxed carefully behind his left jab. Although he showed signs of tiredness from the fifth round, the jab not only sneaked points but also kept the aggressive Belgian at bay. It was not until the final round that Cossemyns got on top again. Staging a big rally, he drove Spinks around the ring convincing the crowd that he had done enough to get the decision. At the end both men were bleeding from the nose, and Spinks also had a cut mouth.

The critics were divided as to who had won, but all agreed that Spinks' masterful boxing had kept him in the fight. Terry was not concerned about the crowd's reaction, and in his dressing room, Mickey Duff told him, 'You want to worry when you think you've won and the other fellow gets the decision.'

Although the situation had been kept very quiet, behind the scenes Spinks had been struggling both physically and psychologically. It was not until the fight against Cossemyns, however, that there were signs that all was not well with him.

During his first six months as a professional he had trained hard, watched his diet and drank nothing but orange juice. 'I lived like a monk,' he recalled, 'but it's no fun being a monk. After that first six months I was back to the booze and the bright lights in a big way. I couldn't do without them.'

The main reason for the playboy behaviour was because Terry started to doubt his ability. Sammy McCarthy was the only person who knew about the problem, and one evening when Spinks had been a professional for about eight months, he went to his house. 'I'm going to pack it in,' said Terry. 'I'm not getting anywhere. I don't think I'll make the grade and I'm not going to end up as a knock-about fighter in the small halls.'

Sammy was extremely concerned, but being a calm and patient man, they talked into the early hours. Eventually Spinks agreed to give it a while longer although they both accepted that the problem with Terry all stemmed from him having won the gold medal. Being an Olympic hero made him a major box-office attraction who promoters wanted. His picture was on the pages of every newspaper and magazine, and the public flocked to see him.

What everyone forgot was that Terry was just an ordinary East End lad who was being rushed to the top with hardly enough time to take a deep breath. Even in the early stages of his professional career he wasn't given any push-overs, although he couldn't complain too much because he always received good purse money.

It wasn't long before he began having weight problems which wasn't surprising because he made no effort to control his diet or his life style. 'Whisky is very fattening,' he once remarked, 'and so were the kind of meals I used to nip through when my manager wasn't looking.'

The Cossemyns fight had been Terry's seventh within five months so he sensibly took a few weeks break. His next contest was set for 15 July at Streatham Ice Rink, and there was an added attraction because his opponent, Terry Toole of Hackney, had also been a stable lad. Since turning professional in 1956, he had won 11 and drawn two of his 19 contests, and in March had outpointed British flyweight champion, Frankie Jones, over eight rounds at Birmingham.

Soon after the contest was signed, promoter Stan Baker got Spinks and Toole together with their former bosses, Marcus Marsh and Ron Smythe, for a photo-call. Both boxers were good ticket sellers and Baker knew the fight would attract plenty of punters from the racing fraternity.

Weighing 8 stone 7½, Spinks held on to his unbeaten record when the referee stopped the contest because Toole had sustained a badly cut right eye. It was an unfortunate ending to what had been an enthralling contest which Spinks was by no means certain of winning.

The fight started at a hectic pace as both lads, urged on by their army of fans, sought to gain an early advantage. Scorning defence, Spinks tore into the attack, but midway through the opening round sustained a nasty cut to his right eye. As the blood seeped into the eye, his cornermen screamed at him to jab and run.

Although Spinks continued to set a fast pace, Toole welcomed his aggression and gave as good as he got. Whilst it was great entertainment for the crowd, it became clear that as the fight progressed, Spinks was ignoring the advice of his experienced handlers and leaving himself open. His orders were to box his man, but instead he chose to mix it with a tough and versatile opponent.

Spinks was probably slightly in front after five rounds, but then began to tire noticeably, something which was becoming a worrying feature. Despite attacking non-stop, he found that Toole could take everything and come back with plenty of punches of his own.

Toole was at his best in the sixth, catching Spinks easily. Although the Canning Town lad recovered well in the seventh, a body attack took the steam out of him and he was forced to hang on. The fight was at an intriguing stage, but came to an abrupt end when Toole sustained a badly cut eye.

Despite his victory, Spinks received a real tongue lashing from Sammy McCarthy and Snowy Buckingham, who at times during the contest cupped their hands over their eyes in despair and exasperation. Their boxer had repeatedly ignored their orders to box his way to victory, choosing all-out aggression instead. Spinks responded angrily saying that he fought according to the way he saw it from the ring, and his methods had resulted in victory.

'Boxing News' were also critical of Spinks, and in their report of the fight, commented:

> If Spinks does not take himself to task in the very near future, that unbeaten certificate will 'go for a burton' and he will have only himself to blame. Brilliant boxer that he can be, Spinks will lose a lot of friends and get no sympathy if he does not do as he is told by his more experienced handlers.

Whatever way he chose to fight, Spinks was a tremendous attraction, Promoters queued up for his services because they knew he would pack in the crowds. Within a week of him beating Toole, it was rumoured that efforts were being made to match him with former British, British Empire and European flyweight champion Dai Dower at Harringay on 30 September.

Having enlisted for National Service, the Welshman had boxed only once since losing to Pascual Perez for the world flyweight title in March 1957. No longer able to make eight stone, he was due to be discharged from the Army on 2 October, and with a style of boxing very similar to Spinks, a contest between them was mouth-watering.

A couple of weeks later, Mickey Duff, acting as matchmaker for Scottish promoter Jim Gilmour, paired Spinks with Billy Rafferty at Paisley Ice Rink on 28 August. Defeat for Spinks was not a consideration, and by mid-August Stan Baker signed him to meet Kimpo Amarfio of Ghana at Streatham on 9 September. The best laid plans, however, can easily come unstuck, especially in boxing, and that is exactly what happened to the former Olympic gold medallist.

Billy Rafferty, a 24 year old from Glasgow, had won 14 and drawn one of his 17 contests since turning professional in 1956. A two-fisted fighter who was sparring partner to British and Empire bantamweight champion Peter Keenan, he held a points victory over Jake Tuli in 1957. To demonstrate how seriously he was taking his opponent, Spinks travelled to Scotland 10 days before the contest and completed his training at a Glasgow gym.

Terry was accompanied on the trip to Scotland by his close friend Terry Gill. He was also managed by Sammy McCarthy and by this time was Southern Area welterweight champion. Apart from keeping Spinks company, he went running with him and acted as his sparring-partner for a few days.

Whilst in Glasgow they shared a room at an hotel in the city centre. One night after they had gone to bed, Spinks decided to have some fun with his room-mate. While Gill was fast asleep with one arm hanging limp outside the covers, Spinks took a pot from under his bed and filled it with cold water. He then took Gill's hand and immersed it into the water. 'What are you doing'? he yelled as he woke up with a start.

'Someone told me that if you put a person's hand into cold water while he is asleep he will wet the bed,' replied Spinks laughing hysterically.

From the opening bell of the fight with Rafferty, Terry knew he was in for a rough passage because the Scot gave him no time to settle. Attacking viciously, he forced the Londoner to retreat for most of the first round and gave him no chance to use his boxing skill.

It was a similar pattern in the second and third, and although Terry tried to keep the fight at long range with left jabs, Rafferty was too strong. Pushing forward relentlessly, he ducked and weaved his way under the Londoner's guard and hammered away to the body with both hands.

Spinks did have some success with good rights in round four, but they had no effect on the tough little Scot. Out of sheer frustration he then tried to mix it and this proved to be his downfall. During a free-hitting melee in the centre of the ring, the injury above his right eye sustained during the fight with Terry Toole, reopened. Although his cornermen patched it up during the interval, it continued to bleed prompting referee Jake Kilrain to stop the contest just before the end of round five. Despite protests from his corner, Terry was well behind on points and looked destined for defeat.

Sammy McCarthy originally planned to lodge an official protest with the British Boxing Board of Control over the stoppage because he considered the injury to be slight. On reflection, however, he changed his mind because as he put it, 'opinions about cut eyes do vary.' The injury did mean that Terry could not go ahead with his fight against Kimpo Amarfio scheduled for Streatham the following week.

* * *

Despite his demanding training schedule, Terry was always thrilled to receive invitations to functions unconnected with boxing. Together with Ryder Cup golfer Bernard Hunt, and Tottenham Hotspur footballer Cliff Jones, he was a guest at the annual Hatter Exhibition staged at a top London hotel. Singularly, and as a group, they paraded along a damask covered platform wearing a variety of trilby hats. The audience included hatters from all over the continent.

Modelling a brown upswept trilby, Terry swivelled round on his toes like a professional to show it from all angles. Even the male models hired for the day applauded his style. Organiser of the exhibition, Mr Lewis Juchall told reporters: 'We could not have had a better model. Terry stole the show. He has a real panache for dressing. He wears beautiful handmade suits and ties with a Stepney flair, and has a slightly broken nose that sets off any hat to perfection.' After the exhibition was over, Terry told reporters; 'I've got two Robin Hood hats at home. I wear them to the races.'

A few days later, the bar of the Black Lion pub at Plaistow was packed to see Spinks push over a *'Penny Pie'* collected in aid of the

National Spastics Society. After performing the ceremony with a left jab, he was presented with a surprise gift of a table lighter and cigarette case in appreciation of his attendance.

On another occasion, Terry accompanied Bobby Neill and Yolande Pompey to the opening of a newsagents shop at Cambridge Street, Victoria, to be run by former Welsh lightweight champion, Willie Lloyd. The press reporters loved Terry because whatever he did was news.

* * *

Back on the boxing front, Spinks was matched with Eddie O'Connor of Dublin over eight rounds at Shoreditch Town Hall on 7 October. He was promised that if successful, he would meet Dai Dower at Harringay on 28 October. His original opponent was Danny McNamee, but after the Scot was beaten by O'Connor at Middlesborough, the Southern Area Council of the Board of Control advised promoter, Harry Grossmith, that he was unsuitable as an opponent for Spinks. O'Connor therefore agreed to replace him.

At the weigh-in at noon on the day of the fight, both boxers were over the stipulated weight of 8 stone 8. Spinks had to shed eight ounces while O'Connor had to sweat off two pounds. It was the first indication that Terry would be unlikely to make the weight for a future title fight at bantamweight.

Although Spinks eventually took a comfortable points decision, there were some worrying moments during the opening round as O'Connor heavily countered his light left leads. Whenever they traded punches, the Canning Town youngster was always first to break off. Once he settled down, however, he remained in command and never looked in trouble.

Spinks showed he could mix it under pressure, and his only fault was a tendency to drop his left hand and leave his chin exposed to a right cross. It looked like a satisfactory nights work until the final minute of the last round when an ugly gash appeared on his left eyelid.

Back in his dressing room after the fight, Terry was devastated and wept openly when the Board of Control doctor told him the injury required stitches. The fight with Dai Dower was only three weeks away, so in the hope that expert medical treatment could save the day, manager Sammy McCarthy rushed him to nearby Moorfields Hospital. Two stitches were inserted after which Terry told Reg Gutteridge; 'My skin heals quickly. After I was out against Billy Rafferty recently, I could have fought again within a fortnight.'

The period of time, however, proved to be too short and with less than a week to go, Spinks withdrew from the contest against the former triple champion. It was a tremendous disappointment to both boxers because not only was it a lucrative engagement, the contest was considered to be such a tremendous attraction that plans had been made to make a film of it to be shown at schools and boys clubs throughout the country. The injury also deprived Terry of the privilege of boxing on what was to be the last night at the nostalgic Harringay Arena.

Dai was devasted when he heard the news because once the fight had been agreed, he decided it would be his last. Had Spinks pulled out earlier, he would have immediately announced his retirement because he had other plans. Since being discharged from the Army, he had agreed to take a position as Physical Training Instructor at Ringwood Grammar School.

'Boxing Terry Spinks before the television cameras on the last night at Harringay would have been a wonderful way to leave the sport,' remarked Dower when recalling events. 'I decided that win, lose or draw, I would announce my retirement from the ring immediately after the fight.'

The Welshman always retained fond memories of the youngster he once boxed on a Stable Lads show. 'I remember he had such a lovely, lovely smile,' Dai once remarked. 'Although he looked too young and gentile to be a fighter, he had wonderful skill and natural ability. He was a credit to the sport.'

Dower remains convinced that it was a loss to both himself and Spinks that they never met as professionals. 'It would have been a great fight for me at the end of my career,' he insisted. 'Even if I had beaten Terry, it wouldn't have been the end for him. He was young and would have gained great experience.'

Although Spinks was temporarily out of action while the injured eye healed, he remained very sought after. Wally Lesley, manager of Len 'Luggy' Reece from Cardiff, placed an advertisement in *Boxing News* on 17 October issuing a challenge over eight or 10 rounds with side-stakes of £100. Efforts were also made to match him with Hugh Riley at Leith.

Meanwhile, Jarvis Astaire and Sammy McCarthy decided that Terry needed to be set new challenges. He was being groomed as a future champion so it was felt that a new trainer would address particular aspects from a different angle and freshen him up.

During recent months there had been some concerns about Snowy Buckingham, who suffered from poor eyesight. On occasions when he applied an adrenaline swab to a cut, the

8 or 10 Rounds Bantamweight
Contest at 8.8

LEN REECE
(Cardiff) v.

TERRY SPINKS
(West Ham)

In ANY ring in Great Britain and REECE wants a £100 sidestake.

All enquiries to :
Manager WALLY LESLEY,
174 Commercial Road,
Staines, Middlesex.
Phone: Staines 3966

Challenge to Spinks in Boxing News of 17 October 1958

solution leaked into Terry's eyes causing him great discomfort. It was also claimed that Snowy's poor eyesight enabled Spinks to cheat on the gym scales when he did a check-weigh. By craftily holding a hand against the wall, he created a false reading.

Although he was a highly respected trainer, Buckingham wasn't strict enough to curb the antics of Spinks or to control his diet. Terry was a happy-go-lucky youngster with a passion for all the wrong food. He ate what he liked and consequently put on weight which was often difficult to shift. Apart from steaks, he loved rice pudding, and thought nothing of sneaking a bar of chocolate from the shelf of his sweet shop at Plaistow whenever he visited.

Snowy had little control over him because whenever the subject of his weight was raised, Terry insisted he ate properly. Sammy McCarthy, however, was well aware of what he was like, but couldn't watch over him all the time. He knew that after sparring at the Thomas A' Beckett, Spinks together with Bernie Dillon, Terry Gill and others from the East End, often stopped off at Joe Lyons Corner House at Aldgate for a bite to eat.

Whilst most of the boys ate sensibly, Terry had very little discipline regarding his diet. He thought nothing of ordering some apple dumplings and a bottle of ginger beer. With a cheeky grin he quickly devoured the lot and insisted that nobody told Sammy. They didn't have to because the manager knew from his weight what Terry was up to. As they left the gym after sparring, he was often heard to call out, 'Make sure he doesn't eat any cream cakes.'

Buckingham was replaced by Jimmy Davis, a former middleweight from Bethnal Green, recognised for his superb boxing skills in the ring. He was considered the ideal man for the job because he was young, well respected and very disciplined. Sammy had known him for some years, and seen him box, so he asked if he would consider training Spinks. Jimmy was about to apply for a trainer's licence so he readily agreed.

On joining the camp, Davis immediately introduced new training methods with the emphasis on Terry switching between boxing and fighting, thereby avoiding situations liable to cause eye injuries.

* * *

On 24 October, Spinks and McCarthy joined fellow boxers, Henry Cooper, Joe Lucy, Dave Charnley, Terry Downes, and a host of other personalities from boxing, stage and screen, at an amateur boxing show at East India Hall, Poplar. It had been staged to raise funds for the dependents of Jimmy Fullerton, a former London Federation of Boys Clubs champion, and member of the St. John Bosco Club, who was killed in a road accident. He left a wife and five children, and the attendance of Terry and Sammy in aid of a worthy cause is something they would continue throughout their lives.

* * *

Terry's place at Harringay was taken by Pat Supple, the bantamweight champion of Canada, who pulled off a massive upset by outpointing Dai Dower, albeit somewhat controversially. Jack Solomons had no hesitation in matching the Canadian with Spinks in the chief supporting contest on his big show at Wembley on 9 December featuring Terry Downes against Spider Webb.

As a warm-up, Spinks faced the French-Algerian, Mohammed Zarzi, a 26 year old Parisian chemist, at Seymour Hall on 27 November. It was claimed he had never been beaten in 101 amateur contests and 18 as a professional. Although he hadn't boxed for nine months, he was rated as the best prospect in France.

The hall was packed for Jack Solomons show in aid of the Mayor of St Marylebone's Fund for the Old Peoples Welfare Association, with many fans anxious as to whether Spinks would survive without getting cut again. From the opening bell, however, there was a noticeable difference about his approach.

Boxing strictly to orders from new trainer Jimmy Davis, Terry boxed brilliantly. Using his lightning left jab to keep the awkward, bustling Zarzi away, he piled up the points for a decisive victory. Although the Frenchman hotted up the pace in rounds five and six, Spinks crashed home good rights to the head and looked a real title contender. It was the perfect preparation for his meeting with Pat Supple eight days later.

Sammy McCarthy and Jimmy Davis knew the fight with Supple was the most important of their boxer's professional career. Defeat would surely mark the end of the road as regards winning a British title, and they were under no illusions about the task Terry faced.

Supple had crammed 134 amateur contests into 10 years and had won 12 titles from City to Golden Gloves. Now a hardened professional, he had mixed it in rings at Tijuana in Mexico, the United States and Canada. On 16 October, he pushed Peter Keenan to a very close decision for the British Empire bantamweight title at Paisley, and then beat Dai Dower 12 days later. On 18 November he soundly beat Spinks victim Eddie O'Connor at Shoreditch, and the manner of his victory convinced the critics that Terry was in for a lively night.

Spinks, however, was a very dedicated fighter and was fortunate to be in the care of an equally dedicated trainer, Jimmy Davis. Although only 32 years old, Davis had the experience of more than 80 professional contests in a career as a middleweight in which he beat quality men such as Arthur Howard (twice), Ron Pudney and Henry Hall. As a fighter he was a good mover, and in the gym passed his experience on to his new charge.

Against Supple, the difference in Spinks was incredible, and a number of critics believed it was by far his best performance as a professional. Looking fit and strong at 8 stone 9, he not only out-boxed the Canadian champion, but also out-punched him to take a wide points decision after 10 rounds.

Boxing in a confident and methodical manner, he looked a seasoned professional as he made every punch count. He lasted the 10 rounds as though he had done it many times before, thus providing the perfect response to his critics.

Although they had not been together for very long, the value of Jimmy Davis in the gym was clear to see. Terry showed many new moves which added to his natural boxing skill, and more importantly, he avoided injury to his suspect eyes. Punching solidly, he used his reach advantage to pump his beautiful left jab into the face of his ever-advancing opponent who was dangerous until the final bell.

After a break for Christmas, Terry returned to action at Earls Court on 12 January 1959 against Sugar Ray, the bantamweight champion of Holland. He had an impressive record with just two points defeats from 26 contests with 12 victories inside the distance. Although most of his fights had been in the Dutch West Indies, he had been nominated by the Dutch Boxing Federation as a contender for the European title held by Mario D'Agata of Italy.

The fight was made at 8 stone 9, but when Spinks scaled two ounces over the stipulated limit, doubts were raised about how long he could continue at bantamweight. Sammy McCarthy, however, assured the press that Terry had no weight problems. It was just that no real effort was being made to restrict his weight.

Terry's eating habits were not general knowledge at this stage, and Sammy certainly didn't want them revealed to the press. He insisted that as Spinks would not be 21 until the end of February it was too early to be concerned with winning titles. Instead they would concentrate on taking fights which generated good purses.

'When the time does come to get title minded, Terry will move up a weight,' he added. It was sound reasoning by a manager who, as a boxer, had his share of weight problems. Despite winning the British featherweight title, he stayed in that division a little too long and consequently paid the price.

Although Spinks beat Sugar Ray by a spectacular knockout in round seven, he did not look in the same condition as he had against Pat Supple in December. For the first few rounds there was very little in it, but Terry needed all his speed to keep away from the wildly swinging but powerful Dutchman. Occasionally he made the mistake of trying to mix it, and by the end of round five sat gasping in his corner, his eyes badly bruised, as Jimmy Davis gave him a stern lecture.

Somehow he managed to survive and in the seventh there was a dramatic turnaround. Backed into a corner, Terry suddenly clipped Ray on the chin forcing him to clinch. Despite referee Bill Williams ordering him to break, the Dutchman still clung on until Williams prized them apart, and severely lectured him for ignoring the instruction.

When ordered to box on, Spinks landed a straight left to the jaw followed by a right cross. Ray fell to his knees and although he didn't look badly hurt, was slow to rise and failed to beat the count. The Dutchman was later taken to hospital suffering from a suspected fractured jaw.

Despite Sammy McCarthy's earlier comments, the extent of Terry's weight problems became apparent within a week of the Ray fight.

He was due to meet Eric Brett at Nottingham on 26 January, but was released from the contest when it was announced that he was to move up to featherweight. Instead, Mickey Duff matched him with Eddie Burns of Liverpool, over eight rounds at Leyton Baths at 8 stone 12, in what would be the first of four contests in 11 weeks.

Although Burns lost seven of his 10 contests during 1958, he had been taking on good class featherweights. He was chosen to assess Terry's strength in the higher division and give him an idea of what to expect.

Scaling 8 stone $11^1/_2$, his heaviest ever, the Canning Town youngster gave Eddie a thrashing. He was utterly ruthless as he pounded away until the Liverpool man sank to his knees prompting referee Bill Williams to call a halt with just five seconds remaining of the fifth round. Burns finished with a bloodied nose, his face red and puffy, and a nasty lump on his forehead.

'I feel fine as a featherweight,' said Spinks as he made his way back to the dressing room. 'The extra weight did not impair my speed and I was punching as hard as ever.'

Spinks was back at Leyton Baths four weeks later to face Con Mount Bassie, a 25 year old Jamaican journeyman boxing out of Birmingham. The fight attracted tremendous interest in the East End, and prompted some incredible scenes. When fans hoping to purchase tickets at the door, discovered that all 1,900 seats had been sold by lunchtime, there were a series of disturbances at the main entrance. Intent on getting in by any means necessary, a large group smashed down a side door and trampled on a steward who tried to stop them. He was taken to hospital with serious head and stomach injuries.

Spinks looked the complete box-fighter, winning all eight rounds against a rugged opponent who never stopped pressing forward. Boxing mostly on the retreat, he jabbed, double-jabbed and hooked viciously to the body. Occasionally he became over-confident and left himself open to wild swinging punches. 'Jab and move Tel, jab and move,' shouted his frantic supporters as the aggressive Jamaican attacked non-stop. Terry's skill, however, was remarkable in a fast absorbing contest, and the packed house roared with excitement at his faultless display. He was cheered all the way back to the dressing room.

'I was very impressed,' said leading featherweight contender Bobby Neill, who was due to meet Charlie Hill for the British title at Nottingham on 13 April. He saw Spinks as a potential opponent in the future, and was therefore keen to see him in action.

The manner of Terry's victory thrilled his manager. 'He is ready for any featherweight of championship class now,' Sammy McCarthy told reporters.

Two days later Terry celebrated his 21st birthday at a lavish party organised by his parents at the West Ham Conservative Club. The place was packed with members of his family, old school mates, friends from boxing and racing, and members of local and national newspapers. It was a typical East End gathering which went on into the early hours.

Despite the late night celebrations, Terry was up early and out on the road doing his running. Satisfied with his progress, he was confident that he was well on the way to a championship contest and was determined to be in the peak of condition when the opportunity came.

When Spanish featherweight champion Jose Martinez pulled out of a proposed fight with Spinks at Wembley on 10 March, Stan Baker attempted to persuade former world bantamweight champion Mario D'Agata to face him at Streatham Ice Rink on 24 March. The Italian, however, was reluctant to make the trip, so Baker brought in Pierre Cossemyns of Belgium. In view of the controversy surrounding Terry's victory when they met at the Empress Hall the previous June, it was a natural rematch. With the show being staged on behalf of the Racehorse Bookmakers Benevolent Fund it was appropriate that Spinks should top the bill.

Since their last meeting, Cossemyns had won only one of his four contests, a 10 rounds stoppage of Eric Brett at Leeds in December 1958. Prior to that fight he drew with Ray Nobile in Italy, then in January 1959, drew with George Bowes over 10 rounds at Newcastle. In his last fight he had taken a real hiding from former world bantamweight champion Alphonse Halimi in Paris on 9 February. After being on the floor four times, he retired at the end of the third round.

Eight years older than Spinks, the Belgian was still one of the most experienced men at his weight in Europe. With his close cropped hair and tattooed shoulders, he looked very much a hardened professional. Nevertheless, he was considered by the Spinks camp to be past his best and a contest against him at this stage was good matchmaking.

Despite the difficulties he encountered in their previous contest, Terry boxed brilliantly and left no doubt about his superiority in what was his first fight over 10 rounds. At the official weigh-in at 12 noon he had scaled 8 stone 11¼, four ounces over the stipulated limit. Once again there were concerns that he was having weight problems, but he showed no ill effects at having had to remove the surplus ounces.

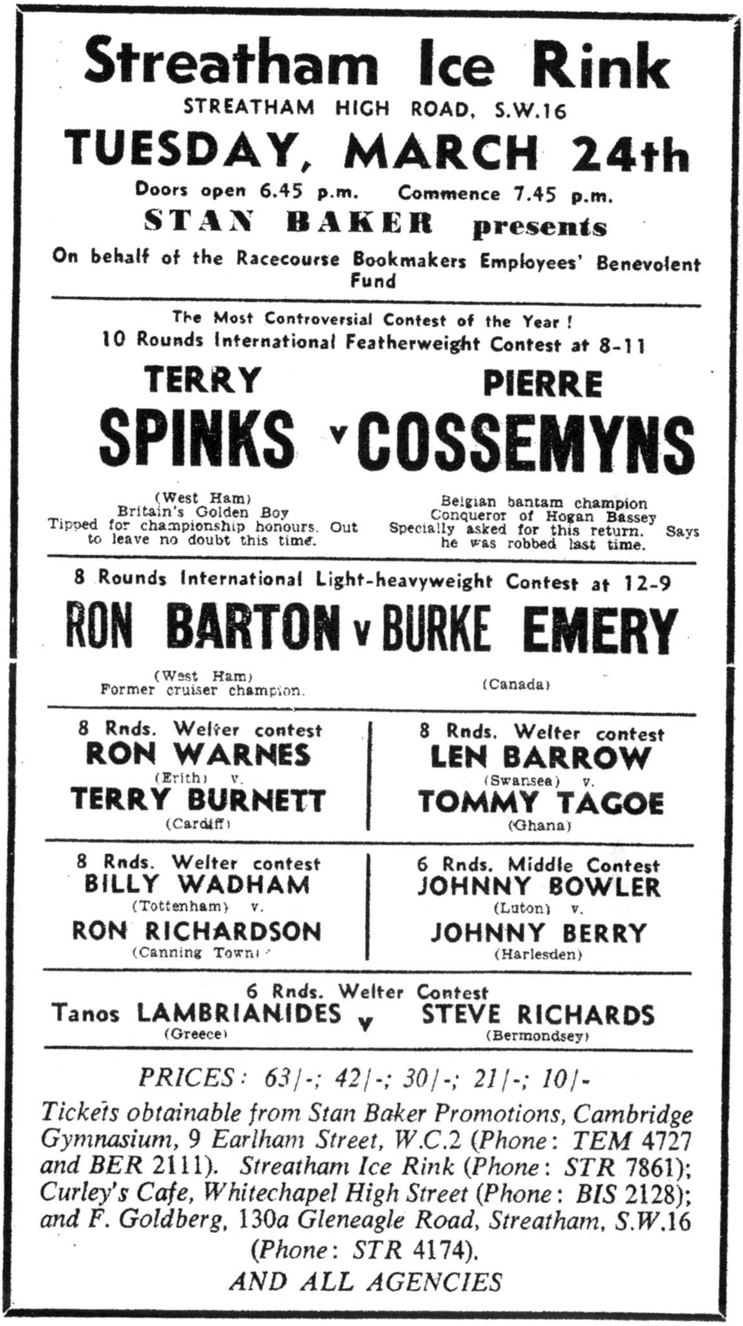

Streatham Ice Rink

STREATHAM HIGH ROAD, S.W.16

TUESDAY, MARCH 24th

Doors open 6.45 p.m. Commence 7.45 p.m.

STAN BAKER presents

On behalf of the Racecourse Bookmakers Employees' Benevolent Fund

---

The Most Controversial Contest of the Year !

10 Rounds International Featherweight Contest at 8-11

TERRY SPINKS v PIERRE COSSEMYNS

(West Ham)
Britain's Golden Boy
Tipped for championship honours. Out to leave no doubt this time.

Belgian bantam champion
Conqueror of Hogan Bassey
Specially asked for this return. Says he was robbed last time.

---

8 Rounds International Light-heavyweight Contest at 12-9

RON BARTON v BURKE EMERY

(West Ham)
Former cruiser champion.

(Canada)

---

8 Rnds. Welter contest
RON WARNES (Erith) v.
TERRY BURNETT (Cardiff)

8 Rnds. Welter contest
LEN BARROW (Swansea) v.
TOMMY TAGOE (Ghana)

---

8 Rnds. Welter contest
BILLY WADHAM (Tottenham) v.
RON RICHARDSON (Canning Town)

6 Rnds. Middle Contest
JOHNNY BOWLER (Luton) v.
JOHNNY BERRY (Harlesden)

---

6 Rnds. Welter Contest
Tanos **LAMBRIANIDES** (Greece) v **STEVE RICHARDS** (Bermondsey)

PRICES: 63/-; 42/-; 30/-; 21/-; 10/-

Tickets obtainable from Stan Baker Promotions, Cambridge Gymnasium, 9 Earlham Street, W.C.2 (Phone: TEM 4727 and BER 2111). Streatham Ice Rink (Phone: STR 7861); Curley's Cafe, Whitechapel High Street (Phone: BIS 2128); and F. Goldberg, 130a Gleneagle Road, Streatham, S.W.16 (Phone: STR 4174).

AND ALL AGENCIES

Poster advertising return contest between Spinks and Cossemyns

His guard held high from the start, Spinks boxed well behind his left jab and sneaked a few good rights to the body and face. He looked sharp and aggressive, and the Belgian's nose and mouth were soon red from the accuracy of his solid punches. Cossemyns pinned his faith on his left hook, but Terry's speed and footwork were incredible. Although there were moments of danger, particularly during round three when he was rocked by a vicious left hook, he took it well and continued to make all the running.

Spinks was even willing to match Cossemyns in any two-fisted exchange. He scored with good shots in round six, and the crowd really got behind him in the seventh when he forced the Belgian to the ropes with hurtful combinations.

As they began round nine, Terry was in unknown territory and took several good shots to the chin as he began to tire. Cossemyns never gave up chasing and always looked as though he had the punch which could turn the fight. Spinks, however, remained cool under pressure and boxed brilliantly to keep out of trouble.

The Belgian was cut over the right eye as he pressed forward in the final round, and despite his great effort could not catch the Canning Town lad with a clean shot. By good scientific boxing and great use of his immaculate left jab, Terry won without argument. It was his 26th victory against one loss, and without doubt one of the most important.

Despite the conclusive manner of his victory, Terry was disappointed with his form. 'I was terrible,' he moaned as he flopped down on a plush couch in his dressing room after the fight. 'Somehow I just lacked my usual zip, but I did seem better in defence.'

Standing beside him, Sammy McCarthy was quick to respond; 'You didn't box at your best Terry, but it shows the improvement you are making to beat an experienced man like Cossemyns on an off day.'

The Belgian had no argument with the decision, but in his dressing room told reporters; 'This has taught me a lesson. When I fought Spinks last time, he was a bantamweight. Now he is a featherweight. I must never again fight featherweights.'

Bobby Neill was introduced from the ring and afterwards stated that if he took the British featherweight title from Charlie Hill, he would be prepared to defend it against Spinks. Provisional plans were already being made for Terry to meet the winner provided he kept winning. An open-air contest at Wandsworth Stadium in June was said to be favourite.

Excited neighbours welcome Spinks home to Morgan Street, Canning town after winning the Olympic gold medal at Melbourne in December 1956.

Watched by his father, Terry reads the greetings telegram from his old school in December 1956.

Behind the counter of the confectionery shop he bought with his mother at New Barn Street, Plaistow in 1957.

Olympic boxing gold medal winner in 1925, Harry Malin, presents Spinks with a certificate to commemorate his Olympic success. Former gold medallists, Harry Mitchell (1925), Fred Grace (1908), and Richard Gunn (1908) look on.

Back stage at the Victoria Palace theatre on 27 December 1956. Spinks is crowned by actress Sonya Cordeau when he visited the Crazy Gang in their hit show "These Foolish Kings".

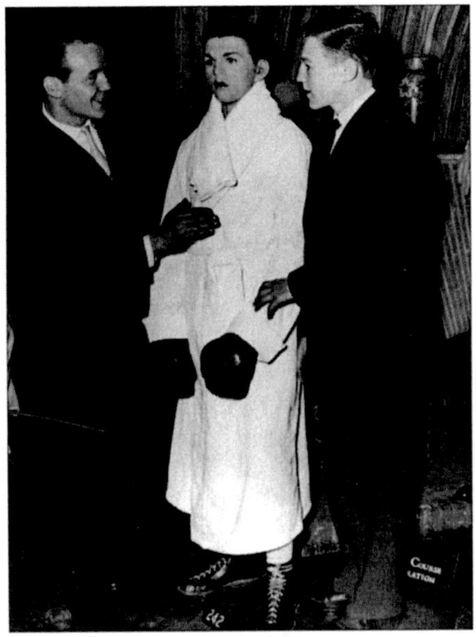

Spinks (right) and Sammy McCarthy admire Terry's effigy in wax on display at Madam Tussauds in London during 1957.

Training session supervised by his manager, Sammy McCarthy, Spinks pounds the heavy bag at the Thomas A'Beckett gym in London in March 1957.

Sammy McCarthy (left) presents Spinks with his award for winning a Stable Lads championship at Newmarket in 1955.

Spinks helps his grandfather Harry Jordan, at his coalyard at Canning Town during 1959.

Terry with "Ching" his pet chow who he named after the owner of a Chinese restaurant at Limehouse.

Spinks (right) shakes hands with his first professional opponent, Jim Loughrey, when they weighed-in at Jack Solomons' Gym in London on 9 April 1957.

Pat Clancy lies prostrate following a terrific attack by Spinks at Shoreditch Town Hall on 16 July 1957. Clancy retired after three rounds.

British welterweight champion, Peter Waterman (left), Spinks and Terry Gill on the sands at Bournemouth where they were training during August 1957.

Sammy McCarthy (left) and Spinks shake hands with promoter, Harry Grossmith, following a meeting at the Boxing Board of Control offices at which Terry agreed not to ride in horse races prior to boxing Ivan McCready on Grossmith's show at Shoreditch four days later.

Ivan McCready (right) attacks Spinks during their fight at Shoreditch Town Hall on 10 September 1957, which Terry won on points.

British Empire lightweight champion, Willie Toweel introduces Spinks to Orlando Zulueta of Cuba at a lunch at the Coq d'Or Restaurant in London on 3 January 1958.

Boxing Writers' Club chairman, Frank Butler (left) with Spinks who was voted the Club's "Best Young Boxer of 1957". Hogan Bassey displays the scroll awarded to him for winning the world featherweight championship.

7

SET-BACKS AND DISAPPOINTMENT

The victory over Pierre Cossemyns had shown Spinks as a genuine featherweight championship contender. It was therefore fitting that he boxed in the chief supporting contest to the British title fight between Charlie Hill and Bobby Neill at Nottingham Ice Rink on 13 April.

Promoter, Reg King, paired him with Eric Brett of Retford who had given him a tremendous tussle at Harringay the previous April. The fight, over eight rounds, was made at 8 stone 11, but once again Terry struggled and came in at six ounces over the stipulated limit.

Brett was a boxer always capable of giving Terry problems. Seeking to cause an upset in front of his supporters, he put everything into his early attacks. A left-right combination early in the second round had the former Olympic gold medallist in a bit of trouble. Twice he slipped to the floor from the impetus of a right hand, taking a count of 'three' on the second occasion.

The Retford man was unable to sustain the pressure or vary his tactics, and once he had weathered the storm Terry's superior boxing skill came into play. Using a variety of quality punches backed by good body movement, he eventually took control of the fight. Although Brett stuck to his task well and delighted his fans, he was well behind at the end and Spinks took a clear points decision.

In the main event, Bobby Neill took the British featherweight title from Charlie Hill. Referee, Jack Hart, stopped the contest in round nine after the defending champion had taken no fewer than 10 counts. With Spinks continuing to win it was generally believed that he would challenge Bobby for the title within a few months. The Board of Control, however, had other ideas.

Sammy McCarthy and Jimmy Davis were called before the Southern Area Council on 22 April to explain why Terry had been overweight for four of his last seven contests. McCarthy pleaded that nature had doubtless been the cause, explaining that on the days prior to the weigh-in's he was within the stipulated weights. Jimmy Davis was also questioned by Council members.

What McCarthy and Davis did not mention was Terry's liking for the wrong food. Despite all Sammy's efforts to get his stable-mates to persuade him to eat properly, Terry still often sneaked a morsel that was bad for his weight. Consequently, he was always fighting to control it.

McCarthy and Davis were told that the Council would carefully monitor the situation. If Spinks continued to exceed contracted weights, a more serious view would be taken. Members agreed to record the fact that Sammy had now decided to arrange contests more suitable to Terry's physical propensity. At this stage, however, Spinks would not be recognised as the official challenger for the British title.

McCarthy was also questioned as to why he had withdrawn Spinks from a proposed contest with Johnny Howard of Holloway for the Southern Area featherweight title. Sammy gave his reasons, they were accepted but never made public.

Despite the Board of Control concern over Spinks, Jack Solomons immediately signed him and Bobby Neill to meet over 10 rounds in a non-title fight on his annual Eve of the Derby show at Wembley on 2 June. Although the contest shared top of the bill with two others, Solomons placed it at the head of the advertising posters, describing it as: 'THE MOST CONTROVERSIAL CONTEST SINCE ERIC BOON V ARTHUR DANAHAR.'

The boxing fans began clamouring for the fight within 24 hours of Neill beating Charlie Hill. Spinks added his voice by issuing an immediate challenge of £1,000-a-side for a title shot or £500 for an over-weight contest. The subsequent stance of the Board of Control meant that he had to settle for the latter.

The fight was made at 9 stone 2 and both boxers agreed to put up side-stakes of £500 to be deposited with the Board of Control. Neill promised that if he lost he would defend his title against Terry with any side-stake he cared to suggest. Contracts were signed at Jack Solomons office in the presence of Teddy Waltham, General Secretary of the Board of Control, and Nat Fleischer, Editor of *Ring* Magazine. Sam Burns the manager of Neill, and

EMPIRE POOL, WEMBLEY
TUESDAY, JUNE 2nd, 1959

Doors Open 6.30 p.m. **Commence 7.30 p.m.**

JACK SOLOMONS presents

THREE MAIN EVENTS ON ONE PROGRAMME

The Most Controversial Contest since Eric Boon v. Arthur Danahar.
£500 a side Genuine Money Match, to be deposited with B.B.B. of C. £500
10 (3-min.) Rounds at 9st. 2lb.
Don't Miss This Intriguing Money Match

BOBBY NEILL v TERRY SPINKS

The Miracle Man of Boxing.
Has survived two car crashes and a broken jaw and then went on to win the British title.

Britain's Golden Boy of Boxing
Can "Baby Face" Spinks beat hard punching Bobby Neill?

International Heavyweight Contest of 10 (3-min.) Rounds

DAVE RENT v FEDERICO FRISO

(Bootle)
The Young British K.O. Specialist
and best British heavyweight prospect seen in years. Can punch with either hand.

(Italy)
Has Had 21 Bouts, Winning 16,
drawn 3, lost 2 points. Never been k.o'd or taken a count in his 21 bouts.

World Class Bantamweight Contest of 10 (3-min.) Rounds at 8st. 8lb.
I have promised Gilroy a World Title Fight against Halimi if he beats D'Agata

FREDDIE GILROY v MARIO D'AGATA

(Ireland)
British and Empire Bantamweight Champion
making his first London appearance.

(Italy)
Former Bantamweight Champion of the World.
Beat Robert Cohen. D'Agata is rated No. 5 World's best.

PLUS FULL SUPPORTING PROGRAMME.

This Programme will be indoors and not, as is usual, outdoors for the eve of the Derby. I realise you have many friends coming to London for the Derby, but please do not ask for more seats than you buy for all my other shows . . . only 10,300 can be accommodated for this super show.

Prices: 10/-, £1, £2, £3, £5

Bookable at Jack Solomons, 41 Gt. Windmill Street, London, W.1. (GER 9195–6): Empire Pool Box Office (WEM 1234).
Public Transport: By Bus: Route 8, 18, 46, 83, 92, (alight Wembley Park Station). Trolley Bus: Route 662 (alight Wembley Triangle). Green Line: Route 703 (alight Wembley Triangle). **Nearest Stations:** Wembley Park–Bakerloo and Metropolitan Lines. Wembley Central–Bakerloo Line and L.M.R. Wembley Hill–Marylebone to High Wycombe, W.R. Alperton–Piccadilly Line (thence by bus).

Poster advertising non-title contest between Bobby Neill and Terry Spinks

Sammy McCarthy for Spinks handed their side-stake cheques to Waltham.

At a press conference, Jack Solomons said it was the most expensive featherweight contest he had ever staged. He was paying Neill and Spinks more than he had to such star performers as Nel Tarleton, Ronnie Clayton, and even world champion, Sandy Saddler whom he had promoted at White City in June 1948.

The event was a throw-back to the old days when big fights were seldom agreed to without side-stakes. Of recent years, however, the practice was seldom heard of, but met with the approval of veteran boxing writer James Butler. 'Spinks and Neill have backed their confidence with cash not words,' he said. 'I hope we see more of these genuine side-stakes. It makes for good fighting.'

The press boys were divided as to who the likely winner would be. Spinks had speed and tremendous boxing skill while Bobby had power and stamina. In his column in the Sunday Pictorial, former British heavyweight champion Tommy Farr wrote:

> Betting boys are running into one another around London's West End trying to convince themselves at what odds they should start.

Farr favoured Neill, claiming that when he watched the two spar several times at the Thomas A' Beckett about 12 months earlier, Spinks was an even money chance for two rounds. 'But in the third and last session Neill made him look like a 33-1 shot,' wrote Tommy.

Both boxers trained at the Beckett, Spinks an hour or so before the champion. When Bobby was working, his trainer Nobby Wallace bolted the gym doors to prevent any Spinks supporters getting in to spy. Nobody was allowed to watch the champion train unless Wallace knew them.

Neill loved boxing, but was extremely fortunate to still be competing. After two road accidents left him on crutches, doctors told him that he would never fight again. Twice, however, he had proved them wrong. After the second accident in 1957, he was so concerned about his future that he visited the offices of the *London Star* newspaper and asked how he could become a boxing writer. He also considered other jobs including becoming a golf professional.

During the course of his recovery early in 1958, Bobby trained at the Beckett, often at the same time as Spinks. Some newspapers claimed that they sparred together and were close friends. The first time they met was when they sat on the same table at the Boxing

Writers' Dinner in January 1957. Bobby had been voted Best Young Boxer of 1956, and Spinks was a guest as the gold medal winner. They got on well, but no particular friendship was formed.

Although the fight with Neill was scheduled for 2 June, the Southern Area Council of the Board of Control granted permission for Terry to box an exhibition bout with Bernie Dillon at Wormwood Scrubs Prison on 27 May. They were accompanied by British heavyweight champion, Henry Cooper, his twin brother Jim, Dave Rent, Joe Lucy, Percy Lewis, trip organiser, Jack Solomons, and Nat Fleischer.

'I felt really weird as we walked in through the prison gates,' recalled Terry. 'It was almost as though I expected to get locked up.'

The boxing ring was erected in the exercise yard, and the boys got changed and gloved up in the prison laundry. The exhibitions were watched by a large audience of appreciative inmates, a number of whom Terry and Bernie recognised from Smithfield meat market and the East End.

'I knew quite a few lads who got locked up for one thing or another,' said Spinks. 'Although it was a bit strange seeing them in there, they seemed really pleased to see us.'

* * *

Spinks against Neill was the most eagerly awaited fight for years. On paper it had everything for the boxing fan – boxer versus fighter, speed and skill against strength, London opposing Edinburgh. Terry had become one of the most popular fighters in the capital, and his 28 professional fights in the space of two years made him one of the busiest boxers in the world at the time. 'I believe I box better if I fight regularly,' he insisted.

Jack Solomons was handsomely rewarded for his enterprise in staging the contest. There was a sell-out crowd who were thrilled by a tremendous contest which culminated with an incredible ending.

Tearing into Neill from the opening bell, Spinks sought to capitalise from his one known weakness. Often referred to as 'The Miracle Man,' Bobby had twice broken his left leg in the road accidents and consequently found difficulty in moving backwards. They were good tactics and Terry was the undisputed master for the first few rounds. As early as the second round a right cross made the champion's knees buckle, and his left glove was rarely out of Neill's face. By the end of the fourth, Bobby was not only well behind on points, but also badly marked about the face.

Neill showed improvement in the fifth and sixth rounds when he slowed Spinks with good left jabs and right uppercuts to the jaw. This should have been a warning to move away from trouble, but Terry ignored instructions from his corner to 'take a rest and run for a while.'

The seventh was an incredible round in which Spinks quickly got back on top. Heavy rights to the head rocked Bobby and he was sent reeling on a number of occasions. His nose badly swollen and his left eye cut, he was pinned on the ropes, in corners, and hammered mercilessly as Spinks sought to end the fight.

The crowd yelled with excitement, and just as it looked as though Neill would be stopped, he hit back bravely. Throwing caution to the wind, the former gold medallist was being lured into destruction, and as they broke away from one hectic exchange he was bleeding badly from a cut above his right eye.

Although Spinks remained in control during the eighth, Bobby's punches were carrying greater weight and Terry showed signs of tiring. He started well in round nine and Neill, his nose bleeding heavily and both eyes badly damaged, was soon gasping for breath. Midway through the round, however, Spinks suddenly fell apart. He slowed almost to a standstill and all the fight suddenly seemed to drain out of him. His arms dropped to his sides as he looked to have neither the strength nor guile to avoid Neill's punches.

In one desperate effort, Bobby seized his chance. Forcing Terry to the ropes, he crashed a right to the head, and a left hook to the stomach almost doubled him up. Earlier in the contest he had taken similar punches without flinching.

Spinks was driven backwards into the champion's corner where two more heavy shots found the target, a short left spinning him sideways. He crumpled, sagged and slid down the ropes in slow motion, to fall on his face. He rolled over, attempted to rise, but as referee Ike Powell spread his arms, he collapsed again flat on his back. It was fully three minutes before he could be taken to his corner.

It was one of the most dramatic endings to the fiercest featherweight contest seen in a British ring for a long time. With just two seconds remaining in the ninth round, it came as a complete shock to the wildly excited crowd.

The drama in the ring, however, was surpassed afterwards when there were serious concerns about Terry's condition. Despite having been attended to for several minutes in the ring by a doctor, he didn't know where he was and had to be helped back to his dressing room.

'What happened?' he asked as he lay writhing on a couch. When told he had been knocked out in the ninth round, he became aggressive and delirious. 'No it wasn't, it was the first,' he screamed as he threatened to fight anyone who disagreed with him.

Despite having dictated the course of the fight he was in a very confused state, and it was more than 20 minutes before anyone was allowed into his dressing room. Dr Philip Kaplin, a Board of Control medical officer, later confirmed that Spinks was suffering from exhaustion.

Sammy McCarthy was extremely disappointed at the outcome, but was critical of his boxers tactics. 'Terry was told to take a rest in the seventh and eighth rounds, but he was too eager,' he told reporters. 'He wanted to go like a racehorse all the time.'

Although very relieved to have won, Bobby Neill was very subdued when he spoke to newsmen. 'I couldn't get going until the ninth round,' he told them. 'Then I knew I would get him and I don't think there is any doubt about it.'

Many boxing writers saw the ending of the fight as a climax that could be compared with the explosions of Eric Boon against Arthur Danahar 20 years earlier. In what is generally recognised as one of the greatest British championship contests of all-time, Boon had stopped Danahar in the 13th round.

Writing in the *Daily Mirror*, Peter Wilson gave Spinks seven rounds with the fifth even. Summing it up, he wrote:

> In all the thousands of fights I have seen, I have never witnessed a finish to compare with this.

Reporters generally had Spinks in front by a wide margin. *Boxing News* gave Neill a share of only two of the eight rounds completed.

Despite the wonderful performance put up by Terry, and the fact that he had lost only one of his previous 28 contests, veteran boxing writer Gilbert Odd subsequently stated that the fight had been of great concern to him. He felt that Spinks was not ready to meet a man of Neill's calibre. 'It is a source of wonder to me why permission was ever given for it to take place,' he wrote.

The ending of the fight was something that Terry never forgot. 'Suddenly in the ninth round he let go a left hook,' recalled Spinks. 'I saw it coming every inch of the way, but just stood there and let it land. I couldn't do anything about it and just before it caught me the thought flashed across my mind, 'he's done me'.'

* * *

Spinks and Neill had been due to go to the Derby at Epsom racecourse the following day with Harry Levene, other leading figures in the fight game and members of the press. 'I was in too much of a mess to go,' said Bobby years later. 'My face was badly bruised and I had two black eyes.'

Although Terry suffered no ill effects from the fight, he didn't feel in the mood for racing either. After a good night's sleep his main concern was getting a return with Neill for the title. Despite the defeat, Sammy McCarthy felt Terry had done enough to warrant a shot at the title. He therefore contacted Neill's manager, Sam Burns, who said they were agreeable provided the money was right and the Board of Control gave approval.

A couple of days later, McCarthy hand-delivered a letter marked 'URGENT' to the Board of Control offices requesting that they order Neill to defend his featherweight title against Spinks. Later the same day, Sammy and Terry called on promoter Jack Solomons and convinced him that a return contest would mean another full house. They agreed terms without too much difficulty.

Solomons invited Neill and Sam Burns to his office a few days later to discuss the possibility of a return with Spinks. 'Not enough,' snapped Burns when the promoter made his offer. After further negotiation, however, the financial aspects were agreed and it was proposed that the fight would take place in October or November. Unfortunately, from Spinks' point of view, that was as far as the matter progressed for the time being.

Being a Saturday, Jack's secretary was not at the office. He was therefore unable to provide contracts to sign. As he was off to Cannes the following day, he asked that the parties left the official signing until he returned from holiday. Usually a meticulous operator, Jack slipped up badly on this occasion. He failed to notify the Board of Control of the agreement he had reached with the two boxers, and to request that they authorise the contest as being for the British featherweight title.

JOHN O'BRIEN
(Glasgow)
Challenges
TERRY SPINKS
(The boy who gets all the chances)
to a contest of Boxing Skill
Any place–Any time
Any number of rounds

John O'Brien challenges Spinks by taking an advert in Boxing News of 31 July 1959.

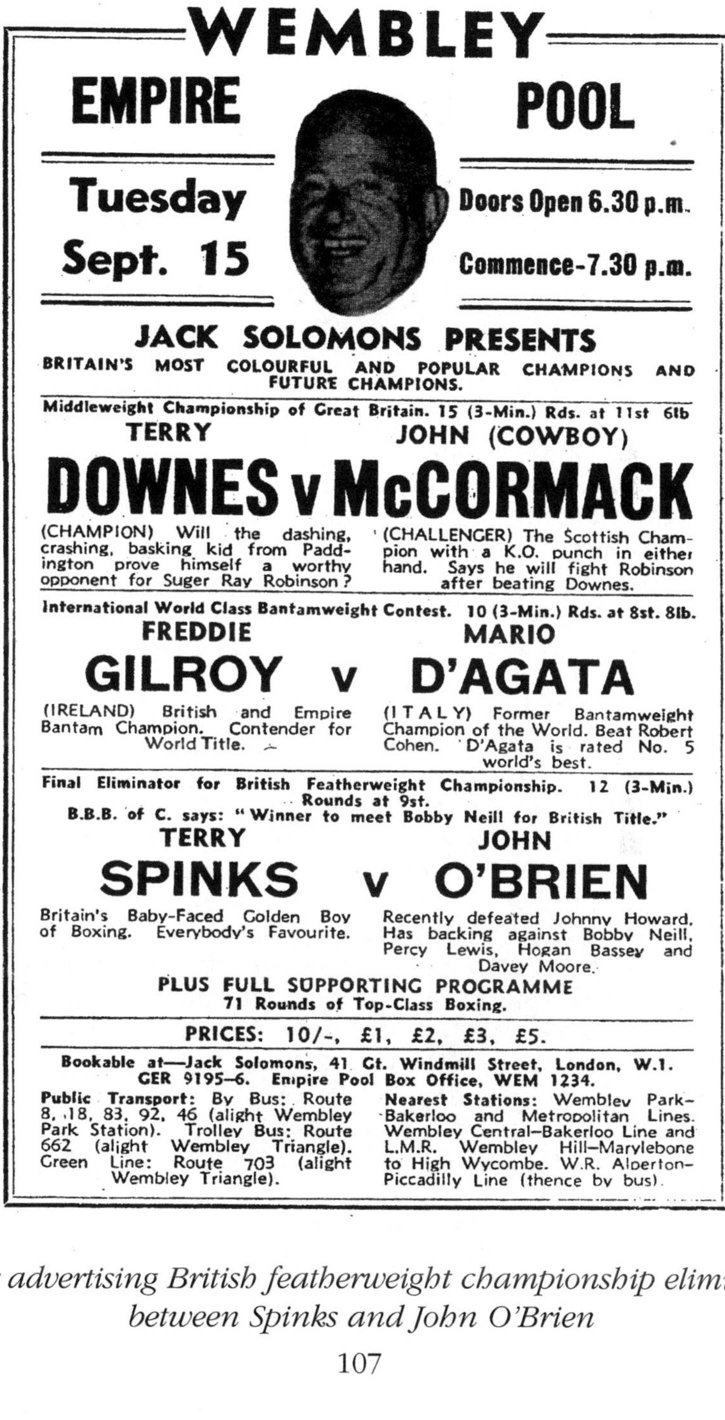

Poster advertising British featherweight championship eliminator between Spinks and John O'Brien

The oversight was to prove a set-back for Spinks because while Solomons was sunning himself in Cannes, the Board announced that Terry must meet John O'Brien of Scotland in an eliminator for Bobby Neill's title. Only a week earlier, O'Brien had taken out an advert in *Boxing News* challenging Spinks to fight him 'any place, any time, over any number of rounds.'

Annoyed and embarrassed by his error, Solomons snapped up the fight as soon as the Board announced it. He added it to his already attractive show at the Empire Pool, Wembley, on 15 September, when top of the bill was Terry Downes defending his British middleweight title against another Scot, John 'Cowboy' McCormack. As soon as contracts were signed, McCarthy offered side-stakes of £500.

As a warm-up, Terry rather foolishly agreed to meet Derry Treanor billed from County Monaghan, Eire, over eight rounds at Streatham Ice Rink on 1 September. Although the contest was made at 9 stone 2, many critics thought he was taking a risk. Treanor was a tough fighter and among his victims was Peter Keenan whom he stopped on a cut eye after six rounds at Paisley in August 1958 on the same bill as Spinks when he was beaten by Billy Rafferty. It was a good performance by Derry who attacked throughout, and as Terry's handlers were at ringside at the show they should have taken note. Treanor had also soundly outpointed Eric Brett in a televised contest at Derby in May. It was remembered that Brett twice gave Spinks plenty to think about.

A week or so before the fight, as if suddenly realising the risk he was taking, Spinks offered Stan Baker £500 to release him from the contest. The shrewd promoter was having none of it because so many people had bought tickets on the understanding that Terry was boxing.

The fight proved to be a disaster for Spinks who was never able to produce the form he showed against Neill three months earlier. He was slow and sluggish and at no stage did he gain control of the contest. The fight was only seconds old when he found himself on the canvas. Caught off balance by a right to the head, he tumbled over in his own corner and rolled under the bottom rope. Before the count could start he was on his feet, but spent the rest of a hectic round defending desperately as Treanor pushed forward hurling punches from all angles.

The fight developed into a maul, and referee Pat Floyd was kept busy breaking them from clinches. Both men were cautioned for holding and dangerous use of the head, and in round five he threatened to throw them both out if they didn't clean it up.

Treanor made sure of victory with a big effort in rounds seven and eight. Several times he shook Terry with hooks to the head, and the Londoner was forced to hold on. At the final bell referee Floyd walked straight to Treanor and raised his arm.

'I have never boxed so badly in my life,' said a dejected Spinks after the fight. 'I just couldn't get going. All my usual zip was missing and now I don't feel as though I've been in a fight.'

Treanor had seen Spinks beat Peter Walsh in the 1956 ABA finals, and whilst conceding that he boxed brilliantly, really fancied his chances. 'Terry was a wonderful boxer with a left hand like a rapier,' said Derry years later. 'Once he got going you couldn't stop him, so the plan was to attack him from the start and not let him get into his boxing rhythm. That's what I did, and thankfully it worked.'

Derry also recalled an incident which occurred during the fifth round of the fight. As they went into a clinch, Spinks suddenly said, 'I'm knackered,' and clung on tightly. 'Well, you're in trouble then,' replied Treanor who could feel that the Londoner was finding the going tough.

Terry's defeat by Treanor saw an incredible swing in the betting odds for his fight with John O'Brien. From being a strong favourite, he suddenly became the underdog as punters put their money on the Scotsman who went into the fight on the back of consecutive victories over Con Mount Bassie, Johnny Howard and Eric Brett. Spinks' defeat had been one of the upsets of the year, especially as the Irishman had lost five of his 16 professional contests.

Spinks was given a wonderful reception as he climbed into the Wembley ring to face O'Brien. Clad in a gold dressing gown and trunks, he was determined to get his career back on track. He opened at a terrific pace, but towards the end of the opening round a perfectly placed right hook to the jaw dumped him on the canvas. Terry looked extremely shaky as he climbed to his feet at the count of 'nine.' Luckily, the bell came to his rescue, but he was so dazed that he walked to a neutral corner.

It was a disastrous start for the Canning Town boy, but he recovered well and by the third round was dictating matters. Setting a fast pace and using his left hand brilliantly, he was looking like the Terry Spinks of old. By round six, O'Brien was cut above the left eye and behind his ear. The Scot though was extremely strong, and with dogged determination turned it into a battle of skill and speed against brawn.

The fight was close as O'Brien, using shoulders, forearms and head, concentrated on attacking Spinks to the body. He tended to be erratic while Terry punched crisply and cleanly and looked the better craftsman. The partisan London crowd roared with excitement in round nine when O'Brien dropped to the floor from a body shot but it was ruled low. After helping the Scot to his feet, referee Jack Hart, warned Spinks to keep his punches up.

As the fight entered the final rounds, O'Brien looked the stronger man. Although they both tired considerably he had just a bit more in reserve. The 12th round saw them stand toe-to-toe in fast, furious exchanges as both desperately sought to swing the balance in their favour. At the final bell, referee Hart gave the decision to O'Brien prompting jeers and boos from all around the arena.

The verdict certainly went against the opinion of those involved in ringside betting. As the fight entered the final round, Spinks was a 3/1 on favourite to get the decision. His co-manager Jarvis Astaire was disgusted with referee Jack Hart, saying it was the worst decision he had ever seen in boxing.

Journalists were divided in their opinions. A number believed the accurate jabs of the Londoner were more telling than the rough-house tactics of O'Brien. Others thought that the Scot's all-out aggression earned him the verdict.

The defeat by O'Brien was a tremendous disappointment to Terry and a serious set-back to his plans, especially as it came only two weeks after the reverse against Derry Treanor. Like the Irishman, O'Brien was far less experienced than Spinks, having won 12 and lost five contests since turning professional in October 1956.

Having now lost three consecutive fights within the space of four months, something had clearly gone wrong. 'You're getting soft – leading too easy a life,' Mickey Duff told Spinks after the Treanor fight.

Duff was absolutely right, but the problem stemmed from the fact that Terry was easily led. This was never more apparent than in the weeks following his defeat by John O'Brien. It was his third defeat in a row, and as always when things get tough, a man needs consolation. Terry always found it at the races so he decided to drive to Newmarket, relax for a few days and do some riding. There, he met up with several of his old mates, one of whom was former stable lad opponent Tony Rawlinson who was staggered to see how low he was.

'You can do one of two things,' remarked Rawlinson. 'Blow your brains out, or come with me and take a holiday on the Scottish circuit.'

Spinks needed no further prompting because he knew the Scottish circuit was extremely popular, with meetings at a number of different courses over a two week period. Many Newmarket trained horses were entered and were loaded on to trains at a special station in the town before travelling north overnight.

Terry knew many of the travelling lads from his days at Marcus Marsh's stable, so he was in his element. He collected a couple of pals, £100 in cash, and set off with high hopes. Before getting off the train in Scotland, however, he had lost all his money playing cards. Undeterred, he cashed a cheque for another £100 and started all over again.

The trip was just what Terry needed to get his head right and forget about his disappointments in the boxing ring. He was very popular in Scotland where many people recognised him because of his gold medal success at the same time as their own Dick McTaggart. In the streets and in the bars, people wanted to speak to him, while on the race courses the bookies, trainers and punters alike loved to be in his company.

After arriving in Scotland, Spinks and his friends booked into The Hydro, a luxury hotel at Peebles, with a swimming pool and golf course. It was a well known meeting place for jockeys from all over the British Isles.

On their first night at Peebles, Spinks and Rawlinson met up with two jump jockeys, Noel Boston and Lex Kelly, and top northern flat race jockey, Teddy Larkin. They quickly became good friends and spent a great deal of time together visiting the race courses, drinking and playing cards. They became the centre of attention at The Hydro and it wasn't long before Terry fell for the charms of an attractive blonde receptionist.

Over the next two weeks Spinks and his group of friends attended meetings at Ayr, Bogside, Edinburgh, Catterick, Perth, Hamilton and Lanark. With the exception of Perth which was a National Hunt meeting, Larkin and Rawlinson both had a number of rides. They stayed at the best hotels, ate and drank well during the evenings, and visited casinos where they gambled heavily. Terry also went to Glasgow where he met up with old opponents Billy Rafferty and Derry Treanor who both enjoyed racing.

During their stay at The Hydro, the group went to race meetings at Edinburgh and Lanark. After returning to the hotel one evening, Teddy Larkin, who had the second retainer for horses owned by Lord Rosebury, introduced Spinks and the others to Manny Mercer. He was first jockey to Jack Jarvis who trained Lord Rosebury's horses. Terry had got to know him well when he worked at Newmarket, but it was the first time Manny had seen him since he won the gold medal.

It was a great reunion, and after a few drinks in the bar they all had dinner together. Mercer ordered top quality wine which was followed by more, paid for by Larkin.

Mercer didn't stay in Scotland for long because he was booked to ride at Ascot on the Saturday, 26 September. Before leaving he gave Terry a couple of horses to back at Hamilton the same day. Spinks gambled heavily on both, and Manny's information didn't let him down. Shuttlecock romped home in the 4.30pm as did Abernicki in the five o'clock.

As Terry was collecting his winnings from the second success, the bookmaker said, 'Have you heard the news?'

'What's that?' asked Spinks.

'Manny Mercer's dead,' replied the bookie. 'He's had a fall at Ascot.'

Terry was absolutely stunned, and for a few moments just stood there looking at the £500 he was clutching – money Manny had won for him.

Gathering his senses, he then ran straight to the weighing room to find Tony Rawlinson and tell him quietly before somebody indiscreetly blurted it out. Terry knew Manny's special pal was Ed Larkin who had ridden the last winner, and thought Tony was the best person to break the news to him.

Mercer had been due to ride in the 4.05pm race at Ascot, the Red Deer Stakes. During the canter down to the start he fell from his mount, Priddy Fair, in front of Tattersalls and was killed. He was only 30, and had ridden 100 winners in a season on five occasions.

'Manny was the one jockey I respected when it came to tipping,' Spinks declared years later. 'Generally, jockeys are the world's worst tipsters. I emptied a lot of cheque books proving the point.'

'But not Manny,' he continued. 'I'd known him a long time and he wasn't often wrong. Come to that, he didn't often tip, but when he did you knew it was the real thing.'

From a gambling point of view, the Scottish trip was extremely successful for Terry. In almost two weeks he picked up about £4,500. Manny Mercer's death was the only thing that marred his enjoyment.

Noel Boston and Lex Kelly also did well during the trip, and once the race meetings had finished they and Spinks decided on the spur of the moment, to go to France. They wanted to have a good time on their winnings, but there was one drawback – Boston didn't have a passport.

'That's not a problem,' Terry assured him. 'We'll go down to London and get you one.' After arriving in the East End, they stayed with Terry's parents at Cumberland Road overnight, and the following day went to Petty France where Noel got himself a passport. Without further delay they went straight to Heathrow, bought open tickets, and flew to Paris.

After three days living it up in the French capital, they went to Chateaux Rou, a United States airbase, to meet up with an American serviceman they had met at Troon. After staying with him and his family for a couple of days, they went to Cannes for a week. There they were like playboys, visiting bars, casinos and dining in style.

One night, in one of the more fashionable establishments, they met a titled lady who recognised Noel Boston as having ridden for a leading northern racing trainer in England. As they were chatting she suddenly recognised Terry. 'You won a gold medal at Melbourne didn't you?' she remarked. The conversation progressed and she eventually invited them to her yacht in the harbour for drinks the following day. It was a luxurious vessel and they were treated to champagne and nibbles while most of the conversation related to racing. It transpired that the lady was well connected to a number of owners and trainers in the North of England.

Although the currency restriction in force at the time allowed a person to take only £100 out of the United Kingdom, Spinks later revealed that he and his pals had nearer £1,000 between them. 'We planned to give the Chemmi a thrash,' he recalled. 'We reckoned that even if we did our £1,000 in, we'd still have a couple of weeks good living out there because you can't lose all the time, or can you?'

They played the tables at night, and at two o'clock in the afternoon collected the English newspapers, went back to the hotel and studied the racecards. Once they had picked their fancies, Terry telephoned a London bookmaker and placed their bets.

Although it was all great fun, the gambling in the casinos, which included shoot pontoon, was heavy and far from rewarding. The night before they planned to return home the trio had only the equivalent of £9 between them, not nearly enough to pay their hotel bill.

Deciding that they had no alternative but to 'do a moonlight,' they booked their seats home. That night after a meal and a drink in the hotel, which would be charged to their account, they went into the casino to gamble their remaining few francs. Terry sat down at the Chemin-de-Fer table and immediately struck lucky. He went on to win a '16 timer' which paid over £300. This time he knew when to quit, and after collecting his winnings, called for champagne.

The next morning they were up early, paid the hotel bill and checked out. Although Lex Kelly wanted to stay on in Cannes, Terry and Noel insisted on returning home because it was Newmarket races the next day. Back in the East End they met some of Terry's mates and all went to West Ham Dog Track. Spinks was given a tip which they all put a tenner on and it won at 6-1. The following day they went to Newmarket races, lost the lot and were skint again.

Over the next two or three years Terry went to Scotland for the races on several occasions. He usually met up with Boston and Kelly, and on one occasion after a jump meeting at Perth, they moved on to Chester. They stayed at The Nags Head Hotel where people watched in amazement at their heavy betting while shooting dice.

Whenever he was in Glasgow, Terry stayed at The Central Hotel and always met up with Derry Treanor and a few others. Regulars at the Piccadilly Club, they loved having a good time and were often partying into the early hours.

Spinks was very friendly with many of the jockeys and was renown for getting tips. If he put £500 on a horse, his mates knew it was a likely winner. They usually followed suit and won a lot of money.

Information, from whatever source, however, was not always reliable. One day, Jock Stein, the manager of Celtic Football Club, was at a Scottish race meeting and had been given a 'hot tip'. Terry was asked by a friend to see what he could find out from the jockeys. 'The word on the inside is that it is no good,' he remarked on returning. Stein decided not to back the horse but seethed with anger as he later watched it romp home at a good price.

At this stage of his life Spinks was a compulsive gambler and some years later revealed his addiction to a Sunday newspaper. 'I've never been a hunch-backer,' he remarked. 'I've always worked on information, which means I've had a lot of bad information to cost me £30,000.'

An example of what Terry referred to occurred at a meeting at Ayr. He was told to back a horse called Grandstand which 'couldn't lose.' Trusting the source, he put £600 on it to win at 11-2. With three furlongs to go everything appeared to be going to plan as the horse hit the front. 'It was the biggest cert I ever saw in my life,' recalled Spinks. 'All of a sudden, however, a 10-1 outsider, Falling in Love, came out of the pack and pipped it. I just stood there watching £3,000 go down the drain.'

To make matters worse, a lot of people who followed Terry's information, had backed Grandstand each-way and got their money back plus a small profit.

Luck though, was generally with Terry on that particular trip. At Hamilton, he was strolling about considering what to back when he bumped into former West Ham United centre half Malcolm Allison, and Arthur Shaw who used to play for Arsenal. They had travelled all the way from London specifically to back a horse called Golden Disc. They advised Terry to go for it which he did and picked up £1,000 on the information.

'But that's how it is when you bet big,' he remarked when recalling the situation. 'One day everything you touch turns to gold, the next you're a candidate for the poor house.'

* * *

Having started his professional boxing career so well, Spinks knew he had to do something different if he was to get back to winning ways and progress to the top. Some people were already advising him to give it up, while a number of newspaper critics thought he was past his best.

Terry accepted that he needed to toughen himself up, so apart from road running and gym work, he also started work at his grandfather's coalyard. Shovelling coal and humping the sacks on and off the lorry were just what was needed to give him the extra edge he appeared to lack, especially after the life he had been living in recent weeks.

After a three month break from competition, Spinks returned to the ring against George Dormer of East Ham over eight rounds at Leyton Baths on 7 December. Dormer had won only one of his four contests during 1958, having been beaten by Con Mount Bassie, Terry Toole and Billy Rafferty, making it very much a make or break fight for Terry.

Despite his recent set-backs Spinks remained as popular as ever, and the venue was packed. He didn't disappoint them, showing plenty of his old form with flashing left leads, nimble footwork and solid counter-punching. Showing no ill effects from his defeats he was always on top in a bitterly contested local derby, and took a clear points decision.

Spinks started cautiously as Dormer scored with several good left hooks to the body. In the second round both attacked the body incessantly and George went to the floor from a blow which appeared low. Referee, Pat Floyd, halted proceedings to allow him to recover, and at the same stage gave Terry a stern warning to keep his punches up.

When Dormer went down again from another body blow in the

fourth, Spinks was warned again. By this time a certain amount of needle had crept into the fight and both men were prepared to mix it.

Another heavy shot to the body in round six caused George to stop and look appealingly at the referee. As he did so, Spinks caught him with a hard right cross. He was on top throughout the last two rounds and ran out a good winner.

The featherweight division had suddenly become wide open and on form there was not much to choose between the top four or five contenders. Champion, Bobby Neill, suffered a severe set-back in October when he was stopped inside a round by world champion, Davey Moore, in a non title bout. Leading contender, John O'Brien, was then sensationally knocked out in two rounds by Percy Lewis for the British Empire title at Nottingham the night Spinks beat Dormer.

Promoter, Harry Levene, gave Terry a massive vote of confidence when, within a week of his victory over Dormer, signed him to meet Scottish lightweight champion, Johnny Kidd at Olympia on 26 January 1960. Levene made application to the Board of Control for the contest to be recognised as a final eliminator for the British featherweight title. The championship Committee of the Board agreed, and the fight was therefore scheduled for 12 rounds.

In the meantime, Neill had agreed to defend his title against O'Brien. The contest was scheduled to take place on 1 February at Nottingham, but with only a week to go, O'Brien surprisingly withdrew. The reasons were not known at the time, but it was generally thought that he was seriously considering retirement from the ring. At first there was talk of putting the winner of Spinks and Kidd in to replace O'Brien, but this was not a practical suggestion as there would be only five days between two major contests.

Despite the importance of the fight with Kidd, matchmaker Mickey Duff, took a real chance by putting Terry on Harry Levene's promotion at Leyton Baths on 18 January. His original opponent was George Carroll of Covent Garden, but when he pulled out to face Welsh champion, Terry Rees at Kingston, his place was taken by Junior Cassidy.

Weighing 9 stone 2, Terry used the contest to sharpen himself up for the vital meeting with Johnny Kidd eight days later. Cassidy, a squat, well-muscled 21 year old Nigerian, who had previously sparred with the former Olympic champion, never stopped trying to land a big punch. Boxing strictly to orders, however, Spinks did only as much as was necessary to take a drab points decision after eight rounds. Much to the relief of his manager and the promoter, he was completely unmarked. 'I told him at the start not to take any chances,' said Sammy McCarthy after the fight. 'I am pleased to say he listened to me for a change.'

The following day, Terry was back in the gym continuing his preparations for the Kidd fight. There was still work to be done to reach peak condition, and with the contest under championship conditions he needed to remove a further two pounds in weight.

* * *

A few days before the fight with Kidd, Terry attended the prestigious Annual Boxing Writers' Dinner at the Criterion Restaurant, Piccadilly. In conversation with journalists he expressed a willingness to help British boxers prepare for the forthcoming Olympic Games at Rome in August. 'I really want to help the boys,' insisted Spinks. 'I learned such a lot outside the ring as well as in it during my five contests in Melbourne.'

He explained that there was too much hanging about doing nothing, and competitors appeared remote from those in charge of them. Although Terry was even prepared to pay his own expenses, his offer of help was never going to be accepted by the ABA. He was now a full-time professional and therefore banned from involvement with the amateur game.

Away from boxing, Terry had built up a good standard of living since becoming a professional in 1957. Apart from receiving good purse money for his fights, sound business deals and his uncanny knack of picking winners at the horses and dogs ensured that he maintained a healthy bank balance. Most of his money was handled by Tich, a shrewd businessman, who made sure it was invested wisely.

'I have seen too many tragic cases of fighters around these parts who have been unable to hold on to their money,' remarked Tich. 'When Terry leaves the game I want him to be well set in life.'

Thanks largely to his father's guidance Terry had considerable share investments, and owned a luxury caravan and speedboat at Burnham-on-Crouch where he loved to go water-skiing. He was an immaculate dresser who always wore stylish clothes, his shirts all bearing his initials on the breast pocket.

He was also the proud owner of a new Ford Consul convertible motor car with personalised index plates TS40 which represented the nickname, 'Forty Winks Spinks' by which he was affectionately known in the East End. His Olympic panama straw hat was always lying on the back window-shelf as a status symbol. He owned two dogs, a chow named Ching and a black poodle called Pierre which he had named after Pierre Cossemyns, the Belgian boxer who gave him so much trouble in May 1958. Such was Terry's sense of humour that the chow was named after the owner of the Chinese Restaurant at Limehouse where he had so many free meals.

Things were going well for the Spinks family. Tich was earning good money from his bookmaking business, and the confectionery shop managed by Doris, had dramatically increased its turnover since Terry helped her to buy it in 1957.

Even at a young age, Terry had an extremely generous nature and desperately wanted to show his parents how much he appreciated the way they had brought him up. In February 1960, anxious that they should have a better standard of living, he negotiated the purchase of a property at 83 Cumberland Road, a short distance from Morgan Street. With three bedrooms, it was a much bigger and more comfortable house with modern conveniences they had not previously experienced.

Terry spared no expense. After making a sizeable deposit, he borrowed the balance of the £1,800 purchase price on a mortgage from Barclays Bank. He also purchased elaborate new furniture including high-back white leather chairs and a white leather bar with stools.

* * *

Johnny Kidd had to be regarded as one of the most dangerous men Terry had been matched with. His manager, Les Maddison lived at 18 Morgan Street, Canning Town, and had been a neighbour of the former Olympic champion. 'Terry and I are quite good pals,' he told a national newspaper reporter. 'I have known him since he was a schoolboy and have followed and supported his rise to the top. Good as he is, I think Johnny will be too strong for him.'

Boxing at lightweight, Kidd had lost just two of his 18 contests in three years as a professional, 11 of his victories coming inside the distance. He won the Scottish lightweight championship in only his ninth contest, and in December 1959, stopped Southern Area champion, Johnny Howard in seven rounds after an explosive battle. His power of punch made him favourite in the pre-fight betting and a lot of money was laid on him.

Once again Spinks had problems making the weight. At the weigh-in at 1 pm on the day of the fight he was four ounces over the nine stone limit. After a good rub-down, he returned to the scales 15 minutes later but was still two ounces over. Only at his third attempt following another rub-down and use of an infra-red lamp did he make the limit.

Sammy McCarthy was baffled and stated that when Terry left the gym the previous day he was three quarters of a pound over the limit. 'I expected he would dry out at least one pound during the night,' he told interested newsmen. What Sammy didn't know was that between leaving the gym and the time of the weigh-in, Terry had eaten a couple of pork pies and drank several cups of tea. A few hours before the weigh-in he had gone to a vapour bath to try and shift more than a pound of surplus weight without anyone knowing.

A big crowd gathered at Olympia where top of the bill was a 10 rounds contest, billed as an eliminator for the world featherweight title, between British Empire champion, Percy Lewis, and Gracieux Lamperti of France, the European champion. Spinks against Kidd, however, was the one they had come to see and both men got rousing receptions as they made their way to the ring.

The fight was an absolute thriller and Terry set a cracking pace from the outset. Boxing mainly at long range, he made Kidd look foolish, and for six rounds it was Spinks at his sparkling best. There was more variety about his work, and throwing good combinations he landed more scoring punches than the Scot. When Johnny found the target, however, his shots carried greater weight, a factor which would tell in the later rounds.

There was plenty of blood about as Spinks bled heavily from the nose from round four and Johnny was cut above his left eye in the sixth. Terry was clearly ahead at the halfway stage, but from that point Kidd came into his own.

In round seven, the Londoner was noticeably slower as the weight of Kidd's punches started to tell. A good shot just before the bell dazed him, and as they broke off he walked to a neutral corner instead of his own.

A swelling came up over Terry's right eye in the eighth after Kidd repeatedly scored with good right hooks. Although Johnny was damaged above his right eye in the following round, Spinks was showing definite signs of tiring. At the end of the 10th he again went to a neutral corner.

The Scot was quickly into action in the 11th, punching away solidly with both hands. The pace was furious, and as they battled hard both men squinted through closing eyes. Although Terry tried desperately to fight back, his strength had drained from him and his feet appeared rooted to the ground. The effects of his weight reducing and the power of Kidd's punches had taken their toll. Just before the end of the round he sank to the canvas from sheer exhaustion. Only the bell saved him when the count had reached 'six.'

It was a similar pattern in the final round as Kidd threw every punch in the book. Spinks staggered on the brink of a knockout for most of the round with only his remarkable courage and will-power keeping him on his feet. Eventually, with the Scot still pounding away, he slipped to the floor. He looked too weary to beat the count, but with McCarthy frantically beating on the boards urging him to get up, he hauled himself to his feet at 'nine.'

Johnny swarmed all over him lashing out furiously with both hands. Most missed the target at a time when one carefully placed shot to the chin must have ended the contest. Incredibly, Terry held on and at the bell his agony was over. Referee, Billy Jones, walked straight to him and raised his arm in victory. Courage had triumphed, yet had it been stopped a minute or so earlier nobody could have complained.

Yet again Spinks had fought himself almost to the point of exhaustion, giving one of the most amazing displays of courage seen in a British ring for a long time. With his legs unwilling to respond to his demands for the last couple of rounds, sheer bravery alone had kept him going. At the end his nose was bleeding heavily and both eyes were almost closed. It would be some days before the swelling went down.

Terry was so exhausted that it was more than an hour after the fight before his handlers finally convinced him he had won. It was not until after the weigh-in that Sammy McCarthy discovered his man had been to a Turkish bath. 'It was a very foolish thing to do and it will never happen again,' he remarked. 'It's a wonder he ever stood up let alone win. Considering his ordeal, it was a wonderful performance.'

Although there were some boos when the decision was announced, most critics thought it a correct, albeit an extremely narrow one. At the final bell nobbins showered into the ring in appreciation of the efforts of both men. 'Give the money to the other fellow,' said Spinks after it had been gathered up.

Victory made the former Olympic gold medallist the leading contender for the British featherweight title, yet neither he nor Kidd would have been in any condition to face the champion five days later as had originally been suggested. It had been a ridiculous idea, but even so Harry Levene said he still wanted to put Terry in with Neill at Wembley on 8 March. McCarthy, however, was having none of it and sensibly insisted that they would not be looking for another fight for several months. His man badly needed complete rest and in order that he recovered fully, it was planned to send him on a good holiday.

In an interview with the *Stratford Express* after the fight, Sammy insisted that Spinks' next fight would be for the British featherweight title. 'He won't fight again unless it's for the title,' he said. Sammy claimed that he spoke to J. Onslow Fane, Chairman of the Board of Control before the fight with Kidd and was told that although the contest couldn't be announced as a final eliminator, the winner would get a shot at the crown. 'Terry really earned a title tilt by this performance,' he added.

McCarthy explained that although Spinks normally made the nine stone limit easily, he misjudged it on this occasion and had a tough and strenuous time getting down to it. 'It makes his win all the more great when you consider he had to go through all that before the fight,' said the manager. 'He had to work off the last few ounces on the day at the weigh-in. All this struggle told – it's a tale of the last few rounds.'

The victory over Kidd really warmed the hearts of Terry's many fans who saw it as one of the most courageous by an East End fighter. It received considerable coverage in the national and local press, with the *East London Advertiser* giving a particularly moving account:

> Hero of East London this week is Terry Spinks. For guts and determination, nobody can hold a candle to the Canning Town featherweight.
>
> Even though he could hardly stand up, he still managed to use his immense skill. Every time Kidd, himself now very tired, measured Spinks for the final right hander, Terry lolled out of trouble.

Despite his courageous victory, the British Boxing Board of Control viewed Terry's physical condition with great concern. Three weeks after the fight he and Sammy McCarthy were called before the Southern Area Council to answer questions about his weight and training.

The point was made that yet again Spinks was overweight at the official weigh-in ceremony. Furthermore, he had given the impression that he appeared unable to remain physically strong during a contest of more than eight rounds.

McCarthy assured the Stewards that Terry could comfortably make the featherweight limit but had possibly not trained with the vigour he should have done. Spinks admitted there had been lapses in various aspects of his training which caused him to misjudge his weight. What he omitted to tell them was what occurred at the West End night clubs.

The sad thing was that the highly talented Spinks was a chancer who was easily led. Rather than conform to the rules set by his manager and trainer, he preferred advice given by hangers-on. The outcome was that he was often out until the early hours of the morning and in no condition to turn up at the gym for a vigorous training session.

Everyone knew that Terry regarded it as a laugh if he could have one over on the manager or trainer. Some years later he confessed to a national newspaper that he loved being a playboy and wasn't as dedicated as he should have been. In an exclusive article he said:

> Poor Sammy! I broke training so many times that he wore out a pair of legs looking for me. He reckoned it would be cruel to handcuff me to a bed-rail so he appointed a spy-ring to watch me. People in the neighbourhood were supposed to let him know as soon as they saw me making tracks for the bright lights.
>
> I beat that one easily. It was a great giggle, except it wasn't so funny sweating the pounds off. Usually I had about a stone to lose. Once when it was even more, I had a couple of secret gym sessions on my way home from the clubs at five in the morning.

After consultation with the Chief Medical Officer, the Council decided that Terry must have two contests not exceeding 10 rounds before any consideration would be given to him meeting Bobby Neill for the featherweight title. Those contests would be observed by Council members, and only if they were totally satisfied with his performance and stamina would he be allowed to take part in a championship contest.

As the matter was of such public interest, the Council agreed that details would be passed to two press agencies. After the meeting, Chairman, Jack Solomons, said that McCarthy and Spinks had agreed to follow an entirely new training programme. In future Terry would go away from home to train, and be more careful about his diet.

McCarthy, however, was angry at the Council ruling, and in an interview with *Boxing News* said: 'Terry will not fight again until he is given a deserved crack at the British title.'

It was originally planned that Terry would go on a relaxing cruise of the Mediterranean to recover his strength after the Kidd fight. At the last minute, however, he changed his mind and decided to spend some time riding at Newmarket instead. 'I find riding horses helps to strengthen the legs,' he told Reg Gutteridge. 'It keeps you fit and stops you getting lazy.'

Once at Newmarket, Terry relaxed with his friends from the racing business and it was not long before a group of them decided to take a trip to Le Touquet in the South of France.

Apart from sight-seeing, they visited the bars and casino's where they gambled quite heavily. Generally, Terry was a lucky gambler, and although they had their share of bad luck, the winnings paid for most of their nights out. Terry's only problem was he didn't know when to quit. Whenever a winning streak came to an end, he would carry on, and also bought drinks for his mates and anyone else who had tagged along.

'I had the time of my life,' he recalled. 'The only problem was, when I arrived back in England I was completely skint so I had to telephone my Uncle Johnny and get him to pick me up at Heathrow.'

Whilst Spinks was away, Harry Levene still wanted him to box on his Wembley show on 8 March. Newspaper reports claimed that he was to meet Sexton Mabena, the non-European featherweight champion of South Africa in a 10 rounder. The problem was, nobody knew where Terry was, not even Sammy McCarthy. Instead, Johnny Kidd faced the South African, although Sammy insisted that he would not have allowed Terry to fight in any event.

During his break from boxing Spinks also underwent a series of medical checks. In recent fights he had experienced difficulty in breathing so he consulted Sir David Davis, a Harley Street specialist to Sir Winston Churchill. Examination and x-rays revealed that his main problem was on the bridge of the nose where bone was blocking the nostrils. Consequently, he was not getting enough oxygen into his lungs. He was told that his breathing and stamina would be vastly improved by an operation.

'He has been passed one hundred per cent fit in every department except his nose,' Sammy McCarthy told the *Stratford Express* when the situation was revealed. 'Terry will be fit to fight next month and our objective is the British title. I shall draft a letter of all the doctor's findings and send it to the Southern Area Council asking them to change their mind.'

Terry underwent the operation at St Johns Wood hospital at the beginning of April 1960. After being discharged eight days later he went to Newmarket where he spent two weeks just relaxing and breathing in fresh air.

'I feel like a new man,' said Spinks when he returned home to Canning Town. 'I had been breathing through my mouth for a long time but the operation seems to have completely cleared my nose. All I want to do now is test it out in the ring.'

Back home with his parents at Cumberland Road, Terry resumed roadwork almost immediately. A week or so later he began light training at the Thomas A' Beckett. Within a few days, Nat Sellar, the manager of Derry Treanor, issued a challenge on behalf of the Irishman with a side-stake of £200. 'As Terry needs to re-establish himself with the Board of Control, we are willing to give him the opportunity to avenge the defeat Derry handed him last year,' said Sellar.

Having already qualified for a title shot the Spinks camp showed no interest in the challenge. Another defeat at the hands of the awkward Treanor would ruin what chance Terry had of facing Neill. Instead they agreed to meet Roy Jacobs of Nigeria on Jack Solomons Derby Eve promotion at Wembley Pool on 31 May.

Nobody could accuse Spinks of taking an easy route back because Jacobs was a highly rated boxer with an impressive record. In March 1957, he won the Nigerian featherweight title by outpointing Rafiu King over 12 rounds at Lagos. Later that year he based himself in Britain under manager Tony Vairo and won his first seven contests in good style.

On his British debut at Blackpool on 1 November, Jacobs was so impressive that many fans saw him as a challenger for the British Empire title. He was busy during 1958, losing only two of 14 contests, one of which was a 10 rounds points decision to Empire champion, Percy Lewis, at the Empress Hall the night Spinks struggled against Pierre Cossemyns. Amongst his victims were Derry Treanor (rsf.7) and John O'Brien (pts), both of whom would defeat Terry in 1959. He also beat Eddie Burns in four, a round quicker than Spinks would the following year.

In November 1959, Jacobs became the first man to defeat South African 'Wonder Boy' Sexton Mabena when he stopped him in five rounds at Earls Court. Going into the fight with Spinks he had won 24 and drawn two of 34 contests.

Jack Solomons stated that provided Spinks put on an impressive display against Jacobs, he would do everything possible to match him with Bobby Neill for the title. Sammy McCarthy was equally determined and confirmed that he had written to the Board of Control asking them to give the go-ahead. 'Terry's recent nose operation has been a great success,' he told reporters. 'I am positive he will no longer have any trouble going 20 rounds yet alone 15.'

Spinks was unusually outspoken and in no doubt about what he should be doing. 'Why shouldn't I fight for the British championship?' he said firmly. 'I all but beat Bobby Neill in a non-title fight last year, and outpointed Johnny Kidd in January. Take it from me, when I do get my chance against Neill I will not make the same mistake as last time.'

Also on the Wembley bill was French flyweight champion, Rene Libeer, who Terry beat in the Olympic semi-final. Unbeaten in 15 contests since turning professional in January 1958, he was matched with Irishman, John Caldwell, who also reached the Olympic semi-finals, losing to Mircia Dobrescu who Spinks beat to win the gold medal.

His training having gone well, Terry looked fit and relaxed for the official weigh-in at Jack Solomons gym, Great Windmill Street at 2.00pm on the day of the fight. Jacobs, returning to Britain after three 12 round contests in Australia, looked equally fit, and on-lookers expected an interesting battle. Both men scaled 9 stone 1, a pound inside the agreed limit.

The fight itself turned out to be a great disappointment, and after 10 uninspiring rounds referee Jack Hart called it a draw. Spinks was only a shadow of the fighter who went so close to beating Bobby Neill on Solomons last Derby Eve show. The only satisfying aspect was that his pacing of the fight had improved and he didn't finish in a state of exhaustion. Although there was some booing from the predominantly Spinks crowd, most critics thought the decision was fair.

After starting confidently but carefully, Terry was generally on the receiving end of Jacobs long jabs in rounds two, three and four. Although he scored well with his own jabs, he showed only flashes of the brilliant boxing his fans had become accustomed to. When he went to the canvas in round six from a flurry of punches to the head, it looked as though the end was near. Spinks looked weary as he climbed to his feet with the count at 'five', but suddenly hit back well to share the round.

Fortunately for Terry, his opponent was not finding his best form either, and many of his punches were wild and out of range. The later rounds of the contest were marred by clinching and prompted frequent orders from Jack Hart to 'break.' Neither boxer dominated the contest at any stage and the referee's decision could not therefore be faulted.

Terry was the first to admit he had given a poor performance. 'I boxed badly,' he told reporters in his dressing room. 'I felt lazy and sluggish – just as I did against Derry Treanor – and couldn't get moving.'

'Terry left all his moves and boxing behind in the gym,' added

Sammy McCarthy. 'He has been worried about this Board of Control ruling that he must improve his stamina, and trained too eagerly. It blunted his bite and skill.'

Board of Control officials at ringside watched Terry's performance closely and after the contest he was given a thorough examination by a Board appointed doctor. Most critics believed that after this performance, his chances of being nominated to fight for the title were very slim.

At a meeting of the Southern Area Council three days later, the Stewards decided that Spinks must engage in a further contest before any decision would be made. There would be no delay because matchmaker, Mickey Duff, had already lined him up to face Nye Ankrah of Ghana over eight rounds at Walthamstow Assembly Hall on 13 June. The Ghanaian was a sensible choice because in his last contest he had outpointed old Spinks' rival, Jerry Parker, and also beaten Eric Brett.

With less than a week to go to the fight, Ankrah injured himself in training. His place was taken by Scottish featherweight champion, Dave Croll, who was in his seventh year as a professional. Croll was far more experienced than Ankrah, having won 27 and drawn five of his 43 contests. In November 1959, he won the Scottish title by knocking out Chic Brogan in two rounds. He had also been a successful amateur.

Spinks knew that this was one of the most important fights of his career. If he failed to impress Board of Control representatives, his chances of a British title fight were gone. Indeed it could be the end of what had promised to be a glittering career.

Weighing 9 stone $1^1/_2$, Terry paced the fight like a master as he boxed his way to a clear points decision. Most ringsiders thought he won every round. Although Croll was dangerous in the opening rounds, flashing left jabs and solid right crosses gave the Londoner a commanding points lead. As he was taking a breather in round four, however, a hard right to the jaw shook him badly. Croll went all out to finish it, but Terry's superb boxing skill got him out of trouble and he was soon hitting back viciously. It was a hectic round in which both men finished with cuts about the left eye.

Spinks was in complete control in the fifth as he dominated the exchanges with his left jab. Hard right crosses wore the Scot down, and although he was always dangerous he couldn't catch Spinks cleanly enough to change the course of the fight.

Blood streamed from a nasty gash on Dave's left cheekbone, and another cut opened above his left eye in the seventh. Terry punched away relentlessly and at the end was covered in blood which streamed from his opponent's injuries.

Referee, Tommy Little, had no hesitation in raising the Londoner's arm at the final bell, and the sporting East End crowd were quick to show their appreciation to an extremely gallant loser.

'Terry was much too fast for me,' admitted Croll after the fight. 'He's still got the speed of a bantam.' His manager, Joe Gans, nodded in agreement. 'He certainly is a corker,' he added.

Spinks said he was delighted with his performance and insisted that he could have gone extra rounds if necessary. 'I boxed much more like my normal self,' said Terry. He added that the nose operation had already cleared up his breathing problems and he was now ready to challenge for the title.

Sammy McCarthy had a broader than usual smile as he told reporters he would be bitterly disappointed if Terry was not now nominated for first shot at the title. 'Johnny Kidd and Terry are regarded as the top challengers for a championship bout,' he remarked. 'Terry beat Kidd in January and that must make him the logical contender.'

Sammy insisted that his man's poor showing against Roy Jacobs should be completely disregarded. 'I take the entire blame for that,' he continued. 'After the Board's ultimatum that he must box two trial contests to prove his staying-power, I ordered Terry to really get down to some hard work. He obeyed my instructions to the letter.'

The manager insisted that Spinks in fact trained too hard and it upset rather than helped him. By over-training, his zip and sparkle vanished. 'For the fight with Croll, we went back to the usual pattern and he returned to form,' said Sammy, but added that Terry sparred only three rounds during the final week of training.

At the insistence of the Board of Control, their medical officer, Dr Paul Saville, examined Terry in the dressing room immediately after the fight. 'There is not the slightest sign of tiredness about him,' he told waiting reporters. 'He lasted well.'

As a separate issue, Dr Saville persuaded Terry to partake in an experiment to further the cause of medical science. The drug Varidase was designed to reduce swelling and promote the healing of injuries. It had been used for some time, especially in America, by Police surgeons and plastic surgeons in selected cases.

Doctors involved in boxing were seeking test-cases in both the professional and amateur ranks. When Dr Saville examined Terry's bruised left eye which swelled rapidly after the fight, he saw the injury as an ideal one on which to test the drug. Spinks therefore agreed to take a four-tablet-a-day course and provide the doctor with a progress report.

* * *

Although he was a full-time boxer, there were plenty of other matters for Spinks to contend with. Two days before he fought Dave Croll, he appeared at St Albans Magistrates Court charged with careless driving. Despite his plea of 'not guilty' he was convicted, fined £10 and ordered to pay £13.2.0 costs. His licence was also endorsed after the court had been told he had a previous conviction for careless driving in 1958.

The case arose following an accident on the southbound carriageway of the M1 motorway at St Albans on 19 April. Terry was returning from a race meeting near Birmingham with a friend when he ran into the back of another car causing it to zig-zag across the motorway, down a bank and into a field.

Giving evidence, the driver of the other vehicle said that he felt a bump and thought one of his tyres had blown. Only when he got out of his car did he realise Spinks had hit him. They had a conversation during which the boxer allegedly said, 'I'm glad you're still alive.'

Terry told the court that he was driving at about 60 miles per hour in the centre lane when the car in front of him suddenly pulled to the offside and seemed to stop. He was about five yards behind and couldn't avoid hitting it.

* * *

Spinks was in constant demand for personal appearances especially in connection with amateur boxing. In August he presented Ivan Drew of Woodford with a cup for winning a National Schoolboy Intermediate championship. Terry, Sammy McCarthy, and a number of Leyton Orient footballers attended the presentation at the Garden City Boxing Club at the Drill Hall, Woodford.

During 1960, Terry became the first and only British boxer ever to be featured on a postage stamp. The Dominican Republic produced a set of stamps depicting great Olympic achievements, and the 5 correos stamp featured him in boxing action. It was a remarkable tribute and demonstrated the esteem in which he was held throughout the world.

8

BRITISH CHAMPION

The day after Terry's fight with Dave Croll, Sammy McCarthy personally delivered a letter to the Board of Control asking that his man be nominated for a title fight with Bobby Neill. This was discussed by the Southern Area Council at their meeting on 22 June and it was decided that the restrictions imposed on Terry in February would be lifted.

Two days later, however, Johnny Kidd threw a real spanner in the works when he stopped Neill in a non title contest at the Royal Albert Hall. It was a rough fight in which both men sustained injuries, but when blood streamed from a bad cut above Bobby's left eye in round five, referee Tommy Little called a halt.

Kidd's manager, Sam Burns, immediately made an application to the Board of Control for his man to get a shot at the title ahead of Spinks. At a subsequent meeting, the championship committee considered the claims of both men. They recommended that Spinks meet Neill for the title on condition that both boxers agreed to waive the customary six months grace.

The featherweight division was really hotting up, and apart from Johnny Kidd, a number of other contenders were waiting in the wings for consideration. Central Area champion, Billy Calvert, and Welsh prospects Phil Jones and Howard Winstone were progressing well. Derry Treanor, who held a decision over Spinks, had taken out British nationality so that he could fight for a Lonsdale belt.

Despite a bid by Jack Solomons to stage the contest, promoter Stan Baker quickly agreed terms with Neill and Spinks for the fight to take place at the Royal Albert Hall on 27 September. Not only would it give Terry the chance he had been after for more than a year, it would also give him the opportunity to put the East End back on the map. This tough area of London, once the hotbed of

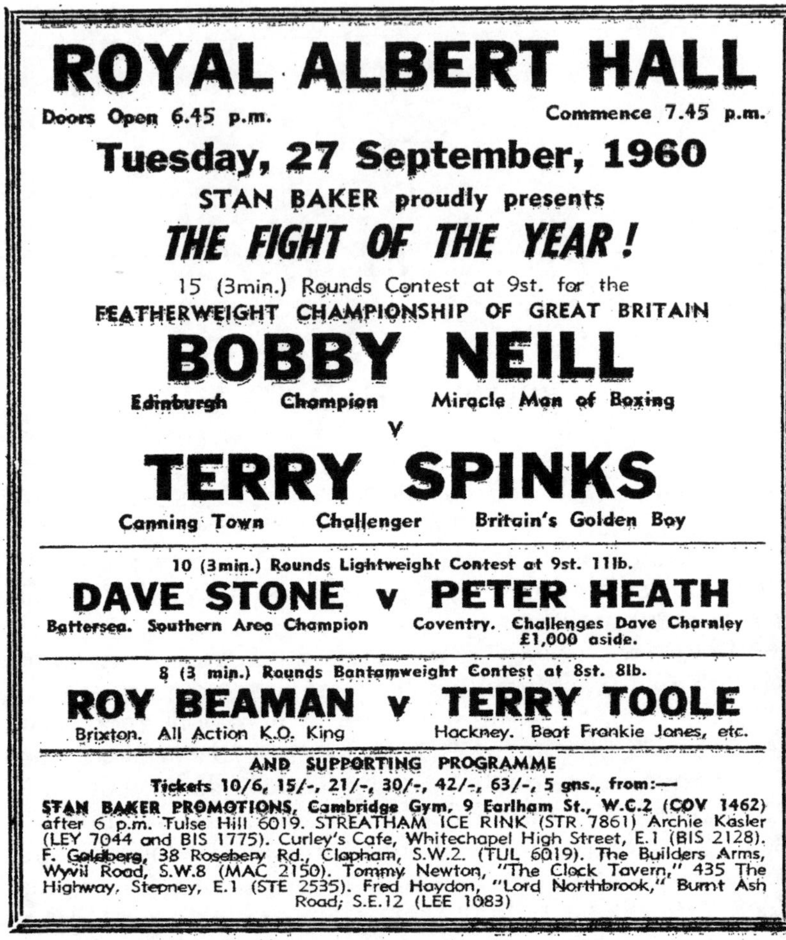

Poster advertising British featherweight championship contest between Bobby Neill and Terry Spinks

boxing, could no longer boast a British champion, but Spinks had a massive following. Success against Neill would make him one of the East End's most popular champions.

Despite his love of the good life, Terry had by this stage got a steady girl-friend. Miss Valerie Pearson was an attractive dark haired 21 year old young lady who lived with her parents at Broxash Road, Clapham Common.

They first met at an open-air swimming pool at Ashford in Kent the previous summer. Valerie and a group of friends who knew each other from the Lyceum dancehall, had gone there by train for a day out. Terry, who was with a crowd of his mates, just sat down beside her and started chatting.

That evening, Spinks and his mates planned to have a meal at a West End restaurant, so he invited Valerie to join him. They got on well together and started dating, although at first it was a rather casual on-off affair. Terry was not very reliable and there were occasions when he didn't turn up at an arranged place.

Despite splitting up at one stage, their relationship gradually developed. Valerie knew very little about boxing, but they shared a number of other interests, in particular jazz, and went to concerts in the West End, including one to see Count Bassie.

They often went out for drives in Terry's car, and one day while driving through Battersea Park, came across a male pedestrian with a small boy frantically waving them down. It turned out to be the Sheffield Wednesday and England goalkeeper, Ron Springett, who had continued to live in London since being transferred from Queens Park Rangers three years earlier. He had taken his little boy for a walk in the park, but when they returned to their car, Ron couldn't find his keys and was unable to open the door. Terry gave him a lift to a locksmith.

As soon as the fight with Bobby Neill was signed, Terry and Valerie went to Jersey for a two week holiday, staying at La Fonteine, a private hotel at St Peters. Local people knew who Spinks was and were very friendly towards them.

It was not Terry's first visit to the island – he had been there on holiday several years earlier, and loved it. It was an ideal setting for a period of relaxation before he got down to the hard training for his title fight in September.

Bobby Neill had also spent a holiday in Jersey having gone there shortly after his fight with Spinks in 1959. He too had been a great attraction on the island and when talking about their fight, praised the splendid display given by Terry.

After the holiday was over, Terry thought about very little other than becoming British champion. He had never been more determined in his life and once he was back in London commenced his preparations at the Thomas A' Beckett. A strict schedule was mapped out by trainer, Jimmy Davis, in which preliminary work and some sparring would take place at the Beckett. Then in order to harden Terry up, the final three weeks work would be done in solitary confinement at the Medway Sports Centre, London Road, Maidstone. It would mean that for the first time in his professional career, Spinks would move away from home to train.

From the first day of preparation, Terry really set about his task.

'Bobby Neill will not catch me this time,' he told a *Boxing News* reporter. 'I'm confident that I can jab his head off the way I did in our first meeting. I will enter the ring fit enough for 20 rounds let alone 15.'

At the Beckett, Terry sparred with old amateur opponent Bernie Dillon, a meat porter at Smithfield market, who had been managed by Joe Lucy since turning professional. They were joined by Hugh O'Neill, Brian Bissmire and Welsh featherweight champion Terry Rees. Despite the hard work put in there were moments of light relief.

Former light-heavyweight Tommy Gibbons had taken over the Beckett from Joe Lucy, and amongst his prize possessions was a pet monkey. Most of the time it was kept in a cage on the pub roof but when let out for exercise often found it's way down into the gym. Spinks took an instant dislike to the animal after it urinated over his leg one afternoon while he was doing his floor exercises. 'It's a filthy, horrible creature and should be kept locked in it's cage,' he told everyone.

Terry's attitude was like red rag to a bull because the boxing game has always had its share of practical jokers, and plenty frequented the Beckett. One day after a sparring session, Spinks and Terry Rees went for a shower, but after only a minute or so Tommy Gibbons called Rees out. The shower cubicle was rather sparse and the door had a large gap at the base. As Spinks continued to refresh himself, Gibbons pushed the monkey under the cubicle door. Terry was petrified and ran into the gym shrieking, pursued by the monkey who thought it was all a game. The more Terry ran, the more the animal chased him, much to the enjoyment of everyone present.

'If that thing comes near me again I'll throttle it,' yelled the naked Eastender. It was not the brightest thing for him to say because it just made him the target for more pranks. A few days later he opened his training bag to put his kit away, and out jumped the monkey.

Once Terry moved to Maidstone for the final three weeks of training his daily programme intensified considerably. He had long, tough spells of roadwork and spent hours climbing trees with the aid of ropes whilst wearing heavy clothing and boots. It was all designed to harden him up and get him on the correct weight. In the gym he did 15 to 20 rounds of exercises and sparring. He looked sharp in the workouts although some critics thought he should control his appetite for work.

Particular attention was paid to his diet and he was given plenty of plain but nutritious food. Because of his weakness for the wrong things, especially cream cakes and chocolate, he was strictly supervised by Jimmy Davis and Sammy McCarthy. They insisted that they were informed if any other member of the camp caught Terry sneaking a luxury.

Spinks described his manager and trainer as 'gaolers' because, 'They tried to keep me under lock and key.' The situation, however, was entirely of his own making with much of his recent weight problems being due to the amount of beer and spirits he was drinking. The hangers-on were taking him to clubs several nights a week because he didn't have the will-power to resist. The whole idea of going to Maidstone was to get him in the right environment away from temptation.

At a press interview McCarthy made no secret of the reasons for their tactics. 'Terry will not be left alone for a moment,' he insisted. 'Either Jimmy Davis or myself will be at his side when he eats, trains and sleeps. In fact, just to be doubly sure he doesn't go on a midnight larder raid, one of us will sleep inside his room and one outside the door.'

Ever since he turned professional Terry had smoked because, in his words, 'it helped to keep my weight down.' Shortly after moving to Maidstone, Jimmy Davis considered his wind and stamina would be greatly improved if he gave it up. Not wanting to fall out with his trainer Spinks agreed with him to his face although in reality he had no intention of giving up smoking.

One day after training he asked one of his sparring partners to go and get him some cigarettes. 'But you told Jimmy Davis you were giving up smoking,' said the other boxer feeling caught up in a difficult situation. 'No, I said I wasn't going to buy any more cigarettes,' retorted Spinks. 'You are going to buy them for me.'

Although he had still not won a professional title, Terry had a tremendous following, especially in the East End. He was constantly asked to attend charity functions and make personal appearances and, subject to commitments, he usually accepted. On 19 September he broke from the toil of training to open a new gymnasium called Club Bongo at Barking Road in Canning Town.

* * *

After completing his training Spinks left Maidstone and returned home four days before the fight. It was a bad mistake because

Local newspaper advertisement of a typical Terry Spinks attraction

Davis and McCarthy could not supervise him 24 hours a day. Although he desperately wanted to become champion, the rigors of the training camp were suddenly a thing of the past and it was like being released from confinement. Although he knew that even the slightest morsel of junk food would affect his weight, Terry could not resist the temptation. At one stage he was so dehydrated that he drank water out of a flower vase.

Despite more than six weeks intensive training and a controlled diet, Spinks was 14 ounces above the featherweight limit of nine stone when he attended the official weigh-in. The rules allowed him an hour to shed the surplus weight, so he was rushed to Joe Blooms gym at Cambridge Circus where he put on a rubber suit. After a spell of skipping and shadow boxing he returned to the scales 50 minutes later and was two ounces inside the limit.

Terry was astounded when told he was overweight. 'I feel there must have been something wrong with the scales when I got on the first time,' he told reporters.

Sammy McCarthy, however, was more forthcoming when he

revealed that although Spinks had been well inside the limit when he weighed himself earlier in the morning, he had admitted having sneaked a light breakfast of poached egg on toast. 'If you are tight on the weight, that's all it takes,' said Sammy. Nevertheless, McCarthy was confident about his man's chances. 'He's a better and more experienced fighter than when he met Neill 15 months ago,' he said. 'I feel he can win.

Sammy's thoughts were shared by Terry's father. 'The thought of losing hasn't entered his head,' said Tich. 'He's so determined, and has never trained like this before.'

Terry obviously knew he was tight on the weight because as he stood on the scales the first time, he held his breath in an attempt to create buoyancy while a Board of Control Inspector studied the reading. It was a careless situation to be in and could have cost him a forfeit of £200 and also his title chance.

Despite having had to work off the surplus weight, Terry went to the fight in good spirits and full of confidence. He was determined to prove that the defeat Neill inflicted upon him 15 months earlier, was a fluke. His confidence was demonstrated by the fact that he had lodged a side-stake of £1,000, the custom with title fights of years gone by. This was covered by Neill who said he was determined to prove he could never box so badly and win. Both cheques were held by the Editor of *Sporting Life*.

Terry's only regret was that his father would not be at ringside to watch him. Tich, despite being his greatest fan, had seen only one of his son's professional contests, that being against John O'Brien the previous year. After the decision went against Terry, he vowed never to watch him again. 'I'm a bogey,' he remarked. Instead, he waited at home by the telephone hoping for a call to say his son was champion.

The day of the fight was of double importance to Spinks because apart from challenging for the British featherweight title, he and Valerie announced that they were to become engaged on what was her 21st birthday. They had arranged a party for later that evening hoping it would be a double celebration.

Terry denied that wedding bells were just around the corner and told interested reporters that they would probably get married the following summer. 'After all,' he said with a cheeky grin, 'she's got to get in a lot of cooking practice because a bloke can't be expected to fight on tins of sardines and salmon.'

The announcement was of great excitement and reporters hounded Valerie for her comments. Showing off her beautiful diamond solitaire engagement ring, she told them she would not be at the Royal Albert Hall to watch Terry box. 'I'm scared of fighting,' she said, 'but I'm keeping my fingers crossed for Terry. If he wins he has promised to bring the Lonsdale belt to the party.'

Big fight nights at the Royal Albert Hall were always special occasions. The design of the tall, circular building was perfect to generate a wonderful atmosphere. This event was no exception as moving renderings of *'I'm for ever blowing bubbles'* from the huge contingent of Spinks fans echoed to the roof as their hero made his way to the ring. Bobby also had plenty of support, and although opinion was divided regarding the eventual outcome, there was a strong feeling that his power of punch could be the deciding factor.

The contest followed the expected pattern between the swarthy, hard-punching champion and his sprightly challenger. Although the highly partisan London crowd made it sound exciting, it did not reach championship standard. Both men were guilty of holding, and on three occasions referee, Ike Powell, called them together and ordered them to clean it up and stop wrestling.

Although Spinks boxed with all his old fire and speed, he had certainly learned a lot since their last fight. Instead of setting himself too fast a pace, he jabbed and hooked in bursts. Then whenever the opportunity arose he dropped into a clinch and rested, sensibly conserving his energy.

During the first few rounds, Spinks boxed brilliantly. He scored with speed and precision forcing the champion to give ground on a number of occasions. Sharp jabs opened a cut on the bridge of Bobby's nose in the third as Terry built up a good points lead.

Confident of his punching power, Neill bided his time, content to wait until Spinks got in close. Then he slammed solid blows to the solar plexus, reddening the area around the Londoner's rib-cage.

Although the pattern of the fight didn't alter, Spinks gained in confidence. For short spells in rounds four and six he appeared willing to stand and trade blows with the champion. Then, as if suddenly remembering his mistake in the previous contest, he sensibly contented himself with making Bobby miss and went back to picking up points from a safe distance.

Although Terry was winning each round, Neill was patiently awaiting his chance. He was confident that when an opening came he would end the fight just as he did 15 months earlier. When Bobby did score, his shots were harder and more damaging than those which Spinks rifled in at great speed.

The champion's patience appeared to be paying off because as the fight reached the halfway stage, Spinks was not slipping his counter-attacks so neatly. In rounds six and seven there were signs that his legs were beginning to tire and the initiative was moving to Neill. Terry was still scoring, however, and a short burst of punches in the seventh rocked Bobby's head from side to side, but without really hurting him.

All around the ringside there were non-stop shouts of the gamblers constantly changing the odds on the eventual outcome of the fight. Yet few could have confidently wagered on the sudden and somewhat controversial ending.

The fight was at a fascinating stage when, almost at the end of round seven, Spinks suddenly scored with a beautiful right uppercut to the chin. Neill, who had earlier received warnings for careless use of his head, lunged forward and they fell into a clinch. When they eventually stepped back, blood was streaming from a cut above the champion's left eye. A clash of heads appeared the most likely cause of the injury because Spinks had a visible swelling above his left eye.

Referee Powell immediately stepped between them and made a spot inspection of Neill's injury. Without wiping it clean or allowing the cornermen the opportunity to work on it, he signalled the end of the contest. The bell had in fact sounded and his action brought about angry protests from Bobby's corner.

It was the first time for many years that a British title contest had been stopped due to a cut eye. Although the controversial ending slightly soured what for Spinks should have been a glorious moment, his fans were ecstatic. The large Canning Town contingent leaped to their feet and roared with excitement when they realised the fight was over. Some jubilant individuals climbed into the ring and tried to lift Terry onto their shoulders as the announcement was being made.

Despite the controversy, Spinks was overjoyed as the Lonsdale belt was strapped around his waist, albeit upside down, by Board of Control President, J. Onslow Fane. Meanwhile, Neill's manager, Sam Burns, stormed from the corner to the press benches. 'It was diabolical,' he shouted furiously. 'They must give him a return.'

Despite his disappointment, Neill walked to Terry's corner to congratulate him. Although the ending to the fight had been controversial, he showed no animosity and warmly embraced the new champion. Holding gloves, they smiled and spoke briefly. They were two fine professional sportsmen with great respect for one another.

'This is the biggest thing in my life since I won the gold medal,' said Terry as he left the ring to be mobbed by his adoring fans. 'It is what I have been working for.' All the way to the dressing room, cockney voices became a massive choir as *'I'm forever blowing bubbles'* again echoed around the Albert Hall.

Irrespective of how the fight ended, Spinks deserved credit for his boxing skill – he was superb. He showed a good variety of swift, accurate punches, and fared just as well inside when he decided to mix it. He showed that he had learned from earlier mistakes and kept his defence tight thus preventing Neill from landing his dangerous left hook.

Arriving back at their dressing room Spinks and McCarthy were annoyed to find that a sneak thief had ransacked their belongings whilst the fight was in progress. Terry was particularly upset when he found that a pair of gold cuff-links had been stolen from his shirt. They had been a 21st birthday present from his friend and advisor, Jarvis Astaire. Money was stolen from Sammy's jacket pocket.

'We left our door wide open never dreaming that anyone would do such a thing,' Spinks told the army of newspaper reporters who crammed into the dressing room seeking interviews.

'I was never hurt during the fight,' said Terry once everything had calmed down. 'I felt I was going to win easily. I had no worries.'

He said he was willing to fight Bobby again, but the remark prompted Sammy McCarthy to interrupt. 'Maybe I'm not so soft-hearted,' he remarked. 'We shall have to wait and see. Terry will have a short rest and then be a fighting champion.

A journalist from the *East London Advertiser* raised the matter of Spinks being overweight. McCarthy said that a set of bathroom scales were the cause of the problem. 'I've asked him to get rid of these scales time and again, but he never has,' insisted Sammy. 'He nipped on to these this morning and thought he had room for a cup of tea and some toast, and that was where he made the mistake – the scales were wrong.'

Spinks became the first man to take the British featherweight title back to the East End since his manager Sammy McCarthy. He won it in 1954 by beating Ronnie Clayton in eight rounds at the White City but lost the title the following year to Billy 'Spider' Kelly in Belfast. It was thought to be the first time that a boxer had won the same title as his manager.

There was a great deal of sympathy for Bobby Neill because there was no doubt that the referee's action appeared somewhat premature. Even while the boxers were still in the ring, his injury had been cleaned up and the bleeding stopped. Showing the inch long cut to reporters in his dressing room, Bobby said; 'When the referee took my arm, I naturally thought he was directing me to my corner. I was amazed when he stopped the fight.'

'Yes, Spinks was ahead, but I was getting stronger and had never felt in any danger,' he continued. 'Everything happens to me. I just hope Terry will put up the title as I did for him.' Bobby was particularly annoyed that neither the President nor General Secretary of the Board of Control visited his dressing room to commiserate with him.

World heavyweight champion Floyd Patterson was a surprise spectator at ringside, but was diplomatically noncommittal when pressed by Reg Gutteridge for a comment. 'I couldn't see how bad the cut was,' he said, 'but in the States they usually leave the decision to the cornermen.'

That was precisely the point made by Sam Burns who, some while later, had still not calmed down. 'That referee took a liberty,' he said angrily. 'I have had the experience of cuts for 25 years and there were two other men in my corner equally well able to look after this very minor injury.'

As he began to relax a little later, Burns remarked, 'I have to say the title couldn't have gone to a nicer fellow, but I hope Terry will give Neill the chance of a return.' He said he would back his offer with a £1,000 side-stake.

British middleweight champion, Terry Downes, attempted to break the gloom in Neill's dressing room. 'I've had worse cuts in training,' he growled, 'And the worst cut of all is when the manager takes his cut of the money.'

* * *

Even as a young boy, Spinks hoped that one day he would emulate his great uncle, Sid Butler, and be talked about for his boxing achievements. He had exceeded his wildest dreams because at the age of 22 he was a British champion and idolised throughout the East End.

At a press conference the following day, he could not contain his excitement. 'If anything I feel slightly more elated than when I won my gold medal four years ago,' he said. 'Perhaps it was because I was such a long way from home then that I wasn't so excited as I am now.'

Being the sportsman he was, Terry was quick to commiserate with the former champion. 'I sympathise with Bobby at losing his championship on a cut eye,' he said sincerely, 'and although I had no doubt that I would master him, I can understand how badly he wants a return. He put his title up voluntarily and deserves another chance, but this is something I must leave for my manager to sort out.'

Terry also expressed his thanks for the support he had received from his parents. 'Mum and Dad have been wonderful pals to me,' he said, 'and although I like a bet and have been known to win the odd bob or two, they've always kept a tight hold on my finances. Mum looks after my sweet-shop and if she's got any worries at all it's keeping my fingers off chocolates and small drinks.'

Although the newspapers gave massive coverage of Terry's title success, his engagement to Valerie also received widespread publicity, including a television appearance. 'The best birthday present I had was Terry winning the title,' Valerie told reporters the morning after the fight. 'I listened to the radio commentary and we took a tape-recording of it at home. I've never seen a boxing match and didn't want to go.'

Valerie worked for a publishing company off Blackfriars Road where she was a secretary in the Trade Subscription Department. The day after Terry became champion she took an extended lunch break to go with him to a jewellers in the West End to have an adjustment made to her engagement ring.

After winning the title, Terry became very sought after by boxers, matchmakers and promoters. Harry Levene was anxious to stage a return between him and Bobby Neill whose manager, Sam Burns, offered to increase the side-stakes to £2,000. At the Piccadilly headquarters of rival promoter, Jack Solomons, it was planned to match Spinks with the winner of a proposed contest between Welsh star Howard Winstone and Derry Treanor.

The featherweight division was bursting with talent. Central Area champion, Billy Calvert, Harry Carroll, Johnny Howard and Phil Jones from Wales who had lost just two of his 23 contests, were all clamouring for a shot at the new champion.

There was a great deal of speculation among the fans and in the press regarding Terry's next opponent, but the most sensible statement came from Sammy McCarthy: 'Money speaks all languages,' he remarked. 'Terry is in the boxing business for a living so he will fight anyone if the cash in right.'

Meanwhile, Sam Burns lodged an official complaint with the British Boxing Board of Control regarding the action of referee, Ike Powell, in stopping the fight between Spinks and Neill. The matter came before the Southern Area Council on 12 October 1960. Burns contended that Powell should have given the corner the opportunity to treat the cut before making his decision. He claimed that the referee was prejudiced against Neill throughout the contest.

Powell told the Council that the cut occurred during the seventh round, but almost at the end Spinks unleashed a fusillade of blows which caused it to bleed profusely. He stopped the boxing and terminated the contest before the bell sounded.

After hearing all the evidence the Stewards were critical of the referee, finding that he in fact stopped the contest after the bell had sounded. In the circumstances he should have followed Board of Control directives in allowing the cornermen time to treat the injury. The matter was then referred to the Championship Committee of the Board who stipulated that Neill must be given the chance to fight for his old title.

Five days later, according to the *London Evening Star* newspaper, Spinks made the sensational offer of a winner-take-all contest. It meant that as champion, he would be laying odds of nearly 3-1 on himself, but as everyone knew, Terry was a gambler.

'Everyone seems to be on Neill's side,' remarked Sammy McCarthy. 'It seems that public opinion is forcing Terry into the return fight, but that is not so. Terry is willing to go through with the return any time, and is confident he can win again.'

'Terry is a betting man, and to show his confidence he made this offer,' continued Sammy. 'He knows he has a lot to lose, but he likes to have a flutter especially when the odds are against him.'

Promoter, Harry Levene, and matchmaker, Mickey Duff, were closely in touch with the situation. Within a few days they had discussions with both camps and an agreement was quickly reached. Both boxers were confident of victory, and after offers of substantial side-stakes, agreed to take the unusual course of a £5,000 winner-take-all fight. Contracts were signed and lodged with the Board of Control for the contest to take place at the Empire Pool, Wembley, on 22 November. 'I will pay the losers training expenses,' said Harry Levene on announcing the details.

One matter which did concern Levene, however, was the appointment of the referee. Although recovering from illness he instructed his office to contact the Board of Control and ask for a neutral official to be appointed. 'Feeling is running high in both camps over the choice of referee,' he told the press. 'It will save argument if the referee comes from as far away from London or Scotland as possible.'

Tremendous interest was being shown in the fight and ITA filmed Spinks in his final workout at the Thomas A' Beckett before he again moved to the Medway Sports Centre adjacent to Maidstone

Station goods yard. 'We liked the set-up there,' said Sammy McCarthy, 'so why change a winning formula?'

The training camp was set up shortly after the contracts were signed. McCarthy and Jimmy Davis again designed a rigorous schedule to ensure that Spinks became totally disciplined from the outset. Probably for the first time in his life there were no cream buns or bottles of pop. They knew his ability and potential, but the hardest task was making him control his diet.

'I suppose I did live it up a bit a year or two back, but now I'm dead serious,' Terry told reporters who visited the camp.

Determined to be at his fittest ever, he was up at 6.00am every morning for a six mile run, and after a good breakfast relaxed until early afternoon. Then he went into the gym for exercises and sparring which increased as the day of the fight drew nearer.

Terry's chief sparring partner was Junior Cassidy, a stocky Nigerian fighter whom he had outpointed earlier in the year. He was chosen because of his aggression and ability to withstand punishment. His job was to attack and make Spinks defend for all he was worth. McCarthy and Davis were also anxious for Terry to improve his punching power. Cassidy, being exceptionally tough, was the ideal man for him to work with. 'Mix it, mix it,' Davis would frequently shout from the side of the ring as he strove to harden his man up.

There was a lot of spare time at the training camp, but it was important to keep Terry relaxed and concentrated on the task ahead. Sammy and Jimmy knew that their boxer was never happier than when he was having a flutter on the horses. As a form of compromise they were prepared to tolerate it provided it didn't interfere with training.

One afternoon in the gym, Terry suddenly stopped working and said to Jimmy Davis, 'Look at the time. Don't forget we have got to get that bet on.' Davis said there was nobody to do it. Spinks then turned to Bob Paget, another boxing trainer he and Sammy knew from the Thomas A' Beckett, and asked him to do it. Bob refused because he knew nothing about betting.

Almost as if wanting to keep Terry relaxed, Jimmy said he would go and place the bet. 'All you have got to do is your skipping,' he told his boxer. 'I can rely on you to do that can't I?' Then turning to Paget, said firmly, 'Stay here and watch him.'

As soon as Davis had left the gym, Spinks threw down the skipping rope and sat in a chair. 'Tel, what are you doing to yourself?' remarked Paget.

'It's bad enough when he's here, but nobody should have to train like this,' retorted Terry.

Although Terry occasionally tried to cheat in training, everyone got on well together. They played a lot of darts and cards. Terry had visits from his parents, but not his fiancee because McCarthy considered she could be a distraction and unsettle him. They shared many things including jazz, dancing and fast cars, but not boxing.

Spinks remained at Maidstone until the morning of the contest, unlike in September, when he went home several days earlier. This time his handlers were taking no chances and they were rewarded. At the weigh-in he was on the limit of 9 stone, as was Bobby Neill.

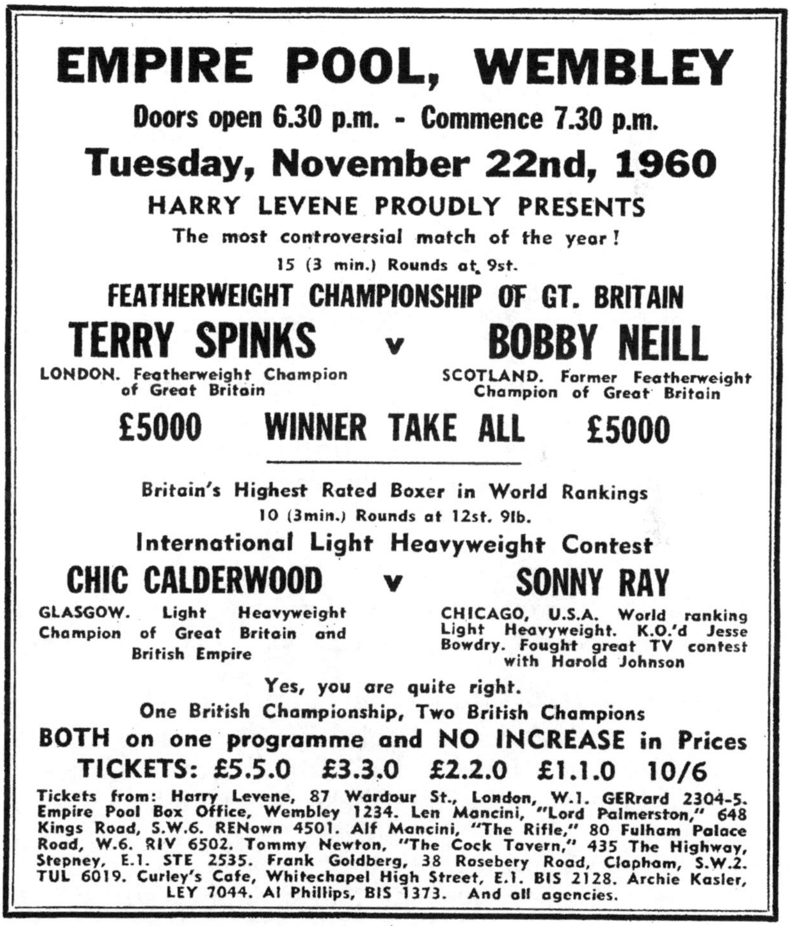

EMPIRE POOL, WEMBLEY

Doors open 6.30 p.m. - Commence 7.30 p.m.

Tuesday, November 22nd, 1960

HARRY LEVENE PROUDLY PRESENTS

The most controversial match of the year!

15 (3 min.) Rounds at 9st.

FEATHERWEIGHT CHAMPIONSHIP OF GT. BRITAIN

TERRY SPINKS v BOBBY NEILL

LONDON. Featherweight Champion of Great Britain

SCOTLAND. Former Featherweight Champion of Great Britain

£5000 WINNER TAKE ALL £5000

Britain's Highest Rated Boxer in World Rankings

10 (3min.) Rounds at 12st. 9lb.

International Light Heavyweight Contest

CHIC CALDERWOOD v SONNY RAY

GLASGOW. Light Heavyweight Champion of Great Britain and British Empire

CHICAGO, U.S.A. World ranking Light Heavyweight. K.O.'d Jesse Bowdry. Fought great TV contest with Harold Johnson

Yes, you are quite right.

One British Championship, Two British Champions

BOTH on one programme and NO INCREASE in Prices

TICKETS: £5.5.0 £3.3.0 £2.2.0 £1.1.0 10/6

Tickets from: Harry Levene, 87 Wardour St., London, W.1. GERrard 2304-5. Empire Pool Box Office, Wembley 1234. Len Mancini, "Lord Palmerston," 648 Kings Road, S.W.6. RENown 4501. Alf Mancini, "The Rifle," 80 Fulham Palace Road, W.6. RIV 6502. Tommy Newton, "The Cock Tavern," 435 The Highway, Stepney, E.1. STE 2535. Frank Goldberg, 38 Rosebery Road, Clapham, S.W.2. TUL 6019. Curley's Cafe, Whitechapel High Street, E.1. BIS 2128. Archie Kasler, LEY 7044. Al Phillips, BIS 1373. And all agencies.

Poster advertising winner-take-all championship contest between Spinks and Bobby Neill

Promoter, Harry Levene, who claimed to have put up a record purse to secure the fight, was an assured winner. Wembley was packed to capacity on the night of the fight. Coach loads of fans had travelled from the East End, and the demand for tickets was so great that touts outside the arena did a roaring trade.

Once again opinion was divided over who would win, with a number of critics predicting that the power of Neill's punch and Spinks suspect stamina would be the deciding factors. Others, however, thought the Londoner would last the distance and win on points. It was a fascinating match-up which it was hoped would erase all doubts once and for all as to who was the better man.

As the lights went out, the Empire Pool erupted as the searchlights picked out first Neill, and then Spinks. As a fanfare heralded them to the ring, fans adjacent to the aisle screamed emotionally for Terry to 'go and do the business.'

The fight followed the familiar pattern of their two previous encounters. Spinks again set a fast pace, scoring with rapid left jabs to the head, while Neill patiently waited like a tiger looking to pounce. As the fight progressed, Terry again showed that he had matured considerably and learned from previous mistakes. Whilst his speed was incredible he always looked to take a breather in the clinches. This clearly irritated Bobby who often looked appealingly to the referee.

It was generally a clean and lively contest with little of the mauling which occurred in their last meeting. In the early rounds, Neill concentrated on body punching in the hope that he could slow the champion down. When he did catch him, Spinks didn't hang around for the follow-up attack. He was supremely fit and his footwork a delight.

Terry brought frequent bursts of applause from the packed audience with his clever bobbing and weaving away from trouble. At times his great skill made the former champion look crude and clumsy.

Spinks built up a wide points lead and at times was so confident that he wanted to stand and trade punches with his challenger. Then as McCarthy and Davis yelled at him from the corner not to mix it, he quickly reverted to the jab, scoring with four or five shots without reply.

It was not until round seven that Neill really hurt Terry. Suddenly, the course of the fight almost dramatically switched to the challenger. A hard left hook flush on the chin sent the champion reeling into the ropes. Angry and frustrated that his man was getting careless, McCarthy again yelled at him to box.

After covering up and re-grouping, Spinks retaliated and fought back, and a solid right to the chin sent Neill's gum shield flying across the ring. As the crowd roared, he peppered the challenger with jabs, but Bobby was prepared to take them in order to score with another good left hook.

Londoners at ringside screamed at Terry to stop mixing it. When he broke away from a toe-to-toe slog in the centre of the ring, there were gasps of dismay because he had a slight cut and swelling above his left eye. 'Box him, box him,' yelled his anxious supporters.

Neill continued to force the pace in the eighth and scored with four good hooks to the chin. Obeying instructions from his corner, Terry sensibly reverted to using his speed and skill and fought the challenger off with short sharp bursts of jabbing. Drawing applause from the crowd, he moved away from Bobby's dangerous left hand and gradually resumed control of the fight, but knew he couldn't relax for a moment.

By round nine both men were showing signs of battle. Neill was bleeding heavily from the nose and Terry's left eye was swelling rapidly. Spinks, however, was showing no signs of weakening or slowing down. By the 10th he was looking the fresher and stronger of the two.

At this stage of the fight, the champion began to back up his brilliant left hand work with solid right crosses. Picking up the pace, he gradually punched Bobby to a standstill.

As they entered the final three rounds, Neill had nothing to offer. McCarthy and Davis, two good former professionals, had been carefully monitoring the situation, and at the start of round 13 told Terry to go all out for victory.

Although his left eye was now a grotesque slit, the champion was still scoring. After carefully manoeuvring Neill to the ropes, he opened up. Bobby had no defence to the lightning bursts of punches from Spinks who pinned him there for what seemed an eternity. Just before the bell a tremendous right to the chin made Bobby's knees buckle, but somehow he stayed upright. The fact was, he was too brave for his own good – only his tremendous pride kept him on his feet. At the end of the round he staggered to his corner and flopped on to his stool.

Neill was a beaten fighter and should have been pulled out at that stage. Instead, his cornermen worked feverishly to revive him, and used swab sticks to check the flow of blood from his nose.

As he bravely came out for the 14th, Bobby was so weak he could hardly defend himself. Boxing with the same speed as in the earlier rounds, Spinks tore into his rapidly weakening challenger and worked him to the ropes. Yet he didn't lose his head and throw a flurry of punches hoping to put Neill away. He was cool and calculating, sized up the situation, and then threw the punches that were required.

Bobby had no resistance and was stunned by a looping left hook which slammed against his chin. He crashed to the canvas, but as the count was tolled over him, nodded to his corner that he was okay.

Clutching the ropes, he hauled himself up at 'eight', but everyone in the arena could sense the fight was over. Peter Wilson, writing in the *Daily Mirror* summed up the obstacle Neill faced:

> Now instead of the golden boy of the amateurs, Spinks was a trained professional killer.

Referee, Billy Jones should have stopped the fight at that stage but allowed Spinks to resume his attack. Showing no mercy, the champion crashed a right-left-right combination to Neill's jaw sending him down for another count of 'eight.' When he bravely rose, another right uppercut sent him toppling back to the floor.

Neill slowly climbed to one knee, looked at the timekeeper, but was too bemused to understand what was happening. Bravely, yet instinctively, he struggled to his feet, but failed to beat the count.

The crowd roared, and Terry's supporters excitedly stormed his corner. As the Lonsdale belt was strapped around his waist, the proud champion waved to his adoring fans who blew kisses back. *'I'm forever blowing bubbles'* again echoed around Wembley, and Spinks was mobbed all the way to his dressing room.

It had been a thoroughly workmanlike performance by Terry who boxed like a champion from the start. He was fitter and stronger than ever before, and whilst Bobby always had a puncher's chance, the fight was very one-sided. Apart from a couple of left hooks which caught him, Terry never looked in any real trouble. He coupled his boxing skill with stiff punching and good ringmanship, and his punches, whether to head or body, were more accurate. He paced himself well – the first time in his career that he seriously tried to do so. He was the boss, and George Whiting of the *London Evening Standard* gave him all but two of the 13 completed rounds.

'I wanted to start shooting more punches from the 10th round, but they stopped me,' beamed Terry pointing to Sammy McCarthy and Jimmy Davis.

Although he thought his hand-made boots, manufactured specially for the fight, had been a lucky omen, Spinks was quick to praise Davis who told him how to breathe and relax between rounds. 'I owe it to him because he did it all for me,' insisted the champion. 'This was everything I have ever wanted to do – prove I can last the championship distance and knock someone out in the process. I desperately wanted to prove my strength and get revenge by beating Neill again,' he continued, 'but I didn't think it would end with a knockout.'

No boxer likes to see an opponent seriously hurt, and Spinks was extremely concerned because he knew Neill had been assisted from the ring in a dazed and exhausted condition. He desperately wanted to know how Bobby was, but was refused admission when he visited his dressing room. Bobby was being tended to by two Board of Control doctors, and when Terry was eventually allowed in he was horrified to find him lying prostrate on a couch.

Stooping to kiss him on the cheek, Terry wished him a speedy recovery. Bobby squeezed his hand, thanked him for giving him the chance to win back his title, and congratulated him on his victory. At that stage it was thought he was only suffering from exhaustion.

Reporters had also been refused entry to Bobby's dressing room, and as he was being examined Sam Burns went outside and issued a statement. Announcing that the former champion would not box again, he said: 'It took real guts for him to be fighting after two bad road accidents. If he had stayed down when Spinks hit him with a left hook, he would not have taken that tremendous barrage of punches. But Bobby isn't the type of fellow to lie down if there is breath in his body.'

An hour or so later, Neill appeared to have recovered. He was dressed and ready to leave the arena when he suddenly collapsed. A doctor rushed to the dressing room and after a brief examination made an emergency call to summon an ambulance. It was just after midnight when he was rushed to Wembley hospital.

Shortly before leaving the arena Bobby vomited causing those around him to think that his condition was due to the fact that he had swallowed a lot of blood during the later rounds of the fight. In the early hours of the morning, however, he underwent emergency surgery for the removal of a blood clot from his brain. The first bulletin issued by the hospital described his condition as 'serious but making satisfactory progress.'

Terry was extremely upset when he heard the news at his home the following morning. He immediately went to Wembley hospital and spent several hours at the bedside of his beaten opponent. He was very emotional because he felt personally responsible for what had occurred. In the privacy of his home, he prayed for Bobby's recovery.

Whilst the next 48 hours were critical for Neill, they were extremely distressing for Spinks. Apart from having to come to terms with the situation, he also had to contend with hate mail sent to his address. Other sick-minded cowardly individuals made anonymous telephone calls to him and his parents saying Bobby had died. He was hounded by reporters who virtually camped in the hospital grounds. They asked how he felt about Bobby's situation, and on one occasion a photographer followed him to the ward. As Terry sat beside Bobby's bed, he took a photograph before being ejected by nursing staff. Neill was furious when the picture appeared in a national newspaper the next day.

Spinks never forgot how his elation at the victory suddenly and dramatically turned into sadness and fear. 'My dressing room was a riot and I laughed and shouted as loudly as the rest,' he recalled. 'Then came the West End celebrations. What I didn't know, was all the time I was whooping it up, the surgeons were fighting for Bobby's life. When I found out next morning that he had been rushed to hospital, I suddenly felt empty and cold inside.'

Terry kept telling himself it wasn't his fault – he was just doing his job. 'I was even saying it when they showed me into his ward after the emergency operation,' he recalled. 'But it didn't mean anything because in my heart I felt I was responsible.'

The person who eventually convinced Terry that he shouldn't blame himself, was Bobby's father. He telephoned Spinks the night after the fight telling him not to worry because it could have happened to anyone.

'Those must have been the most generous words ever spoken by a fighter's father to his son's opponent,' said Terry with tears in his eyes.

Bobby made a remarkable recovery and was soon sitting up in bed. One day Spinks visited him wearing a pair of sunglasses. 'Bobby couldn't help laughing when I took them off and showed him the black eye he gave me,' recalled Terry. With warmth and reassurance he told Terry not to worry about what had occurred. 'It wasn't your fault,' said Bobby, 'It was just one of those things.'

As professionals, the two fighters already had tremendous respect for one another, but a friendship was also developing. It would be maintained as the years passed by, and there are warm embraces whenever they meet at functions. This was typified one night in February 2001 at a gathering of champions at Charlie Magri's pub in Mile End. Terry was comfortably seated in a corner of the bar when Bobby pushed his way through the dense crowd just to embrace him.

'Bob and I always made a good fight,' remarked Spinks years after they had both retired. 'I was lucky enough to win two out of three, and my successes were both title shots.'

* * *

Bobby Neill was luckier than most other boxers who collapsed from blood clots on the brain. He made a remarkable recovery and left hospital on 17 December. He even had a telephone debate with Dr Edith Summerskill, at the time, boxing's most committed opponent. He made it clear that despite his injuries, and the fact that he would never box again, he fully supported the sport and wouldn't have changed anything.

Bobby was undoubtedly one of the bravest men ever to have graced a boxing ring. He was badly injured in two road accidents, the second of which resulted in him having a steel plate inserted into his left thigh. Despite having been told by doctors that he would never box again, he fought his way back to full fitness, and winning the British featherweight title from Charlie Hill was just reward.

Neill also suffered other setbacks including a fractured jaw, broken wrist and rheumatic fever. Not surprisingly the press called him 'The Miracle Man.'

Like Spinks, Bobby also suffered badly from trying to make the featherweight limit. After beating Charlie Hill he told Sam Burns it was his last fight at the weight because he was terribly drained. 'The problem was, the fight everyone in London wanted was Neill against Spinks, so I was offered a huge purse to go through with it,' said Bobby when describing the situation years later.

He had real problems making nine stone and admitted he would have struggled had the fight gone much longer than seven rounds. Yet the shrewd Sam Burns kept his fighter's problems from the press who were concentrating on Spinks' well documented weight and stamina problems. It was the same for their third fight – Bobby went through hell making the weight. 'I was dehydrated,' he remarked, 'and that's why I finished with a blood clot.'

When he retired from the ring, Bobby had the credible record of 28 victories from 35 contests, 23 coming inside the distance. In March 1962 he took out a manager and trainers licence and his first signing was Frankie Taylor, followed by Alan Rudkin. He also managed and trained Johnny Pritchett and Joe Tetteh, and was an influential member of the teams who guided Alan Minter and Lloyd Honeygan to world championship honours.

* * *

Terry's popularity appeared to grow after every contest, and hardly a day went by without him receiving an invitation to attend a function. Even as a very young man, he was always keen to support charity functions. It was something his father had encouraged him to do. 'There are many people out there far worse off than we are so always do what you can to help them,' Tich once told him.

A few days after the successful defence of his title, Terry was one of a number of leading sports personalities to attend a special benefit dance at Canning Town Public Hall. Fight fan, John Hetherington, a stevedore, had been badly injured in an accident at the Royal Albert Docks, and his work mates organised the event to help raise him financial aid.

Spinks, together with international footballers Jimmy Greaves and Peter Brabrook, volunteered to attend to help boost the attendance and proceeds. Throughout the evening they charged a small fee for autographs and the amount they raised helped swell the fund considerably.

* * *

Having defended his title against Bobby Neill just 56 days after he won it, Terry deserved a break from the rigors of training. His pal Terry Downes was due to fight Paul Pender for the world middleweight title in Boston on 14 January 1961, so arrangements were made for Spinks to join a party flying from London to support him.

Shortly after the Neill fight, Sammy McCarthy revealed that he had received a fairly substantial offer for Spinks to fight at St Nicks Arena, New York, on 23 January. His opponent had not been revealed, but Sammy delayed his decision pending the outcome of the bout with Neill. Once that was over, he resumed talks with the American promoter, but in late December the plans fell through.

Terry was not alone in Boston because he knew a number of people who made the trip, including Harry Levene, Shoreditch promoter, Harry Grossmith, and Board of Control General Secretary, Teddy Waltham. Whilst there he visited Downes at his training camp and volunteered to give him a workout for speed.

Although the main purpose of the trip was to support Downes, Terry stayed in America for 10 days as a holiday. He and Downes went to New York where they were guests at a Boxing Writers' Dinner. They went sight-seeing, and among the places they visited were Jack Dempsey's Restaurant on Broadway, and the Latin Quarter.

Although he had not boxed there, Spinks was well respected in the United States, particularly by world heavyweight champion Floyd Patterson. 'The fighter who made most impression on me during my recent stay in Britain was Terry Spinks,' he told reporters when he returned home. 'I saw him at the Albert Hall the night he took the title from Bobby Neill and I thought he made a real good job of it.'

Patterson was also a former Olympic gold medallist, having won the middleweight division at Helsinki in 1952. Like Spinks, he moved up two divisions in order to win a professional title.

'In British boxing during 1960, Terry Spinks looks outstanding to me,' continued Floyd.

Arriving back in Britain, Terry was refreshed and itching for action. It was hoped that he could be matched with either Floyd Robertson of Ghana for the British Empire title, or Gracieux Lamperti for the European crown. 'Now that Terry has silenced the critics who reckoned his stamina was suspect, he can start aiming at bigger prizes,' said Sammy McCarthy.

The British Boxing Board of Control, however, were not prepared to support Spinks in his quest for further honours. Instead, they directed that he defend his British title against Howard Winstone before 29 April. Knowing that Terry would need to be in top condition, McCarthy asked the Board for a two month extension to allow them to fit in two 10 round warm-up contests. His application was refused.

In early February, Harry Levene announced that Spinks would face a leading American at the Empire Pool, Wembley, on 7 March. Belfast promoter, George Connell, also made an offer for the cockney idol to meet British and Empire bantamweight champion, Freddie Gilroy, at catchweights. McCarthy rejected the offer because even if his man was successful it would not necessarily progress him towards further honours. Victory over Winstone, however, would give him the Lonsdale belt outright.

Meanwhile, Spinks and Winstone met at the annual Boxing Writers' Dinner at the Criterion Restaurant, Piccadilly, and were photographed together. Howard had recently outpointed British Empire champion, Floyd Robertson over 10 tremendous rounds at

Cardiff. The quality of his victory made the prospect of a fight with Spinks even more mouth-watering.

Terry's opponent for the Wembley bill on 7 March was 20 year old Canadian featherweight champion, Dave Hilton from Montreal. It was claimed that he was unbeaten in an amateur career of 72 contests in which he won several Golden Gloves championships. He turned professional in April 1959, and won the Canadian title in only his second contest after a gruelling 12 rounder. He had lost only one of his 12 pro fights and agreed to box in England because he had run out of opponents at home.

Hopeful that Spinks would emerge from the contest unscathed, matchmaker Mickey Duff also booked him to top his Eve of the Grand National bill at Liverpool Stadium on 23 March. It was planned that he would meet Scottish champion Dave Croll who had knocked out Johnny Kidd in one of the biggest upsets of 1960. It was an ambitious plan, and Spinks would eventually withdraw from the promotion as would Chic Calderwood who was also on the Wembley bill of 7 March.

A week before facing Dave Hilton, Terry celebrated his 23rd birthday, and the Canadian champion presented him with a birthday cake in the shape of a boxing ring. The presentation was made at a luncheon given by Harry Levene at the Black Angus Restaurant, Great Newport Street, to welcome overseas boxers appearing on the Wembley bill. Apart from Hilton, Americans, Von Clay and Willie Green, were scheduled to meet Chic Calderwood and Terry Downes respectively.

Spinks made a particularly nice gesture by donating his cake to Bobby Neill. Although his old opponent was making a fine recovery, he still felt in some way responsible for what occurred. With Terry's blessing, Bobby gave the cake to the nurses at Wembley hospital who had looked after him during his stay there.

The fight with Dave Hilton was made at 9 stone 3, and at the official weigh-in at Bloom's Gym, Spinks was exactly on the limit. He had again trained at Maidstone where Jimmy Davis and Sammy McCarthy put him through the same demanding schedule as for the Neill contest.

Spinks was far from impressive during the opening few rounds when the Canadian more than held his own. On several occasions he unleashed good left hooks to remind the British champion that he was no pushover. In the third Terry looked distinctly uncomfortable as powerful hooks brought blood streaming from his nose.

Both men received warnings following close-quarter mauls in

Promoter, Jack Solomons, sits between Spinks (far left) and Bobby Neill as they sign for their non-title contest scheduled for Wembley on 2 June 1959. Nat Fleischer (second from left) and Teddy Waltham look on.

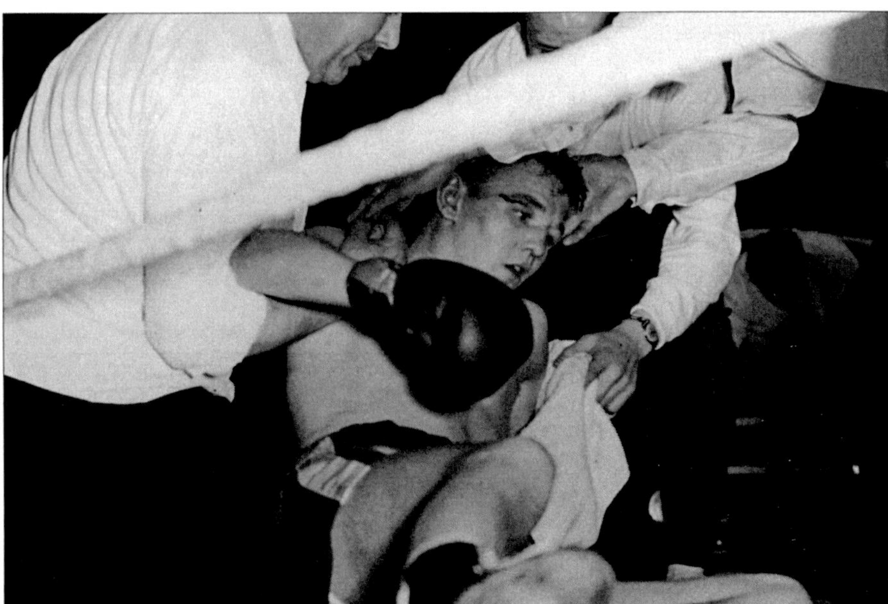

Spinks is assisted by his cornermen, Jimmy Davis (left) and Sammy McCarthy, after being knocked out by Bobby Neill in the ninth round at Wembley on 2 June 1959.

Spinks works at a century-old forge at West Ham as part of his preparation for his fight with Eric Bret at Harringay on 15 April 1958.

Spinks (left) shakes hands with Derry Treanor when they weighed-in at Blooms gym for their contest at Streatham on 1 September 1959, won by Treanor on points.

Spinks cuts a cake presented to him at the Thomas A'Beckett gym on his 20th birthday by fellow professional boxers, Alex Buxton (left) and Dave Charnley.

Spinks is floored by Pierre Cossemyns during their fight at Empress Hall, London, on 20 May 1958. Terry won a disputed decision.

Johnny Kidd floors Spinks during their British featherweight championship eliminator at Olympia on 26 January 1960. Terry got up to win on points.

Spinks with his unsuccessful greyhound Coar Pete.

A day at Hamilton races in 1959. From the left - Derry Treanor, Terry Spinks, Lex Kelly, Tony Rawlinson, Billy Rafferty and Noel Boston.

Spinks (left) with trainer Jimmy Davis in 1961.

Spinks (left) and Bobby Neill shake hands after signing contracts at promoter Harry Levene's office in London for their winner-take-all contest at Wembley on 22 November 1960.

Canadian featherweight champion, Dave Hilton, (right) presents Spinks with a cake to commemorate his 23rd birthday at the Black Angus Restaurant in London 28 February 1961.

Spinks (front right) and Howard Winstone sign contracts at the Dorchester Hotel in London on 4 April 1961 for their British featherweight championship fight to take place at Wembley the following month. Promoter, Harry Levene (standing left) and Teddy Waltham, General Secretary of the British Boxing Board of Control, look on.

Howard Winstone (left) ducks under a left from Spinks during their championship contest at Wembley on 2 May 1961, won by the Welshman in 10 rounds.

Terry and Valerie toast each other at their wedding reception in the West End of London on 19 July 1961.

Spinks (left) on his wedding day with best man Sammy McCarthy.

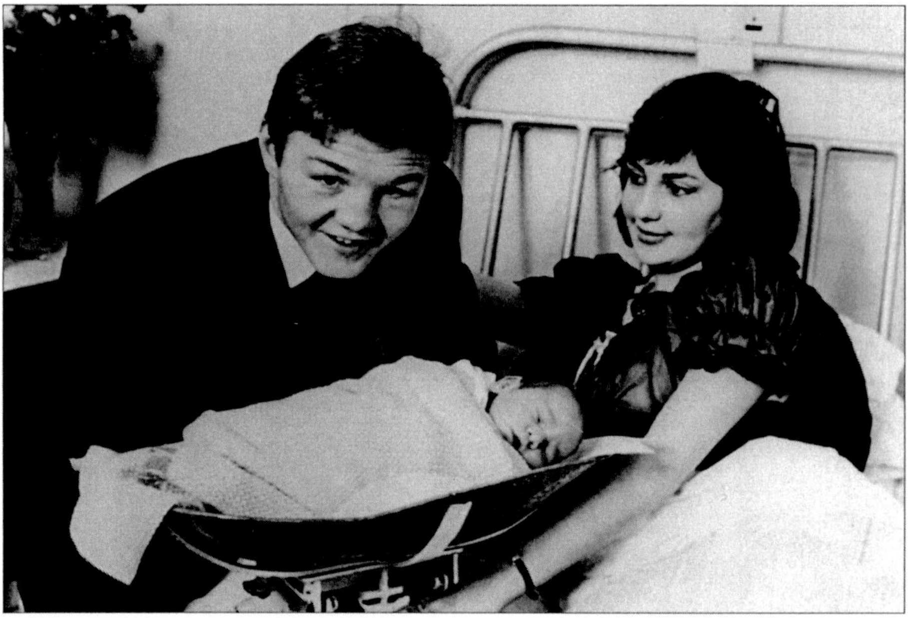

Terry and Valerie admire their baby son Jarvis who was born at Thorpe Coombe Hospital, Walthamstow, on 21 May 1962.

Proud, loving parents - Terry and Valerie at home with their son Jarvis.

the first and fourth rounds. As Hilton sought to attack, the British champion smothered his aggression making it untidy and not pretty to watch. As the fight progressed, however, Spinks became the stronger of the two. He picked up the pace in the fifth, cut Hilton's left eye, and showed glimpses of the brilliance for which he was known.

By round six the Canadian had run out of steam. A solid right to the chin early in the round had him reeling, and he held on desperately. As he struggled to survive, he continued to grab and hold bringing several stern warnings from referee Pat Floyd. Spinks was at his best in this round as he shook Hilton with solid left leads and right crosses.

He continued the good form in the seventh and Dave had no answer to his accurate jabs. The cut over his left eye had worsened, and his nose, injured in round four, streamed blood as Spinks poured in punches from both hands. Despite repeated warnings from Mr Floyd, Hilton continued to hold. He was a spent force and eventually the third man lost patience and disqualified him for persistent holding. Dave was in tears as he was led to his corner.

Many people thought the fight had been stopped because of the ugly gash above the Canadian's left eye. The power of Terry's punches had undoubtedly taken their toll, and had Hilton not been disqualified it would only have been a matter of time before he was stopped.

It had been a good workout for Spinks although there had been signs of ring-rust early on. Only in the last three rounds did he dominate the fight. He looked relatively unscathed, but had again experienced difficulty with his breathing. The following day he saw his specialist again, but was assured that there was no lasting damage. Nevertheless, his proposed contest with Dave Croll at Liverpool was called off. His next contest would be against Howard Winstone, and his fans knew that a vast improvement in form would be required if he were to emerge victorious.

9

DEFEAT THEN MARRIAGE

Although the Board of Control had given Spinks a deadline to meet Winstone, Harry Levene was convinced he could get the East End lad a shot at the world featherweight title. Since bringing champion, Davey Moore, to London to meet Bobby Neill in a non-title contest in October 1959, Levene had kept in touch with his handlers. Apart from beating Neill inside a round, they thoroughly enjoyed their stay and indicated they would like to return for a title defence.

Levene knew a world title fight involving Spinks would fill any arena in the capital, so he discussed the possibility with his camp. It was an attractive proposition, so the day after the fight with Dave Hilton, Sammy McCarthy wrote to the Board of Control asking for a postponement of the Winstone contest deadline. The Stewards refused the application because they did not consider Spinks a suitable contender for world championship honours.

Unperturbed by the attitude of the Board, Levene immediately set about securing the contest between Spinks and Winstone. Back in January while they were in Boston for the Downes - Pender fight, the promoter promised Terry he would do everything possible to secure him home ground advantage.

The Board of Control invited promoters to submit purse offers for the fight already dubbed by the press as 'The Battle of the Golden Boys.' Apart from Spinks having won gold at Melbourne, the Welshman took a gold medal at the 1958 Empire Games at Cardiff. He had a tremendous following in Wales and Levene knew the fight would be a guaranteed sellout.

True to his word, Harry secured the fight for London with a purse of £12,055, a record for a British featherweight title bout, as was Spinks purse of £7,233. Levene easily outbid his rivals, Jack Solomons (£10,800) and G.R.G. Promotions (£6,275), but he considered it worth every penny. Announcing that the fight would go ahead at the Empire Pool, Wembley, on 2 May, he knew the financial rewards would be substantial. Of equal importance was the fact that Spinks would be boxing in front of his adoring London fans.

Contracts were signed on 4 April at a lavish ceremony at the Dorchester Hotel in Park Lane in the presence of Teddy Waltham, General Secretary of the British Boxing Board of Control. Both boxers used gold pens, and posters advertising the contest were elaborately printed in gold and red.

On paper it was an even money affair although in London, Spinks was very much the pre-fight favourite and huge numbers of bets were placed on him to retain his title. In and around the mining centre of Merthyr Tydfil, however, Winstone's army of fans were equally confident that he would be the winner.

Aged 22, the challenger was a year younger than Spinks, and although he was less experienced, had fulfilled all expectations. Under the careful guidance of former British and European welterweight champion Eddie Thomas, he had gone from strength to strength. Since turning professional in 1959 he had won all of his 24 contests.

Winstone had also been a top class amateur, having won 84 of his 86 bouts. He was a Welsh international, and in 1958 won the Welsh and ABA bantamweight titles as well as a gold medal in the Empire Games. Guaranteed a purse of £4,822, he set up his training camp at the Dowlais Club at Penydarren near Merthyr as soon as the match was made. Full of determination he enlisted the help of sparring partners Gordon Blakey, Phil Jones, Ayree Jackson and Darkie Hughes.

Sammy McCarthy knew that the Welshman was a quality opponent so he searched hard for the best possible training camp for the champion. At the end of March he went to Brighton and inspected Billy Butlin's gym at the Ocean hotel. He also checked other locations at Bognor and Bournemouth. After careful consideration they decided to return to their old camp at Maidstone.

'Terry was yawning after a couple of hours at Bournemouth,' Sammy told a *Stratford Express* reporter. 'The air is so heavy down there it wouldn't have been any good for training.' He said that whilst conditions at Brighton and Bognor were ideal, the facilities available did not match up to those at the Medway Sports Centre. 'Maidstone had been lucky for us in three fights,' continued McCarthy, 'so we are going back there.'

As for previous fights, Terry did his initial training at the Thomas A' Beckett before moving to Maidstone on 12 April for the hard graft. With the credible record of just three defeats from 39 contests, the incentive for victory could not have been greater. Not only would it win him a Lonsdale belt outright, but also put him in line for a shot at British Empire champion Floyd Robertson or the European title held by Gracieux Lamperti of France.

A couple of weeks before the fight Harry Levene gave Terry an even greater boost by saying that if he beat Winstone he would meet Lamperti at Wembley in September. The promoter added that he planned to have the contest recognised as a final eliminator for Davey Moore's world title. The announcement was well timed and Wembley was sold out days in advance of the fight. Although Terry had personally ordered more than £2,000 worth of tickets from the promoter's office, many of his fans were disappointed.

Spinks trained rigorously at the Maidstone camp. He looked very sharp during tough workouts and shook his sparring partners with fast left jabs and combinations. During one brisk session, Phil Lundgren, also an ex-Olympic entrant who had been hired to impersonate Winstone, suffered a damaged nose.

Despite the fact that his fiancee Valerie was restricted to just one visit a week, Terry was extremely happy and relaxed. When Jimmy Davis suggested certain moves during a particular workout, he replied, 'Okay Jim, I'll do that. Who won the 2.30? I bet that bookmaker down here will be glad when I go home. I've really been tuning him up.'

Onlookers loved Terry's constant chatter and cockney humour. 'I suppose I'll back myself for a few quid,' he told Reg Gutteridge. 'I usually do. I love a gamble. Well, I'm getting married ain't I? Mind you we'll have to draw up a contract that suits me.'

Amongst the audience were three National Hunt jockeys who were friends of Terry. 'I give them a hand getting a bit of weight off,' said the champion.

Spinks was a real hit with the club hostess, Mrs Harris, who had real motherly admiration for him. The former school secretary told Reg she had learned plenty about life from characters in the fight game, especially from Spinks. 'He's such a lovely boy, you'd never think he was a boxer,' she remarked as she phoned for the latest race-result for him.

With less than a week to go before the fight there were irritating rumours that Spinks was once again having weight problems. This was angrily denied by Jimmy Davis and Sammy McCarthy who told press men that the champion was fit enough for 20 rounds let alone 15.

'The old weight ain't giving me no trouble, I'm a natural feather,'

EMPIRE POOL WEMBLEY
Tuesday, 2nd May, 1961

Doors open 6.30 p.m. Commence 7.30 p.m.
Matchmaker : MICKEY DUFF

HARRY LEVENE proudly presents the two GOLDEN BOYS in a GOLDEN MATCH for a GOLDEN PURSE

15 (3 min.) Rounds at 9st. for the Featherweight Championship of Great Britain

TERRY SPINKS v **HOWARD WINSTONE**

London. Champion — Merthyr. Challenger

10 (3 min.) Rounds International Middleweight Contest

Terry **DOWNES** v Tony **MONTANO**

British Champion — Champion of Arizona, U.S.A.

8 (3 min.) Rounds Empire Welterweight Contest

TONY MANCINI v **BOSWELL ST. LOUIS**

Hammersmith. Southern Area Champion — Trinidad. All-action fighter

USUAL GREAT SUPPORTING BOUTS

Prices : 12/6, 25/-, 50/-, £4, £6

Tickets obtainable from : Harry Levene, 87 Wardour Street, London, W.1 (GERard 2304-5); Empire Pool Box Office (WEMbley 1234); Archie Kasler (LEY 7044, BIS 1775); Alf Mancini, "The Rifle", 80 Fulham Palace Road, W.6 (RIV 6502); Tommy Newton, The Cock Tavern, 435 The Highway, Stepney, E. (STE 2535); Frank Goldberg, 38 Rosebery Road, Clapham Park, S.W.2 (TUL 6019); Curley's Cafe (BIS 2128); The Builders Arms, Wyvil Road, S.W.8 (MAC 2150); Al Phillips (CAN 5852); AND ALL AGENCIES

Poster advertising British featherweight championship contest between Spinks and Howard Winstone

Terry remarked. 'It's just that I used to take liberties, but I'm getting a big boy now.'

Jimmy Davis was totally dedicated to the fight game and took it for granted that his fighters would be too. Behind the scenes, however, Spinks was doing things his way whenever the opportunity arose.

As soon as Davis left him for his afternoon rest, on would go the television for the racing. With a phone at his side as he relaxed in an armchair, Terry would lay bets with a London bookmaker on whatever horses he fancied. He gambled because he liked it, and a little matter of a few hundred quid wouldn't stop his fun. He knew that his purse money of more than £7,000 was still to come.

On Sundays, Terry had a good meal at a restaurant in the town, putting on weight behind Jimmy's back. 'All week I'd been a slave to the weighing machine and this was my chance to catch up with all the good things I'd been missing,' he admitted years later. 'First soup, then the fish. After that the meat course, as many vegetables as I could eat, and naturally a bottle of wine.'

Every time Terry got on the scales on a Monday morning his weight was right up. Davis would shake his head and mutter because he couldn't understand how it happened.

As Spinks sweated away in a rubber suit to reduce weight again, he told himself it was all worthwhile. 'As I shook the moisture out of my eyes, I'd cheer myself up working out what I'd have for dinner next Sunday,' he remarked. 'I know it wasn't the ideal preparation to meet a man like Winstone, but that's the way I was.'

Normally, a fighter doesn't do much during the day before a fight other than gentle exercise and relaxation. Spinks decided that the most relaxing place he knew was the racecourse. He was fed up with watching racing everyday on television, and as there was a meeting at Wye, about 30 miles into the Kent countryside, he was determined to go. The only problem was how to get there.

Everyone at the camp was dedicated to keeping him lying down resting. To divert attention he therefore persuaded a mate who visited him, to start a big argument in the next room. At that point he disappeared and joined up with some friends who took him to Wye.

As for his last fight with Bobby Neill, Terry was kept at Maidstone until the morning of the fight. After a light breakfast and some gentle exercise he, Davis and McCarthy took a leisurely walk before making their way to London for the weigh-in at 1 pm. Spinks scaled exactly 9 stone and Winstone 8 stone 10¾. Both men looked relaxed and toned to perfection as they smiled and posed for cameramen.

* * *

The Empire Pool was packed, not only by Spinks' supporters, but also a huge contingent from Wales who had hired a special train for the journey to London. Posters and programmes had been printed in gold and red to mark the special occasion, and by the time the boxers entered the ring the atmosphere was electric.

The fight opened at a terrific pace and from the first bell the sharply divided crowd roared with every punch. Although he was three pounds lighter, Winstone was an inch taller than Spinks and had a longer reach, an advantage which he used to maximum effect.

Spinks attacked viciously using good jabs coupled with hooks to head and body from both hands. He was anxious to take command early, but his enthusiasm brought him warnings from referee Ike Powell, firstly for a low blow and then a rabbit punch.

Winstone remained calm under pressure, but when he used his immaculate left jab the champion had no defence to it. So many good punches were thrown by both men in the opening round that it was hard to separate them. The crowd screamed in appreciation as they returned to their corners at the bell.

The champion opened round two by ramming three sharp left jabs into Howard's face and outboxed him for the first minute. Midway through the round, however, the Welshman got on top. His punches appeared to carry more weight and as jabs poured into Spinks' face, he clinched at every opportunity.

Although Terry hit back with occasional heavy rights, Winstone took them well and continued to pile up the points with his deadly left jab. Almost in frustration, the champion tore into Howard just before the bell, forced him to the ropes and lashed out with a wild right. Again the Welshman remained calm and skilfully replied with good shots of his own.

Spinks took the fight to Winstone at the start of the third, stabbing his left flush into the face. Again Howard was equal to it and caught the champion with good counters. It was a close round and again the huge crowd roared their approval at the bell.

In the fourth Terry was again on the receiving end. His jabs and hooks generally fell short due to the evasive skills of the Welshman. Good combinations to the face slowed the champion and momentarily he looked to be in trouble. He rallied briefly, but was again under pressure during the last half minute of the round. Although Spinks scored with good lefts of his own, Winstone looked well in control by this stage of the contest.

The pace dropped in the fifth as both men began to feel the effects of their efforts. As in previous rounds, Winstone put on a spurt during the last half minute to edge the round.

Round six began in familiar fashion with Spinks doing the early attacking. He was soon in trouble, however, as the challenger used his left hand to good effect. In desperation Terry charged in head down forcing Winstone to the ropes, but unable to do any damage. Howard was superior in every sense and made him miss badly. When they stood and traded punches it was Spinks who broke it off and retreated. Blood streamed from his nose as testimony of the accuracy of the Welshman's punches.

Terry took a lot of punishment in round seven and it was at this point of the fight that his fans realised he had little chance of victory. Winstone went straight on the attack, doubling his jabs and throwing stiff right crosses. Spinks stumbled to the ropes where the Welshman hit him with every punch in the book. Gallantly the champion moved away and hit back with his own stiff shots, but his attacks were quickly halted by accurate counter-punches.

A terrific left smashed against Terry's already bloodied nose. Then, after standing off momentarily, Winstone scored with good shots to the head from both hands. With Spinks in serious trouble neither heard the bell and referee Ike Powell had to pull them apart. As he walked to his corner Terry shook his head as though resigned to defeat. His face was a reddened mass from the effects of Winstone's jabs, his nose bled heavily and there were lumps around both eyes.

Davis and McCarthy worked desperately to revive him during the interval, and looking refreshed, the champion was quickly off his stool at the bell for round eight. With great courage he jabbed well to the Welshman's face, but his success was short-lived because Howard was soon back in command. A four punch combination had Terry reeling, and stiff rights had him in serious trouble on the ropes near his own corner.

Winstone had brought his right into play more as the fight progressed and repeatedly caught Spinks flush in the face. The fading champion defended desperately as he was hammered along the ropes by a stream of quality punches. It was a tribute to him that despite the pressure he was under he still tried to hit back whenever Howard paused for breath. His punches, however, lacked power and the Welshman took them without flinching.

Desperate to cling on to his title Terry refused to go down. Then displaying incredible courage he suddenly hit back. With about a minute of the round to go they stood toe-to-toe and traded punches. For a moment it looked anybody's fight. When two rights from the plucky champion slowed Winstone noticeably, it suddenly looked as though he was running out of steam. The fans yelled frantically as Spinks drove the Welshman to the ropes as he somehow found reserves of strength.

As the excited London fans urged their man on, Winstone dramatically turned Terry on the ropes and caught him with a volley of punches. As there were less than 10 seconds to go he survived, but at the bell the weary champion again shook his head in despair as he slumped to his stool. It had been a tremendous round in which fortunes swung both ways. The fans were certainly getting value for their money.

Despite the efforts of his cornermen, the champion's nose was still leaking blood as he left his corner for the start of round nine. Again he was quickly into action forcing Winstone to the ropes, and his excited fans screamed encouragement as he slammed a right to the Welshman's chin. Howard's left leads were missing their target and Spinks was able to get inside and mess him about.

With the challenger appearing to be tired it looked as though the fight might be turning in Terry's favour. There was, however, a touch of desperation about his work. His two-fisted attacks to the head were wild and off target, and he was unable to land punches to seriously hurt Winstone.

Despite his tiredness Howard was boxing strictly to orders. As the champion was lured into a false sense of security, he cleverly picked his punches while trying to conserve his strength. A few rapid shots to the head soon had Spinks back on the receiving end again and he was looking in a bad way. Some referees would have stepped in at this point, but Mr Powell was anxious to give the champion every possible chance.

Towards the end of the round, Winstone gradually picked up the pace and his shots became more accurate. A steady stream of left jabs just before the bell gave him the round, and the packed crowd rose to Spinks who showed the courage for which he was renown.

As they came out for round 10, Spinks' face bore clear signs of battle. Yet he still refused to give up and attacked the Welshman with a couple of good hooks to the head. Cleverly avoiding the full impact, Winstone resumed control with his jab. They were sharp and accurate, and again brought blood streaming from Spinks' nose which had bled almost continuously since the sixth.

Good uppercuts slowed the champion midway through the round, and when Howard really turned on the pressure, a volley of hooks almost floored him. His left eye closing rapidly, the courageous champion never gave up trying, but by this stage he was shipping a lot of punishment. He had no answer to Winstone's wonderful left jab.

Spinks was terribly weak, but somehow he managed to cover up and roll along the ropes as Howard threw everything at him. Although the action was halted when Mr Powell sternly warned Winstone for using the elbow, it was only temporary respite for the fading champion. Three sharp left jabs flush in the face without reply left him in serious trouble on the ropes.

Winstone was scoring at will and did everything except put Spinks on the floor. At the bell, the spirited little fighter tottered to his corner on unsteady legs. His left eye closing, he looked up appealingly at trainer, Jimmy Davis, as he slumped on his stool. After a brief word with his fighter, Davis called Ike Powell to the corner to say they were pulling Terry out. He had given everything, but on the night it wasn't enough to overcome the brilliant undefeated Welshman.

Spinks had taken a real beating and how he managed to stay on his feet during the last two rounds defies imagination. Although he kept up a fast pace and never stopped trying, nothing seemed to go right for him. His punches lacked power and he was unable to avoid the deadly accuracy of Winstone's punching.

Howard boxed with the skill of a veteran and turned in a truly wonderful performance. There were wild scenes as his arm was raised, and excited fans and members of his family, including some women, climbed into the ring to congratulate him. On the opposite side of the ring a fierce fight broke out after some indiscreet Welsh supporters were heard to make adverse comments about Spinks' ability. Angry East End fans set about those responsible until it was broken up by police and security men.

As the Lonsdale belt was strapped around Winstone's waist, Spinks quietly left the ring and made his way back to his dressing room. After being examined by a doctor, he faced reporters. 'Winstone surprised me,' he told them. 'I couldn't breathe through my nose so my mouth was open, and every time he hit me I felt it jar my head. But don't put that down as an excuse,' he insisted. 'He beat me fair and square.' It was a sporting remark so typical of Spinks, an honest young man who never complained in his life.

Despite looking terribly battered around the face, Terry remained quite chirpy. 'It was just one of those nights,' he continued. 'I just could not get going.' Then, turning to Sammy McCarthy, he asked, 'I'm not finished fighting am I?' Smiling broadly, the manager assured him that he wasn't.

There was no doubt that Terry's nose was still giving him problems, but McCarthy revealed that he had also suffered from a cold in the days leading up to the fight. Before going into the ring to face Winstone they had given him something to help him breathe. There certainly appeared to be substance in Sammy's claim because, writing in the *Daily Mirror* the following day, Peter Wilson commented that Spinks had gone into the ring with what appeared to be cold sores around his mouth.

About half an hour after the fight was over, Spinks had a surprise visitor to his dressing room in referee, Ike Powell. The Board of Control originally appointed Eugene Henderson from Scotland to officiate, but due to business commitments he had to withdraw at short notice. Neither fellow Scot, Frank Wilson, nor Andrew Smythe from Belfast were available.

A neutral referee was always appointed for a championship contest to ensure impartiality, but in discussions with the Board, Spinks and his handlers had suggested Powell. For a Welshman to officiate in a fight involving a fellow countryman was almost unheard of, but the London camp had insisted that they were quite happy for Mr Powell to take charge.

'Thank you very much for having such confidence in me to put my name forward as the referee,' said Powell shaking hands with Terry. 'It's the greatest compliment I've been paid in 40 years of boxing. I'm sorry it turned out the way it did for you.'

'Was there much in the fight Mr. Powell?' asked Spinks rising up from his couch. 'Well, I'm not allowed to divulge points of course,' replied the official, 'but I cannot mislead you Terry. Winstone had a convincing lead.'

Another visitor to Terry's dressing room was the new champion himself. They shook hands and Winstone thanked him for a good fight. 'Keep that Lonsdale belt nicely polished,' said Spinks with a smile. 'I want it as a show-piece for my new home.'

It was no disgrace for Terry to lose to Winstone, whose display was acclaimed by practically every national newspaper in Britain as being one of the finest for years. In the *Daily Mirror*, Peter Wilson described the Welshman as: 'the finest British nine-stone boxer I can recall seeing – and that includes the late great Nel Tarleton.'

Another tribute to Howard's skill came from veteran boxing correspondent, George Whiting of the *London Evening Standard*. An ardent fan of Terry's, he wrote: 'I have never seen Spinks made to look so ordinary in all departments save that of gallantry.'

A few days after the fight, Harry Sheppard, manager of Canadian champion, Dave Hilton, told *Boxing News* he was not surprised that Winstone won. 'Dave took more out of Spinks in their fight on March 7th than people realised,' he insisted. 'Hilton's strong body punches did the former champion a lot of harm and that was why Spinks held him in the clinches.'

Some critics believed that the defeat by Winstone should convince Terry that it was time he retired from boxing. It was a view privately shared by a number of his fans, but not by Nobby Wallace, the Plaistow man who successfully guided Bobby Neill to the British featherweight title. He predicted that Terry could win the title back from the Welshman. 'People who say Spinks should retire are talking nonsense,' he told the *Stratford Express*. 'He is a great little fighter and I reckon he can get back to the top after he has settled down to married life.'

Wallace recalled an occasion when Terry visited him in June 1959 just after he had been knocked out by Neill. He was confident he could still beat Bobby, and aimed to prove it. 'Terry kept his word,' said Wallace. 'He beat Bobby twice and convinced me that on his night he is one of the best boxers in Britain.'

Meanwhile, Terry paid another visit to his specialist because he was convinced that his troublesome nose contributed to him losing the title. 'Once I can breathe freely again I know I can beat Winstone,' he told the *Stratford Express*. 'My aim is to regain the title. I will think about my future when I have won a Lonsdale belt outright.'

Years later when he reflected on the fight with Winstone and his preparation, Terry admitted that the Welshman had little to beat. 'My high living had seen to that,' he remarked. 'It wasn't just the Sunday dinners or the breaks in training that finished me. It went back further than that.'

'When I fought Howard, I fought years of drinking, gambling and refusing to go to bed,' he continued. 'And then there was the constant weakening as I sweated off the weight. Suddenly it all caught up with me. I don't make any excuses for my performance against Winstone. I got what I deserved.'

* * *

In the weeks following the Winstone fight Terry and Valerie were making plans for their wedding scheduled for July. Much of their spare time was taken up looking for somewhere to live and window shopping for furniture. In the days leading up to the wedding they spent a lot of time at Terry's house at Cumberland Road sorting out their presents.

For relaxation Terry went horse riding at Newmarket and was also granted a Pony Turf Club Rules licence. 'I love horse racing,' he declared. 'Riding will help take my mind off boxing. I want to forget about the gloved sport for a few months, but I'll be back.'

Sammy McCarthy was amused when he heard of Terry's plans to take up pony racing. 'Well, at least it will help keep his weight down,' he laughed.

The first outing of Terry's new pursuit was on Whit Saturday at

Rayleigh in Essex where he was scheduled to have three rides. Much to his embarrassment, however, he found that ponies were much more difficult to handle than the full grown race horses to which he was accustomed.

In the first race he rode Nazim, a tiny grey pony which despite having good speed on the straight was not so good rounding the sharp bends of the track. Consequently, they finished last of the six runners.

The second race turned out to be an even greater disaster. Terry's mount, Paddy's Chance, a young Irish pony, was having its first competitive gallop on a racecourse. In a hectic journey from the saddling enclosure to the starting tapes, the boxer was thrown to the ground on four occasions. Watching among the 7,000 holiday crowd was Terry's fiancee, Valerie. 'It's worse than seeing him box,' she told a *Stratford Express* reporter as she watched him crash unceremoniously, to the ground for the fourth time.

Showing his true fighting courage, Spinks eventually managed to steer his mount to the starting tapes, but his troubles were far from over. As the tapes shot up to signal the start of the race, Paddy's Chance didn't move, leaving Terry to sit and watch as the other five starters galloped away.

When the stubborn pony finally decided to move forward it was only in a trot and too late to be part of the race. Realising his hopeless position, Terry sportingly cantered along the course grinning broadly as he was cheered home by the good humoured crowd. He scratched from his third ride because the effects of his tumbles made it exceedingly uncomfortable to sit on a saddle.

'I will ride again,' he told a *Stratford Express* reporter. 'Even now I consider pony riding great fun and I hope to race at Hawthorn Hill next month.' The following day the boxer was confined to a cosy arm chair nursing huge bruises, particularly to his backside.

Despite his disappointment at losing to Howard Winstone, Terry was back in the gym by early June. Although his wedding day loomed, he said he was keen to have further contests as soon as possible. In considering the best way back for their man, Sammy McCarthy and Jimmy Davis let it be known that they would like to manoeuvre him into a fight with Empire champion Floyd Robertson who had been outpointed by Winstone in a non-title bout in January. It was a sensible ploy because victory over Robertson would qualify Spinks for a return with Winstone in October or November.

Although Terry no longer held the British title, his popularity remained as high as ever and there were plenty of offers of fights.

At one stage negotiations got underway for him to box in Australia where he had a massive following.

Boxing agent, Benny Huntman, acting on behalf of London Representative Stadiums Limited of Sydney, approached Sammy McCarthy in early June. The proposal was for Terry to travel to Australia after his wedding, for a tour taking in three fights in late August or September. The offer included all expenses paid for his new wife and trainer Jimmy Davis. Opponents short-listed included Australian featherweight champion Wally Taylor and lightweight George Bracken.

McCarthy believed the change of scenery would be good for Terry especially as he had fond memories of Australia. 'It would be a big gamble for him, but one I think could pay off with handsome dividends,' he said when announcing proposals to the press. 'They are boxing crazy in Australia and always turn out in their thousands when a name fighter tops the bill.'

Although Sammy negotiated for Spinks to receive a guaranteed purse, the promoters preferred to agree on a percentage of the gate. This proved to be the stumbling block and after three weeks of discussions no agreement could be reached, and the plans fell through, leaving Terry free to concentrate on his forthcoming wedding.

* * *

Terry and Valerie were married at noon on 19 July 1961 at St James Church, Piccadilly. It was a massive occasion, fashionable and stylish, just like a society wedding. Outside the ring it was unquestionably boxing's event of the year.

Throughout the morning, crowds gathered at the church entrance and in the street, while newspaper reporters and cameramen jostled to gain the most advantageous positions. With an hour still to go before the principals arrived it looked as though there were representatives from every national newspaper and fashion magazine in the country, and some from abroad as well. Pathe News cameras were also in position early because despite Terry no longer being British champion, he remained high profile.

Accompanied by her father, Mr Leslie Pearson, and four bridesmaids, Valerie arrived at the church on the stroke of noon. She wore a crinoline-skirted white net dress and carried a bouquet of white orchids and a silver horseshoe on which a miniature pair of boxing gloves were tied. Terry and his best man, Sammy McCarthy, had arrived a few minutes earlier, but to avoid the bustle of the excited crowds, had entered the church through a side door.

Before setting off for the church Terry became very nervous and his plight was not helped when he saw a group of reporters waiting outside the house at Cumberland Road. 'I've got butterflies in my stomach just as if I was about to go 15 rounds,' he told Sammy.

When approached by a reporter who asked how he felt, Spinks made no secret of the daunting experience he faced. 'Blimey, I'd rather face a championship fight anytime,' he remarked. 'I feel dreadful.'

St James was packed for the 30 minute service conducted by the Rev J S Brewis. Among the guests was new world middleweight champion, Terry Downes, who had taken the title from Paul Pender just eight days earlier. Other boxers included Bobby Neill, George Walker, Terry Murphy, Terry Brown, Peter Waterman and West Ham welterweight Johnny Kramer, a close friend of Spinks. Mr and Mrs Bill Parkinson had travelled from Newmarket for the occasion. Outside, the crowds grew to incredible proportions. When the bride and groom emerged from the church there was tremendous cheering. Standing shyly on the steps, Terry faced an army of cameramen shouting for him to kiss the bride. He needed an awful lot of persuading and would much rather have been in a boxing ring.

After leaving the church, Terry and Valerie went to a champagne reception at the fashionable Trocadero where there was music and a splendid buffet for more than 200 guests. The three-tier wedding cake had been specially made and donated by Lyons Corner House at Coventry Street in the West End.

During the evening the couple were joined by about 400 friends at a reception at Woodford. Many were from the East End, and the boxing and racing fraternities who had been unable to attend the Trocadero celebration. It was a real East End knees-up which developed into a heavy drinking affair. By the end of the night Terry was so drunk that he had to be taken home. Valerie was looked after by Sammy McCarthy and his wife. and slept on the sofa at their flat at Woodford.

For their honeymoon, Terry and Valerie had booked a week at Le Touquet, but it became a disaster. After flying from Lydd Airport in Kent a couple of days after the wedding, they returned home after only a few days because Terry lost all their money in a casino. They were in fact so broke that Terry had to get Tich to pay the taxi-driver they had hailed at the station.

As they still had nowhere to live Terry insisted that they stayed with his parents at Cumberland Road until they got their own place. This, however, proved to be yet another set-back to their marriage.

A few days after returning from Le Touquet, Valerie made Terry a cup of coffee. She boiled the milk in a saucepan and tipped it into a cup. As soon as he drank it, Terry said, 'Come on, leave the cup, we're going out.' They spent the day at The Kingfisher, a swimming pool and club at Epping, which was one of their favourite haunts.

When they returned to Cumberland Road, Valerie was confronted by Doris who was furious because she had not washed Terry's coffee cup. An obsessively house-proud woman, she was extremely hostile and even threatened to hit Valerie. The situation between them became so difficult that within just a week of being married Valerie had to go and stay with her parents at Clapham.

Although they saw each other regularly, she and Terry lived apart for several weeks until they managed to rent a ground-floor flat at 2 The Limes, High Road, South Woodford. Sammy McCarthy and his wife Sylvia lived upstairs at number 6.

* * *

Shortly after he returned from Le Touquet, Terry was told that his next fight would be at Wembley on 5 September. Harry Levene had matched him with Paddy Read, the featherweight champion of New England, USA, over 10 rounds at 9 stone 4.

Following his marriage there was a great deal of speculation regarding Spinks' future in boxing. It had been rumoured that he would move up to lightweight, or even retire. Some critics, already concerned about his dedication, believed married life would cause him to lose all ambition to continue as a fighter.

At a press conference, however, he insisted that he had all his old appetite back and was raring for action. Valerie gave him her total support. 'Because we are married does not mean Terry is going to give up boxing,' she remarked. 'It's his life, and after all it's our living.'

Terry wasted no time in getting back into training. Within a few days he was back into his routine of getting up early and doing his roadwork before going to the Thomas A' Beckett for sparring.

Between training Terry continued to attend fund raising events, and was a member of a celebrity cricket team at a fete at Cumberland Road, Canning Town, on August Bank Holiday Saturday. The event attracted a crowd of more than 600 and raised £200 for the Mayor of West Ham's Roundtable. After he was out for a duck, Spinks amused the crowd when he took the microphone and said, 'I've fallen off ponies, kicked a penalty over the bar in a football match, and now this. I think I'll stick to boxing.'

Although his training for the Read fight had gone well, Terry suddenly lost concentration with just a few days to go. Firstly, he had to go to Poplar hospital where he was given penicillin injections for three nasty boils. Then there were rumours that the Wembley promotion had been cancelled. The story was quickly denied in the national press at the weekend, but by that time the damage had apparently been done. Instead of trying to verify the situation, Spinks carelessly relaxed his diet and took a lot of liquid which badly effected his weight.

On the morning of the fight he was two pounds overweight. He telephoned Sammy McCarthy who wasn't surprised because he'd got used to this kind of news. 'I'll come and get you,' said Sammy, 'You'd better go to the gym and try to box it off.'

Spinks said he would prefer to go to a Turkish bath and get rid of it. He knew that for the first time in his life he was too weak to train, but didn't tell Sammy that.

They went to the baths at Jermyn Street where Terry had a long hot sweat. Afterwards they decided to sit in the gardens at Leicester Square until it was time to go the weigh-in at 1.00pm. Sammy started talking about a film that was showing at one of the cinemas, but within a few minutes he was talking to himself. Terry had fallen asleep. When Sammy woke him to go to the weigh-in he was still tired and listless. 'They've buried livelier bodies than I was that day,' recalled Spinks.

When he stepped onto the scales Terry was still 1lb 2oz overweight. The American camp demanded that he paid the forfeit of £25, but McCarthy refused because Paddy Read had arrived at the weigh-in 15 minutes late. 'No money, no fight,' insisted the Americans. The only other alternative was for Spinks to go to the gym and shift the surplus weight. Not being able to face another hour of sweating and working he told Sammy to pay the forfeit which he reluctantly agreed to do.

Terry's problems were far from over. A few minutes after being passed fit to box by a Board of Control doctor, he went to a restaurant at Leicester Square. After just a few mouthfuls of food, he suddenly complained of feeling unwell. He was taken to a doctor who found that he had a high temperature, high pulse rate and an inflamed throat. He was promptly withdrawn from the fight and sent home to bed.

'I expect they will have an enquiry,' said Sammy McCarthy, 'but we have nothing to fear.'

Terry's non-appearance was a great disappointment to many in the 10,000 crowd at Wembley, and there was concern in the East End about his health. 'He is upset that he let his fight public down,' his father told local reporters who enquired about him. 'He is itching to get into action.

Terry was going through a very difficult period, and a few days later he and trainer, Jimmy Davis, split following a heated discussion over future training plans. Explaining the situation to the *East London Advertiser*, Sammy McCarthy said: 'It is unfair to say that Jimmy was sacked. The three of us had a long talk and decided it would be best if Terry went back under Snowy Buckingham's guidance.' Davis would, however, continue to train all other boxers in Sammy's stable.

Another concern to Terry was a vicious attack on his 74 year old grandfather, Harry Jordan, at his home by a thug who stole £200. It was the second burglary he had suffered within six months. On the previous occasion, £2,000 had been stolen within a few days of his wife passing away.

Harry, who still ran his coal business, lived alone at Beckton Road. On a Sunday evening in mid-September, he went out for some food, but when he returned found the man in his house. Although he struggled with him he finished up with two black eyes and bruising.

Meanwhile, the British Boxing Board of Control were concerned that Spinks had yet again failed to make a stipulated weight. The Southern Area Council decided that his future urgently needed to be considered and ordered him and Sammy McCarthy to appear before a special meeting on 4 October.

Evidence was heard from Spinks, McCarthy, Jarvis Astaire, boxing trainer Frank Duffett, and Board of Control Medical Officer, Dr W Kelsey. The Council drew the following conclusions:

1) that Spinks' explanation for withdrawing from the fight with Paddy Read be accepted,
2) that disciplinary action be taken for failing to make the stipulated weight. In view of his past record his licence was suspended for a period of 12 months.

Afterwards, Council Chairman, David Hopkin said: 'The decision was taken after careful consideration of the fact that Spinks has appeared before us on other occasions for being overweight.'

Terry broke down and cried after the decision to suspend him was announced. It destroyed original plans for him to have a fight every two weeks as a path towards a return with Howard Winstone. In the East End there was great resentment over the Board's decision, although many people held the view that it was their way of telling Spinks he should retire.

'I was stunned by the Council's verdict,' said Sammy McCarthy. 'At the very most I was expecting a fine or perhaps a two months suspension. They have been far too severe and Terry is very upset, but determined to box on.'

Within a few days Spinks was composed but angry. Determined to fight back he contacted the Board of Control and lodged a notice of appeal. 'I am determined to box again,' he told the *Stratford Express*. 'Their decision is ridiculous and I hope to get the sentence wiped out or at least reduced.

* * *

The evening before he was suspended, Spinks had his first fight since losing to Winstone. His opponent was Kimpo Amarfio, an unsung Ghanaian. The intention was to ease the former Olympic champion back with a couple of undemanding contests, and victory was expected to be a formality.

Managed by Al Phillips, Amarfio had only a moderate record. Since arriving in Britain in 1958 as bantamweight champion of Ghana, he had won seven, lost eight and drawn one, most of his contests having lasted the full distance. His last fight was in April 1960, and apart from some rough and tumbles in the fairground booths, he had been inactive. His ambition had in fact been so low that he had to be reminded to renew his licence.

It was sad to see Terry having to fight such an undistinguished opponent to try and prove that he still had the ambition and ability to force his way back to the top. Writing in the *London Evening Standard*, George Whiting made no secret of the fact that if Spinks couldn't reduce Amarfio to 'tattered impotence,' it could be time for him to retire from the ring. A close friend of Terry's since his amateur days, Whiting concluded his article:

> I would sooner see Terry Spinks behind his sweetshop counter or help run his father's bookmaking business than being harried and hammered by lesser men at job-lot rates.

The fight against Amarfio took place at the National Sporting Club near Piccadilly Circus. When referee, Harry Gibbs, raised Terry's arm at the end of the eight rounds, there was an outburst of booing, something which was unheard of at the club.

It was a rough and tumble affair and for most of the time Amarfio was the aggressor. Had he been more accurate with his punching Spinks would have struggled to last the distance. The Ghanaian also landed too many shots with the open glove for which he was sternly warned by Mr. Gibbs in round seven. When Terry went to the floor for a count of 'three' in this round it appeared to be from a push.

Although he was never in full command, the Canning Town boxer's punches were landed correctly. He won the first two rounds with ease, but after that it was all-out aggression from his opponent. He threw long arm jabs, hooks and right uppercuts almost at will except during the fifth when he took a breather.

Although he was often caught flat-footed by Amarfio's non-stop slugging tactics, Terry was fighting back all the time. His best work was on the inside with good two-fisted combinations making each round close and difficult to score. It was the Ghanaian's tactics which caught the eye, however, and at the end the dinner-jacketed audience had no doubt who had won, and it wasn't Spinks. The usually reserved club members covered their faces with their hands and turned away booing and jeering at referee Gibbs decision. Despite their reaction, Spinks said he was pleased with his performance, and claimed that his legs had taken him where he wanted to go.

Terry's appeal hearing was set for 27 October and until that date he was free to take other contests. He therefore agreed to face Con Mount Bassie at Cardiff on 25 October. Two days before the fight, a statement was issued by Messrs Anthony Leader & Co, solicitors acting on behalf of Spinks:

> We have been asked by our client, Mr Terry Spinks, to make it clear that his decision to take part in a contest at Cardiff on Wednesday next, should not in any way be construed as contempt of the Southern Area Council's decision to suspend him from boxing for 12 months.
>
> Indeed, our client has full respect for the competence of the Southern Area Council, and furthermore wishes us to state that his Appeal is only in respect of the penalty imposed upon him, and will not now be against the findings of the Council for breach of regulations.
>
> We understand that at the time the pending contest in Cardiff was arranged, our client believed that his Appeal would not take place for at least another month, and in view of the Provisions of Regulation 16, para. 8 of the British Boxing Board of Control Regulations which expressly state that pending an Appeal no penalty shall attach unless the Council otherwise ordered; and the Council having not so ordered, we advised our client that he should enter into contests pending the

Appeal being heard, and he still feels justified in accepting the engagement.

The fight against Con Mount Bassie took place at Sofia Gardens, Cardiff, and again Terry really struggled at stages during the middle rounds. Having won every round of their fight at Leyton Baths in February the previous year, it was a contest he should have won comfortably. The fact that he didn't was a clear indication that he was well past his best.

Spinks showed his best form in the first and last rounds, and in the latter rocked Bassie with a vicious right hook. Setting a fast pace he scored well at close quarters with two-fisted attacks. His left jab was effective, but he never looked like bringing the fight to an early conclusion.

At the end of the fight Terry danced around the ring in jubilation blowing kisses to the crowd as referee Joe Morgan raised his hand. Although he finished with a swollen left eye he was a clear winner, and the crowd gave him a great ovation.

'I'm very satisfied,' said Sammy McCarthy. 'Terry boxed really well. He is in fine shape physically and mentally.'

* * *

Terry's appeal against his suspension was heard by the Stewards of Appeal at the Board of Control offices on 27 October 1961. His Honour Judge Herbert QC was Chairman, and the panel included one other judge and two QCs.

Spinks, who was represented by eminent barrister, Robin Simpson, knew that if the period of suspension was not reduced, it would almost certainly be the end of his boxing career. As the appeal was against the length of suspension only, Sammy McCarthy and Jarvis Astaire made impassioned pleas on his behalf. Teddy Waltham, General Secretary of the Board, commented favourably on Terry's showing against Con Mount Bassie at Cardiff two days earlier.

After considering the evidence of all parties, the Appeal Stewards were sympathetic. They quashed the original suspension and made an order that Spinks be suspended for three months to take effect from the date of the hearing. He was also fined £100.

After the 70 minute hearing a spokesman for the Board of Control told Sydney Hulls of the *Daily Express*:

The Appeal Stewards have taken the plea of mitigating circumstances into consideration, but have warned Spinks that they take a very

> serious view of the offence and have told him of the grave consequences of any repetition.

Terry was a very relieved man when he emerged from the Board offices to face a group of reporters who had been waiting for several hours to hear the result. 'It was a bit scary in there because I didn't know what to expect,' he told them. 'I am very grateful to the Stewards for giving me another chance, and I want to thank Mr Astaire and Sammy for all the support they gave me.'

McCarthy was also happy with the outcome. 'We were given a fair hearing,' he said, 'and I think Terry now realises that if he is ever overweight again it will be the end of his boxing career.'

'We reckon three months will cost us about £2,500 in purse money, but justice has now been done,' continued Sammy. 'We feel the punishment fits the crime and Terry will be back in the ring in three months. In the meantime he will continue to work hard in the gym.'

As he walked away accompanied by his wife Valerie, Terry's cockney humour came to the fore. 'I shall back Sticky Case in the Cambridgeshire,' he said with a grin, 'because I have just won mine.'

Despite the reduction of the period of suspension, Terry's problems were not completely over. The Southern Area Council issued a statement saying that when he returned to the ring, his next three contests would be carefully monitored. If there were any concerns, he would be called back before the Council.

Although he would be free to box again at the end of January 1962, the break gave the former champion the chance to reflect on his situation. He never denied the fact that he was lacking in discipline when it came to diet. A bar of chocolate, a cream bun or a bottle of pop were lethal to a fighter trying to control his weight, especially a man as small as Spinks. The only explanation he could ever give for his indiscipline was: 'I couldn't help myself and just loved eating the wrong things. If I hadn't been a boxer I think I'd have looked like a barrel.'

The overall situation regarding Terry's weight problems was always far more serious than people generally knew. Much of what really happened was only known to those really close to him. There were many occasions, in the days leading up to a fight, when he went running wearing a plastic suit and hob-nailed boots. If the surplus weight hadn't come off he would sleep in the plastic suit and lose as much as two pounds during the night. The next morning he would go to the bathroom, take off the suit and pour the water down the drain.

Valerie was fully aware of the situation and had to be extremely careful about eating and drinking in front of Terry before a fight. 'It was a 24 hour thing,' she recalled. 'I couldn't drink a cup of tea in front of him when he was training. I often had to go to the bathroom and drink from the tap.'

Although Valerie eventually went to Terry's fights, she lived on her nerves before and during them. When he was in the ring she often spent long periods with her hands over her eyes. His mother never once watched him fight, although she often attended the shows. Generally, she left the ringside before he made his entrance. Tich didn't watch him for another reason – he thought he brought bad luck on Terry. He was, nevertheless, his greatest fan. 'It was marvellous in those days,' he once remarked. 'There couldn't have been a prouder dad in the country than me.'

Despite the tremendous hardship and sacrifices he had to make Terry still loved boxing and couldn't bear the thought of giving it up. He was still only 23 and was convinced that provided he became totally dedicated there was no reason why he shouldn't get back into championship contention.

10

NO WAY BACK

Throughout the period of his suspension, Spinks went to the Thomas A' Beckett gym for light workouts. 'I've got to keep my weight in check,' he told local reporters who frequently asked him about his plans. Despite there being rumours that he was contemplating retirement, he was defiant. 'I aim to fight again in the New Year and want to be in tip-top condition.'

Terry also relaxed a great deal by decorating his new flat, and continued to attend charity functions, particularly in the East End. In November, he was one of a number of celebrity guests when the Repton Amateur Boxing Club staged a special boxing show at York Hall, Bethnal Green. It was in aid of the Mayor of Stepney's appeal on behalf of the elderly people of the borough. Other guests included film star, Vera Day, comedian, Harold Berens, British heavyweight champion, Henry Cooper, former world flyweight champion, Terry Allen, as well as the Mayors of Stepney, Poplar, Bethnal Green and Shoreditch.

A collection in the arena raised £150 of which £50 came from the Kray twins who also donated all of the trophies. Reports of their generosity appeared in local newspapers, and an article in the *East London Advertiser* was illustrated by a photo of Ronnie Kray with West Ham boxer Billy Walker. It was claimed that Ronnie had purchased more than £200 worth of tickets and his guests included Joan Littlewood, Barbara Windsor, Victor Spinetti and Terry Spinks. Other invitations had been extended to actor Sir John Gielgud and jockey Charlie Smirke.

It was well known that the Krays loved to be seen with people well known in show business, films, politics and boxing. They mixed with them mostly at functions they sponsored because it increased their popularity and status in the East End. They were frequently photographed with the stars, and guests at their clubs included world class boxers, Joe Louis, Sonny Liston, Barney Ross and Billy Conn. From show business came Billy Daniels, Sophie Tucker, Ronnie Fraser, Dickie Valentine and a host of others.

The twins were great supporters of the Repton club based at Victoria Park Square, and sponsored a number of their shows. Well known personalities were always invited to guarantee sell-out attendances. Spinks was idolised in the East End following his success in the Olympics, and was often invited to present prizes at Repton club shows.

Terry first came to the attention of the Krays when he was boxing for West Ham on a show at Manor Place Baths. They were also present at York Hall in 1956 when he won the North East London Divs championship, and recognised that he had real talent. One of their associates was instructed to speak to West Ham trainer, Billy Walker, to try and get Spinks to join Repton.

The ploy didn't work and Terry remained at West Ham, but when he returned from the Olympics he was extremely high profile. The twins interest in him became even greater as his professional career developed. He was invited to many of the functions they staged or sponsored in the East End to raise funds for Boys Clubs, pensioners, hospitals and hospices.

Spinks and Len Harvey were among many celebrity guests at a Jewish club in Commercial Road where a benefit night had been organised by the Krays for St Joseph's Hospice. They invited Terry to present trophies at a boxing event at the Kingston Club in Surrey, and he was often a guest at wrestling events they staged at York Hall.

At the end of March 1960, Spinks and Sammy McCarthy were joined by former champions Jack 'Kid' Berg, Ted 'Kid' Lewis and Terry Allen at the opening of a plush new gymnasium at the Double R Club which the Kray twins owned at Bow. He also attended events at the Kentucky Club when they staged charity functions in aid of Bancroft Hospital and Queen Elizabeth's Hospital for Children at Hackney Road.

There was no denying that the Kray twins raised huge amounts of money for worthy causes. They operated on the principle that the attendance of celebrities from show business and boxing would ensure that their events were a success.

Terry was also a regular visitor to the Astor Club at Berkeley Square, a fashionable Mayfair establishment frequented by the Krays and many other well known figures from the underworld. Some people sought to make an issue of his association, and there was speculation that there was more to his involvement with them than just fund raising.

Such suggestions, however, have always been refuted by associates of the twins. They suggested that Terry was in fact not very street-wise. There were a number of occasions when he innocently asked what line of business they were in because they always had a lot of money. His questions were generally avoided and the subject changed.

'I only knew the Krays as straight guys,' insisted Terry when asked about them. 'Whatever they did, they never involved me.' He was typically modest when explaining his association with them. 'We were all East End people. I was popular, they were popular, and they wanted to be seen with me. There was nothing more to it than that.'

The fact was that anyone living in the East End during the 1950's and 60's would have known the Kray twins or come across them. Being a high profile boxer, it is a certainty that they would have made Terry's acquaintance. They had been professional fighters and were tremendous fans of the fight game. They put a lot of money into amateur clubs in the East End, particularly the Repton. They had tremendous respect for Spinks, and he was more use to them than they were to him.

* * *

During the period of Terry's suspension annoying rumours of his retirement persisted despite categorical denials by both himself and Sammy McCarthy. Over the Christmas period they were in fact in negotiations with a number of promoters regarding a comeback campaign in which it was hoped that Spinks would have a fight a month.

The original plan was for Terry to have his comeback fight at West Ham Baths on 15 February 1962. Matchmaker, Benny Huntman, wanted to put him in against local man, Ron Jones who, on 14 December, surprisingly beat Welsh prospect Phil Jones on a cut-eye stoppage after eight rounds. In his dressing room after the fight Ron issued a challenge to his East End rival.

'I hear Spinks is searching for an opponent for his comeback contest in the New Year,' he remarked. 'Well, he needn't look far because I am ready and willing to meet him.'

Jones' manager, Sam Burns, and trainer, Nobby Wallace, were in full agreement. 'He will give Terry a lot of trouble,' said Wallace.

Although Sammy McCarthy and Huntman were in close

negotiations to stage the fight, Harry Levene suddenly wanted to use Spinks on his big show at Olympia on 23 January, despite the fact that it was four days before Terry's suspension expired. Application was made to the Board of Control for him to meet Danny O'Brien of Kilburn, but the Board refused to relent, insisting that the suspension be served in full.

Agreement was then reached with promoter, Ronnie Ezra, for Spinks to make his comeback at Seymour Hall on 7 February against Roy Beaman of Brixton over eight rounds. A few days later it was announced that he would face Ron Jones over eight rounds at West Ham Baths the following week.

'This should quash all the rumours about Terry having retired,' Sammy McCarthy told the *East London Advertiser*. 'Apart from Jones, we were also in discussions to meet George Judge and Johnny Howard. It has taken a lot of work to sew up the final details and complete the contract.'

Although Spinks had kept himself in good trim, Snowy Buckingham devised a tough fitness programme for him which they commenced at the beginning of January. McCarthy believed his man would benefit by doing his training at Brighton because there would be fewer distractions than if he stayed in London. After a few days, however, Terry found it was too cold and returned to his regular quarters at the Thomas A' Beckett.

With just a few days to go before the former champion's eagerly awaited return to the ring, Roy Beaman pulled out of the contest with influenza. Former French bantamweight champion, Eugene Lecozannet, was brought in as a substitute. The 30 year old Parisian panel beater had the experience of 42 professional contests and had faced top continentals Piero Rollo, Robert Tartari, Elyee Castre, Pierre Vetroff and Pierre Cossemyns.

In the first boxing promotion at Seymour Hall for 10 years, a packed house saw Spinks gain a convincing points victory over eight rounds. Earlier he had surprised everyone by weighing in at 9 stone 2, two pounds inside the stipulated limit, which was a tribute to his commitment.

Although he finished with swellings above both eyes, he dominated the fight against a rough, bustling opponent who relied mainly on rushes, hooks and wild swings. The Frenchman offered little resistance to Terry's determination to silence those people who said he should retire.

Spinks took a few rounds to find the range, but once he did, he pumped his left jab to the face with monotonous ease. The Frenchman's only successes came in round four, when he brought blood from the Londoner's mouth, and in the sixth when he rocked him with hooks to the head.

Although he never looked like winning the fight, Lecozannet was tough and always ready to trade blows, giving Spinks very little time for a breather. The Frenchman's aggressive, head-down style earned him warnings from referee Bill Williams in rounds five and seven, and after rolling their heads in a clinch in the seventh, both men were warned.

Spinks showed great composure and refused to be drawn into a fight. He was content to box and move, picking up the points with his left jab. It was an impressive performance and convinced many of his critics that he still had plenty to offer.

'It felt a bit strange out there first of all after four months without a fight,' said Terry afterwards. 'I think I boxed tonight the way I always used to. It was great to be back again. I had to take it a bit easy because I have got another fight next week.'

West Ham Baths was packed the following week for the local derby between Spinks and his former amateur club mate Ron Jones. Although there was not much between them in experience, Terry had mixed in better company and had by far the more impressive record. Jones did have the distinction of winning the Southern Area bantamweight title in 1957 in only his seventh professional contest, but had not progressed as well as had been expected. When he faced Spinks his record was 18 victories, 18 defeats and three draws.

Despite Ron's mediocre record, the Spinks camp knew he would be no pushover. Apart from Phil Jones, who he beat in a 'nobbins' contest in December, he had also beaten good featherweights Chris Elliott and Freddie Dobson earlier in 1961. He had been preparing for the fight for some time and was eager to put up a good show before the sellout crowd.

The promoter of the show was East End man, Bill Meyer, who ran a flourishing wholesale bakery business. A few months earlier, when Spinks was preparing for his comeback, Bill offered to provide him with a gymnasium in luxury surroundings for his exclusive use. The place he had in mind was his own farm in the Essex countryside 15 miles outside London. Although it was an extremely generous offer, Terry refused it because he didn't want to train outside London again.

Despite having returned to the Thomas A' Beckett towards the end of 1961, Terry eventually moved his training camp to the Duke of Fife gymnasium at East Ham. There he showed some flashes of his old brilliance in hectic sparring sessions with undefeated West

Ham featherweight Bobby Davies who was trained by Terry's old coach Bob Galloway.

Against Ron Jones, Spinks continued his impressive return to the ring and never gave Ron the slightest chance of causing an upset. As his arm was raised at the end of the eight rounds, the fight was accurately summed up by a fan in the gallery who shouted: 'Bad luck Ron, you were beaten by class.'

At 9 stone $2^1/_2$, a pound lighter than Jones, Terry was again well inside the stipulated limit of 9 stone 4. He sneaked most of the rounds with quick, precise punching, the best of which was his left jab. There were flashes of the old Spinks as he moved well throwing good punches from all angles and spearing Ron's guard with lightning jabs.

Although Jones was handicapped from round three by cuts around both eyes, he pressed forward and continuously drew applause from the appreciative audience for his gameness. At certain stages of the fight he tried to land punches from point blank range, but Terry ducked and weaved in brilliant fashion. By round six Spinks was well on top, and in the seventh Ron's gum shield went flying across the ring from a powerful right cross to the chin.

Although Spinks was a clear winner it was never a one-sided contest because Ron's solid counter-punching often had him back-pedalling. It was a fight strictly for the connoisseur featuring two men who learned their trade as amateurs at the West Ham club.

Spinks and McCarthy were delighted at the victory because in the space of just eight days Terry had completely silenced his critics. He had shown that he still possessed tremendous skill and speed, and his return to the ring was not as forlorn as some people had predicted.

Snowy Buckingham, however, was far from satisfied with Terry's performance. 'He was boxing brilliantly at times tonight, but did some silly and reckless things that could have proved fatal against a lethal puncher,' he grumbled as he untied the gloves.' 'Terry took ridiculous risks. Several times he threw his right when well out of range.'

'Terry again proved tonight that when he boxes to his true potential, he is unbeatable,' interrupted McCarthy. 'Two or three more warm-up contests and he will be ready to challenge Howard Winstone.'

Spinks himself was more than satisfied with his performance. 'The mood I was in tonight, I felt I could beat anyone in the world,' he said. 'I thought Ron Jones was a sporting and strong opponent. I caught him with good punches that he took very well.'

Further praise for Spinks came from Ron's trainer, Nobby Wallace, as he tended to four cuts around his boxer's eyes. 'If Winstone is better than Spinks, then he must be a really good fighter,' he remarked. 'Terry is always moving and a hard man to pin down.'

* * *

Apart from being a successful boxing manager with a stable of promising young fighters, Sammy McCarthy also became a show-business agent. By January 1962, he and his wife Sylvia already had two Stepney boys who were ballad singers under 'Show-biz' contracts.

Suddenly, he was approached by song-writers, Tony and Irvine Hiller who were fight fans, and wanted Terry Spinks to make a record. Whilst Terry had a good voice, he started giggling and couldn't stop once he got in front of a microphone. The intended side-line to his boxing career therefore didn't get off the ground.

Sammy always believed it was important that his fighters were relaxed. He therefore often took them for days out away from the boxing environment. He was a keen golfer, and one day took Spinks, Terry Gill and Terry Brown to Hainault Golf Club. Although none of them could play golf they all said they would like to learn, so Sammy hired clubs and accessories for them.

After a few holes the trio of pupils became bored. They cheated by moving the position of balls which annoyed Sammy who was very serious about his game. Eventually Spinks and the others said they'd had enough. When Sammy tried to persuade them to stay a little longer they threw all the clubs and bags into a lake. As they laughed hysterically, poor Sammy waded waist-deep into the silt-ridden lake to retrieve all the equipment he had hired. As it had to be returned to the club-house in perfect order, he spent the next hour cleaning and drying everything.

Another of their forms of relaxation was horse-riding. Spinks couldn't get enough of it and frequently persuaded other boxers to join him. They hired horses from riding-schools around Epping Forest and in the Essex countryside. Although none of the others could ride they always got horses by saying that Spinks was a jockey.

Terry rarely took life seriously, but the others were nearly as bad. On one occasion he, together with Sammy, Joe Lucy, Terry Murphy, Terry Gill, Terry Brown and a few others, galloped their horses through Epping Forest all wearing bandanas and waving water pistols. 'People we passed didn't know what to think,' said Spinks. 'We were all grown men with broken noses playing Cowboys and Indians.'

Despite the tough business he was in, Terry was always full of fun. He was impish, a rascal and practical joker who, as a youngster, was always getting up to mischief. One weekend when he was in his early twenties, he went on a coach trip to Eastbourne with a group of mates from the Red Sail Drinking & Dining Club at Clapham. It was a typical lads day out and took a predictable course. By lunchtime they were all in a pub.

During the afternoon, Spinks and several others went for a walk along the beach. The tide was in, and as it was a hot summer's day, they jumped into the sea fully clothed. Terry pulled himself up on to a jetty where a pleasure boat was moored. Suddenly the skipper of the boat, dressed in uniform, walked along the jetty only to be pushed into the water by Spinks. As he floundered in the water, he was subjected to shouts of: 'You're improperly dressed – you should wear your cap.'

'Do your jacket up or you'll get cold,' laughed Spinks as the man hauled himself out of the sea.

An on-looker called the police who arrived in numbers within a few minutes. Although the lads were sitting quietly on the sea wall drying off, they wanted to know when they were leaving. 'Soon,' was the solemn reply.

'Well clear off and don't let's have any trouble,' remarked one copper.

Meanwhile, the owner of a local dry-cleaning business recognised Terry who, despite being fully dressed, was still soaked. He introduced himself and started talking about boxing. 'Why don't you come with me and get smartened up?' he said. When the former Olympic champion re-joined his mates about half an hour later his clothes were pressed and dry, and he looked immaculate.

That evening they took over the bar of the Pier Hotel – singing, dancing and drinking. One of the lads played the drums, and it was 4.00am before they left. Although there was no further bother, a local newspaper referred to their visit with the exaggerated headline – 'LONDON TEDDY BOYS RAID THE BEACH.'

* * *

The victory over Ron Jones put Terry back into the Boxing News ratings at number five after having been omitted for three months while he was suspended. His return to the ring sparked genuine excitement amongst East End boxing fans because he looked to have turned the corner. Not only had he boxed well in his last two contests, but also appeared to be controlling his weight. Ronnie Ezra wasted no time and signed him to meet Jean Biosca of France over eight rounds at Seymour Hall on 6 March.

The 29 year old Frenchman turned professional in 1957 and had campaigned in Spain, Finland and Switzerland as well as at arenas in his own country. Whilst his record was incomplete, he was known to have won 12, lost 13 and drawn seven of 32 contests until the end of 1960. His biggest claim to fame was that in October 1961 he lasted nine rounds with world-rated Rafiu King in Geneva.

At 9 stone 0¾, Spinks gave away almost four pounds, and for the first few rounds boxed brilliantly to make his task look easy. Accurate left jabs drove the Frenchman around the ring giving the Londoner little more than a workout. Yet as the fight progressed he appeared to get lazy and bored. Hands held low, he became careless during the last three rounds and allowed himself to be caught by right crosses to the head.

Encouraged by his success, Biosca attacked throughout the final two sessions which spurred Terry into action. Accurate left jabs brought blood streaming from the Frenchman's nose, and at the end the decision in his favour was a formality. There was some booing from a section of the crowd who expected more from him after the promise he had shown in his previous two contests.

Back in his dressing room Terry took off his right boot and showed reporters three blisters the size of penny pieces on the sole of his foot. They had caused him a great deal of pain during the last few rounds, and although he made no excuses, must have slowed him down.

Although it was a disappointing fight, it was a sensible one to take. Biosca, who was rated above Eugene Lecozannet, was an awkward and evasive opponent although not particularly formidable. He was chosen so that Spinks' handlers could assess his progression.

Neither Spinks nor McCarthy disguised their disappointment after the fight. 'Terry didn't get going tonight and we shall have to step up the class of opponents now,' said Sammy. Nodding in agreement with his manager, Terry said: 'I fell into one of my oldest faults of trying to win with the minimum of effort. It's always the same when I meet lower class opponents. I need a better fighter to help bring out the best in me.'

Trainer, Snowy Buckingham was, however, satisfied with Terry's

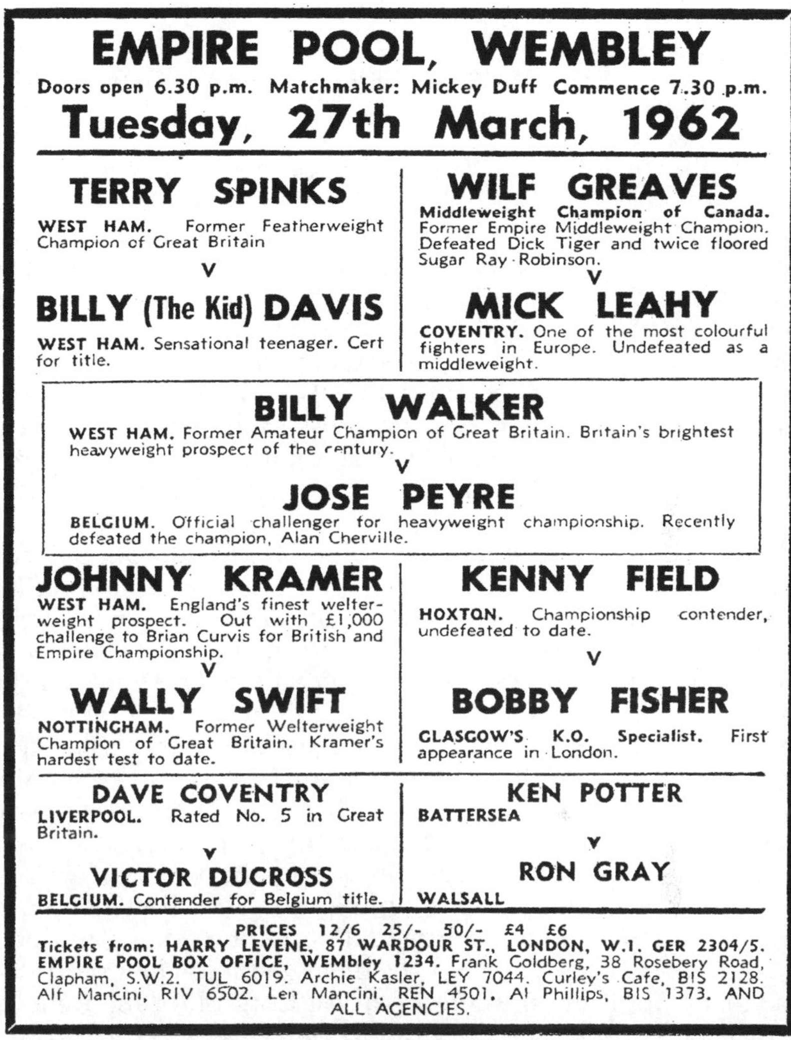

EMPIRE POOL, WEMBLEY

Doors open 6.30 p.m. Matchmaker: Mickey Duff Commence 7.30 p.m.

Tuesday, 27th March, 1962

TERRY SPINKS
WEST HAM. Former Featherweight Champion of Great Britain
v
BILLY (The Kid) DAVIS
WEST HAM. Sensational teenager. Cert for title.

WILF GREAVES
Middleweight Champion of Canada. Former Empire Middleweight Champion. Defeated Dick Tiger and twice floored Sugar Ray Robinson.
v
MICK LEAHY
COVENTRY. One of the most colourful fighters in Europe. Undefeated as a middleweight.

BILLY WALKER
WEST HAM. Former Amateur Champion of Great Britain. Britain's brightest heavyweight prospect of the century.
v
JOSE PEYRE
BELGIUM. Official challenger for heavyweight championship. Recently defeated the champion, Alan Cherville.

JOHNNY KRAMER
WEST HAM. England's finest welter-weight prospect. Out with £1,000 challenge to Brian Curvis for British and Empire Championship.
v
WALLY SWIFT
NOTTINGHAM. Former Welterweight Champion of Great Britain. Kramer's hardest test to date.

KENNY FIELD
HOXTON. Championship contender, undefeated to date.
v
BOBBY FISHER
GLASGOW'S K.O. Specialist. First appearance in London.

DAVE COVENTRY
LIVERPOOL. Rated No. 5 in Great Britain.
v
VICTOR DUCROSS
BELGIUM. Contender for Belgium title.

KEN POTTER
BATTERSEA
v
RON GRAY
WALSALL

PRICES 12/6 25/- 50/- £4 £6
Tickets from: HARRY LEVENE, 87 WARDOUR ST., LONDON, W.1. GER 2304/5. EMPIRE POOL BOX OFFICE, WEMbley 1234. Frank Goldberg, 38 Rosebery Road, Clapham, S.W.2. TUL 6019. Archie Kasler, LEY 7044. Curley's Cafe, BIS 2128. Alf Mancini, RIV 6502. Len Mancini, REN 4501. Al Phillips, BIS 1373. AND ALL AGENCIES.

Poster advertising the professional debut of Billy Walker. Spinks featured in the joint top of the bill contest

performance. 'As far as I am concerned he did all that I wanted him to do tonight,' he remarked. 'Unless a boxer comes out of the ring covered in blood, some people regard it as an ordinary fight. Terry wasn't brilliant, but what he did was adequate.'

The plan was to keep Spinks busy, and his next fight was on Harry Levene's bumper show at the Empire Pool, Wembley on 27 March. His original opponent was Mick Greaves of Leicester, but he sustained a badly cut eye against Phil Lungdren at Seymour Hall and had to withdraw. Within a few days, however, matchmaker Mickey Duff, made an even more attractive fight when he persuaded Spinks to meet the exciting teenager Billy 'The Kid' Davis from West Ham.

The highlight of the Wembley promotion was the eagerly awaited professional debut of West Ham heavyweight, Billy Walker. It was one of the biggest attractions for years and really captured public imagination. Billy had a tremendous following, and with Spinks against Davis being a mouth-watering local derby, a huge number of tickets were sold in the East End.

Spinks and Walker had been friends for several years, and it was Terry who originally encouraged the 'Blond Bomber' to take up boxing. Walker made incredible progress and Terry was present at most of his fights at club and international level. It was therefore fitting that he should box on the show when Billy launched his professional career.

Billy Davis was another East End lad with an incredible following. He joined the West Ham club at the age of 13 and made rapid progress under Spinks' old trainer, Jackie Gubbins, winning 80 of 86 junior contests. Since turning professional in October 1960 he had won all but one of his 17 fights. His only defeat had been in September 1961 when a cut eye ruled him out of a fight he was winning against George Judge at Finsbury Park. His victims included Ron Jones, Phil Lungdren, Jimmy Carson and Con Mount Bassie. In his last contest he beat his first overseas opponent, Marcos Morales from Puerto Rica at Olympia in January.

Davis was rated number four in the featherweight division by *Boxing News*, one place above Spinks. An all-action fighter who never gave his opponents a moment's rest, he was considered a very dangerous obstacle for the former Olympic champion. Harry Levene made application to the Board of Control for the fight to be over 10 rounds, but as Billy would not be 19 until 11 April the Board insisted that it be limited to eight.

Meanwhile, Spinks received a challenge from Johnny Morrisey, the former Scottish bantamweight champion and one-time contender for the British and Empire crowns. After a nine month lay-off he had returned to stop Bobby Fisher in two rounds, and said he had backing of £500 for a fight with Terry.

Morrisey wanted the fight to be over 10 or 12 rounds at nine stone. It was an attractive proposition and some critics believed that should agreement be reached it could be approved by the Board of Control as a final eliminator for the British featherweight title.

Spinks and McCarthy, however, showed no interest in the challenge. Billy Davis was a huge threat to their future plans so all their concentration went into preparing for that contest.

Wembley was sold out days in advance of the show which had a real East End flavour. Apart from the appearances of Spinks, Davis and Walker, welterweight prospect Johnny Kramer from West Ham was up against former British champion Wally Swift, while Kenny Field of Hoxton was paired with tough Scot, Bobby Fisher.

At 9 stone 0¾, Spinks was three quarters of a pound lighter than Billy. Determined to prove his fitness and stamina he set a fast pace, scoring with lightning left jabs to the head and good rights to the body. Davis, however, was a complete bundle of energy and always ready to stand and trade punches. His shots, however, lacked authority and Spinks grew in confidence.

As the fight progressed, Davis began to do all the forcing and hardly took a backward step. The exchanges were fast and furious, and in the middle rounds it was noticeable that Terry was beginning to feel the pace. He chose to hit and run while his teenage opponent was like a human windmill, throwing an incessant stream of punches from every angle.

Despite constantly chasing Spinks around the ring, Billy was too impetuous and a lot of his punches missed the target area. The former champion was a skilful ringman and despite being on the retreat for long spells, took many punches on the arms, elbows and shoulders. In return, he countered well with his own crisp, accurate shots.

Realising the fight was extremely close, Terry changed tactics in round seven and instead of retreating, stood his ground and started trading punches with his aggressive young rival. It was the same in the final round as, roared on by the excited crowd, they punched it out toe-to-toe in the centre of the ring. It was a furious round in which both men fought desperately to snatch victory.

At the final bell, referee Harry Gibbs walked straight to Spinks and raised his arm. The decision brought a mixed reception, with Billy's fans screaming that he had been robbed. Press reaction was mixed, but there was a feeling that many of the teenager's punches were wide of the target area, a fact not missed by Mr Gibbs. In reality, it was such a close contest that whatever decision had been given it would have been booed. Everyone did, however, agree that it was one of the finest contests seen in London for years. There were very few infringements, and Mr Gibbs rarely had to issue any kind of warning.

In the dressing room after the fight, Jim Wicks, the manager of

Davis, was furious. 'It was a diabolical decision,' he shouted. 'I honestly don't think Spinks won even one round yet alone the fight.'

It was a poor assessment of a closely fought contest, but Wicks remained defiant. At a press conference the following day he continued his protest. 'I'm not being biased when I say this was one of the worst decisions I have known after 50 years in the fight game,' he said angrily.

Wicks said that despite his anger he would not lodge an official complaint. 'There were goodness knows how many Boxing Board officials and inspectors round the ringside,' he remarked. 'Unless they had their eyes closed, they must realise what happened. So what's the use of a manager like myself objecting?'

'I shall be very interested to see what does happen,' continued Wicks. 'It's no use the Board shutting their eyes to these things. What chance does boxing in this country have if they won't recognise what is going on?'

Wicks stressed that he didn't blame Spinks for what had occurred, but wanted the chance of a return contest for Davis over 10 rounds. 'I am so certain that Billy would stop him over the extra two rounds that I would be willing to put up £5,000, or more if they like, for a return.'

Immediately after the fight, Norman Giller of the *Stratford Express* went to Spinks' dressing room and was brave enough to remark that he thought Davis had done enough to win. 'Then you must be a poor judge of boxing,' Terry was quick to counter. 'I was blocking most of his punches. I thought I was a clear winner.'

* * *

On 10 April, Howard Winstone successfully defended his British featherweight title by stopping Derry Treanor in the 14th round. Spinks had attended the weigh-in for the fight and spoken to both boxers. Politely and privately he asked Winstone for a return if he retained the title. Howard said it would be a matter for his manager.

Treanor, who was born in Eire, had lived in Glasgow since he was two years old and had taken British citizenship in order to fight for a British title. Since their fight in 1959, he and Spinks had become good friends. The former champion wished him luck and said he hoped Derry would defend the title against him if he beat Winstone.

The following day a £5,000 challenge was issued to the Welshman on behalf of Spinks, although it was just one of a number received by the champion. When Howard agreed to defend his title against fellow Welshman Harry Carroll at Cardiff on 30 May, Spinks and McCarthy resumed business with Harry Levene.

The London promoter promptly signed Terry and Billy Davis to meet in a return contest over 10 rounds at Wembley on 22 May. It came as something of a surprise to some critics that Spinks agreed to the return, although his purse of £2,000 no doubt went a long way to counter-balance the risk of defeat and prestige. When the fight was announced it was the news that every boxing fan in the East End had hoped for.

The contest was the chief support to a 10 rounder between former world middleweight champion Terry Downes and Don Fullmer of the USA. With Billy Walker also in action it was an attractive bill, but an expensive one for the promoter. Although he was a master at selling a fight, Levene wanted a sell-out crowd. Spinks against Davis was a huge attraction, but as if to remind the punters of what lay in store, the promoter had a caption inserted on all of his advertising posters:

> On March 27, at my last promotion here, these two fought. Spinks won on points. Some thought Spinks won; some thought Davis won. Everyone agreed it was the best fight seen in years.

'If Davis happens to turn the tables, I will put on the 'rubber' between him and Spinks on my next promotion,' said Levene at a press conference. 'This, of course, is only providing that this second contest is a good fight.'

Terry was as keen as Davis for the return and said that another victory would put him in line for a return with Winstone. He badly wanted the title back, insisting he had only lent it to the talented Welshman. He added that if he beat Billy he would make an immediate offer of £1,000-a-side for a return.

Following their last contest, Billy's trainer Danny Holland had been called before the British Boxing Board of Control and fined £200 for allegedly striking referee Harry Gibbs. In the build-up to the return contest Billy said that he would help pay his trainer's fine. 'I beat Terry last time but didn't get the verdict,' he said at the press conference with a determined look in his eyes. 'I'll beat him this time, and believe me, there will be no doubt about the result.'

'I'm fitter now than I've ever been,' countered Spinks. 'I'll beat Davis for the second time and then I want my British title back from Winstone.'

By this time, Terry's wife Valerie was expecting their first child.

When asked by a reporter if he felt worried, Spinks replied, 'My wife has told me she will do all the worrying in that department. She has ordered me to worry about the fight.'

Despite all his domestic distractions and responsibilities, Spinks trained rigorously at Joe Bloom's gym in the West End of London where he sparred daily with Ron Jones. As he wound up his preparations, Valerie was admitted to Thorpe Coombe Hospital at Walthamstow where she gave birth to a baby boy the day before Terry faced Billy Davis. Weighing 8½lbs, they named him Jarvis after Jarvis Astaire who had been so solidly behind Terry's professional career from the start.

On the day of the fight, Spinks weighed nine stones, a pound lighter than his opponent. Again, the Empire Pool was packed to the rafters as Spinks walked to the ring to a fanfare of *'Oh Mein Papa.'* The fight was very similar to their last, and fought at a fast and furious pace with neither man prepared to let up throughout the 10 rounds. In front of a wildly enthusiastic crowd, it proved to be everything that had been hoped, and again only a fraction divided the two brilliant young fighters.

Spinks started quickly with good combinations to the face, and Davis immediately responded with a series of hooks to the body. The pattern was set and the crowd got behind their fighters. The emphasis was on speed from the start, and as with their first fight, the rounds were exceptionally close.

Spinks did well in the second, round three appeared even, and Davis took the fourth. Billy showed more composure during this contest, and was less erratic. He made more of his punches count and didn't allow Terry the room to be so effective.

In the fifth Spinks moved well as he looked for openings to prod home his left jab, but when he did land, Billy was quick to counter. There was one terrific toe-to-toe exchange midway through the round with neither man prepared to give ground.

Fortunes fluctuated in round six as first Spinks, then Davis, had success. Although Terry rocked his rival with a sweeping right cross in the seventh, Billy boxed his way out of trouble brilliantly and edged the round. Spinks looked to have taken the eighth, and in round nine he really piled on the pressure only for Davis to again meet him blow for blow.

The crowd roared as the two boxers rose from their stools to await the bell for the final round. Neither gave an inch as they battled bravely for victory. Jabs, hooks, they gave everything they had because both knew it was extremely close. Spinks did slip to the floor briefly, but was up in a flash and straight back into the action. They pushed themselves to the limit for the entire three minutes of what was a pulsating round. At the bell it was Davis who got the decision. Again there was some booing because it was extremely close, but it had been a clean, sporting contest which was a credit to both men.

'It was one of the finest exhibitions of boxing I have ever seen,' said Sammy McCarthy. 'If Terry and Billy fought each other a hundred times I think every fight would be better than the one before.'

Sammy said they were disappointed with the decision and thought Terry had done enough to get at least a draw. 'But it was such a brilliant fight, I don't think it has upset Terry's ambitions at all,' he added.

Spinks also questioned the decision. 'Billy thought he won the first fight, but I got the verdict,' he said in his dressing room. 'I thought I won tonight, but he got the decision. Surely the only way to decide who is the better boxer is for us to meet a third time.'

Then, throwing a playful punch at Sammy McCarthy's smiling face, Spinks said, 'I lost tonight because I took it too easy in the middle rounds, but next time I'll make no mistake.'

As soon as he was dressed, Terry went to a telephone and put a call through to the hospital to check on the condition of his wife and baby son. In the meantime, Valerie received a visit from Terry's mother who wanted to see the baby. It was only then that they started to get on together and healed the rift between them.

Shortly after Jarvis was born Valerie received a telegram from Terry's friend Kenny Lynch saying: *'Congratulations – hope the baby looks like me.'*

Despite his defeat by Davis, the crowd showered their appreciation and sympathy on Spinks. Ringside veterans remarked that it was the most skilful featherweight contest they had seen since the scientific era of Nel Tarleton. Harry Levene was quick to confirm that he was willing to put up a substantial purse as an inducement for the two brilliant East End fighters to meet for a third time.

Spinks, however, still badly wanted to meet Howard Winstone again. After the Welshman successfully defended his title against Harry Carroll at Cardiff on 30 May, he re-issued his challenge. Having won a Lonsdale belt outright, Winstone said he wanted to make as many defences as possible. His preferred opponents were Kenny Field and Spinks. 'If Spinks is willing to lodge his £1,000 challenge money with the Welsh Area Council, we are ready to meet it,' said his manager Eddie Thomas.

Terry was delighted with the news, but as attempts were being made to get Winstone a European title fight, he knew he needed to keep busy and get back to winning ways. Apart from tiredness, he suffered no ill-effects from the Davis fight, so he got back into training within a couple of weeks. Mickey Duff matched him against Bobby Fisher of Craigneuk over eight rounds at the Majestic Ballroom, Finsbury Park on 17 July in what looked an intriguing contest.

Although he had lost in two rounds to Johnny Morrisey, Fisher was a known puncher and much better than his record of five victories and a draw from nine professional contests. In March he drew with Kenny Field at Wembley, and in his last fight beat George Judge in four rounds. In a pre-fight summary *Boxing News* commented:

> Bobby loves causing surprises, and respects none of his opponents reputations. A classy box-fighter with a dig, Fisher is quite capable of causing an upset.

It was an accurate prediction because in one of the biggest upsets of the year, Fisher pounded Spinks to defeat in the seventh round. Referee Jack Hart's humane decision to stop the contest was greeted with only mild protest from the usually turbulent Spinks supporters.

Although he started quickly, Terry made the mistake of ignoring his brilliant left hand which once tamed the best amateurs in the world. As early as the first minute he decided to try and out-punch the hard-hitting Fisher and this was his undoing.

Stiff right crosses from the Scot thudded against Terry's chin in round two and he reeled backwards across the ring before crashing to the canvas. He was on his feet at 'eight', but looked badly shaken. A volley of lefts and rights soon put the bemused West Ham idol back on the floor and he remained in a sitting position before rising at 'nine.'

Bravery was something Terry never lacked and using all his experience he held, mauled and laid-on as the over-exuberant Fisher tried to finish him. Just before the bell he even bravely tried to fight back.

With the crowd solidly behind him, Spinks desperately tried to get back into the fight in rounds three and four. Boxing strictly to orders he jabbed and moved, but there was no power in his punches. The earlier punishment had badly weakened him and defeat looked inevitable.

Fisher completely dominated the exchanges in rounds five and six both at boxing and fighting. He even dropped his hands to his sides and invited Spinks to hit him. The crowd jeered, but it was a sad sight to see the former 'Golden Boy' being taunted in such a way by a relative novice.

By round seven all the bounce and ambition had left Spinks and he was wobbled every time Bobby landed his clubbing shots to the head. His eyes swollen and bleeding badly from the nose, he was taking a terrible hiding from a man having only his 10th paid fight. Everyone in the hall must have been relieved when Jack Hart eventually stepped in and stopped it.

Spinks was a shadow of the once great boxer, and there was no protest from him or his corner at the intervention. As he walked sadly back to his dressing room, many people felt they were witnessing the last act in his great career. It was his seventh defeat and the fourth at the hands of a Scotsman. Evidence of his condition came in the dressing room when he asked his sympathetic audience if he had been floored more than once.

Despite the shattering defeat there was no talk of Terry retiring. 'We will plod on,' insisted Snowy Buckingham. 'Sure this defeat is a setback, but we must keep on trying.'

Sammy McCarthy agreed with the trainer. 'We shall be carrying on,' he told reporters. 'Remember Terry once got caught by Pierre Cossemyns. He got knocked down but he came back. He will come back again.'

Within a few days there was talk of trying to match Terry with new Welsh featherweight sensation, Lennie 'The Lion' Williams, at Newtown or Carmarthen in the autumn. Fortunately, common sense prevailed and the Spinks camp resisted the offer. Williams was young and powerful, and had the fight gone ahead it could have been an undignified ending to a wonderful career.

Many critics advised Terry to quit before he got badly hurt. He had many close friends and admirers in the press, experienced men who had travelled the world with him and loved him like a son. The last thing they wanted to do was report a tragic ending to the career of a former Olympic gold medal winner. He had dropped to number eight in the *Boxing News* ratings, just behind Bobby Fisher. He had nothing to prove, but was now the target for other up and coming young prospects anxious to put a name fighter on their records.

One of the sad things about boxing is that a fighter is often the last person to accept when it is time to give up. Terry thought long and hard about his position, but was convinced he still had plenty to offer. After a few months break he went back to the gym determined to have one more shot at reviving his career. He reached agreement with promoter Mike Barrett to meet Johnny Mantle of Battersea over eight rounds at the Royal Albert Hall on 11 December.

Mantle, a 20 year old barge builder, was another promising young featherweight with no respect for reputations. Since turning professional in May 1961, he had won 15 and drawn one of his 17 fights. His only setback occurred in his third bout when he was knocked out in the first round by Steve Ellwood.

Although he had trained hard Terry weighed in at 9 stone 4, two pounds above the agreed limit. Mantle scaled 9 stone $0^3/_4$. Before going to the ring a journalist asked Spinks what the future held for him. 'A good turkey and Christmas pudding dinner,' he replied with a cheeky grin. 'After that, I'll decide on my 1963 fighting programme.'

The fight was a rousing affair from the start, with youth and exuberance matched by experience and know-how. It turned out to be the fight of the night.

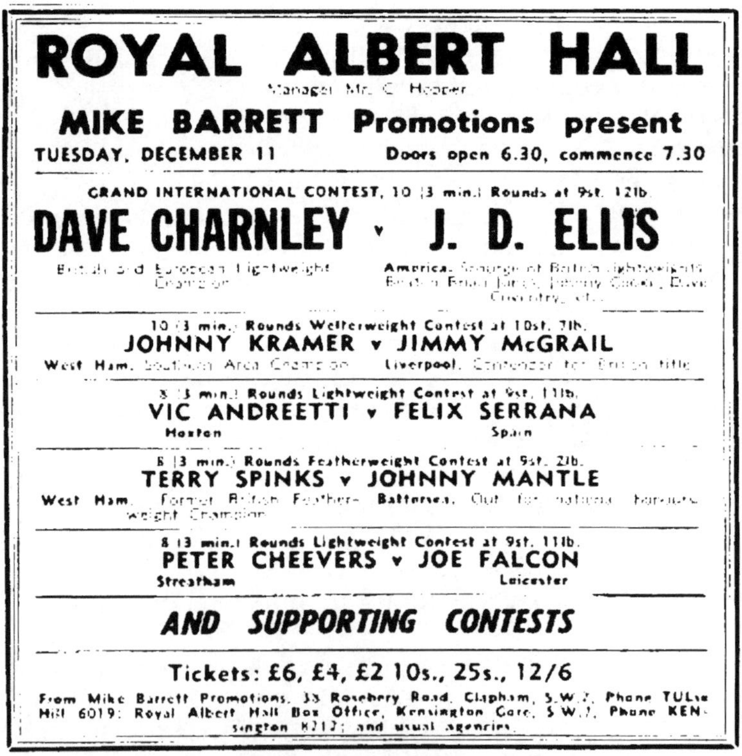

Poster advertising Terry Spinks last professional contest

Mantle started in whirlwind fashion as he tried to rough Spinks up and sap his strength with all-out aggression. Looking slow and rusty, Terry took a terrible battering and did well to survive the opening round. The fact that he did so without going to the floor was a testimony of his wonderful spirit and gameness.

The fireworks continued in round two as Spinks hit back with rapid bursts of jabbing, although his punches lacked the power of his opponent's. The crowd roared as they punched it out toe-to-toe for most of the round. The action was so intense that Spinks landed a right to the jaw after the bell. Mantle was furious and retaliated with a hard right to the chin before they were pulled apart and dragged to their corners.

Throughout the third there was a clear indication that Mantle had the 'needle,' and in round four he smashed away to such an extent that at one stage Spinks looked about to fold. Terry, however, was never short of courage, and when the going got tough he hit back. Urged on by the crowd he smashed away furiously and began to show some of the form that took him to the British title. It was a hectic round and at the bell both men looked totally exhausted.

They continued to slam away at each other as the fight entered the second half. In the seventh, Terry sensed that Mantle was weakening. Using all the strength he could muster he hammered away relentlessly to pull back the points deficit.

As they touched gloves at the start of the final round, the fight was evenly poised. As the bell sounded they set about each other, slamming punch after punch from every angle. Urged on by Bethnal Green man Charlie Page in his corner, Johnny staged a grandstand finish. It was a real tear-up, nothing short of a street fight as both went for victory.

A cut suddenly appeared above Spinks left eye, then almost immediately Mantle suffered a nasty gash above his left eye. Blood poured down his face prompting referee Ben Stitchbury to halt the action. After a careful inspection of the injury he stopped the contest, ruling that it was too serious for Johnny to continue.

There was some criticism of the referee's decision because only 45 seconds of the contest remained. With the outcome in the balance Mantle's handlers argued that he should have been allowed to continue. Mr Stitchbury's action, however, was fully supported by the Board of Control doctor. When he examined the boxer in his dressing room he found the injury too serious to treat effectively and advised him to attend hospital.

Although Terry had triumphed, it had been so very close against a fighter he would have toyed with a few years earlier. His purse of £500 was peanuts compared with the big money he earned when he was at the top. Spinks knew this, and in his dressing room strongly hinted that he was contemplating retirement.

''While I was swapping punches with John I actually asked myself what I was doing in the ring?' he told reporters. 'There's no future in it and all I am doing is taking punches I could have avoided with ease a couple of years ago. There comes a time when every fighter has to think about retirement, and I'm packing up now.'

After long and careful discussions with his family and close friend Sammy McCarthy, Spinks officially announced his retirement from the ring on 17 December 1962. It had been widely predicted a year earlier, but he had insisted on continuing much against the wishes of many of his close friends. In the comfort of his home, and with his seven month old son Jarvis on his lap, Terry spoke exclusively to his journalist friend, George Whiting.

'I've been boxing for 14 years and enjoyed every minute of it, but now I've had enough,' he said. 'I made up my mind to quit after I beat Johnny Mantle last week. Like a fool, I stood there slugging it out with him, taking punches that would never have touched me in the old days. After it was over I figured that if that was the best I could do I should be in some other game.'

'Would you care for your son to become a boxer?' asked Whiting.

'Not on your life,' replied Spinks.

Paying tribute to Terry in the *London Evening Standard*, Whiting wrote:

> The rise and fall of Terry Spinks offers a perfect cameo of all the things that can happen to a kid with an itch to fight – and the ability to do it well. He gave us the lot – from gore to glory, and from medals to misery.

When Terry's golden reign as a box office star came to an end he had the impressive record of 41 victories and a draw from 49 contests. Billy Davis was the only Englishman to beat him, and he never lost to a foreign boxer. He left the fight game with a host of wonderful memories and a huge number of friends. As a professional, he was believed to have earned over £32,000 in less than six years.

Despite everything he had achieved, Terry was quick to pay tribute to his handlers, particularly Sammy McCarthy and Jimmy Davis: 'A great deal of my success was due to the skilful way I was managed by Sammy McCarthy, the great encouragement he gave me, and the way he and Jimmy Davis looked after me in the corner,' he remarked. 'I think I am lucky to have had the benefit of their combined experience,' continued Terry. 'Jimmy was one of the most talented middleweights a few years ago who just missed out on being a champion, while Sammy was British featherweight title holder. I could not have been better trained or coached, and I take this opportunity of paying full tribute to them.'

The fans always remembered Terry because he never failed them. Not once did he give a dud performance, and whenever he climbed through the ropes they were assured of thrills, courage and an abundance of skill. There was great sadness when he decided to retire, but at least he had the satisfaction of going out a winner in a memorable battle on a big stage and before a packed house. He was a true professional in every sense of the word and deserved nothing less.

11

FINANCIAL RUIN

Boxing had been Terry's life ever since he returned from Newmarket at the end of 1955. Having been a full-time professional since April 1957, he had no educational qualifications nor a trade he could turn to once he had retired. Although the confectioners shop at Plaistow was doing well, it was being run by his mother and had been put into her name. In any event Terry was still a lad who always wanted to be out and about. Becoming a full-time shopkeeper did not appeal to him in the slightest.

Apart from boxing his only other love was horse-racing so he decided to open a betting shop. By this time his father was in partnership with another bookmaker and they owned a shop at Cyprus Place, North Woolwich. Terry successfully applied for a licence, and with financial help from a close friend, opened a shop at 362 Leabridge Road, Leyton, in January 1963.

Unfortunately, he couldn't have picked a worse time to launch his new venture. Heavy snow and freezing conditions throughout the British Isles meant there was no horse-racing for three months. The only action was on the dog tracks.

To try and make a living, Spinks foolishly laid off many bets, and things soon went horribly wrong. The debts built up and after only a few months he was left with no alternative but to close the shop. It was badly sited at the wrong end of a main road, and with a staff of three he was losing £50 a week in wages alone.

The final decision to quit came after he had lost more than £400 in a day at Ascot in June. The business was sold the following month, by which time he had exhausted his capital.

The venture was in fact so unsuccessful that years later Terry's most vivid memory of his time there was of being refused entry to the cinema next door. One afternoon business was so poor that he decided to shut shop and go to see an 'X' rated film. As he stopped at the cash desk the assistant told him he was too young to be admitted. 'Don't be stupid,' he replied, 'I own the betting shop next door.'

Terry's personal gambling was not just confined to horses. He also won and lost plenty on the dogs, and loved going to evening meetings at the East End tracks, particularly Hackney, West Ham, Walthamstow and Romford. Wherever he went, he met dozens of people, many of whom were connected to the boxing world.

During the early 1960's, he bought a greyhound named Coar Pete for £300. At first he automatically backed it every time it ran, but the dog was never successful. After he had lost about £900, Terry started asking the trainer before a race, what the chances were. On two occasions he was told, 'Not a chance tonight. He couldn't beat my grandmother.' Thinking he was being shrewd, Terry didn't back him, but they were the only two occasions when the dog won.

Encouraged by the sudden success, Terry took Coar Pete to a 'flapping' track near Newmarket where dogs from all over the country raced under false names. He was familiar with the set-up because he ran a book at a similar track at Rayleigh. It was unlicensed and illegal, but by then he didn't care as long as the dog won him some money.

A lot of Spinks' jockey pals went along as well and asked about the dog's chances. 'He'll walk it,' Terry told them. 'He's in a class of his own.' He genuinely believed he was doing them a favour in return for good information they had given him in the past. Everyone backed it and Spinks confidently laid £150 himself.

Under an assumed name, Coar Pete was quickly out of the trap and went straight in front. Each stride took him further ahead. 'He'll lap the field at this rate,' thought Terry believing the dog was at last going to bring in some money. Suddenly, however, he stopped and waited until the rest had passed him, then quietly trotted after them. Terry couldn't believe it, but enough was enough. Having had the dog for only three months, he sold him for £150.

Despite loving a bet, Terry never backed himself in a fight. 'I reckon it's bad for a fighter to put money on himself,' he once remarked. He did, however, put money on other boxers. He picked up £200 when Carlos Ortiz beat Dave Charnley in October 1958, and £100 following Joe Erskine's victory over Willie Pastrano at Wembley in February the following year.

His bread and butter fighter, however, was Terry Downes. The only time Spinks lost money on him was at Boston in January 1961, when Downes was beaten by Paul Pender for the world middleweight title. By the time the fight was over, Spinks was out of money and had to borrow off him to pay the losing bet.

* * *

The beginning of 1963 was the start of a very difficult period for Spinks. Shortly after he retired from boxing he lost a very special friend in Ernie Jarvis, the boxing correspondent for the *Sunday People*. He passed away suddenly at the end of January, aged 58. Terry was extremely sad because apart from reporting all of his fights since he won the ABA title, Ernie always visited his dressing room after a contest. They also met at each others homes on many occasions and discussed matters far removed from boxing.

A few days later there was more sadness for Spinks when Fred McCarthy, the father of Sammy, also passed away. Terry had known him since the days when, as a schoolboy, he sat on their doorstep at Commercial Road waiting for Sammy to return home.

Like Terry's father, Fred was also known as Tich to boxing followers all over the country. A former amateur boxer himself, he taught Sammy all he knew and rarely missed one of his fights. When Spinks turned professional he gave him tremendous support as well. Fred's funeral took place on 4 February, and traffic in Commercial Road, Stepney, came to a standstill. Terry was among the mourners, together with other former boxers Eddie Phillips, Jack 'Kid' Berg and Billy Palmer, son of the great Pedlar Palmer.

Although he had stopped boxing Terry remained high profile. Sammy McCarthy continued to look after some of his affairs, and he earned good money travelling all over the country making personal appearances. He opened pubs, clubs and shops, and gave speeches about his life in boxing. Amateur clubs clamoured for him to attend dinners as guest of honour and present prizes. It seemed that everyone wanted to meet an Olympic gold medal winner.

In the East End the Kray twins continued to invite Spinks to functions they staged. On 6 March 1963, he was one of their guests at a wrestling show at York Hall organised by Empress Promotions, with which they were associated. He and Terry Downes, who had beaten Jimmy Beecham of America in nine rounds the previous evening, were given rousing receptions when introduced. Other guests included Ted 'Kid' Lewis, Lord Effingham and the Mayor of Bethnal Green.

Later in the year, Spinks was one of several celebrity guests to attend a function organised by the Krays at the Cambridge Rooms on the Kingston-by-pass. The main attraction was world heavyweight champion, Sonny Liston.

During the evening a racehorse named Solway Cross was auctioned, the successful bidder being actor, Ronnie Fraser. The twins had originally bought it as a present for their mother, but it was never successful. When they first became interested in the horse, Terry gave it a trial ride over Epsom Downs as a favour.

Terry also spent more time at the races. One of his regular companions was Joe Lowery, a professional gambler, who lived at Woodford near Sammy McCarthy. One day they invited Sammy to join them just for a day out. He knew nothing about racing and it was the first time he had ever been into a racecourse betting ring. He was astonished when Spinks suddenly laid a bet of £500 on a particular horse.

'A lot of people in the racing game knew Terry and gave him tips,' recalled Sammy years later. 'He always gambled heavily if he fancied a particular horse or had been given a tip.'

Whenever Spinks put a large amount on a horse, Lowery did likewise, but usually with a different bookie. 'I was horrified to see what they were doing,' said Sammy, 'but when I saw they were winning I started to fancy my luck.'

Urged on by Terry and Joe, who told him what horses to back, Sammy began betting as well, despite having a degree of apprehension. 'It was as though I felt I had to follow suit because I was with them,' he recalled.

That day they really took the bookies to the cleaners and won between £5,000 and £6,000 which was an absolute fortune. Sammy was stunned because he had only taken about £500 with him.

Two days later they attended another race-meeting. They again gambled heavily, often on tips given to Terry by people he met on the course. The outcome was the same and they returned home with a profit of several thousand pounds.

Like most gamblers, Terry didn't know when to quit. The more he won the more he laid out on new bets. A few days later, he, Joe and Sammy had another successful trip, and on returning to the East End went straight to Hackney Dog Track. 'It seemed as though everyone knew Terry there as well,' recalled Sammy. 'He was given a few tips and again we were quite lucky.'

After going dog-racing Terry and his cronies usually finished up at a drinking and gaming club for a late night game of cards. Such establishments were scattered all over London and usually situated in basements or backrooms of legitimate properties. Although he knew places throughout London, Spinks usually headed for Soho or the East End. Most were unlicensed dens of iniquity often frequented by members of the criminal fraternity. Nevertheless, he was always treated with great respect whether he won or lost.

Because the clubs were unlicensed they were often the subject of police raids. Despite the frequency of his visits Terry was only caught up in such a raid on one occasion. He was in a club at Notting Hill with several of his mates from the East End when police stormed in shortly after midnight. 'Don't give your right name, Tel,' said one of his mates. 'We're all going to give wrong 'uns.'

The police told everyone to stand still and then asked for their personal details. 'Name please,' said a constable to Spinks.'

'John Smith,' replied the boxer.

'Yes, thank you very much Terry. Stand over there,' was the response.

Everybody in the club was arrested, taken to Notting Hill Police Station and charged with frequenting a common gaming house. Spinks appeared at Marylebone Magistrates Court next morning, pleaded guilty and was fined £2.

On the racecourses Terry was often a reckless gambler. Even when he lost a lot of money he still appeared unconcerned. Sammy McCarthy, however, was much more cautious and level-headed. In his heart he knew that whatever he won would eventually finish up going back to the bookies, which is exactly what happened. Despite the incredible amount of money that Sammy won, all that remained one day was an amount he had sensibly left at home.

Heavy losses, however, never seemed to deter Spinks who continued to lay large bets wherever they went. He had accounts with several bookmakers on the courses and subsequently there were many occasions when no cash changed hands. He encouraged Sammy to do the same, but when their luck eventually dried up, Sammy unexpectedly received a bill from a bookmaker for £1,500. He didn't have the money, which in those days was enough to buy a house. 'Don't worry, we'll see to it,' Joe told him when he asked what would happen.

Spinks and Lowery were professional punters so if they were banned from the courses the bookmakers would never get their money back. Sammy, however, was different. He couldn't pay the money he owed and never did. Under the rules of racing, anybody could be reported to Tattersalls, who would then warn them off the courses if their conduct was deemed to be undesirable. Eventually, Sammy received a letter advising him that he would be refused future credit, and that he was banned from racecourse betting. He never went racing again.

* * *

On the domestic front, Terry and Valerie's son Jarvis was baptised on 14 April 1963 at St Lukes Church, Victoria Docks. Known as the Cathedral of the East End, it had opened in 1875. Tich and Doris were married there, and Terry christened at the church in 1938.

Despite being a family man, Spinks continued to be attracted by the bright lights and West End clubs. The hangers-on did him no favours by dragging him out night after night, and more often than not he was the one who did the paying.

While he was boxing, Terry had an account with the Black Angus Restaurant in the West End. Unfortunately, certain individuals knew about it and took advantage of his easy going nature. Quite often groups of up to 12 would go to the restaurant for meals and say, 'Terry Spinks said we can charge it to his account.' Bills of several hundred pounds were often received by Terry who was being used as a meal ticket by certain people he thought were his friends.

During the early hours of 18 May 1963 after a night in the West End, Terry fell foul of the law. He was arrested and charged at Islington Police Station with being unfit to drive through drink, and dangerous driving. At a preliminary hearing at Old Street Magistrates Court on 1 July, Prosecuting Counsel, Mr William Howard, said that the former boxer was seen by police to drive through two sets of red traffic lights.

Dr Abraham Matthews told the court that he was called to the police station to examine Spinks who told him he had drunk three or four lager and limes and a scotch. The doctor asked Terry to add up nine, seven, six and eight. After 26 seconds he answered, '33'. When told it was the wrong answer, Spinks said, 'I left school at 15. I was a dunce. I was in the bottom class.'

He was then asked to do some subtractions but couldn't. After a short period, Spinks allegedly remarked, 'It's a long time since I went to school.'

In September that year, during a three day trial at the London Quarter Sessions, doctors called by the prosecution and defence had differing opinions regarding certain medical aspects appertaining to Terry's condition.

Police evidence was that the former boxer was talking to a female passenger and not paying much attention to his driving. His van swerved frequently, and it was alleged that he went through two sets of red traffic lights.

Dr John Clougherty of Silvertown, east London was called by the defence. He told the court that after Terry's last fight in December the previous year, he had told him it would be advisable to consider retiring from boxing. When he examined him at that time certain symptoms were beginning to show. 'There was a slight alteration of gait, swaying and nystagmus – an eye disorder,' said Dr Clougherty. 'These changes were undoubtedly due to multiple knocks to the head.'

At this point, at the request of Mr Robin Simpson, Counsel representing Spinks, Dr Clougherty and Dr Abraham Matthews, a prosecution witness, went into the dock and conducted independent examinations of Terry's eyes.

Returning to the witness box Dr Clougherty said: 'Very definite nystagmus was present in both examinations.' He told the court that Spinks had swayed when he stood with his feet together and his eyes closed. Had he continued with his boxing he would have risked complete punch-drunkenness.

In answer to Mr Roger Frisby, Prosecuting Counsel, the doctor said: 'Driving at night is not the best for a nystagmus condition.'

Dr Matthews' further evidence contradicted that of Dr Clougherty. He said Spinks had 'no true nystagmus.' When he examined him at the police station in May there was a definite mark of nystagmus – an involuntary movement of the eyeballs. 'The movement I saw in Mr Spinks' eyes this morning was, in my opinion, voluntary,' said Dr Matthews.

The jury took just 18 minutes to find Terry not guilty of driving whilst unfit through drink. A previous jury had acquitted him of a further charge of dangerous driving, but failed to reach a verdict on the drink-driving matter. A re-trial was therefore ordered.

As soon as he was released from the court Terry rushed to a telephone to call his wife. 'I've been cleared,' he said excitedly. 'See you later.'

Outside the court a crowd of well-wishers and friends were waiting to congratulate him on his acquittal. 'Good luck Terry,' they shouted, 'well done mate.' He was hugged and slapped across the shoulders, and among those who shook his hand were the police officers who had arrested him and given evidence at the trial. 'Naturally I am delighted with the verdict,' said the jubilant Spinks as he set off for a celebration drink.

The publicity the court case received brought about a number of letters from cranks, while other writers suggested Terry should join the Salvation Army or Alcoholics Anonymous. Although he liked a good drink, he was not that bad and no different to many other young men who liked the atmosphere of pubs and clubs. His biggest problem was that by not having a steady job he had too much time on his hands.

Despite no longer being a boxer, people still wanted to be seen with Terry, and because of his exceptionally generous nature many took advantage. Although he had grossed more than £32,000 during his professional boxing career, it was always a case of easy come, easy go with him. He gambled heavily and lived lavishly, automatically buying drinks for anybody when he was in the clubs. When he retired from the ring in December 1962 his fortune had dwindled to just a few hundred pounds.

Towards the end of 1963 there were rumours in the East End that he was contemplating a comeback. To many people this did not come as a surprise because it was well known that he was experiencing financial problems. When contacted by a reporter from the *Stratford Express*, Spinks made no secret of his plans. 'I've been training for some weeks now,' he said. 'I am confident I can get back to the top. Apart from Winstone, the featherweight division is weak.' It was a brave prediction but fooled nobody.

Any plans Spinks might have had for a quick return to the ring were, however, shattered when, on 9 January 1964, he was involved in a nasty accident at Barking Road, Plaistow. His Austin A30 van was virtually a write-off after being in a collision with a lorry. Although he was taken to Queen Mary's hospital at Stratford with a dislocated hip, Terry could easily have been more seriously hurt. His van finished up partly under the lorry.

'This has upset my plans a bit, but once they get me out of here I'll be heading for the gym,' he optimistically told a reporter who visited him.

Sammy McCarthy, who was sitting at his bedside, confirmed that Terry was serious about the comeback. 'I have applied to the Board of Control for the renewal of his licence,' he remarked. 'Terry is confident he can regain his old form, and so am I.'

The injury, however, eventually made Spinks realise that it would be a long time before he was fully mobile again. Even after three weeks in hospital he still required regular physiotherapy and therefore abandoned all thoughts of a comeback.

Tich had by this time become extremely concerned about his son's welfare. Although he still had his betting shop at North Woolwich, he planned to open another at Pelly Road, Plaistow. He wanted Terry to run it as soon as he was discharged from hospital. The former champion's run of misfortune, however, continued. The West Ham Betting Licenses Committee refused Tich's application on the grounds that there were enough betting shops in the borough.

'Terry had his heart set on the job. I feel really cut up about the decision,' Tich told the *Stratford Express*. 'I suppose he will now have to look around for another job when he is better.'

It wasn't the first time that Terry had failed in an attempt to run a betting shop. The previous year, he and Sammy McCarthy had planned to go into business together from premises at 33 Plashet Road, Plaistow. On 30 July 1962 a company entitled 'Spinks & McCarthy (East Ham) Limited' was registered, but didn't trade because their application for a licence was refused.

The whole situation was getting to Terry and he became very low as disappointment and disasters continued. 'If only I could turn the clock back seven years,' he muttered to a reporter as he lay in his hospital bed. 'I am a no-hoper at just 25. I'm in the boxing dustbin. I'm all washed up.'

'My life isn't just the story of a boy going off the rails a bit,' he continued. 'No-one has heard about the real Terry Spinks.'

Desperate for cash, Terry began writing down notes of his experiences as he lay in hospital. A Sunday newspaper had jumped at the opportunity to publish his exclusive account of how he had gone wrong. He was paid £1,500 to reveal everything about his drinking and gambling exploits.

The story ran for four weeks during January and February 1964, but did far more harm than good. Headlines of; 'I'M WASHED UP AT 25'; 'I COULDN'T SAY NO TO THE BOOZE'; and 'I LOST £30,000 ON SLOW HORSES', were splashed across the pages. The former Olympic champion was shown in such a poor light that Valerie was too embarrassed to leave their flat because everyone was staring at her. They had reached such a low point that they had little more than bread and jam to eat. The electricity had been cut off and was only re-connected because Terry Downes took the overdue bills and paid them.

Terry's financial problems had been building up for some while. In September 1962, when he was short of money, Doris repaid him the £1,000 he invested in the purchase of their confectionery business at Plaistow. She took complete ownership and would continue to run the shop for many years until forced to give it up due to ill health.

By mid-1963, Terry was having difficulty keeping up the repayments on a mortgage of £2,500 with Barclays Bank in respect of the property at 83 Cumberland Road. When the bank threatened him with bankruptcy, the house was sold to Tich.

Although Terry talked about taking a job as a boxing trainer, and of writing his autobiography, neither came to fruition. He and Valerie also talked about taking over a pub, but only on condition that it was away from the East End and all the hangers-on. That proposal didn't materialise either because more trouble was looming.

During February the Board of Trade brought six summonses against a company known as Terry Spinks Limited, of which Terry and Tich were Directors. It was alleged that they failed to submit annual returns for the year 1960 to the Registrar of Companies within the permitted period. Having pleaded guilty by letter, neither appeared in court. They were each fined £5 with £2 costs. No separate penalties were imposed in respect of summonses relating to the years 1961 and 1962.

At the hearing at Old Street Magistrates Court, Prosecuting Counsel described the company as Boxing Agents and Managers. Although it had existed for three years, it never traded. Consequently, no returns were sent as required by law.

Meanwhile, Terry and Valerie had negotiated the purchase of a small newsagents shop at Paul Street in Shoreditch. They used the money Terry received from the series of Sunday newspaper articles, paying it into their account one day and withdrawing it the next. There was a flat above the shop, and although the property cost only £1,000, there were massive pit-falls. It failed to become the cosy family business venture they had hoped for.

As they couldn't afford a solicitor, Terry's mother insisted they used the same one as the vendor. Doris had become very much the guiding light in the enterprise, but this proved to be terrible advice. Part of the deal was that they had to purchase all of the existing stock for a further £500. It transpired that most of it was very old, therefore unsellable and had to be thrown away.

Part of the problem was that Valerie, on her own admission, was afraid of Doris, a strong-minded and often domineering woman. Consequently, she went along with her suggestions but with dire consequences. The £1,500 from the Sunday newspaper had gone, and Terry and Valerie still had to purchase new stock for the shop which was not in a prime position. Trade was dependent on people walking by, many of whom were workers at a nearby printing company which employed about 2,000. What Terry and Valerie didn't know was that it was already ear-marked for closure, something they would have been made aware of had they engaged an independent solicitor.

Once they settled into running the shop, Valerie opened up at 6.00am because a high proportion of their business was early in the morning from people going to work. They remained open until about 7.00pm except at weekends when there were very few customers.

By this time, Jarvis was aged three and a half. He was an active little boy who didn't like being couped up in the shop all day. He was therefore enrolled at The Gatehouse, a private school at nearby Goswell Road. Even this attracted attention, and photographs appeared in newspapers of Terry taking him in on his first day.

Within a few weeks of taking over the shop at Paul Street, Terry was hit with more trouble. His revelations in the Sunday newspaper about his ring earnings and gambling had attracted the attention of the Inland Revenue who were already investigating him over unpaid tax on his purse money. He and Valerie were questioned about how they managed to buy the shop, and although they were allowed to carry on running it, the Official Receiver was appointed. A Receiving Order was made on 14 May 1964 on a creditors petition, and Terry was adjudged bankrupt on 16 June. The act of bankruptcy was his failure to comply before 5 March 1964, with the requirements of a Bankruptcy Notice.

Procedural matters began on 15 January 1963 when the Inland Revenue obtained judgement against Spinks for an amount of £1,042-two shillings in respect of unpaid income tax and interest. In due course, bankruptcy proceedings were instituted on which the Receiving Order was subsequently made. Notice of the Order was published in the London Gazette, with Terry's occupation being described as 'at present not known, but lately a professional boxer'.

The first meeting of creditors was held on 11 June 1964, and Terry's public examination conducted at The London Bankruptcy Court at Victoria House, Kingsway, London WC2, on 7 July.

Subjected to vigorous questioning regarding his financial affairs, Spinks attributed his insolvency to heavy expenses; to drawings and gambling losses during the six years he was a professional boxer, and to the failure of his betting shop business. He admitted gross personal extravagance, and to having been negligent and irresponsible as regards his Inland Revenue affairs.

Official Receiver, Mr J L Williams, told the court that Terry's Statement of Affairs showed liabilities of £2,062 against assets of £26. According to the accounts, his gross earnings were £32,680 during the six years he was a professional boxer. Spinks agreed that the net amount he received was a matter of conjecture, but accepted that £16,000 to £17,000 was a fair estimate.

He explained that he received his pay from his manager after the relevant percentages had been deducted. He had to pay for his own gym fees, bandages and tapes, and never kept a record of these expenses or of his fares and petrol which must have been quite considerable over the six year period. The main problem was, there were no proper accounts.

Addressing Spinks, Mr Williams said, 'I have read that by the time you were 19 or 20 you had drunk so much scotch whisky that you spoke cockney with a Scots accent. Did you say that?'

'No,' replied Spinks.

Mr Williams was referring to the Sunday newspaper articles in Terry's name where there was a clear statement in the words referred to. Whether Terry actually said them is open to speculation, but the Official Receiver had made his point.

Spinks also claimed that figures quoted in the newspaper articles regarding his gambling losses, were exaggerated. He estimated that he lost about £12,000, not £30,000 as had been quoted.

Terry told the court about the injury he had sustained in the car accident and stated he was receiving £6 per week accident insurance. He was still attending hospital two, and sometimes three times a week, and could not therefore find regular work.

Doris and Valerie accompanied Terry to the hearing, taking Jarvis in a pushchair. During the proceedings, Valerie was asked why she wasn't working to pay off her husband's debts. The whole situation was humiliating and degrading for the once proud Olympic champion and his wife. Only when he left the court did he realise just how low he had sunk.

It wasn't long before bailiffs, appointed by the court, turned up at The Limes looking to seize anything of value. Fortunately some of Terry's wiser East End friends anticipated what would happen and removed some of their better belongings before the bailiffs visit. These were replaced by old bits from Grandpa Harry Jordan's house and weren't of interest to the bailiffs because they were of little value. Valerie was allowed to keep Jarvis' cot, and paid 25 guineas for their living room suite.

Being declared bankrupt was the saddest moment in Terry's life, but it had come about because of his happy-go-lucky attitude. 'That's the type of character I am,' he remarked. 'I don't worry over many things.'

When he reflected on his situation some years later he readily admitted having indulged in extravagances during his boxing career. 'I had four new cars in five years, and hand-made suits costing £30 to £40 a time,' he said. 'I went on luxury holidays to

Italy and Cannes, cruises to Madeira and Portugal. I also went to night clubs a lot.'

Although he saved money during the early part of his career and invested in shares, he sold them because they were slow making a profit. 'I guess most of my hard-earned ring money was spent,' he admitted. 'When you are a famous personality in the public eye, you've got to act like one. You've got to be seen in smart places with important people.'

What Spinks didn't reveal was the fact that too many hangers-on took full advantage of his generosity and desire to impress. Many boxers, before and since, have had plenty of so-called friends when they were at their peak, but when the going got tough and the cash ran out, they were nowhere to be seen.

There were many occasions when, in the days leading up to a fight, Terry went into a pub and gave tickets to his friends. Others who wanted to buy them often asked, 'Alright if I pay you in a couple of days Tel?' They rarely did. On other occasions, associates sold tickets on Terry's behalf, but failed to pass on the money, often amounting to hundreds of pounds, thereby seriously effecting the purse money he eventually received.

Long after he had finished with boxing Terry was frequently asked how much he earned in the ring. Invariably his answer was the same, 'My money is my own business.'

Despite his financial shortfalls, the only debt Terry had was to the Inland Revenue. It arose because during his boxing career he didn't pay sufficient tax from his purse money. 'It takes an ordinary man 25 to 30 years to make £30,000 and he can pay his income tax over the whole of that period,' he remarked. 'A boxer's life is short, usually only five years or so. Yet he has to pay all his tax in that time which has always seemed unfair to me.'

Spinks offered to pay off the debt at the rate of £10 a week but it was refused. Although his friends rallied round and offered help, he was not a man to accept charity. Terry Downes, who at the time ran a chain of betting shops, told Spinks there was a full-time job for him if he wanted it. Like other offers, Spinks refused it, choosing instead to try and work things out himself.

Within a few weeks of the bankruptcy, Terry and Valerie gave up their rented flat at The Limes and moved into their own above the shop at Paul Street. Although it saved them money on rent and petrol, they were no better off because Terry was still gambling and often took money from the till to fund the habit. As money was very tight, they could no longer afford to keep Jarvis at the private school so he left after only a few months.

Concentration and determination are etched on Terry's face as he pounds the heavy bag in training at the Thomas A'Beckett gym.

Spinks discusses the finer points of boxing with His Royal Highness, The Duke of Kent, Patron of West Ham Boxing Club.

Spinks training a South Korean squad boxer in Seoul for the 1972 Olympic Games in Munich.

"The Spinks Brothers". Terry meets former Olympic gold medal winners Leon Spinks (left) and his brother Michael at Liverpool Stadium in March 1977.

Spinks and his good friend Billy Walker at a dinner in London during the late 1990's.

Spinks (left) with former world lightweight champion, Carlos Ortiz, at the International Ex-Boxers Convention in London during October 1998.

The Princess Royal chats to former Olympic gold medal winners, Terry Spinks (1956), Dick McTaggart (1956) and Chris Finnegan (1968).

Spinks meets world heavyweight champion, Lennox Lewis, in London during 1999.

London ex-Boxers Association President, Stephen Powell (centre) with Vice-Presidents, Sammy McCarthy (right) and Terry Spinks who display awards made to them for services to the Association.

Spinks (left) with his great friend and rival, Howard Winstone, in London during 1999.

Spinks (left) and former opponent, Bobby Neill, show the fondness which exists between them at a meeting of the London ex-Boxers Association in 2000.

Throughout his life, Spinks has worked for charitable causes, and on many occasions has been invited to public houses and clubs to knock over piles of coins.

Spinks (left) and Bobby Neill congratulate Joe Calzaghe after he had been presented with the Geoffrey Simpson Award for the "Best Boxer of the Year" at the Boxing Writers' Dinner at the Savoy Hotel in April 1996.

Terry and his cousin Rosemary relax at Charlie Magri's pub at Mile End during November 2001.

Whenever Terry and Valerie wanted to go out for an evening they had to get a baby-sitter for Jarvis. One lad who performed the task was John Stracey from nearby Bethnal Green who was an extremely talented boxer. He won a National Schoolboy championship in 1965, National Association of Boys Clubs title the following year, and a Junior ABA championship in 1967. As a professional he progressed to the very top and became WBC world welterweight champion by stopping the great Jose Napoles in six rounds at Mexico City in a never to be forgotten fight on 12 December 1975.

From a very young age Stracey was fanatical about boxing. He spent hours in local libraries searching for information about former champions from the East End. Despite his admiration for Ted 'Kid' Lewis and Jack 'Kid' Berg, Terry Spinks became very much his favourite. He was absolutely thrilled when he got to meet him, and jumped at the chance to baby-sit for Jarvis. Apart from visiting the flat at Paul Street, he also sat for Jarvis while Terry and Valerie were having a break at a holiday camp. John had just won his Junior ABA championship and was on holiday at the same camp.

Spinks knew the dedication it took to win a Schoolboy championship, and had tremendous admiration for Stracey. They talked a lot about boxing, and the former Olympic champion gave the youngster great encouragement just as he had received from his idol, Sammy McCarthy, more than a decade earlier.

John's baby-sitting duties were the start of a great friendship. In later years he always claimed that he modelled himself on Spinks and had always wanted to be like him.

Whilst living at Paul Street, Terry became involved in training young boxers at the West Ham Club on a part-time basis. His appointment in 1964 came a few weeks after the North East London Divisional Boxing Committee decided to allow former professionals to assist in the affairs of amateur clubs. 'I have been thinking about teaching youngsters since I quit the ring,' Terry told the *Stratford Express*.

For a short period he was also involved in training promising West Ham featherweight, Don Weller, a professional managed by Jarvis Astaire. During their period together, Terry took him away from the Duke of Fife gym to Joe Bloom's in the West End so he could get better quality sparring.

Despite the commitment required to run the shop at Paul Street, Spinks still found it difficult to settle into a routine. Since retiring from the ring he had become restless and always wanted to be out with his mates. Although he had been declared bankrupt, he continued to gamble because, in reality, he had little sense of responsibility. Soon after they took over the shop, Valerie virtually ran it single-handed because Terry was always out, often at the races.

The shop proved to be a terrible investment. After less than two years they sold it at a financial loss and moved into a rented unfurnished flat at Oaks Avenue, Dulwich. Although Terry continued to visit his parents on a regular basis, he avoided most of his old haunts in the East End.

Deeply embarrassed by the fact that he and his family were living on the bread-line, he desperately wanted to break free from his old habits and build himself back to respectability. Although there were plenty of occasions when mates offered him some dodgy gear to help him along, he would never touch it. He preferred to remain straight and muddle his way through his financial crisis.

Valerie took a job with Lonsdale Sports while Terry went mini-cabbing with a company based at the Elephant & Castle. He also began working for John Branch, a close friend who was a specialist contractor in sculptural and architectural preservation.

John's company, Antique Bronze Limited, had huge contracts with the Greater London Council, and the Boroughs of Kensington and Westminster, to preserve and maintain statues situated throughout Central London. There were also contracts with County Hall, Festival Hall and Queen Elizabeth Buildings, all on the south bank of the Thames, to maintain and clean marble and bronze work.

A sculptor by trade, Branch was a stabling influence on Spinks who had great respect for him. He had been a Physical Training Instructor with the Army Physical Training Corps, and after being discharged took out a British Boxing Board of Control trainer's licence. He worked mainly at Klein's gym, Fitzroy Square just off Tottenham Court Road, and among the professionals he trained was Ernie Fossey, a good lightweight from Islington whom he had known in the Army.

John first met Spinks shortly after he won the National Schoolboys championship in 1953, and from that time followed his career closely. He also knew many of Terry's boxing mates from the East End including Terry Murphy, Dave Salmon and the Enifer brothers.

When Terry started working for Branch during the mid-1960's his task was cleaning statues. The job really suited him because he loved being out in the open air and meeting people. Many who recognised him stopped for a chat, but foreign tourists became a nuisance once they discovered he was a former Olympic gold medallist. He was pestered for autographs and expected to stop work to pose for photographs.

One particular job Terry was involved in was the cleaning and restoration of the Eros statue at Piccadilly Circus which took two months. One day he arrived for work wearing a very smart sports jacket which was far too good to work in. He told John he was short of cash and asked for a loan of £20. 'Don't get that jacket dirty Terry,' said Branch as he handed him the money. Terry immediately removed the jacket and laid it on the steps of the statue.

Part of the Eros job required cleaning off old gold coating to bring out other colours. Terry was so involved that when John and the other workers said they were going to get some breakfast, he said he wanted to finish what he was doing and would join them later. He never did.

As the group were walking back from Leicester Square about half an hour later, they spotted a tramp wearing Terry's jacket. Without hesitation they grabbed him and accused him of stealing it. 'No, no, the bloke gave it to me,' screamed the terrified vagrant. Then, pulling a note from his pocket said, 'And look he gave me ten quid as well.'

Not believing a word he said, Branch and his mates marched the man back to Eros where Spinks confirmed the story. 'I felt really sorry for him,' he remarked. 'He looked so down on his luck that I told him to take the jacket, and gave him a tenner to get something to eat.'

Recalling the story years later, Branch said: 'That was so typical of Terry. He was the kindest, best-hearted man I have ever known. The trouble was he got taken advantage of because of his generosity.'

Apart from cleaning and restoring statues and monuments, Terry was also trained by John to make moulds required to do complicated repairs. 'He had a special talent of being able to look at an object in reverse as opposed to face on,' recalled Branch. 'That would ensure that the mould was a perfect reproduction.'

Terry spent a lot of time at sites taking impressions of items such as statue heads which required repair. Most were made of clay so he made an impression by pouring a solution of rubber over damaged areas. Back at the company workshop he would then make a jacket which had to fit perfectly. Hot wax would then be poured in to create a new impression which he used to replace the damaged part.

Terry did all manner of jobs for Branch and was good at

whatever he did. He got on well with people and gained their respect. John therefore eventually made him a manager. His task was mainly to supervise work being carried out inside a number of large buildings in London. In particular, the company had a big contract to maintain County Hall. So as not to interfere with the day-to-day business, all work had to be carried out at night.

To check that the workmen arrived on time, Spinks was always at County Hall long before the shift began. John always briefed him about the jobs to be done and it was his responsibility to ensure they were carried out. Terry was the ideal man for the job because he got on with everybody. Throughout the night he and his team worked on the flooring of the building. As the manager, he made a number of spot checks to make sure nobody was slacking.

County Hall, however, was an extremely big, dark and lonely place at night, and on his travels Spinks frequently became the target for practical jokes. There were a number of occasions when the men would wrap themselves in curtains and move about in the shadows or jump out at him from under tables. Despite the hi-jinks the work still got done according to schedule.

Terry had a good sense of humour. He could take a joke and knew how to play a few himself. One evening, all the lads had arranged to go dog-racing before starting work and he knew there was a chance they would be late. Earlier the same day he went to a fancy dress shop and hired a gorilla suit which he sneaked into County Hall when he arrived for work. After dressing up in it he hid in a dark corridor in the basement outside the tea-room and waited for the men to arrive.

Suddenly, he saw the site electrician who he only knew as Jack. He was doing some work, but had his back to Terry who crept up and tapped him on the shoulder. 'Hey Jack,' he said, 'Do you know where the boys are?' The sudden tap on the shoulder terrified the man, but when he turned around to be confronted by a 'gorilla' he was petrified. He had to sit down and recover, but even then couldn't stop shaking and had to go home. 'I'm so sorry Jack, I really am,' said Spinks repeatedly as Jack left the building.

Whenever a large job was completed at County Hall there was a party with plenty of drinks. Terry always consumed his share, but whenever he started to sing everyone knew he'd had enough. Although there was always someone willing to drive him home, nobody knew where he lived and had to rely on his directions. The problem was when he got drunk, not only was he incoherent, but his memory often became jaded. Sometimes he directed cab drivers to addresses from his past such as Cumberland Road and The

Limes. One night he asked to be dropped off at the shop in Paul Street, despite the fact that he and Valerie had sold up and moved to Dulwich two years earlier.

Another night he was driven to Dulwich and eventually told the driver to stop in a particular road. 'That's my house,' he slurred pointing to a particular semi-detached. As Terry was very much the worse for wear, the helpful driver went and knocked on the door only to be confronted by an irate lady who had been woken from a deep sleep. 'Not him again,' she screamed on seeing Spinks sitting in the car. 'He don't live here. Go and tell him so will you, because every time he gets drunk he turns up here in the middle of the night.' Although Terry lived only a short distance along the road it had happened on a number of previous occasions.

Although he wasn't a big man, Terry was exceptionally strong, and this was demonstrated on a couple of occasions while he was working at County Hall. One day he noticed a man in a wheelchair having difficulty getting into the building. There were steps at the front, but no slope. In an instant he walked up to the man, put his arms around the wheelchair, and with him still in it, lifted it to the top of the stairs. 'Are you okay now mate?' said Terry before returning to what he was doing.

On another occasion he almost single-handedly unloaded a consignment of 50 gallon drums of liquid seal used for the floors, from the back of a lorry. Without any obvious difficulty he lifted them onto his head and carried them into the loading bay. One of his work-mates was a huge muscular man built like a power-lifter. Because Terry looked so small, he offered to help him, but when he tried to carry a drum he collapsed under its weight.

Terry was fortunate to have a friend like John Branch who, apart from giving him work, also allowed flexibility. To supplement his earnings, he continued mini-cabbing and also became involved with Lonsdale Sports, a company set up by former boxer, Bernard Hart. He and Spinks had known each other since 1953 when they both won National Schoolboy championships.

In August 1960, Spinks, Sammy McCarthy, Terry Downes and Johnny Kidd were all present when Hart opened his first shop at 21 Beak Street in Soho. The company built steadily, and by the late 1960's had opened another shop at Acre Lane, Brixton. In November 1969, a third shop was opened at 546 Kingsland Road, Dalston, and managed by former Tottenham Hotspur and England footballer Alan Mullery. The opening was a big occasion and police had to hold back crowds for most of the day.

Terry Spinks was one of the first visitors to the shop. That day he was chauffeur to European gold medallist Lillian Broad who told journalists she hated boxing. Because of his popularity, and close friendship with Bernard Hart, Terry became very much a figure-head with Lonsdale. He gradually became more involved, and in October 1970 took over the daily running of the Dalston shop. His cheerful personality was soon a hit with the customers, many of whom went into the shop just to meet him. Not many left without being persuaded to make a purchase.

In May 1971, Spinks was one of 23 former boxers, all of whom were sponsored, to compete in a five mile charity run organised by Lonsdale. The event started in the City of London and finished at the Lord Palmerston public house at Kings Road. An amount of £272 was raised towards the ABA training fund for the forthcoming European boxing championships.

'I'm always willing to take part in charity events,' said Spinks who was sponsored by Alan Mullery. 'But being more than two stone over my fighting weight makes me realise I should think about something other than running. I'm absolutely shattered.'

Three weeks later, Terry was one of a number of top class former professional boxers to attend a musical event in aid of charity, organised at the Thomas A' Beckett by the licensee, Beryl Cameron-Gibbons. The evening was light relief for Spinks who had been distressed for several days. Earlier that week he had attended a memorial service at the Church of St Bride in Fleet Street for his close friend George Whiting. The former boxing correspondent for the *London Evening Standard* had adored Spinks since he won a Schoolboy championship in 1953. 'He was a good man and I was very close to him,' said Terry. 'What I liked about him was that he didn't write any bullshit. If I boxed badly, he said so.'

In June 1971, Spinks met up with world heavyweight champion Joe Frazier who was on a tour of Britain with his musical group The Knockouts. Like Terry, Joe was also an Olympic gold medal winner and the two got on well as they compared experiences. They were also joined by Terry Downes, and the three of them amused crowds of people outside Lonsdale's shop in Soho as they played musical instruments, albeit not very harmoniously.

Spinks was still a great supporter of boxing and continued to follow both the amateur and professional sides closely. He was a great admirer of Henry Cooper and frequently praised his massive contribution to the sport.

Following Henry's retirement from the ring after his controversial defeat by Joe Bugner in March 1971, the trade paper *Boxing News* suggested he should receive a knighthood in the Queen's Birthday

Honours list. Many boxing fans agreed, and Spinks was quick to add his views. 'Henry's a smashing fellow and I think the fight game will badly miss such an upright and popular man,' he said in an interview. 'If you can get a knighthood for public service, why not for a contribution for sport?'

Cooper was eventually knighted in 2000 and became the first boxer to receive such an honour. Years earlier he had been awarded an OBE, and many people felt that Spinks should also have been decorated for his gold medal success in 1956. Many sportsmen and women are rewarded for their achievements and contributions, but for some unaccountable reason he was overlooked. As the years passed by there was increasing anger at the omission. Eventually a campaign was formed on his behalf and a number of representations were made to Members of Parliament. The sheer magnitude of what was to occur was a demonstration of the popularity of Terry Spinks.

12

BACK INTO BOXING

Whatever their sport, Olympic gold medallists are rarely forgotten, and Terry Spinks was no exception. Almost a decade had passed since he retired from boxing and during that period he had not participated in the sport in any great capacity. Suddenly, however, in January 1972, he was asked to become coach to the South Korean national squad for the Olympic Games at Munich.

An approach was originally made to ABA coach David James, but as he was unable to take the job, he asked Terry if he would be interested. At the time he was still working for John Branch, and was also involved with Lonsdale Sports. At first he was uncertain about what to do, but John convinced him to take it. He assured him that he would still have a job when he returned.

Terry flew to Seoul as soon as his appointment was confirmed by the South Korean authorities. Alone on the flight, however, he began to have reservations about what he had let himself in for. On arrival in Seoul his anxiety soon disappeared because he discovered that many people spoke English. The organisers were very professional, and he was given his own interpreter, a local man who was with him most of the time.

Spinks joined up with the boxing squad almost immediately. Most were students who trained regularly before and after their studies. Others were in the Army based in Seoul and were given virtually permanent leave in order to prepare for the Olympics.

Spinks stayed with the boxers in quarters at a fine training camp with good facilities very similar to those in the United Kingdom. A fitness programme had been designed, and whilst Terry's job was to teach boxing, he joined in with everything the squad did. Each morning they went on a three mile run which was broken up by sprints and short bursts of shadow boxing. The afternoons were spent in the gym where Terry put each boxer through eight rounds of sparring sessions on the pads, and bag work.

He worked with the squad non-stop until the end of May when he went home for a short break. He looked younger and much fitter than when he went away four months earlier.

Soon after arriving back in London, Terry was contacted by representatives from the West Ham Boxing Club and offered a position of coach to the seniors. A vacancy had arisen because his old trainer, Billy Walker, had resigned to go to Australia. Although he was under contract to the South Koreans to take their squad to the Olympics, Spinks agreed to take up the position in September when he returned from Munich. 'Since going abroad I have got back all my zest for the sport,' he told newsmen. 'This will be an ideal opportunity for me. I am looking forward to it even more because I used to belong to the club.'

Spinks was still high profile, and while he was in London a number of reporters tracked him down seeking interviews about his venture to Korea. Before returning for the final three months of preparation leading up to the Olympics, he said that he believed some members of the South Korean squad had a good chance of winning a medal at Munich.

'Watch out for Chong-Man You,' he remarked. 'This kid can strike gold at the Games. As far as I am concerned he's one of the hardest hitting amateurs I've seen at his weight.'

'I know the draw will have a lot to say about his chances,' continued Spinks, 'but I still rate him highly.'

The period in Korea was a major event in Terry's life and he was regarded there as a man of great importance. His original appointment was to coach the boxing team for the Olympics, but he created such a fine impression that he was eventually asked to take complete charge of the team in Munich.

Apart from being well paid, he was very well looked after in Korea. Although he worked very hard he had an incredible social life. Everyone wanted to be his friend and he was wined and dined in exclusive establishments. The Korean ladies idolised him and many sought his affections.

Whilst he was living in Seoul there was a curfew from midnight until 4.00am. The authorities, however, were unconcerned about Terry and it was as though he had the freedom to do exactly as he liked. There were many occasions when he was stopped on the streets during the early hours. The police, however, always treated him with great respect and courtesy. 'Ah, Mr Terry Spinks, it is you,' they would say. He was often given a lift back to his quarters in the luxury of a police car.

Despite the hard work he put into the training, Terry was very relaxed and frequently played practical jokes on the boxers and other members of the training staff. Eventually, however, they decided to get their own back. One morning a fellow instructor called Spinks to a building adjacent to the training camp. 'I have bad news Terry,' he said solemnly. 'The North Koreans have heard how you are helping our boxers and they are going to hang you.'

Before anything else was said a man dressed in camouflage gear, with coloured stripes painted down his face and a knife gripped between his teeth, crashed through a door into the building. He and a colleague grabbed Spinks, tied his arms behind his back and marched him to an adjoining room where a gallows had been erected. He was led up on to a platform and made to stand beneath the noose.

Terry was petrified, but as he screamed for mercy another door was flung open. There, through misty eyes, he saw all his boxers and training staff screaming with laughter.

'You are a funny man Mr Terry Spinks,' said one instructor. 'Now we get our own back on you.'

Sweating profusely, Terry fell to the floor laughing. After lying there for a few moments, he jumped up, and with the voice of a Sergeant Major, yelled: 'You lot, into the gym now. You've all got extra training.'

Six boxers were eventually selected to represent South Korea at the Olympics at weights between light-flyweight and light-middle. Terry travelled to Munich with them during August. On arrival at the Olympic Village they found themselves housed in a block immediately opposite the Israeli delegation. This would become a matter of great significance within a couple of weeks.

The South Korean boxers did exceptionally well in the competition, winning a total of nine contests between them. All won their opening bouts, with Chong-Man You (flyweight) and Tai-Ho Kim (lightweight), who was beaten by the eventual silver medallist, both reaching the quarter-finals. Bantamweight, Saing-Keun Koh was eliminated in the third series. Terry was very satisfied by the success of the squad and thoroughly enjoyed his role as the national team coach.

Unfortunately the trip to Munich was marred by atrocities which occurred on 5 September. At about 4.30am, under the cover of darkness, five members of a Palestinian Terrorist Organisation calling itself 'Black September', climbed a wall into the Olympic

Village. Their faces blackened, they made their way to 21 Connolly Street and burst into the three storey building which the Israeli squad shared with athletes from Hong Kong and Uruguay. A few minutes later a 33 year old trainer of the Israeli wrestling team was fatally wounded by sub-machine gun fire as he attempted to raise the alarm. An Israeli weight-lifter was also shot dead, and nine other athletes and officials taken hostage.

The alarm was raised at 4.48am, and by 5.00am West German police swarmed all over the village, a complex of concrete buildings housing about 12,000 athletes and support staff. The area was sealed off and the gates of the village closed.

At about 6.00am, police marksmen wearing bullet-proof vests, moved into the village. Some were armed with sub-machine guns while others carried rifles fitted with telescopic sights. The riflemen climbed on to roofs overlooking the building in which the Arabs were holding their hostages.

Completely unaware of what was occurring, Spinks had got up early to take one of his boxers out for a run because he was slightly overweight for his quarter-final contest later that day. As they walked out into the street they were ordered back inside by German police. At first they had no idea why, but later received a telephone call from the village security centre explaining the position.

The authorities eventually got everybody out of the South Korean quarters by putting ladders up to the rear windows. They were taken to a huge gymnasium some distance from the location of the seige, while events unfolded.

Throughout the day the terrorists made a number of demands. They said that Israel had to free 200 Arab prisoners, and that Germany was to provide three aeroplanes to take them and their hostages to an unspecified country. The German Security Forces, however, stalled them through several ultimatum deadlines during the day. It was not until 10.15pm that there were any signs of movement. A minibus carrying the terrorists and some of their hostages, was driven to a helicopter which then took off for the airport.

The horrifying saga eventually ended in gun-fire and death in the darkened spaces of a NATO airfield outside Munich during the early hours of the following morning. When it was over three guerrilla's had been shot dead, another committed suicide by blowing himself up with a grenade, and a fifth was wounded, but escaped across the wide expanse of waste land surrounding the airfield.

The terrifying events in the Olympic Village, and particularly the deaths of the Israeli athletes, turned the rest of the Games into an anticlimax. Competitors and spectators alike were stunned, and memories were of all the wrong things. Although Terry remained in Munich to see the boxing finals, he never forgot how the atmosphere changed. 'Even after it was all over, there was a lot of tension,' he remarked. 'It was very sad because instead of achievements in the events, all people talked about were the shootings.'

Terry returned home in mid-September to be with Valerie and Jarvis for the first time since May. The trip to Korea had been an incredible experience and got him back into boxing in a big way. Sadly, it was over-shadowed by the events in Munich, and Spinks knew just how close he had been to the atrocities.

'That morning when we went out of our block to go for a run we were confronted by all these blokes in camouflage gear who ordered us back inside,' he recalled. 'We didn't know what was going on, but it was a bit scary once we were told. I keep thinking that if we had gone out a bit earlier we could have been taken hostage or even shot.'

Boxing had become increasing popular in South Korea, and from the mid-1970's onwards a number of professionals became world champions at the lower weights. Spinks could take satisfaction from the fact that he made a massive contribution to the amateur sport during his nine months there. This was confirmed in 1976 when a book entitled *'Boxing Guide for Coaches, Officials and Athletic Directors'* was published in Korea. Terry was so highly regarded that he was asked to write a foreword.

The book, which contained 390 pages, was written in the Korean language, but his foreword remained in English. Terry outlined the need for a firm understanding of training and revealed his observations from the time he spent in Seoul:

> ...No other sport can compare with boxing when it comes to attaining physical fitness and endurance. Boxers are capable of participating in numerous other sports, but non-boxing athletes such as marathon runners, footballers and baseball players do not have the stamina to box three rounds. Many have tried, but after two or three rounds of sparring, collapsed from sheer exhaustion...
>
> ...Being a newcomer to Seoul I have not had the opportunity to watch all of the Korean boxers, but those I have seen are all strong, courageous and full of fighting spirit. These essentials are all excellent qualities in developing into a first class boxer...
>
> ...This book offers a complete course of instruction for boxing hopefuls from the first day of training until they enter the ring as

experienced competitors. My congratulations to Mr Hyung-Ku Sohn, a former boxer, for doing such an excellent job of translating the basic principles and fundamentals of modern boxing. It has been a pleasure to add my comments on this well written book.

Terry Spinks

A signed copy of the book was sent to Terry by the author with whom he has always remained in contact. It serves as a reminder of good times spent in Korea.

* * *

The success of the South Korean team in Munich made Spinks one of the most sought-after coaches in amateur boxing. Before leaving Munich he met a delegation from Singapore who made him a really tempting offer to train their team for the world championships. He was invited to spend a year in Singapore, taking Valerie and Jarvis with him.

'The offer is very tempting,' said Terry when he returned to London, 'and I am going to give it very serious thought. There are a lot of things to iron out yet and it still has to be approved by the Singapore government.'

At the end of September, Terry took up his post with the West Ham Club and teamed up with Bob Galloway and Len Welham training the seniors. He also received offers from a number of other clubs in and around London. The South Koreans wanted him back again, and there was also an offer from Bermuda. After a great deal of thought, however, he rejected them all, including the offer from Singapore. 'It was a really great offer,' said Spinks, 'but after discussing matters I just couldn't afford to quit my job and take up a new post.'

After being home for a couple of months, he did join up with Bob Paget to coach a United States Air Force team. Soon after returning from Korea, Terry had resumed working with John Branch who gave him licence to almost come and go as he pleased. John knew he had to be fully occupied otherwise there was a danger that he would go astray. The US Air Force job was ideal for him.

Spinks and Paget had known each other well since Terry first turned professional and trained at the Thomas A' Beckett. It was Bob's local gym and he was always there with fighters. Apart from boxing they knew each other through Lonsdale Sports. Bob was a general manager with the company and toured the shops to ensure all was well. He frequently met Terry and Valerie while they were at the Brixton shop.

Bob was also a boxing instructor to United States Forces based in the United Kingdom, and each year ran a training camp to prepare novice boxers for a prestigious dinner show in Germany. In previous years he had been assisted by former top amateur Bruce Wells, but as he was no longer available Bob invited Spinks to assist him.

After attending a two day instructors course at RAF Heyford, Paget, Spinks and two other instructors flew to the US Forces Boxing Training School at Rhein Main Air Base in Germany. They were there for four days and stayed in a first-class hotel. Bob and Terry shared a room, and as both liked a drink the first thing they did was to open the mini-bar. The other two instructors were in the next room, but didn't drink. Spinks couldn't bear the thought of drink going to waste, so as soon as they left the room he removed bottles from their mini-bar and replaced them with his and Bob's empties. By the end of the week, however, there were real ructions because the others were given a bill for drinks they hadn't touched. All they drank was orange juice.

The boxing training took place at a gymnasium inside a huge aircraft hanger, and the squad was divided into four groups of eight boxers, each with one instructor. Most had never had a fight and Paget's team was there to teach them the basics. There was a break at the end of the first session, but when they resumed Bob found there were 16 lads in his group instead of eight. When he asked where the extra lads had come from he was told: 'Mr Spinks said we were to join you for this session because he has some business to attend to.'

For the rest of the day Bob had a double squad to look after. When he got back to the hotel that evening he found Terry lying on his bed. A girl was also in the room. 'Tel, what happened this afternoon?' asked Paget.

'They can't fight,' replied Spinks. 'I can't get no interest in people who can't fight.'

'But that's why we are here,' said Bob. 'We're being paid to teach them.'

When Bob asked who the girl was, Spinks replied, 'Oh, she's the piano player from the night club.'

Although Terry worked the following day, he took the girl along as well. Everyone in the camp was after her, but she was besotted with him. Paget eventually finished up with a double squad again because Terry was too busy entertaining the young lady.

CERTIFICATE of RECOGNITION

IS AWARDED TO

IN RECOGNITION OF

SUCCESSFULLY COMPLETING ALL REQUIREMENTS OF THE 1972 USAFE BOXING CLINIC

1-2 NOVEMBER

RHEIN MAIN AIR BASE, GERMANY

PETE DAVIS
TERENCE G. SPINKS
ROBERT PAGET
NOORIE HENDERSON

BUEFORD E. MOSS
DEPUTY CHIEF, SPORTS BRANCH

Certificate awarded to Terry Spinks by United States Air Forces in Europe

By the night of the boxing tournament, two contests were cancelled because boxers pulled out through injury. Spinks was therefore asked to box an exhibition with a US Services middleweight. Although he was happy to oblige, Paget knew Terry was well past his best and not very fit. He therefore advised him against it. He was concerned that as the American boxer would be performing in front of his fellow servicemen, he was likely to take liberties, even though it was only an exhibition. Instead Bob persuaded the organisers to allow him to box the exhibition with Terry.

They put on a good show, but at one stage to make everything look as though it was for real, Bob bundled Spinks into the ropes. As he lightly pummelled him to the body, Terry suddenly whispered, 'Ease up mate.'

'But I'm not hitting you,' replied Paget.

'No, you are laying on me you fat bastard,' retorted Spinks.

At the end of their three rounds Bob and Terry received a great ovation for their efforts. After the show both were presented with a trophy on behalf of the US Forces in Europe for the work they had done.

* * *

Spinks continued to enjoy the popularity he had when he was boxing, and regularly attended amateur club dinners and charity events. One of his favourite nights was the Annual Boxing Writers' Club dinner where he could mingle with past and present champions, old opponents and leading figures within the sport. He occasionally attended the London ex-Boxers Association meetings at Charlie Webster's pub, The Tollington Arms, Holloway, and in 1973 organised a darts match against a team from the Thomas A' Beckett.

The training assignments to the South Korean Olympic squad and the United States Forces in Germany had really motivated Terry and got him actively involved in the sport again. He was considered by many observers to be an excellent trainer when he set his mind to it. With his undoubted talent, it was such a waste that he had been away so long.

Although he spent a couple of evenings a week training youngsters at the West Ham Club, Spinks was still very much involved with Lonsdale. At night he often worked for John Branch and consequently found it more difficult to maintain his commitment to West Ham. After only a year with the club he therefore decided to stand down.

'I think it only fair if I step down for a while because I cannot devote enough time to the club at present,' Terry told a local newspaper reporter just before the 1973-74 season got underway. As a Life Vice-President of West Ham he went to the Black Lion every Sunday and remained in close contact with events at the club.

Terry's association with Lonsdale was very much as a figurehead. Apart from the shop at Beak Street, the company had others at Hammersmith, Brixton, Crystal Palace Sports Centre and Bangor. Valerie, who was a general manager and subsequently director of the company for a couple of years, ran the Brixton and Crystal Palace shops. Terry spent a great deal of time helping her deal with orders and often delivered some of the larger ones to customers in and around London.

One day Valerie received a large order from Wings musical group for fitness equipment, including a rowing machine, to be delivered to Abbey Road Studios at St Johns Wood. The items had to be collected from different shops within the company, but once everything was ready she told Terry to use her car and make the delivery.

Before he left, Valerie explained who the clients were and made particular mention of Paul McCartney. When Terry returned she asked him how he got on and who he delivered the goods to. Although he was a bit vague he produced an autograph of McCartney signed to their son Jarvis. Terry said that although everyone at the studio had recognised him, he didn't know them.

'You didn't recognise Paul McCartney?' said Valerie in amazement.

'No,' replied Spinks. 'Actually I feel a right idiot because I've been calling him John all afternoon. I wondered why they kept laughing at me.'

Working with Lonsdale kept Terry closely involved with boxing and eventually presented him with the opportunity to become a professional trainer. Dennie Mancini, an established manager with his own stable of fighters, ran the company's Beak Street shop. He came from a real boxing family – his uncle, Alf Mancini, having been a top fighter during the 1920's and 30's. After taking out a British Boxing Board of Control managers licence in 1959, one of the first boxers he handled was Johnny Mantle, the last man to fight Spinks.

During the latter part of 1973, Dennie asked Terry if he would train his fighters, and he readily agreed. 'I was really flattered,' he recalled. 'Dennie was a young manager and worked with all the right people so I thought we could do well.'

Shortly after agreeing to work with Mancini, Terry received a letter from the South Korean authorities asking if he would be prepared to train their international squad again. He had created a wonderful impression in that country, not only by his skill as a boxing trainer, but also as a person. He made many friends and was constantly invited back for holidays.

'I enjoyed my eight months stint in Seoul helping them prepare for the Munich Olympics,' Terry told Sydney Hulls of the *Daily Express*, 'but I can't spare the time to go back there at the moment. I am too busy here on my own manor.'

Spinks was granted a Board of Control trainer's licence and set up his training camp at the Thomas A' Beckett. One of the first boxers he took under his wing was Johnny Claydon, a 20 year old lightweight from West Ham who had just turned professional. They got on well and by the end of the year Claydon had won his first two contests.

The following year another West Ham boxer, 20 year old middleweight Alec Tompkins also joined the camp, followed by 19 year old Albert Hillman, a welterweight from Orpington. Established professional, Johnny Cheshire, and self-managed Liverpool heavyweight Billy Aird, also engaged Spinks to train them.

Terry's relationship with Cheshire was not an instant success because in his first contest with Spinks in his corner, Johnny was knocked out in three rounds by Alan Buchanan. The fight in Glasgow in March 1974 was for the vacant Scottish lightweight title, and shortly after his defeat there were rumours that Cheshire had retired. Spinks, however, convinced him he still had plenty to offer, and got him back into the gym.

Johnny was a porter at Covent Garden market which meant that he had to be up by 4.00am to fit in a run before going to work. Spinks then put him through a gruelling work-out at the Beckett each evening. The tactics worked, and within the space of 14 days in June, Johnny secured two victories. Noel McIvor was outpointed at Manor Place Baths in a 'nobbins' fight, and then Brian Jones was knocked out in four rounds at Port Talbot. It was sweet revenge over a man who had stopped him in two rounds just six months earlier.

Cheshire had always been regarded as a good prospect, but questions were raised as to whether he had left it too late. Spinks, however, was confident he could still make it. 'He should just be coming into his prime now,' he told *Boxing News*. 'He's taking it seriously at last and still has chances.'

Crediting Spinks with his change of attitude, Johnny said; 'Terry had the high life himself. He's been there and he has put me right. He has changed my whole approach to the game and made me realise that I was wasting my time before.'

The Board of Control clearly agreed with Terry's assessment, as in September they announced that Cheshire would meet Jim Watt for the vacant British lightweight title. Following a series of delays the fight eventually took place on 27 January 1975 at the St Andrews Sporting Club in Glasgow. Despite a brave performance, Cheshire was stopped with just five seconds remaining of the seventh round.

Ironically, referee Wally Thom's intervention came after Johnny had enjoyed one of his best spells of the fight. Although he had looked well beaten in the previous round after taking two long counts, he had fought back well. When he took two solid jabs to the face, the referee called a halt much to the displeasure of Spinks in the corner. He jumped into the ring angrily protesting that it was premature and unjustified.

Spinks had got Johnny into the best shape of his life, and whilst the beaten boxer took the referee's decision with good grace, Terry would not relent. 'What has the game become?' he demanded furiously of Board of Control secretary, Ray Clarke, in the dressing room later. 'Is it a game for pansies now, where we stop a fight just because a man is taking a couple of lefts to the face?'

Although there was no victory celebration, Terry had a few drinks with his good friend Dick McTaggart and old opponents Billy Rafferty and Derry Treanor who had been at the fight. They had waited behind to see him, so it was a good reunion before he returned to London the following morning.

Meanwhile, the careers of Claydon, Tompkins and Hillman were progressing well. By the end of 1975, Claydon had lost just three of his 12 contests, Tompkins four from 15, and Hillman looked the brightest prospect with a draw being the only blot on his 11 fight record.

In May that year, former British and European bantamweight champion Johnny Clark, joined Dennie Mancini's stable as a trainer. The plan was for him to bring in and develop young boxers of his own rather than take over any of Spinks' work. Terry was the established trainer developing the boxers under strict supervision and training schedules.

Johnny Claydon, a stocky, bustling box-fighter was closer to Spinks than anyone else in the camp. Their association had been built at the West Ham club where Johnny won an NABC championship in 1972. He went on to win 38 consecutive senior contests before losing a disputed decision in the 1973 London ABA semi-finals. He was originally coached by Terry's old trainer Billy Walker, but when he emigrated to Australia, Spinks took over. 'My success as a senior was due largely to Terry,' insisted Claydon. 'He was a brilliant trainer and very similar in style to Billy Walker.'

One of a family of seven, Johnny had been a bit of a tearaway as a youngster and was made to take up boxing at the age of nine to keep him out of trouble. 'I was a right little terror,' he recalled openly. 'Being brought up in the back streets of Canning Town, I was always getting into scraps. It was part of life.'

Having come from the same tough environment, Spinks knew how to handle Johnny, and a close understanding developed between them. Angry at not progressing beyond the London ABA championships, Johnny decided to turn professional. Although he had offers from other managers, including Terry Lawless who had his camp at the nearby Royal Oak at Canning Town, Spinks suggested he went with Dennie Mancini. They had a meeting at The Lord Palmerston, the Mancini's family pub, and a week later Johnny signed a professional contract with Dennie. The move coincided with Terry taking out a trainer's licence, and Johnny became the first professional boxer he coached.

Johnny's father was delighted with the situation because he had long been an admirer of Spinks. He told his son of the time they got on a bus at Canning Town one day when Johnny was about three years old. Spinks, who lived only a minute away from them, had just returned home with the gold medal, sat opposite them. He smiled as Johnny fidgeted on his father's lap, then held out his arms and said, 'Give us him here.' The youngster was comfortable despite being on the lap of a stranger, and in years to come he was just as comfortable as he put his faith in the former Olympic champion to guide him during his ring career.

Claydon progressed well under Terry's guidance, and in October 1976 won the Southern Area lightweight title by beating Tommy Dunn of Reading over 12 rounds. A month earlier they had boxed a draw over the same distance, a decision which Spinks and Claydon vigorously disputed.

Johnny was an exciting all-action fighter, and in June that year beat Jim Watt on a cut eye stoppage after three rounds at Wembley. Earlier in the year he had two rousing battles with Johnny Wall of Merthyr, winning both over 10 rounds. They were 'nobbins' fights, as was the draw with Tommy Dunn.

The following year, Johnny was ranked number two in Britain and challenged Jim Watt for the lightweight title at Glasgow in

February. He put up a game display, but was stopped in the 10th round. In October he returned to winning ways by outpointing Tommy Dunn in defence of his Southern Area title at the Cunard Hotel, Hammersmith. It was a great performance because only after the fight did Spinks reveal that Johnny had injured his back in training. 'He got hit in the kidneys accidentally during sparring,' Terry told *Boxing News*,' and that meant the sparring sessions had to be cut short.'

In February 1978, Claydon again fought for the British lightweight title, but was stopped in 12 rounds by Charlie Nash in Derry. The ending was controversial because under a scoring system in use at the time, Johnny was too far behind to win on points.

Claydon was always appreciative of Terry's style of training and discipline. 'He tightened me up,' he said. 'He made me keep my hands high, and bob and weave my way in.'

They also shared some amusing moments, not least in September 1974 when they were travelling to Solihull in Terry's car. When they reached Birmingham he remembered that they needed to get some bandages for Johnny's hands, so he parked the car and went to a Boots store. As Terry stood at the counter, the female assistant looked at him and said, 'Excuse me, but I know who you are.' As he was about to tell her, she said, 'No, don't tell me because it's on the tip of my tongue.'

Spinks was very proud and stood upright as he smiled at her, but became utterly deflated when she suddenly said, 'I know, you're Charlie Drake.' Claydon burst out laughing and the poor girl couldn't understand what she had said wrong. Terry told her who he was, signed an autograph, but was never allowed to forget it. Back at the Thomas A' Beckett he soon became known as 'Charlie'.

While Claydon was an amateur, Spinks accompanied him and a team of boxers to Wrexham for a match. As they were about to board the train home to London, Johnny saw a strikingly attractive lady struggling with a large suitcase. He was about to help her on to the train with it when Terry pushed him aside. 'Leave it John, I'll do that,' he insisted. He carried the suitcase on to the train and sat next to the woman for the duration of the journey to London. She was a smart, high class lady from South Kensington, and was overwhelmed by Terry's charms.

That night several members of the party, including Spinks and his new friend, ended up at The Angel pub at Stratford. After a long drinking session they stayed at a nearby flat where they remained until awoken by the occupiers next morning.

'There are so many stories about Terry because he attracted so many people around him,' recalled Claydon. 'Even fighters went up to him, many of them old fighters, because of what he achieved in the Olympics. He became an instant celebrity, and it stuck.'

Albert Hillman, a stylish upright boxer, also progressed to a British title fight. He had been a good prospect since turning professional, and in *Boxing News* of 3 January 1975, was listed in the ten boxers to watch during the year. He was described as '...a useful looking welterweight who is learning fast under the guidance of trainer Terry Spinks.'

On 1 February 1977 Hillman put up a brave display before his corner retired him after seven rounds against Jimmy Batten for the British light-middleweight title. The previous year he had won the vacant Southern Area light-middleweight title by outpointing Mickey Ryce over 10 rounds at Manor Place Baths. He successfully defended the title at the same venue in November, forcing Tony Poole to retire after seven. In May 1977, he lost on points to Tony Hudson for the vacant Southern Area title, and although he boxed infrequently until 1980, achieved nothing further.

Alec Tompkins was the most aggressive boxer Terry trained. He was also the busiest, taking part in 39 contests in a nine year career. He reached his peak in 1977 with a shock defeat of the talented Billy Knight whom he stopped in four rounds at the Royal Albert Hall. At the same venue three weeks later he won the Southern Area middleweight title by knocking out Peter Cain in the first round. That, however, was his peak because the aggressive Frankie Lucas stopped him in six and then Jan Magdziarz beat him in five rounds to take his Southern Area title.

One of the gamest boxers Spinks trained was Dave Smith from Eltham. He made his professional debut in November 1976, and after seven victories and a draw, faced Charlie Magri for the vacant British flyweight title at the Royal Albert Hall on 6 December the following year. Despite being floored five times, Dave boxed competently, intelligently and bravely, but simply lacked the power to keep Magri at bay. When the fight was stopped in the seventh round, Smith just shrugged his shoulders and smiled ruefully. Magri, another fighter from the East End, was a bit special and had been admired by Terry Spinks since he won Junior ABA Championships in 1972 and 1973.

In his next fight, in April 1978, Smith was outpointed by Gary Davidson at the Royal Albert Hall for the vacant Southern Area bantamweight title. On 21 November the same year, at Wembley Conference Centre, Dave got revenge by beating Davidson who retired after six rounds with bad cuts to his left eye.

Knowing that his title was slipping away, Gary launched a tremendous attack in the sixth and had Smith unsteady on a number of occasions. Dave, however, was extremely fit and had plenty of heart. He dug deep and hit back with heavy shots of his own in what *Boxing News* described as one of the most exciting rounds of the year.

The contest was also a final eliminator for the British bantamweight title. The following year Smith faced Johnny Owen at Caerphilly, but was forced to retire after 12 rounds in a fight which was also for the Commonwealth title. Two years later Smith again challenged unsuccessfully for the British title, being stopped in eight rounds by John Feeney at York Hall, Bethnal Green. When he retired from the ring in 1981 he had the credible record of 16 wins and a draw from 23 fights.

Other boxers Spinks trained included Harrow bantamweight Wally Angliss, Paul Davis, a good welterweight from Stepney, Dave Cammiss of Eltham, and Billy Williams from Barking who started his career as a light-heavyweight in Miami.

Angliss was another entertaining, all-action fighter. He had 21 contests during his three year career, including three tremendous battles with Gary Davidson. His losing fight at York Hall in March 1977 was a cracker which had 'nobbins' flying in from all sides of the ring.

All the boxers Spinks trained went into their fights extremely fit. During their daily training schedules each man did four or five rounds of shadow boxing, bag work, ground work, skipping and sparring. Terry knew all the dodges and this made him a better trainer. He didn't allow anyone to slack or become indisciplined as he had been during his fighting days. Johnny Claydon rated him alongside Billy Walker, whom experts considered to be amongst the best, certainly in the amateur sport. The fact that a number of boxers reached British championship level was testimony of his ability.

Apart from training the boxers most days of the week, Terry still did the mini-cabbing, and at night worked for John Branch to earn extra money. He also involved himself in many events for charity and was always prepared to travel all over the country at short notice.

In February 1977 he assisted in raising money for Leroy Herriott, a former middleweight boxer from Tredegar, who had become paralysed following a car accident. In two years as a professional he had won seven contests and lost eight. One of his defeats was a fifth round stoppage in May 1976 to Alec Tompkins who was trained by Spinks.

At a promotion at Manor Place Baths, Dennie Mancini made an appeal from the ring. A team of boxers including Spinks, Alan Minter, Bobby Neill, Chris Finnegan and Billy Aird made a collection which realised more than £500. A number of other events were organised in different parts of the country and, subject to commitments, Terry was always willing to attend.

In July the same year, Muhammad Ali made a four day visit to Tyneside aimed at raising £70,000 for Tyne and Wear boys clubs. An incredible amount of effort went into making it an event to remember. Invitations were sent to some of the biggest names in British boxing to join Ali on a Parade of Champions. Terry Spinks was one of them.

The parade was held in the Mayfair Ballroom at Newcastle and attracted a huge crowd despite the high cost of tickets. There was a seven-course banquet, and cabaret starring Frankie Vaughan. Spinks was accompanied by two of the boxers he trained – Johnny Claydon and Albert Hillman. Also in the star-studded parade were Bobby Neill, Chris and Kevin Finnegan, Richard Dunn, Dave 'Boy' Green, Alan Rudkin, Terry Downes, John Conteh, Vic Andreetti, Vernon Sollas, Andy Smith and Danny Holland.

The London based boxers met at the Thomas A' Beckett, and were taken by coach to Heathrow for their flight to Newcastle. For the duration of the event they stayed at the Holiday Inn as guests of the organisers.

During the evening Ali and his entourage sat at a massive table on the stage. He delighted his audience with his usual act of shadow boxing and dancing entwined with screams of 'I am the greatest.' At one point he jumped from the stage and walked amongst the diners. Suddenly he stopped, pointed at Johnny Claydon, and invited him up to spar with him. Before John could react, Spinks stood up and said, 'Hold on, I'm his trainer, I look after him.' Ali was momentarily taken aback, but then smiled broadly before throwing a playful jab at Terry. The two men then fell into a warm embrace.

The following day the boxers joined Ali on a ride to South Shields aboard an open-top bus. Cheering crowds lined streets all along the route and were greater than two weeks earlier when the Queen and United States President, Jimmy Carter, visited the city. After a civic reception at the Town Hall, the party returned to Newcastle for the Muhammad Ali Talk-In hosted by Reg Gutteridge.

That evening the boxers attended an event at the Washington Sports Centre. More than 1,500 turned up to see Ali box a series of exhibition bouts in aid of charity. Supporting bouts included

MUHAMMAD ALI

ROUND 1
All Star Exhibition Boxing at
The Washington Sports Centre
on Saturday July 16th at 7.30 pm

Exhibition contests include
Alan Minter v Albert Hillman
Terry Spinks v Bobby Neil
Howard Winstone v Alan Rudkin
Kevin Finnegan v Chris Finnegan
Dave "Boy" Green To be announced

Also present
Ex World Light Heavy weight Champion
John Conteh
ALL TICKETS £5
Proceeds in aid of N.A.B.C. Boys Clubs on Tyne and Wear.
Tickets available at Dixon Sports, Grainger St, Newcastle. Sunderland F.C. Ticket Office, Roker Park. Rippans Sports, Charlotte Terr, South Shields, Washington Post House Hotel. Joseph Sports, Sunderland, Nairn Travel, The Galleries, Washington, J & J Stanley, Longrigg Road Swalwell.

ROUND 2
at the

MAYFAIR BALLROOM
Newgate Street, Newcastle on
Friday July 15th at 6.45 pm

Parade of Champions with

Frankie Vaughan
plus Supporting Acts

TICKETS £50 AND £30
available from The Mayfair

Proceeds in aid of N.A.B.C. Boys Clubs on Tyne and Wear

Poster advertising Muhammad Ali's visit to Tyneside. Terry Spinks and Bobby Neill featured in an exhibition bout.

exhibitions between Terry Spinks and Bobby Neill, Johnny Claydon v Vic Andreetti, and Kevin Finnegan v Albert Hillman.

Whilst the tour was quite demanding it was not without moments of amusement. Terry was accompanied by Valerie and Jarvis who joined in the activities including the open-top bus ride. At one stage each member of the group had a photograph taken with Ali, including Jarvis who was dressed in a Hawaiian shirt, mohair jumper, pink sandals, and had a mod style wedge haircut. 'Who is this young lady?' asked Ali as Jarvis stepped forward to pose.

The night before they were due to return home, the London based party had a good drink-up in their hotel bar. In the early hours of the morning Spinks fell asleep in an armchair. When he awoke at about 5.00am he found himself covered in make-up.

Spinks and his colleagues returned to London on the Sunday morning. Muhammad Ali, who was accompanied on the trip by his wife Veronica and their baby daughter Hanna, attended a mosque at South Shields to have their recent marriage blessed at a special muslim ceremony.

The Newcastle trip was a massive event, but whenever there was a special boxing function Terry was generally invited. No matter what the size, he was usually very much the centre of attention.

In 1975, together with Mark Rowe, John H Stracey, Alan Minter and a host of other boxing personalities, Spinks attended the opening of Danny Peacock's new gym above The Rose & Crown public house at Morden. He continued to be a regular guest at the annual Boxing Writers' Club dinner, and was present at the last promotions at the nostalgic Shoreditch Town Hall and Manor Place Baths.

Distance was no object to Terry, and among the well-publicised charity events he attended was a Variety Club of Great Britain – Liverpool Committee Night of Champions Dinner on Merseyside on 10 October 1973. He boxed an exhibition with former Northern Area bantamweight champion Gus Foran.

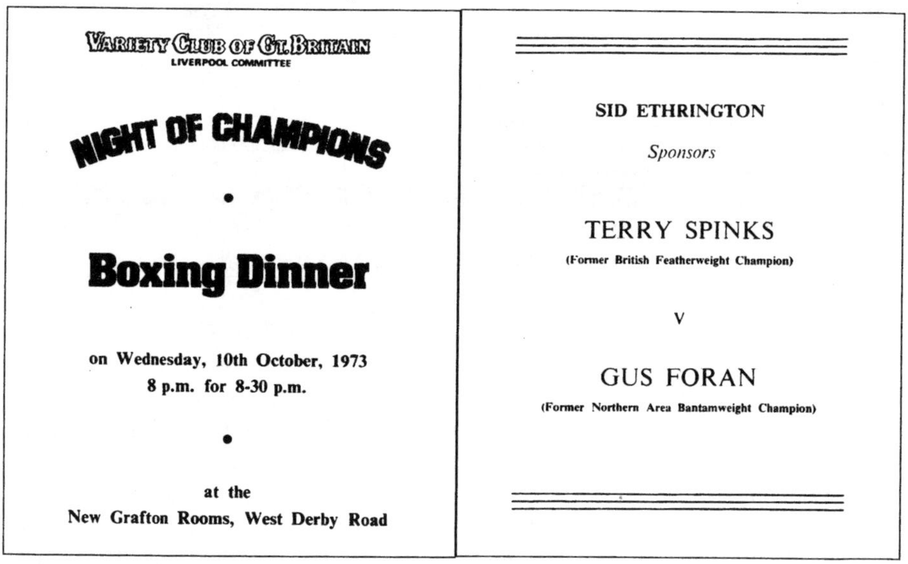
VARIETY CLUB OF GT. BRITAIN
LIVERPOOL COMMITTEE

NIGHT OF CHAMPIONS

•

Boxing Dinner

on Wednesday, 10th October, 1973
8 p.m. for 8-30 p.m.

•

at the
New Grafton Rooms, West Derby Road

SID ETHRINGTON
Sponsors

TERRY SPINKS
(Former British Featherweight Champion)

v

GUS FORAN
(Former Northern Area Bantamweight Champion)

In March 1977 he was a guest of the promoters at Liverpool Stadium the night that John Conteh successfully defended his world light-heavyweight title against Len Hutchins of America. On the same bill Leon Spinks of the United States faced Peter Freeman of Bolton at heavyweight, in only his second professional contest.

Leon had won a gold medal at light-heavyweight in the Montreal Olympics the previous year. He was accompanied by his brother Michael who won gold at middleweight and was due to turn professional the following month.

During the evening Terry was introduced to the two Americans, both of whom would go on to become professional world champions. They discussed their Olympic successes of 20 years apart and were photographed together. Some years later a picture of the trio was displayed in the saloon bar of The Queen Victoria pub in the East End. It bore the caption – '*The Spinks Brothers.*'

Terry's popularity was not just confined to the United Kingdom. On 14 April 1976, he boxed an exhibition in Helsinki with former European lightweight champion Elis Ask who, 10 days earlier, had celebrated his 50th birthday.

Ask, who took part in more than 50 professional contests, had boxed in London on five occasions during the late 1940's. An extremely popular man in Finland, he was matchmaker for a professional show comprising of four contests, one of which featured Trevor Francis from Basingstoke. To the delight of the packed house, Ask and Spinks boxed six, two minute rounds and showed they still possessed many of their former skills.

Although Spinks was incredibly well known, cases of mistaken identity sometimes occurred. During the summer of 1975, one of his old sparring partners, Terry Rees, took his family on holiday to Portugal. Shortly after arriving at their hotel, a man walked up to Rees and said, 'Hello Terry, I haven't seen you for a long time.' Rees, a former Welsh featherweight champion, had no idea who the man was, but went along with the conversation. 'I saw your fight with Winstone,' continued the stranger. 'Pity you got beat.'

Terry had in fact lost to Winstone in 1960 on a stoppage in the eighth round, and from the way the stranger talked, felt he should know him. Yet he was convinced he had never seen him before.

A few days later, Rees bumped into the man again. 'I saw your fight with Con Mount Bassie which you skated,' he remarked. 'You were good that night.'

The former Welsh champion became even more puzzled because although he had boxed Mount Bassie in August 1960, it was on a small hall show at Torquay. In only his third professional fight, Terry had won on points over six rounds, but was badly marked up at the end. He concluded that the stranger was an avid boxing fan so he continued to humour him and engage in brief conversation.

The situation eventually became clear when a number of other holiday makers approached Rees for autographs. In the conversations which followed it became clear that they thought he was Terry Spinks. There were in fact similarities between them because like the former Olympic champion, Rees had a round chubby face with a prominent flat boxers nose. He was about the same height and had a London accent having lived at Catford for many years.

Nevertheless, he was in something of a quandary, but decided the easiest thing to do was sign autographs in the name of Spinks. Having done so he was on edge for the remainder of his holiday and couldn't wait to get away from the hotel. As soon as he got home Terry telephoned Spinks and told him what he had done. 'That's alright with me,' replied Spinks, 'As long as you didn't sign any cheques in my name.'

Despite the passing of time, Terry's popularity never diminished one iota. In 1979, *Boxing News* ran a competition inviting readers to rank their best ABA champion of the past 25 years. Spinks polled the greater number of votes in the flyweight division ahead of Walter McGowan and Charlie Magri.

Sadly, the demand for his services heaped tremendous strain upon Terry's marriage because his lifestyle was not conducive to maintain a solid relationship. For a number of years he had done almost as he liked socially with the inevitable consequence that he and Valerie grew apart. There had been doubts almost from the start because they were different people from contrasting backgrounds. Valerie, a former grammar school girl, admitted years later that she knew on her wedding night she had made a mistake by marrying Terry. After leading virtually separate lives for some while the inevitable break-up occurred in 1978. Their Degree Absolute was granted on 10 April 1980.

Terry moved out of their flat at Dulwich and went back to his parents at Cumberland Road. Jarvis, who was 16 at the time, felt extremely sad and lonely as he watched his father leave with his belongings in a suitcase. Although he saw him once a week when he visited his grandparents, it was not the same as having him at home.

13

CAREER CHANGE

The success and satisfaction Terry gained from training boxers made him want to become a manager. During 1976, he contacted the Board of Control with a view to applying for a manager's licence, but was told it would not be granted. He was still an undischarged bankrupt, and as a manager handles the financial affairs of his boxers, it was a natural and justifiable rejection.

On 14 July that year, Spinks went to the London Bankruptcy Court at Queens Buildings, Royal Courts of Justice in The Strand, and made application before Mr Registrar Parbury for discharge from the Bankruptcy Order imposed during 1964. The court was told that his debts, mostly to the Inland Revenue, had risen to an estimated £5,087 against assets of £432. The increase was due largely to accrued interest on the original debt which had never been paid.

'This, in my view, is a bad case of tax evasion and extravagance,' said the Assistant Official Receiver. 'He squandered the money in all directions, spent £1,500 on his wedding and incurred gambling losses of £15,000.' The court was told that although Spinks wanted his discharge from bankruptcy, he had made no effort to pay his creditors in the 12 years since the Order was made.

Addressing the court, Terry said he wanted his freedom so that he could apply for a boxing manager's licence. He explained that he worked for a sports equipment company of which his wife was a Director. Between them they earned about £74 a week. He said he was unable to support his family on his own, and his wife was not prepared to pay off his debts.

'It looks to me as though the bankruptcy is beginning to bite now,' remarked the Registrar. 'Mr Spinks has been able to live with help from his wife. He now thinks he would like to become a boxing manager and he needs a licence, but to get a licence he has to have his discharge.'

'A bankruptcy discharge is a privilege,' continued Mr Registrar Parbury. 'I am not prepared to grant this discharge unless a monetary proposal is made.'

In answer to questions from the Registrar, Spinks said he would have to talk to his wife before he could commit himself to paying anything. His application was then adjourned for three months to enable him to consider making an offer for the benefit of his creditors.

The matter came before the court again on 29 October 1976. By this time Terry had provided the Official Receiver with an amended schedule of income and expenditure, and submitted an offer to pay £2 per week for two years.

In passing judgement, the Registrar said that the court took into consideration Spinks' conduct and affairs, including his conduct during the proceedings under his bankruptcy. After hearing from Mr T G White, Assistant Official Receiver, and Mr G Lazarus, Solicitor for Spinks, the application for discharge was refused. The decision was advertised in the *London Gazette* dated 11 January 1977.

* * *

By the end of the 1970's Terry had lost his appetite for training boxers. Since becoming divorced from Valerie, he badly wanted a change of environment and set his heart on running a pub. Knowing he would require an amount of security behind him he therefore often worked 10 or 12 hours a day to build up his capital.

'I've been thinking about taking a pub for sometime,' he told John Branch. 'I don't mind how hard I work because all I want to do is get a bit of money together.'

The new venture, however, proved far more difficult than Terry had anticipated, and his applications to three breweries were rejected. Apart from the fact that he had no previous experience in the pub trade, some sceptics thought that breweries were reluctant to take him on because he had been photographed with the Kray twins.

Determined not to give up hope, Terry decided he needed to get experience of the licensing trade. He was helped considerably by Teddy White, licensee of The Golden Lion, Barking Road, who was a great friend of Tich. He taught Terry the basics of cellar work, bottling-up and how to clean the pumps. He learned quickly and when Teddy went on holiday the former boxer was left to run the pub.

Terry also worked part-time, or as required, at The Rose & Crown, Hoe Street, Walthamstow. There he learned about catering as well as gaining further experience of bar work.

By this time he had formed a close relationship with divorcee, Barbara Suter. They lived with Terry's parents at Cumberland Road, and she fully supported his ambition to take a pub.

As it was a general policy of breweries only to employ married couples to manage public houses, Terry and Barbara considered their position. Without saying a word to Tich and Doris, they were married at Worthing Registry Office on 28 January 1981. Although his parents were furious when Terry eventually told them, it proved to be a sensible decision.

Later that year, Romford Breweries offered them The Crown at Upchurch, a village near Rainham in Kent. John Branch gave Terry a reference, and after attending a five day course in London covering all aspects of running a pub, he and Barbara took up residence on 21 September 1981.

Coach loads of Terry's friends travelled from London for the grand opening. A number of former boxing champions were in attendance including Alan Minter, Terry Downes, Gary Davidson, Jimmy Revie, Johnny Claydon and five-times ABA champion Terry Waller. The village kids were thrilled, and dozens laid siege to the pub seeking autographs.

Situated close to the estuary of the River Medway, east of Chatham and Gillingham, the pub was very run down. A lot of money therefore needed to be spent on it, but to the delight of local people, Terry and Barbara were determined to make it a success.

By this time, the restraints of Terry's Bankruptcy Order were behind them and they successfully applied for a £29,000 bank loan. Within a few weeks the pub was closed for renovation. It was ripped apart, and three bars were converted into one, black beams attached to the ceiling and walls, and new carpets fitted throughout. New furniture graced the bar, and new ovens were installed in the kitchen. The initials of Terry and his wife were even engraved into the wood of the bar. After being closed for more than two months, The Crown became a cosy family pub with a garden.

Despite everything that had been done, there were still some concerns. Being situated next to a graveyard, locals claimed that the pub was haunted. There were bulges in the cellar walls said to have been caused by the movement of coffins as a result of the tidal

River Medway. Other strange things occurred, including the movement of barrels in the cellar and the flickering of lights. Spinks found the situation very spooky and eventually called in a local vicar to perform an exorcism.

Terry was very much at home running the pub and loved being 'mine host'. He became extremely popular with local people and was soon in demand for personal appearances, in particular presenting trophies at boxing clubs throughout Kent.

He attended many charity events including rugby matches and sponsored walks. Within a few weeks of taking over the pub he and Barbara were guests at a function aboard HMS Pembroke at Chatham which raised £600 for charity. As landlord of The Crown, Spinks sponsored the first ever car to run on liquid petroleum gas and compete a world championship event – the Lombard RAC Rally.

In November 1983, Terry and Barbara became the proud parents of a baby daughter, Claire Marie. She was born at All Saints Hospital, Chatham and weighed-in at 8lb. At the time they had two dogs, a Pointer and an Old English Sheepdog named Ben. If the baby woke up during the night and Terry or Barbara didn't hear her, Ben would go to their bedroom and tug at an arm.

Not long after they took over The Crown, Ben began putting on weight and eventually scaled eight stone. The problem was that he loved crisps, so Terry put him on a crisp-free diet and hung a notice around his neck saying 'DON'T FEED ME'. Although the customers relented from giving him the odd morsel, the dog was no fool. When left alone, he frequently sneaked behind the bar and nosed into the crisp boxes. Quite often he removed a bag, tore it open and devoured the contents.

Regulars at the pub found it amusing, particularly when the story appeared in a local paper with a picture of Terry and Ben. 'I suppose he's a bit like I used to be,' remarked Spinks. 'When I was boxing I always had weight problems because I ate all the wrong things.'

Local reporters loved Spinks because, apart from him still being a household name, he was always very receptive towards them. Since he took over The Crown they watched him like vultures. Whatever he did, they reported it and generally illustrated their articles with photographs.

Terry and Barbara remained at The Crown until 1987 when they became tenants of The Coach & Horses at Worthing. A country pub set back off the busy Arundel Road, it was a much bigger establishment with a restaurant. Terry was as popular there as he had been at Upchurch. While he ran the bar, Barbara dealt with the catering and they soon built up a good business.

Not long after they took over The Coach & Horses, a group of local self-styled hard boys started visiting the pub and causing trouble. Whenever customers complained, however, Terry just told them to ignore it. They even tried taunting Spinks with comments like; 'Call yourself a gold medallist, you're nothing.' Terry was too laid back to react to their childish jibes so they usually gave up and went away.

One day, however, two members of the group walked into the bar and started upsetting the customers. When Spinks spoke to them, they subjected him to a torrent of abuse. 'Out the back now,' snapped the former fighter moving purposefully from behind the bar. As one of the yobs was considerably bigger than Terry, a couple of his regular customers offered to go with him. 'It's alright, I can handle this,' he remarked insisting that they remained in the bar.

The smirking nuisances fancied their chances, two against one, but were in for a shock. Within a few seconds a loud crashing noise was heard from the back of the pub as Terry put the yobs in their place with a short sharp dose of old-fashioned punishment.

The mouthier of the two tried to escape by the back entrance to save face, but Spinks was having none of it. 'You're leaving by the way you came in,' he snapped dragging the individual by his collar, with his mate close behind. They were made to go through the main bar to show them up for what they were – bullies.

Terry wouldn't tolerate bullying, and didn't care how big an offender was. He dealt with the situation effectively, and none of the group ever returned to the pub.

After only three years at The Coach & Horses, Terry and Barbara experienced difficulties with their marriage. Despite this they went to Melbourne for a three week holiday, which for Terry was a trip down memory lane. He visited the Olympic Stadium where his name was still displayed, and was interviewed on Australian television.

Although more than 30 years had elapsed since his gold medal success, he was recognised wherever he went. He was shown around the Olympic Village and taken to the house where he and the British boxing team stayed. He met the family who lived there, and was treated like royalty.

While Terry and Barbara were away, Barry Noonan, a close friend of Spinks, ran the pub. He had idolised Terry since he was a lad of 15 with St Augustine's Boxing Club at Fulham. 'The greatest moment of my life was when he presented me with a prize,' recalled Barry. 'Everyone wanted to meet Terry.'

About two months after they returned from Australia, Terry and Barbara split up. Although he continued to run The Coach & Horses, Spinks relied heavily on Barry and a group of close friends for support. Without them the pub would have ground to a halt and the brewery would have taken it from him.

The breakdown of the marriage hit Terry badly, in particular losing his daughter Claire who was only seven. He drank heavily, smoked about 60 cigarettes a day and didn't eat properly. As a result his health deteriorated rapidly. It was the start of the most difficult period of his life because shortly after he and Barbara broke up, his mother became ill with Alzheimer's disease.

Terry loved Doris dearly, and as a young amateur boxer had bought her a gold charm in every country he visited. She wore them on a bracelet throughout her life. Although Tich often took her to The Coach & Horses for a day out, she didn't recognise her son. He was extremely distressed at seeing her in such a condition, and as his depression deepened, so he drank more. People close to him knew that he had often consumed a bottle of scotch by mid-day.

As the months passed by, drink controlled Terry's life. It became his only comfort, but at a price. One Saturday night after a heavy session in the bar of The Coach & Horses, he fell down the cellar steps, hit his head and knocked himself out. By the time someone reached him he was lying in a pool of blood which was pouring from a cut to his neck. An ambulance was called and he was taken to Worthing hospital where he was detained overnight.

The following morning Spinks telephoned Barry Noonan and asked to be collected from the hospital as he had discharged himself. Barry was horrified when he saw him. Wearing a neck-brace, his eyes were bruised and swollen, and he looked in a worse condition than after any of his battles in the ring. Although he had been advised to have an operation, Terry was determined to leave the hospital. All he wanted to do was get back to the pub for a drink.

That morning a group of ex-boxers from London were due to visit The Coach & Horses. Despite his condition, Terry was determined to entertain them. After arriving back at the pub at around 10.00am, Barry helped him get dressed, prepare the bar and provide a buffet lunch.

Most of the boxers knew Spinks from his days at the Thomas A' Beckett. They included former world middleweight champion Alan

Minter who was a particularly close friend. Together with their wives, they had spent a number of holidays abroad together over the years, as well as socialising nearer to home.

'What's up with you?' asked Minter when he saw the state of Terry's face.

'He beat me up,' replied Spinks pointing at Barry with a deadpan expression.

For a few seconds the visitors thought Terry was serious. They stared angrily at Barry who later admitted he had never been so frightened in his life. He knew how much they all adored Spinks, and thought he was about to get a hiding. Then with a broad grin Terry said: 'I fell down the cellar – I think I must have been pissed.'

During the Spring of 1991, Terry received an invitation from the BBC to be a guest on a *'This is Your Life'* programme for sports commentator, Harry Carpenter. As this was during the period when he was drinking heavily, it was essential that he stayed sober to avoid making a fool of himself.

One of his regular customers at The Coach & Horses was an East End policeman who had a house at Worthing. On the morning of the recording, he took Terry to Arundel and bought him lunch before taking him back to the pub at about 2.00pm. Barry Noonan then took over whilst they awaited a chauffeur-driven car sent by the BBC. He then accompanied Spinks to the London Studios where they met up with Chris Finnegan. When the guests were called to the make-up department, Barry asked Chris if he would continue to mind Terry as he had not touched a drink all day.

Barry didn't see him again until he walked on to the stage. Straight away he knew Terry had been drinking. Fortunately he was amongst a group of former boxers consisting of Dick McTaggart, Terry Downes, Howard Winstone, John Conteh, Alan Minter, Charlie Magri, Lloyd Honeygan and Finnegan. All had won Olympic gold medals or world professional championships, and down the years Harry had written about them or commentated on their fights.

After the show the BBC put on a free bar, so Spinks and most of the others had a good drink. Later, as they left the studio, Terry stopped and spoke to Frank Bruno who had been the principal guest. Spinks was expecting a car to take him home and when he saw a chauffeur standing beside a vehicle, decided it must be for him. The driver, however, said he was waiting for Bruno. 'I am Frank Bruno,' retorted Spinks as he jumped into the back of the car, pulling Barry in with him.

After a brief protest the driver relented. 'Where would you like to go sir?' he asked nervously.

'Worthing,' replied Spinks.

By the time they reached Box Hill on the A3 near Dorking, Terry urgently needed to visit a toilet. They came across an isolated pub in the country and told the driver to pull in. As Terry dashed into the bar in search of the toilet, the landlord called out, 'Terry Spinks – do you remember me?'

'Of course I do,' shouted Spinks, 'I'll have a scotch.'

It transpired that Terry and the landlord knew each other some years previously in London. They sat in the bar reminiscing until well after closing time whilst the poor chauffeur sat outside in the car. Nobody thought to invite him in. It was 1.00am before Terry decided it was time to head for Worthing. On arriving home he apologised to the driver and rewarded him for his patience.

* * *

On 26 June 1991, Terry drove to London to see his mother who by then was a patient at Goodmayes hospital. He collected Tich from Cumberland Road, and after the visit took him home again before returning to Worthing.

While Terry was away, Barry looked after the pub, but had some terrible news for him when he returned. Since leaving the hospital his mother had passed away, so he had to return to Cumberland Road to be with Tich. Having driven all the way to London and back, and then being told the news, Spinks was in no condition to drive again. Being the true friend he was, Barry took him.

The funeral service took place at Plaistow Memorial Baptist Church, Barking Road, the following week. There was then a procession to East London Crematorium, Canning Town where Doris was laid to rest in the family grave. Afterwards, family and friends gathered for a wake at West Ham Conservative Club situated beside the church.

Unable to control his emotions and loneliness, Terry was drunk throughout the proceedings. His mother's death was another devastating blow which caused him to drink even more, as he tried to shut out his sadness.

The Coach & Horses only continued to operate because of the support Spinks received from friends like Barry Noonan. As his drinking got heavier, so Terry spent less time in the bar with his customers, and more upstairs in the living quarters sleeping off effects of the booze. Although there were always bar-staff on duty, he was living on borrowed time. With his condition worsening, he slid into debt through not keeping proper records.

Eventually a number of regular customers, concerned for Terry's welfare, alerted the brewery to the problem. After inspections, it was decided that when his licence came up for renewal, the brewery, in conjunction with the local police, would oppose his application for an extension.

Informing Spinks of the decision was left to the Area Representative. It was a difficult task because he had become extremely fond of the former boxer. The news was therefore broken to him gently over a period of weeks with the emphasis being on his deteriorating health and the fact that he lived alone.

Getting up on the morning he was due to move out, Terry seemed oblivious to what was occurring. He had done nothing towards leaving and acted as though it was just another day. The tills in the bar were still full with the previous evening's takings because he had made no effort to tally up for banking. Fortunately a few of his close friends arrived at the pub early to help him pack.

'Come on Tel, it's your money,' said one of his friends as he emptied the till drawers into a carrier bag. 'Let's clear it out before the brewery people get here.'

A relief manager was installed to run the pub, but soon encountered a problem. 'I've got no small change,' he remarked as he served a customer.

'Well you'll have to go to the bank and get some then won't you,' remarked Spinks, who continued to go behind the bar and help himself to a scotch from the optic.

Once the reality of what was occurring registered with Terry, he was heart-broken. He reacted in the only way he knew – to have a drink. As he had nowhere to go, his good friends, Tony and Eve Townsend, insisted that he stayed with them for the night. They were regular customers at the pub and owned a farm at nearby Castle Goring.

The following morning Tony drove Terry to Tich's house at Cumberland Road, and his belongings followed in a van. It was a sad end to the former Olympic champion's licensing career, but many people knew it was for his own good. Had he been allowed to stay at The Coach & Horses, the likelihood was that he would have drunk himself to death.

Moving back to Cumberland Road, however, was no pleasure for Terry and did nothing to improve his health. From having a lovely country pub, it was yet another backward step because since Doris died, Tich was lonely and in poor health himself. He smoked a pipe for most of the day and consequently everywhere stank of stale tobacco. The curtains and windows were filthy, and there was rarely any food in the house.

Although Terry took jobs with a security company in London, as a guard at a mansion house in Bromley, and as a security guard with the Co-operative bank at Cornhill, his mind was never fully on his work. He was often vague and forgetful, and one day took his Olympic umbrella to work, but forgot about it. He never saw it again.

Despite his drink problem and an undiagnosed illness, Spinks was still extremely well thought of. In July 1992, he joined former champions Howard Winstone, John H Stracey, Henry Cooper, Charlie Magri and Alan Minter at a royal garden party at Buckingham Palace. Yet again he relied on his friend Barry Noonan to escort him.

He also attended an event in Manchester organised to support the city's bid to host the 2000 Olympic Games. Terry was amongst more than 800 former Olympic heroes at a unique gathering at Mottram Hall. During the proceedings he was called upon to present a special commemorative badge to Tom Farrell, a member of the Great Britain 1956 Olympic athletics team.

Ever since he was a child, birthdays had always been special occasions for Terry. People close to him knew his health was failing, so as he would be 55 on 28 February 1993, a special surprise party was arranged. It was staged at The Crooked Billet public house, Chadwell Heath, which was run by former ABA lightweight champion, Dennis Hinson, a former West Ham club-mate of Terry's.

A car was sent to Cumberland Road to collect Terry and Tich, and by the time they arrived, the guests were already there. Dick McTaggart had travelled from Scotland especially to see him, and Howard Winstone made the journey from Wales. Other guests included Billy Walker and fellow Olympian, Nicky Gargano, who ran a pub at Putney. He and Spinks had not seen each other for many years.

The pub had been specially decorated for what proved to be a moving occasion. There was a huge birthday cake with coloured icing depicting Olympic circles as a tribute to Terry's success 37 years earlier. A scrap book of his boxing career had been lovingly created and was presented to him during the party.

Although it had been a wonderful evening, there was great concern about Terry's health. Some people even doubted whether he would survive long enough to have another birthday celebration. Tich was the only member of the family who knew of his condition, but was incapable of doing anything about it.

Son Jarvis only became aware of the problem after arriving at

Cumberland Road to take his father out for the day. This was some months after Terry had left Worthing. Jarvis had planned to take him to Dulwich, but when he arrived to collect him Terry was shaking badly and was sick before he got into the car. Seeing him in this condition was distressing and frightening for Jarvis who was accompanied by a friend. As it was the first time he had taken his father out for three years, Jarvis decided they should continue.

During the journey, Jarvis' friend pointed out a spider in the car, whereupon Terry immediately panicked and screamed. They went to a pub for lunch, but within a short while Terry was sick again. Being very embarrassed, and unaware of how ill his father was, Jarvis sent him home in a cab. Later, however, he related the story to another friend who immediately recognised Terry's symptoms. He persuaded Jarvis to go to his father and try to get him to seek help. Despite talking to him for a long time, Terry either didn't listen or failed to understand.

Although his health continued to deteriorate, Spinks still went to functions, but relied on the hospitality of friends to take him. In June 1993, he and Sammy McCarthy attended the London Ex-Boxers Association monthly meeting. There Terry met his great friend Reg Gutteridge for the first time for several years.

Whilst everyone was delighted to see him, the most noticeable aspect was how frail and weak he looked. A few years earlier he had been a lively, rotund character weighing about 12 stone. Now he was just a skeleton, weak and lacking in ambition, and lighter than when he won his gold medal more than 37 years earlier. Everyone knew that Terry Spinks was extremely ill.

14

SERIOUS ILLNESS

Terry seemed oblivious to the deterioration in his health which had worsened since he moved back to Cumberland Road. He didn't eat properly and spent hours every day drinking at the Cumberland Arms just a short distance along the road.

By this time Tich was an old man in his 80's. He had also gone downhill rapidly since his beloved wife Doris passed away two years earlier. This was reflected in the state of the house which was dirty and cold. There was very little food, and Tich was unable to provide the care which Terry so desperately needed.

They lived in virtual squalor, and for Terry every day became a routine. With no ambition and nothing to get up for, he often laid in bed until lunchtime sleeping-off the effects of the previous night's boozing. When he did get up, more often than not he would have a lunch time drinking session at the Cumberland Arms until closing time.

Tich always walked to the West Ham Conservative Club in the afternoons for a quiet drink and some company. Returning home at about 4.30pm, he usually found Terry fast asleep either in bed or in an armchair. During the evenings he went back to the pub until closing and rarely ate a proper meal between sessions. Week in, week out, it was the same routine.

The sad thing was that nobody seemed to care. Most of the friends he once had seemed to have disappeared, and the former East End idol was being left to his own life-destroying devices. Although some of his old boxing colleagues occasionally visited him and gave him money to help him through his difficult times, Terry just spent it on booze. There were times when Tich gave him as much as £50 only for him to return home the same night penniless. Tich couldn't understand how he got through so much money in one evening. The sad fact was, that whenever Terry had money he bought anybody a drink, and there were always plenty of takers. There were other occasions when he lent money never to see it again.

Quite often Terry was so drunk at closing time that other regulars at the pub carried him home. Several nights, after getting into the house, he collapsed in the hall and slept on the floor still fully dressed. More than once Tich got up in the morning and found him lying prostrate, with the front door wide open. Unaware of how ill his son was, he lost his temper one day and kicked him as he lay on the floor. 'You wouldn't do this if your mother was still here,' he shouted out of sheer frustration.

By this stage of his life, Tich was very deaf. Every evening he watched television and had it on full blast until very late. One night, Terry staggered home from the pub at closing time, but couldn't find his front door key. Despite hammering on the door for all of 10 minutes, Tich couldn't hear him.

With nowhere else to go, Terry made his way back to the pub, but it was closed and in darkness. Desperate to put his head down, he tried the doors of cars parked in the street. A few yards from his house, he found the back door of one car unlocked so he climbed in and fell asleep on the back seat. When he awoke the next morning he couldn't get out because the car was fitted with child-locks. Eventually, a neighbour walking his dog saw him and let him out.

Boxing fans in the East End who knew Terry at this stage of his life, should have been reminded of the tragic story of Teddy Baldock from Poplar, who in 1927, was recognised as bantamweight champion of the world. Like Spinks, he was tremendously popular, and during the 1920's earned more than £20,000 from the ring. He owned a dozen suits and two cars, rubbed shoulders with the rich and famous in the oyster bars and plush restaurants in London's West End, yet when he died in 1971, had nothing. His friends had all deserted him, and during the last years of his life he slept rough on the streets or in dirty common lodging houses of the East End.

Terry Spinks was not quite that bad, but he was heading rapidly in the same direction. By mid-1993 the once wealthy, immaculately dressed young man was just a shadow of his former self. He was scruffy and unkempt, losing weight rapidly, and only a skeleton of the fit, powerful athlete who had graced British boxing rings with great pride more than 30 years earlier.

Although Terry had some difficult and painful times ahead, he was far more fortunate than Baldock. His life suddenly took what would prove to be a fairy-tale twist, and rescue him from obscurity, if not an early death.

In August 1993, his cousin Rosemary, with whom he had spent many school holidays as a boy, suddenly became a big part of his life. Despite having seen each other only three or four times during the past 20 years, Rosemary was well aware of Terry's health problems. When she lost her father six months earlier the funeral arrangements were handled by Cribb Funeral Directors of Canning Town. The proprietor, Stan Cribb, was a close friend of Terry's father, and during the course of conversation mentioned to Rosemary that the former Olympic champion was in a bad way. She was told that he had great difficulty in walking and always appeared to be drunk.

The last time Rosemary had seen Terry was at his mother's funeral two years earlier. She remembered that he was very drunk, but had assumed that it was due to the loss of his mother. She had no idea what had been going on since, or how much he had deteriorated.

Although Rosemary's mother, Iris, had kept in touch with Tich by telephone, she had no idea either. Whenever she enquired about Terry she was told he was fine. The problem was, that being an extremely proud man, Tich couldn't bear the thought of his sister and other members of the family knowing the state Terry was in.

Iris, however, was extremely concerned about what Rosemary had been told. She therefore telephoned Tich and made arrangements for them all to meet one Sunday evening at the West Ham United Supporters Club in Castle Street adjacent to the Upton Park ground.

Tich had a routine whereby three of his friends would call for him regularly at 7.00pm every Sunday evening and go the the club. On the day in question, Rosemary and Iris were unable to get to Cumberland Road by 7.00pm so Tich arranged for Terry to stay behind, meet them at the house and show them the way. When he opened the door it was obvious to them that he was very ill. He was extremely thin and barely mobile, walked with his legs wide apart and tilted back on his heels.

One of the first things he did was to ask Iris if she could lend him £50. She didn't have such an amount of money, so Rosemary gave it to Terry knowing full well she would never get it back. She would have given him anything because she was devastated to see him in such a condition.

Rosemary asked Terry if she could have a photograph of him

because she was the only person in the family who didn't have one. He told her to go upstairs and take them all because he didn't want them any longer.

Unprepared for the shock that awaited her, Rosemary was absolutely stunned as she walked into the bedroom. It was as though the place had been vandalised by burglars. The bed was filthy and unmade, Terry's clothes were lying in heaps all over the floor, while cupboard doors and drawers were wide open. A pair of trousers caked with dried blood were so stiff that they could have been stood against the wall. Rosemary couldn't believe it, because in reality the once proud fighter was living like a tramp.

Hundreds of beautiful boxing photographs given to him over the years by friends in the media, were strewn all over the room. They were precious memories of Terry's glory days so, with tears streaming down her face, Rosemary packed as many as she could into a cardboard box for safekeeping. 'I will never forget that day as long as I live,' she recalled. 'I felt extremely sad because I knew how particular Terry had always been about his clothes and appearance.'

After composing herself, Rosemary rejoined her mum and Terry downstairs, and the three of them went to meet Tich and his friends at the club. Once he realised they knew all was not well, Tich explained how Terry was drinking too much and not eating.

Rosemary's immediate concern was that she was going to Cyprus the following week for two weeks holiday. She even considered cancelling it because she was convinced that something terrible was going to happen to Terry. Although she eventually decided to go, she left her hotel telephone number with Iris with strict instructions to call if anything happened.

The holiday passed without a call, but on 10 September, her first day back, Rosemary's worst fears were realised. She was at work in her office at Greenwich when her mother telephoned to say she had received an emotional call from Tich. Terry had been rushed into hospital. An hour or so earlier he was found by Sammy McCarthy and Ronnie Jacobs in a state of collapse. A doctor was called, but after taking a quick look at him, had called an ambulance.

Terry was admitted to Newham General Hospital. He was in such poor health that he couldn't wash or dress himself. Weighing only seven stone, he was virtually at death's door. Rosemary rushed to the hospital and found Terry Brown, his former boxing colleague and lifelong friend, at his bedside. Spinks didn't recognise her and was hallucinating badly. He became excitable as he talked about bombs, machine guns and aeroplanes.

Rosemary later discovered that before she arrived at the hospital Terry Brown had bathed Terry and washed his hair. He even went and bought him two pairs of pyjamas because he hadn't got any.

Terry underwent extensive examination, including brain scans, and about a week later the family were told that he had permanent brain damage. The consultants predicted that he was unlikely to recover. His brain was already soft from having been a boxer, but when he started drinking excessively the alcohol attacked it quickly. In describing the situation to Rosemary, the doctors compared Terry's brain to a bruised pear eventually becoming rotten as it was affected by the alcohol.

Word soon got around the East End about the former Olympic champion's condition. He had literally hundreds of visitors, many of whom were ex-boxers. He was in a general ward, and hospital staff estimated that more people visited him than the rest of the patients put together.

From the day Terry was admitted to hospital, Rosemary visited him every evening on her way home from work. Despite her long and difficult journeys driving between Chadwell Heath and Greenwich, and working all day as a Sales Representative, she still found the energy and patience to sit at his bedside trying to persuade him to eat.

Once he was allowed out of bed, Terry was given a walking frame, but his movement was very restricted. He was still not eating properly and consequently remained extremely weak. On occasions when the weather was fine and warm, Rosemary took him into the hospital grounds in a wheelchair. To give him hope for the future, and assure him that he was loved, she talked to him non-stop. Once he started eating small amounts she even took him to her home at weekends.

Despite the fact that he could hardly walk, there was an occasion when Terry gave his father the fright of his life. When Tich opened his door to go out one evening he found Terry standing on the doorstep in his pyjamas. 'What are you doing here in your pyjamas?' he asked. 'They are not pyjamas,' replied Terry, 'It's my lightweight summer suit.' Tich called a neighbour who agreed to take Terry back to hospital which was about a mile away. How he got to Cumberland Road remained a mystery.

After a few weeks the doctors decided that nothing more could be done for Terry. Physically, he was fit and could therefore leave hospital, but it was stressed that one more drink could kill him. The immediate problem, therefore, was where he could live. Tich was not physically capable of controlling him if he returned home, and with the Cumberland Arms just a few yards along the road, it would only be a matter of time before he was drinking again.

It was eventually arranged for Terry to stay with Iris and her husband at Tollesbury in Essex. Rosemary collected him from the hospital and took him there, but after only two nights he became too difficult to handle. He kept getting up in the middle of the night trying to leave the house, saying he had to catch a plane because he had a fight in Ireland. Iris was in her 70's and couldn't cope, so she telephoned Rosemary saying she was taking Terry to her.

As she worked full-time, Rosemary was not in a position to look after him either. It was a desperate situation so she immediately contacted his doctor to see if he could go back into hospital. After dogged persistence an appointment was made and Rosemary arranged to meet Tich at the doctor's surgery. When she arrived she found him sitting alone in the waiting room crying. The reality of the situation was too much for the old man who had adored Terry since the day he was born.

Although the doctor was unable to get Terry back into Newham hospital, he did eventually find a bed for him at St Andrews hospital at Bromley-by-Bow. Tich was still distraught and couldn't face taking him there, so Rosemary did it. She hated leaving Terry, but accepted the fact that there was nowhere else for him to go.

The journey from Cumberland Road to the hospital was difficult for Tich, so after leaving her house at Chadwell Heath for work each morning, Rosemary picked him up at Canning Town and took him for visits. After spending some time with Terry, he made his way home by train. In the evenings Rosemary visited Terry after work, and during the day another cousin went to the hospital, did his laundry and helped wash him.

Terry remained at St Andrews while a decision was made regarding his care. It was an extremely difficult situation because he was unable to look after himself and was too young to go into an Old Peoples Home. In an attempt to do what was best for him, there were meetings with Welfare Officers, and Terry cried bitterly when he realised the extent of his problem. He pleaded to be allowed to return to his father, but for his own good this was impossible.

Everyone involved was extremely emotional, and one evening when Rosemary and Tich visited together, they held hands and wept openly. Memories of Terry as a boy, his achievements in the ring, and his cockney humour all came flooding back. Looking at him lying helpless in a hospital bed was heartbreaking. Despite everything, Rosemary was determined to do whatever she could for Terry, and continued to take him home with her at weekends.

Eventually a meeting was held at the hospital which the social worker, ward sister, Terry and members of his family all attended. The social worker suggested he be transferred to Sutton Manor Clinic at Stapleford Towney. It was a high class establishment caring for patients suffering from brain damage as a consequence of motor accidents, alcohol or drug abuse, and nervous breakdowns. The social worker explained that if he did go there it would be long-term. Terry became very distressed and kept saying he wanted to go back home and be with his dad. 'Please don't let them put me in a home,' he begged Rosemary as she sat beside him holding his hand.

The situation was extremely distressing for everyone. Even the social worker and sister had tears in their eyes because they had become very fond of Terry. He was always polite and well-mannered and they hated seeing him in such a helpless situation. Rosemary assured him that whatever happened she would always visit him every night and continue to take him home at weekends.

The family were invited to view the clinic, and after doing so were agreed that it was ideal for Terry to hopefully make a recovery. Unfortunately, it was far too expensive. After further discussions, however, Newham Social Services which was responsible for West Ham, agreed to pay the fee of £1,200 a week.

Before anything could be finalised, Terry had to agree to become a patient at Sutton Manor. It took a great deal of persuasion, particularly by Rosemary, but even then he said that as soon as he was better he wanted to go home and live with Tich. Everyone knew that would never happen, and it wasn't until Terry went to hospital that Tich accepted just how ill he was.

Terry was transferred to Sutton Manor Clinic on 4 November 1993, and his situation was re-assessed every month at meetings which Tich had to attend. It was a big occasion when he left St Andrews hospital and many photographs were taken of him with members of staff who adored him. He was so popular that a framed photo of him still hangs in the ward which cared for him.

Before he left St Andrews, a request was received for Terry to appear on a *'This is Your Life'* programme which ITV were producing about Reg Gutteridge. The script writer was Norman Giller, a great admirer of Spinks, who had reported many of his fights for the *Stratford Express.* The consultant, whom Terry was under, agreed to his participation on condition that Rosemary went with him. He stipulated that under no circumstances must he touch alcohol.

The programme was being recorded at Teddington Studios on 10

November, by which time Terry had been transferred to Sutton Manor Clinic. The first thing Rosemary had to do was buy him a complete new outfit of clothes because he had nothing decent enough to wear.

On the morning of the recording she collected Terry from the clinic and took him to her home at Chadwell Heath. ITV sent a chauffeur-driven car which took them to the studios in time for the recording which was due to commence at 4.00pm. On arrival, they were shown to a room and left alone for more than an hour. While they were waiting for the programme to commence, Rosemary walked Terry up and down like a racehorse to keep his legs loose. If he sat still for any length of time they became stiff and painful.

Just before Reg arrived at the studios they were called to an area immediately behind the stage. There Terry met the other surprise guests including boxers Terry Downes, Henry Cooper, Frank Bruno, John Conteh, Jim Watt, Ron Barton, Barry McGuigan and Dickie O'Sullivan, as well as Harry Carpenter and Norman Wisdom.

At the relevant moment in the programme all the boxers, with the exception of Spinks, were called on stage in a line and introduced. He was held back and called separately because the producers knew that Reg had always regarded him with special affection.

Everyone present knew how ill Terry had been and he was given a wonderful reception. Reg was amazed and delighted to see him because it was his first day out since being taken ill. Although he had great difficulty walking, he knew exactly where he was, and with great concentration and determination, did exceptionally well. A photograph, collected by courier from Rosemary's house a couple of days earlier, showing Terry holding his gold medal, was flashed on to the screen as he walked out. Reference was made to Reg's campaign which led to Spinks finally being selected to box in the Olympics.

The producers originally wanted Terry to speak, but Rosemary was terrified he would make a fool of himself. After an embrace and a few words from Reg, he went and sat next to Jarvis Astaire for the remainder of the programme. He later joined the other guests at a party, and looking very smart, stood up to it remarkably well. After a couple of hours, however, he suddenly became very tired, whereupon Rosemary called for their driver to take them home. That night Terry stayed with Rosemary and she took him back to the clinic the following morning.

* * *

Set back off a country road amid secluded tree-clad grounds, Sutton Manor Clinic was an extremely impressive establishment. It had a swimming pool, sauna, and exclusive restaurant which could be reached through a covered walkway from the main building.

The day Terry was transferred there, he, Rosemary and another cousin, Fay, were met by the Director of Nursing, Frank Rugeley. He commented on how smart Terry looked, and gave them a conducted tour before showing Terry to his own en-suite room.

To try and help him settle in, Rosemary and Fay had lunch with Terry in the restaurant, but leaving him later in the day was extremely difficult. He became very emotional and insisted that Rosemary did all his washing. He was like a little boy lost, and couldn't remember a thing. She knew that when he woke up the next morning he wouldn't know where he was.

Although conditions at Sutton Manor far exceeded those in hospital, Terry's condition continued to deteriorate. Extremely concerned about him, Rosemary still visited him every evening on her way home from work. He was very low, and one night told her he had nothing to live for. He said that in the days when he was drinking, all he wanted to do was die.

Although the clinic was difficult to reach without a car, Terry still had a lot of visitors. Sadly, he was unable to hold a conversation which resulted in a number of people not going again. Sammy McCarthy and former ABA lightweight champion, Ron Cooper, however, never gave up on him. Despite the difficult journey, and not having a car, Sammy visited Terry two or three times every week.

Fortunately, Rosemary got on very well with all the staff at Sutton Manor, so apart from visiting Terry every evening, she was in and out whenever she could. Every Friday evening she took him home with her for the weekend, and this helped to brighten him up. As a special treat on Sunday evenings she took him to the West Ham supporters Club to see his dad. Terry had been an honorary member since he was 18 and knew many of the regulars. Although people were kind and tried hard to make conversation, there was rarely any response from him.

As the weeks passed by, Rosemary realised that he deteriorated after she had taken him back to the clinic after the weekends. Part of the problem was that when he first went to Sutton Manor many of the patients had illnesses resulting from nervous breakdowns, alcohol or drug abuse. Despite their poor health most were able to talk to one another. Suddenly, however, more and more patients were admitted with severe brain damage sustained from violent incidents, such as road accidents. Many required one-to-one care, and as a result Terry was often left alone with no stimulation.

Rosemary couldn't bear the thought of him spending Christmas at the clinic so she took him home to spend it with her family, including her mother and step-father. They also invited Tich who was on his own, and did everything they could to try and make Terry happy. For most of the time he was oblivious to what went on or what time of the year it was.

Two months later, Rosemary arranged a party at the West Ham Supporters Club to celebrate Terry's 56th birthday. She bought him a new suit, shoes, shirt and tie, and he looked immaculate. The place was packed, and amongst the guests were his son Jarvis, Tich, many friends from his boxing days, and even some who knew him from Worthing. There was a beautiful birthday cake with candles, and everyone stood and sang '*Happy Birthday*' to him.

Terry, however, was completely unaware of what was happening. He looked blank for most of the time, and was oblivious to the occasion, as had been the case at Christmas. Rosemary was devastated, because in her mind the party was a disaster. She had hoped it would brighten Terry up and lead people to believe that he was getting better. Sadly, everyone could see he was in very poor health.

One of the most worrying aspects of Terry's health was that for months he had bouts of hallucination. He was convinced the police were after him. He repeatedly told staff at the clinic that he had been taken to Ongar Police Station where he had to make statements against some of his friends. He gave vivid descriptions of the police officers, how many there were, and even told the doctors and nurses that Rosemary was really a policewoman, not his cousin.

The situation was so bad that Rosemary would often receive telephone calls at her office in Greenwich from staff at the clinic saying they didn't know what to do with Terry. Because she worked as Sales Representative, she was often out on the road and not available to receive the calls. There were a number of occasions when messages were left with clients she was due to visit, asking that she made urgent contact with the clinic. Desperately worried about Terry, she often dropped what she was doing, raced to Sutton Manor to find him in a state of hysteria. Time and again he pleaded with nurses, doctors and Rosemary to take him to the police station.

In an attempt to put his mind at ease, Frank Rugeley and Sammy McCarthy took him to Ongar Police Station one day and explained the predicament to a desk sergeant. At the conclusion of a searching, but sympathetic interview, Terry was told that at no time had he been required to make any statement regarding incidents involving friends of his. There were no outstanding matters relating to him, and a letter confirming this was subsequently sent to him at the clinic.

Frank Rugeley gave Rosemary tremendous support and let her do whatever she liked to try and help Terry. Quite often she picked him up from the clinic and took him with her when she was delivering to clients. Even then he kept hallucinating and it was clear that the visit to Ongar Police Station had done absolutely nothing to ease his in-built fears.

At times when he was hallucinating, he scratched himself so badly that blood dripped from his injuries. One day Rosemary walked into his room at the clinic to find him lying on his bed wearing only a pair of boxer shorts. A nurse was carefully rubbing cream into his legs which were bleeding badly as a result of him scratching.

Quite often Terry was terrified to go to sleep because he said that the police used to go into his room at night and take him away. There were many evenings when Rosemary sat in an armchair at his bedside until he was soundly asleep. Sometimes she didn't leave Sutton Manor until well after midnight, then drove through the pitch-black country lanes to get home.

Not having a mobile phone, she was always afraid of breaking down. One night, miles from any houses, she got a puncture, but was terrified to stop and drove all the way to Romford on the wheel rim. When she eventually stopped, the tyre was in shreds. Only then did she use a public call box to get her husband to meet her and change the wheel.

Before leaving the clinic late at night, Rosemary always left Terry a note. She told him where he was and what day it was, who would be coming to see him, and that she would be there in the evening. Once she arrived home, however, she couldn't sleep for worrying about him. Most nights she lay in bed worrying and wondering what he would be like when he awoke the next morning not knowing where he was.

Although the situation placed enormous strain upon her, Rosemary was determined to support Terry come what may. Apart from effecting her family life, it also created difficulty with her employer. Her job was demanding enough, but because of the frequency of calls from the clinic she had difficulty maintaining the required level of performance. In an attempt to rectify the situation she therefore often got up early in the morning and went to the clinic just to reassure Terry that he wasn't alone.

Because there were no signs of his health improving, Rosemary was anxious to get a second opinion to see if anything more could be done for him. On 22 March 1994 she took him to see Dr Robert King, a Psychiatric and Psychological Consultant at 14 Devonshire Place in the West End of London. After a series of tests, Terry was diagnosed as suffering from cerebral and cerebellar atrophy due to alcoholic consumption and dementia. In simple and factual terms, Rosemary was told that his brain had three patches of dead cells. This meant that other parts of his brain would have to adjust and learn to do the work originally carried out by the dead areas.

Rosemary paid the consultant's invoices herself, but professional photographer Derek Rowe, a close friend of Terry's since his boxing days, later asked her for them. A few weeks later she received a letter from John Morris, General Secretary of the British Boxing Board of Control, together with a cheque from the Board's Benevolent Fund, fully reimbursing her.

Although Terry badly needed stimulation, it didn't always work. Sutton Manor had a mini-bus which was used to take patients for a ride each day. Although he sometimes went, Rosemary was terrified that somebody would recognise him and it would get into the newspapers. She had already heard that one boxer made a remark about him being in a 'nut-house'.

One day while out on a trip Terry started shouting that he wanted to get off because the police were after him. He was hallucinating so badly that he had to be taken back to the clinic. Rosemary was contacted and went straight there to try and pacify him. He felt safe with her because it was as though she was his mother.

Apart from Sammy McCarthy and Ron Cooper, two other regular visitors to Sutton Manor were Terry Bay and Don Dirs. They had been mates with Terry since they were all teenagers, and remained very loyal to him. Throughout the period he was at the clinic there was only one evening when Rosemary didn't visit him, and that was because Don had said he was going. That night she stayed at home, but at about 10.00pm her telephone rang. It was Don saying that he was afraid to leave Terry because he was hallucinating badly and in an emotional state.

Rosemary immediately got dressed and went straight to the clinic. Terry was sitting in an armchair beside Don and two nurses. He was in a terrible state, but she managed to calm him down and get him to bed. She stayed with him until he was asleep, and then drove home tired and exhausted.

While he was at Sutton Manor, Terry saw a doctor every Monday morning. One day Rosemary was told that they were going to put him on a course of tablets to stop the hallucinating. The doctor warned that there would be side-effects in that Terry would keep looking upwards to his right, and also dribble.

Being very uncomfortable about what she had been told, Rosemary established the name of the tablets, then contacted a friend of Tich who was a hospital nursing sister. Her advice was not to allow the clinic to give them to Terry because, in the long term, they could cause a stroke because they paralyse the part of the brain that hallucinates.

When Rosemary told the doctor Terry was not to be given the tablets, an argument developed. He said it was Terry who was suffering not her, but she stood her ground. Later that day, Frank Rugeley returned to the clinic from leave and supported Rosemary's opinion. He confirmed that Terry needed stimulation, not tablets. The worst situation for him was to be left thinking he was on his own.

Frank adored Terry and was extremely kind to him. From that day he often took him for a ride in his car and they even visited a country pub for lunch. There was no harm in this because Frank was adamant that despite his problems Terry had never been an alcoholic. In any event, he had lost his craving for drink and was content just sipping fruit juice or water. The important thing was getting him out into a social environment which was good for him.

Encouraged by what Frank was doing, Rosemary started taking Terry out for a couple of hours some evenings. The first place she took him to was The Woodman, a pub just a short distance from the clinic. The licensee was Eddie Johnson, a friend of Terry's since they were teenagers. Although they hadn't seen each other for many years, Eddie recognised Spinks the moment he walked into the bar.

'Hello Terry,' he called out, 'It's been a long time.' Eddie had no idea how ill he had been, and was shocked when Rosemary told him the sorry story. Eddie, however, was a true friend and spent hours recalling the times they spent together as lads. It was hard work for him because Terry still couldn't hold a conversation, and just stared vacantly throughout. The licensee, however, was always pleased to see him and wanted to do anything to try and make him comfortable.

Eddie also had another pub, The Two Puddings at Stratford

Programme cover of Boxing-Dinner Evening held in honour of Terry Spinks on 12 September 1994

Broadway. On 1 December 1994 he organised a benefit night for Terry, and in typical East End fashion, people rallied round to support the former champion in his time of need. There were a host of celebrities, an auction, raffle and karaoke. More than £2,500 was raised, demonstrating once again the depth of Terry's popularity.

'Terry cheered us up in those grim and austere post war years,' Johnson told a local newspaper reporter. 'He gave heart to all cockneys. Despite his difficulties he has never once complained. The gala night is an opportunity to show how much we love him.'

Three months earlier the Anglo-American Sporting Club staged a tribute night for Spinks at the Marriott Hotel in London. There were four professional contests, with West Ham boxer Jason Rowland appearing in the main event. Many former boxers were in attendance including Sammy McCarthy, Chris Finnegan, Dave Charnley and Herol Graham. Amongst items under the hammer in the auction was Terry's Olympic blazer. The successful bidder was Jarvis Astaire who later gave it back to Spinks saying it didn't fit him.

The plight of the former Olympic champion touched the hearts of many people. Johnny Branch contacted Rosemary offering financial help for anything Terry needed, and The Jack Solomons Trust made a donation after Reg Gutteridge referred to his illness in one of his columns.

* * *

Although Terry's inability to respond to people was of great concern to Rosemary, she didn't allow it to deter her from trying to stimulate him. Irrespective of her work commitments, she persevered because getting him out and about was far more important than allowing him to sit alone in his room at the clinic. She always knew there was never going to be a magic cure for his problem, and any improvement would be very much long term.

It was perhaps somewhat unfortunate that some of Terry's closest friends were licensee's. To a cynical minded person, taking him into a public house could have been construed as being irresponsible. The situation, however, was quite the reverse because meeting people was of paramount importance to his recovery. He no longer had a drink problem and was quite content drinking alcohol-free beer which looked more manly than fruit juice.

Rosemary also took Terry to Dennis Hinson's pub, The Crooked Billet at Chadwell Heath, when he stayed with her at weekends.

They knew each other from their amateur days at West Ham, and Dennis always had special affection for Spinks. Again, the visits to the pub were purely for the purpose of seeing an old friend in the outside world.

Meanwhile, the Peacock gymnasium, a modern and much-needed establishment, had opened at Caxton Street North in Canning Town just below the Silvertown flyover. Situated just half a mile from where Morgan Street once stood, it boasted the best training facilities in the East End as well as catering and restaurant areas for the comfort of visitors. Re-development of the area meant that the part of Morgan Street once made famous by Spinks' success at the Olympic Games, no longer existed. It had been replaced by modern housing.

One of the proprietors of the Peacock was Terry's old school-mate Jackie Bowers. In April 1994 he contacted Rosemary and asked her to take Terry and his father to see the new gym. As it was another outlet in an environment with which Terry was familiar, she took a day off work to take them. Despite him being very limited in his conversation, people made a real fuss of Terry as they sat drinking coffee in the restaurant area of the gym. His popularity remained as high as ever.

Jackie Bowers introduced him to Bradley Stone, a young Canning Town boxer who was training for a contest with Richie Wenton for the vacant British super-bantamweight championship at York Hall the following week. Spinks was one of Bradley's heroes and he was thrilled to meet him. He told him all about his life and how excited he was to be fighting for the title. 'You will be there to see me on Tuesday won't you?' he pleaded before leaving the gym for a run.

'Yes', replied Spinks. 'Good luck son.'

Although Terry was very ill, Rosemary recognised the respect Bradley had for him. She therefore decided to take him to York Hall on 26 April. That night she rushed home from work, changed her clothes and then drove to the clinic to collect Terry. They had ringside seats, and throughout Stone's fight she kept him interested by commenting on the action.

Although Bradley boxed well for most of the contest, he fell apart in round 10 and was stopped. Before they left York Hall, Rosemary suggested that Terry went to the dressing room to commiserate with the Canning Town youngster. When he got there security men refused him admission.

Rosemary took Terry back to Sutton Manor Clinic, but early next morning received a telephone call from a journalist saying that

Bradley Stone was seriously ill in hospital. Despite having been stopped, he had left the ring of his own accord and in the dressing room afterwards there were no indications of what lay ahead. At 2.30am the following morning he collapsed at his girl friend's house. He was taken to the Royal London hospital at Whitechapel where he underwent an operation to remove a blood clot from his brain. He was in a critical condition on a life-support machine.

The following day, Rosemary received another telephone call advising her that Bradley's life-support machine was about to be switched off. Conscious that the young boxer's death was bound to be a prominent news feature, she immediately telephoned Frank Rugeley at Sutton Manor Clinic and told him not to let Terry watch television. She then drove straight there and broke the news to him herself. He was very upset and cried bitterly.

Rosemary took Terry to Bradley's funeral at Ascension Church, Custom House on 9 May where they were met by Jackie Bowers. Smartly dressed in a dark suit and tie, he was well aware of the situation despite his poor health.

* * *

With the passing of time Terry stayed with Rosemary and her husband every weekend. Initially they had him from Friday until Sunday evening, but eventually it was Monday morning before he returned to the clinic.

It was a tremendous responsibility because he needed careful supervision. One Sunday morning he fainted and fell off a chair at Rosemary's house. On returning to the clinic the doctors were told. A blood test revealed that he had a salt deficiency so he was put on a liquid diet, given a tablet of sodium chloride each day and also vitamins.

Sometimes when he was very upset, Rosemary also took Terry home with her during the week. Throughout the day, he accompanied her on her rounds, and many of her clients got to know him. Everywhere they went, people became fond of him and she took the view that at least she was giving him a life and contact with the outside world.

Often on a Friday evening after picking Terry up from the clinic Rosemary took him straight to Poplar. One of his old boxing colleagues, Terry Brown, was the licensee of the Royal Charlie public house at Crisp Street. He and his wife loved seeing Terry, as did one of their regulars, former Southern Area welterweight champion, Albert Carroll.

As well as looking after Terry, Rosemary automatically started to care for Tich as well. She visited him every morning on her way to work, did his washing, and helped him to tidy the house. He was heartbroken about Terry, and admitted that he was lonely and depressed believing he would be in care for the rest of his life. The situation placed an extra burden upon Rosemary to the extent that it became even more difficult to do her job.

* * *

By March 1995, after spending more than 15 months at Sutton Manor clinic, Terry's condition showed no sign of improvement. Although he still needed full-time care, Rosemary was convinced that if he stayed there he would never get better. Believing that she could give him a better quality of life, she therefore decided to have him live with her permanently.

As she worked full-time, Rosemary discussed the situation with Tich. It was agreed that she would drop Terry at Cumberland Road on her way to work in the morning. He could spend the day with his father and she would then pick him up on her way home in the evening. Tich was thrilled because he never expected Terry to ever come out of the clinic. He told Rosemary that when he went to bed at night he prayed that Jesus would send an angel to look after him and Terry. 'My prayers have been answered,' said the old man. 'He sent us you.'

One of Tich's few social outlets was a daily visit to the West Ham Conservative Club in Barking Road just a short distance from his house. For years he walked there every afternoon at 1.30pm for a quiet drink and chat with his friends. Although Terry wasn't very mobile, he could walk short distances with support. Tich therefore decided to take him to the club because it would provide him with a much needed change of scenery.

Holding the arm of his father, who walked with a stick, Terry managed the 10 minute journey every afternoon. It was a moving sight for neighbours because Tich was so proud having his son alongside him again. Although at first Terry was only going through the motions, it gave him the stimulation he needed. All the regulars at the club were local people who had known him since he was a boy. They made a fuss of him and helped him if he needed to stretch his legs or go to the toilet. The surroundings were comfortable and relaxed, and Tich and Terry stayed there each day until 5pm when Rosemary collected them.

Once Terry became more steady on his feet, he and Tich went

to West Ham Supporters Club every Friday for a fish and chip lunch. They caught a bus from the end of Cumberland Road, and in the afternoon were driven home by Charlie Rogers, a friend of Tich's who worked at the club.

Terry was certainly getting a better quality of life. He was going to places and meeting people who were genuinely concerned about him and wanted to help. By living with Rosemary, he gained a new circle of friends, and her neighbours took an instant liking to him. Whenever she had a pressing business engagement there was always someone willing to look after him. People loved having him in their houses or taking him for short walks.

The care and stimulation that Terry had received since going to live with Rosemary at last appeared to be paying dividends. Within about six months, he started to show slight signs of improvement both in his mobility and response to other people. Whilst this was pleasing, everyone knew there was a long way to go and that a great deal of love and patience would be required.

15

ROAD TO RECOVERY

Terry's illness was of great concern to many people in all walks of life. In November 1995 he received a letter from the Private Secretary to Her Royal Highness, the Princess Royal, saying how sorry she was to hear that he was unwell.

The Princess Royal knew all about Spinks and his achievements having met him at functions involving former Olympians. As Chairman of the Olympic Games Committee, she hosted a reunion event every four years for men and women who had represented Great Britain.

Along with Chris Finnegan, Terry attended one such event in the early 1990's whilst he was still living at Worthing. During the proceedings the guests lined up to meet his Royal Highness, Prince Philip.

'Hello my lord, how are you? It is lovely to see you,' said Spinks as the Prince stopped to shake hands with him. 'Do you remember my lord, when I won my gold medal?' continued Terry. 'I've got to thank you for sending that case of champagne.'

Prince Philip asked Spinks how his father was, even referring to him as Tich. He remembered him from a visit to West Ham Boxing Club during the 1980's.

Despite his health problems Terry's popularity remained as high as ever. During 1996 he was asked to sign hundreds of Post Office First Day Cover envelopes designed to commemorate the forth-coming Olympic Games in Atlanta. All British gold medal winners from 1956 to 1992 were listed on the back of each envelope.

That year, Terry was also a contributor to a BBC television film, *'Rings within the Rings'*, a history of Olympic boxing. Part of it was filmed at the Peacock Gym at Canning Town, and was shown on BBC 2 on 16 June.

On 22 May the same year Spinks was a guest at The British Olympic Association Sports Ball at the Grosvenor Hotel in London. His letter of invitation was addressed to 'Terry Spinks MBE' because, like many other people the organisers believed he had been honoured. Mysteriously, this was not the case.

* * *

After Terry left Sutton Manor clinic to live with Rosemary and her husband, it was important that he got good exercise as part of his rehabilitation. The Bowers family invited Rosemary to take him to the Peacock gym as often as possible. It was an offer she couldn't refuse because, not only would Terry get good exercise, but he would be in a familiar environment and meet people who genuinely cared for him.

Several times a week Rosemary took Terry to the gym on her way to work. She waited until he changed and then had a cup of coffee with him while he settled. Once she had left, the gym staff supervised him as he exercised on the treadmill and pedalled an exercise bike. After about an hour one of Rosemary's work colleagues collected Terry and took him to his father's house at Cumberland Road.

Terry's illness, however, was far from over, and one morning after a work-out he went missing. He was eventually located sitting in the showers with no clothes on and looking extremely frightened. Unable to function sufficiently to dry himself, the first thing he said on being approached was: 'Where's Rosemary?' He still had no confidence without her, so from that day he only went to the gym if she or somebody he knew well could stay with him all the time.

Gradually Terry's health began to improve although for a long time he continued to lack confidence. Whenever somebody offered to take him out he always asked if Rosemary was going as well. Fortunately her close friends and neighbours were a great support and Terry got on well with them all.

In July 1996, a group of 10 went to Florida for a holiday. They wanted it to be a special treat for Terry so instead of staying at an hotel, they hired a villa with a swimming pool, and also a 15 seater minibus. It was a perfect situation because everyone gave him great attention and shared the responsibilities of looking after him.

They went to Disneyland and water parks, and as there was a lot

Terry with Rosemary (left) and his son, Jarvis, outside Buckingham Palace on 2nd May 2002.

Rosemary, Terry and Sammy McCarthy (right) with friends and family outside Buckingham Palace on 2nd May 2002.

Terry (centre) with former world flyweight champion, Charlie Magri, Rosemary and guests outside the Phoenix Apollo Restaurant, Stratford, before his celebration party.

Prince Charles talks to Terry at his MBE investiture at Buckingham Palace on 2nd May 2002.

Spinks (left) with his close friend and "minder" Chris Carr.

Spinks at the launch of his biography in 2002.

Richard Barber presents Terry with his edition of 'This is your Life' at the celebration of his 70th birthday.

Spinks (left) with former Southern Area
Bantamweight Champion, Mark Goult.

Spinks (left) with his first senior amateur opponent, George Rix.

Spinks at West Ham Amateur Boxing Club annual presentation 2010.

Spinks with leading British lightweight boxer, Kevin Mitchell, (West Ham) in 2010.

Terry (centre) with neurosurgeon Mr Fary Afshar (left) and neurologist Dr John Jestico at the Gold Medal 50th anniversary celebration in 2006.

Terry (left) with former 1956 Olympic Games opponent Sammy Harris in April 2008.

Terry and his daughter Claire in November 2011

Spinks with Rosemary and her husband Terry on New Years Eve 2011

of walking to do, a wheelchair was hired for Terry. Most people took turns pushing him, although several times each day he walked and pushed the wheelchair to aid his balance. He even insisted on giving the ladies a ride. Terry was taken on most of the rides, reminding him and Rosemary of the days they spent as kids at fairgrounds.

Back home, Rosemary often took Spinks to Terry Brown's pub at Poplar. One evening they were joined by Albert Carroll and it was suggested that Terry was taken to the London Ex-Boxers Association meeting at Kings Cross the following Sunday. Although she knew nothing about it, Rosemary believed it would be a wonderful opportunity for him to meet old friends and also give him something new to think about.

That Sunday morning they all met at The Royal Charlie and drove to Kings Cross in one car. Not surprisingly, word had already reached committee members that Spinks would be attending the meeting, and as he walked into the St Pancras Conservative Club he was given a wonderful reception. As he was introduced by Chairman, Mickey O'Sullivan, the entire gathering of almost 200 stood and clapped him all the way to his seat. Everyone knew he had fallen on hard times, but they were delighted to see him on his feet again.

Rosemary had no doubts about the significance of that day. 'It has been the best thing he ever joined,' she remarked with some emotion. 'It's good for him and he is good for LEBA because so many people go to see him. He is loved.'

Spinks was immediately made a member of the London Ex-Boxers Association, an organisation which typifies everything that is good about boxing and many of the people involved with it. In particular, it supports a number of worthy charities, and the camaraderie between old fighters is incredible. The Association is aptly described by its motto, *'It's nice to belong'*, a saying so often used by former President, Jack Powell.

It was fitting that Sammy McCarthy was also a member of LEBA, and it was not long before the Association recognised the importance of two such influential figures. Both were appointed as Honorary Vice-Presidents, and during recent years represented the Association at numerous functions, particularly funerals of ex-boxers and members. They were frequently invited to be guests of honour at prestigious luncheons and dinners, and regularly attend amateur boxing shows and presentation nights. Spinks and McCarthy were a good double act and it was hard to split one from the other. Both were London men born and bred, loved and respected since they first laced gloves.

In appreciation of his dedicated service to the London Ex-Boxers Association and its members, Terry was presented with the Jack Powell Award in November 1999. 'Whenever we need a senior representative to attend a function, we can always rely on Terry,' said LEBA President, Stephen Powell. 'It only takes one phone call - he never lets us down.'

As Terry's mobility and confidence improved, he began to go out on a regular basis with Sammy and Ron Cooper. Affectionately known as *'Last of the Summer Wine,'* the loveable trio often spent a day in the west end of London visiting old haunts and friends. Each outing proved to be another step forward for Spinks because his progress started to become noticeable. Always extremely clean and smart, his old cockney humour gradually returned as did his awareness to life around him.

In February 1998, Terry attended the funeral of his old opponent Pancho Bhatachaji who had idolised him since their fight in 1957. Pancho, who had lived at StJohns Wood, even named his son after the former Olympic champion. Throughout the duration of Terry's illness, he frequently telephoned Rosemary asking how he was.

After the funeral service, Terry spoke to Pancho's son who was thrilled to meet him. He said his father always told him how much he loved and respected Terry. Holding his hand firmly, Spinks assured him that his father was also a very special man and a talented boxer.

A fortnight later it was Terry's 60th birthday. For several years there had been a celebration at Terry Brown's pub at Poplar, but as this was a special milestone in his life, a party was organised at the London Ex-Boxers headquarters at Kings Cross. Such was his popularity that it was not possible to cater for everyone who wanted to attend and at least 100 had to be turned away.

It was a massive event and guests included former boxers Billy Walker, Charlie Magri, Sammy McCarthy, Billy Wadham, Terry Gill, Ron Cooper, Kenny Field, Albert Carroll, Dave Charnley, Dennis Hinson, Billy Aird and Mickey O'Sullivan. A surprise guest was Dick McTaggart who made the journey all the way from Scotland just to be with his friend on his special day. It was an emotional reunion.

Other members of the Scottish Ex-Boxers Association also made the trip and presented Terry with a unique trophy in the shape of a boxing glove. He was highly regarded in Scotland and for many years had kept in touch with former opponents who lived north of the border.

A number of sporting journalists also remembered Terry's

birthday. Neil Allen who, as a young reporter for *The Times,* had covered the Olympic Games in Melbourne, sent him copies of reports he wrote of his contests leading to the gold medal.

During the course of the evening a beautiful birthday cake was unveiled. A replica of a gold medal made of marzipan was expertly moulded in the centre. Entertainment included a song and dance act, and the function which was due to end at 1.00am, was in full swing until 2.30. The LEBA monthly meeting took place at the same venue eight hours later, but Terry was too exhausted to attend. He was at home in bed fast asleep.

West Ham Football Club also acknowledged the former Olympic champion's 60th birthday. He was a VIP guest at the Upton Park ground at a match which marked the home debut of new £2 million signing Trevor Sinclair. Terry had been an Honorary member of the Supporters Club for many years and was a life-long 'Hammers' fan.

In December 1998, Terry was one of 600 guests at the Sports Writers' Association of Great Britain 50th anniversary dinner, at the Hilton Hotel, Park Lane. He was joined by fellow 1956 Olympic gold medal winners Judy Grinham and Dick McTaggart. During the evening they were all presented to the Guest of Honour, Her Royal Highness, The Princess Royal.

* * *

Just when things seemed to be going well for Terry he suffered yet another set-back. On 27 January 1999, his father, who had been in poor health, passed away aged 87.

Two years earlier Tich underwent an operation for bowel cancer, but made a marvellous recovery. Eventually, however, he became unwell again and was confined to his bed at home. Despite the fact that he was almost blind and lived alone, all efforts to get him back into hospital failed. It was left to Rosemary to care for him. Under extreme pressure, she visited him every day, taking Terry with her.

Eventually Tich became so ill that he was omitted to Newham General Hospital where he died from pneumonia two weeks later. Terry visited him each day and had been with him just three hours before he passed away.

Rosemary knew it would be extremely difficult explaining to Terry that his father had died, so before doing so she persuaded a neighbour to sit with her. Predictably, he became very emotional, but Rosemary's greatest fear was that it would cause him to seek comfort from drink as he had when he lost his mother. That didn't occur, however, because his short-term memory was very poor due to the damage to his brain.

The consequence was that every morning Terry asked to go and see Tich. Each time Rosemary explained the position to him he reacted as though it was the first time he had been told. He only fully understood three months later when his father's name was added to the gravestone erected for Doris.

There was a massive turn-out for Tich's funeral which took place at Plaistow Memorial Baptist Church. He was an extremely popular man having lived and worked in Canning Town all of his life, never moving more than three miles. He had been a member of West Ham Boxing Club for 60 years, many as President. He was also President of West Ham Conservative Club where the flag flew at half mast for several weeks following his death.

After Tich's funeral a reception was held at the Conservative Club identical to that arranged for his wife eight years earlier. During the gathering a friend gave Terry a pound coin to put into the fruit machine. He won the jackpot of £120 prompting a remark, 'Tich did that for you son.'

Tich was buried at East London Cemetery alongside his wife in the family grave, and Rosemary took Terry there every two weeks. His passing, however, caused her a major problem because it meant that she had nobody to leave Terry with while she was at work. Although his health and confidence had improved dramatically since living with her, he still needed 24 hours a day supervision. Because it was important that he continued to progress, she decided to give up the job she had held since 1973.

Terry then lead an active life and Rosemary took him everywhere with her. She also ensured that, as far as possible, he attended most events to which he was invited because it kept him stimulated and motivated.

During the early part of 2000, Terry and Rosemary took part in the production of *Shiner,* a new film starring Michael Caine and Coronation Street actor Matthew Marsden. It had a boxing theme and much of the filming took place in the East End including seven days at York Hall, Bethnal Green, the venue for a fight scene.

A number of other former boxers joined the cast or acted as extras. They included Sammy McCarthy, Charlie Magri, Prince Rodney, Ron Cooper, Dave and Johnny Ould, Dave Parris, Roy Francis and Fred 'Nosher' Powell, who originally contacted Rosemary on behalf of the producers inviting her and Terry to become involved.

Throughout rehearsals, Sammy looked after Terry just as he had

40 years previously as his manager. One morning they were filming at Bray Studios in Berkshire and had to be up at 4.00am. Since his illness, Terry needed a lot of sleep and was not at his best at that hour. Sammy, however, livened him up with jokes about still being on 25 per cent of his fee.

The filming took almost three months, during which time Michael Caine became very fond of Spinks. Despite his massive success as a movie star, he was very down to earth and made a point of shaking hands with him each morning.

Terry's 62nd birthday fell during the making of the film, and on the day everything stopped. Everyone gathered round and sang *'Happy Birthday'* to him. He was presented with four cakes, one of which had been made by a member of the cast and had a marzipan figure of a boxer sitting on the top.

Spinks was also the centre of attention at the wrap party held on 21 March 2000 aboard *'The Elizabethan'*, a floating restaurant on the Victoria embankment. Most of the girls involved in making the film wanted photographs taken with him.

The preview of *'Shiner'* was held at the Curzon Cinema, Mayfair on 24 October 2000. It went on general release in September the following year, and was also sold to the United States.

'Shiner' was not Terry's first experience of acting. Shortly before his illness he was offered work as an extra in the ITV series *'The Bill'*. The Locations Manager, Mickey Moynihan, knew he had fallen on hard times, and thought his involvement would help occupy his time and also earn him some much needed cash. The producer of the programme was a real boxing fan who adored Spinks and was thrilled when he met him.

The original idea was for Terry to be a member of a jury, although eventually he was asked to be the jury foreman. There were a number of rehearsals of the particular set in which all he had to say was 'we find the accused guilty.' Suddenly, however, Spinks lost confidence and on the day the set was due to be filmed, he didn't turn up.

When Mickey telephoned him, Terry said he couldn't say the words. He was told that he could read them from a card, but he was still reluctant to go through with it. Eventually he agreed and a car was sent to Cumberland Road to collect him. At the time, most people thought Terry's shyness was the problem. Nobody knew just how ill he was and that his brain was not functioning correctly.

Due largely to Rosemary's love and patience, Terry kept in touch with everyday life. When British boxer, Audley Harrison, reached the Olympic Games super-heavyweight final at Sydney in December 2000, Terry sent him a telegram:

I did it in 1956 - now it's your turn. Good luck and best wishes. Terry Spinks.

In May 2001, Terry joined a party of 30 members from LEBA on a three day trip to Glasgow where they were guests of the Scottish Ex-Boxers Association. At an international boxing dinner he met up with old opponents Derry Treanor, and Peter Walsh whom he beat in the 1956 ABA final, and also Dick McTaggart. There was also a reunion with American heavyweight Freddie Mack, a former sparring partner to Billy Walker, who had made his home in Scotland. Back in the 1960's, he had used Spinks at the Thomas A' Beckett to speed him up for some of his fights in Britain.

Two months later, Terry and Sammy McCarthy were among LEBA members to attend the funeral of former Kilburn featherweight, Danny O'Brien who sparred with Spinks on many occasions during the early '60's. At a gathering afterwards Sammy bumped into Irish comedian, Frank Carson. 'Where's Terry Spinks?' he asked. Sammy called Terry over whereupon Frank remarked, 'It's great to see you again. You were the greatest amateur boxer I ever saw.'

A few days earlier Spinks had been the centre of attention at West Ham Boxing Club's presentation evening. Shortly after his father's death, he and Rosemary purchased a trophy which they donated to the club in his memory. Named 'The George "Tich" Spinks Memorial Cup', it was presented annually by Terry to the club 'Boxer of the Year'.

West Ham was still a thriving club and Terry posed for photographs with every award winner. He spent a long time signing autographs, and one lad reminded him that at Clacton the previous year Terry gave him a signed photograph. 'I keep it on our mantelpiece,' he said proudly.

Spinks always kept in touch with boxing and had great respect for all of his former opponents. In particular, he frequently spoke with great affection about Howard Winstone with whom he developed a close friendship in later life.

On 8 July 1974, Howard was guest of honour at the World Sporting Club in London. He presented the Lonsdale belt to Evan Armstrong at the conclusion of his gruelling battle with Alan Richardson for the British featherweight championship. Spinks was in the audience and as soon as Howard spotted him he went and asked for his autograph. 'It's the first time I've seen him since we fought 13 years ago,' he remarked.

There was genuine respect between the two men as they stood shaking hands. 'Howard was an all-time great,' said Terry with great sincerity. 'He had the fastest and most accurate left jab ever. Although when we met for the title I had bother making nine stone, I don't think I could have licked him on my best night.'

From that moment their friendship blossomed and they kept in touch. During interviews over the years they complimented each other with warmth and sincerity. Terry was about to go on holiday to Spain in October 2000 when he received news of Winstone's death. He was very distressed, but immediately contacted a friend and asked that flowers be sent to the funeral on his behalf.

In February the following year Spinks travelled to Merthyr to be present at a Memorial Dinner staged to raise funds for a statue of the former world champion to be erected in his home town. He donated two framed photographs of himself and Howard, and also a framed poster advertising their contest. The items raised the princely sum of £1,900.

Spinks was a tremendous attraction and treated with great affection by the Welsh people. He signed so many autographs that at one stage he had to have a rest because his wrist was aching. Not that he minded because he was delighted to support any cause in aid of his former opponent and friend.

Charity was always high on Terry's agenda. For many years he travelled extensively throughout the British Isles supporting events staged to raise money for a wide variety of worthy causes.

During the early 1960's, he became one of the original committee members of the Freddie Mills Club. It was founded by Freddie and Stan Johnson just before the former world light-heavyweight champion's tragic death in 1965.

In the early days it was a club for muscular dystrophy sufferers, but with the passing of time became open to those suffering from other mental and physical problems. In recent years it has become open to all ages ranging from eight years to over 50's. When the club started it operated from the Army drill hall at Pimlico, but money raised by Bob Hope in America was later used to build new premises called Clubland at 54 Camberwell Road in south east London.

Harry Carpenter was the club's first President and held the position for 30 years. When he retired in 1997 he was succeeded by former European heavyweight champion, Dick Richardson. Apart from Terry Spinks, original committee members included Terry Downes, Johnny Shannon, Roy Francis and Larry O'Connell. Former boxers Billy Aird, Mark Rowe, Bobby Neill and Billy Walker have also given great support to fund raising events, as did Reg Gutteridge OBE.

Some years later 'Angels with Dirty Faces' was formed, it being an off-shoot of the Freddie Mills Club. It consists of the fittest and more able members of the Freddie Mills Club, pupils from Cumber Grove Junior School, adults from the world of boxing, and city workers.

With a club motto *'You'll do a good turn and not get found out, if you do it does not count',* the object of the Angels is to integrate members of the Freddie Mills Club into the general world of sport, leisure and social society.

The club organises trips to the coast, days in the country and five-a-side football matches, all of which cost money. No financial support is received from government or local council, so it relies entirely on support from private donations and fund raising events. Terry Spinks and Sammy McCarthy were committee members since formation and attended many club functions.

The most popular and successful events were boxing shows comprising of 'contests' involving Angel members, many of whom suffer from Downs syndrome. Most of their 'opponents' were active and retired professional boxers who were always outclassed and never lasted the distance. Spinks and McCarthy were among those to have been knocked out over the years.

Another event which Terry and Sammy supported was the annual Boxers and Blind Golfers challenge match. Organised in support of the Freddie Mills Club and Angels with Dirty Faces, it has been staged for almost 20 years. Each team comprised of a boxer, English blind golfer and two other players.

Another strong supporter of the organisations was former British lightweight champion Joe Lucy, who everyone always described as a 'nice guy'. When he passed away in 1991, Bob Paget, the club Activities Organiser and Fund Raiser, decided it was important to keep his memory alive. He therefore donated a trophy which he named 'The Joe Lucy Nice Guy Award', which is presented each year at the golf day. It was awarded to Terry Spinks in 2000 and the previous year had been won by Sammy McCarthy.

One of the most popular characters around the British fight scene in recent years was Gary Davidson. He was also one of the bravest. A once successful boxer, trainer, manager and promoter, who at one time owned the Thomas A' Beckett, he suffered from Motor Neurone Disease for several years. Despite being confined to a wheelchair in the later years of his life, Gary continued to attend functions due largely to the tremendous support he received from members of the boxing fraternity.

For a number of years a benefit golf day was held near Sevenoaks to raise funds to help support Gary. Once he had recovered sufficiently from his own illness, Spinks gave his support. Although the event was for men only, Rosemary took him and busied herself with the raffle.

In 1999, the year before Gary died, Terry sat beside him on the top table at dinner. During the evening a letter of thanks which Gary had written, was read on his behalf. It said:

> I am so grateful to everyone for coming tonight. I've got Wally Angliss and Dave Smith here and they both boxed me. I've also got my friend Terry Spinks here who trained them both. I've got to laugh when I think about it because Terry could have fought us all together with one arm tied behind his back.

The last comment drew tremendous laughter whereupon Spinks put his arm around Gary and kissed him.

Terry was extremely fond of him and when Gary passed away on 7 February the following year, he became very distressed. At his funeral 10 days later at All Saints Church, New Cross in south London, Spinks stood with his mates Sammy McCarthy and Ron Cooper, and wept openly.

Over the years Terry attended countless amateur boxing club dinner shows staged to help keep the sport alive at grass roots level. In November 1970, he drove from his home in south London to Anglesey to present trophies to amateur boxers of the local club. No matter how far the journey he rarely accepted expenses for his attendance.

Yet his charity work was not just confined to boxing. In the early 1970's he was the guest speaker at a Hackney Rotary Club dinner where he engaged in a question and answer session. Asked by the local Padre how he felt when being hit, Terry replied, 'Well Padre, I feel like you do - it's better to give than receive.' His quick witted response brought roars of laughter from the audience of about 150.

Among the events Spinks attended during the 1980's was one in aid of the Pegasus Bed Fund staged annually in Sussex. It was claimed that the government would not provide much needed financial aid to the project. An event was therefore hosted by Sussex based Southwick Association Football Club of the Southern Counties League in conjunction with a local boxing club. Terry's presence helped to raise over £5,000 for the charity. He took his

Olympic gold medal for people to see and charged 50p for an autograph or photograph, all of which he donated to the cause.

For many years Spinks participated in football, cricket and darts matches for charity. Despite not being very talented, he was a regular member of a football team known as 'The Boxer's Eleven' which travelled all over the country. Sponsored by Lonsdale, they were captained by Tosh Chamberlaine, a former England schoolboy and youth international, who had spent 18 years with Fulham in the days of the legendary Johnny Haynes.

Terry rarely took the games seriously, and consequently he was involved in many amusing incidents. One Sunday, the team were due to play a game at Billericay. It was raining when they arrived at the ground, and in the dressing room, Spinks said he didn't want to play.

'Why not?' asked Chamberlaine. 'What's wrong?'

'It's raining,' replied Spinks. 'I don't want to get wet.'

Thinking he was joking, his team mates just laughed and started making their way to the pitch. 'No, I'm serious,' shouted Spinks. 'I'll only play if I can take an umbrella.'

A few minutes later, he ran on to the pitch carrying an umbrella. 'Put that thing away Terry,' said Tosh. 'You'll poke somebody's eye out.'

'No,' retorted Spinks. 'I'll only put it down when it stops raining.'

Onlookers believed the whole episode was part of the entertainment. Only when the umbrella was taken from Terry and thrown to the touch-line did it become apparent that he was serious.

On another occasion, he was invited to kick-off a charity match at Littlehampton. As he walked on to the pitch he was given a tremendous reception. Nobody, however, noticed his footwear until a young girl suddenly shouted out, 'He's got odd shoes on.' Terry was wearing one black and the other brown, but refused to disclose if it was deliberate or by accident.

Throughout his boxing career and the ensuing years, Terry visited hundreds of public houses and clubs all over London and the Home Counties to knock over piles of coins collected in the bars in aid of the blind, cancer research, the British Heart Foundation and a host of other charities. Even when he was very ill he attended a number of functions in aid of the Bradley Stone Trust. The young Canning Town boxer was buried at East London Cemetery, and whenever Terry visited his parent's grave he always walked the few yards to stand beside Bradley's for a few moments.

Following his recovery from ill health, Terry continued to work for charity. Within the space of three weeks during November 2000, he attended events organised by Bournemouth Rotary Club for breast cancer and children's charities, and by Clacton Round Table. Each event raised approximately £5,000.

Spinks had many mementoes for the good work he did. Each year between 1980 and 1985 he was presented with a trophy by Jersey Dinner and Sporting Club for attending charity events on the island. The Uppercut Club, of which Terry was President, and Johnny Shannon the Chairman, presented him with a trophy inscribed *'For all his help in helping others.'* The club was set up by a group of ex-boxers as a charity organisation to help people in boxing who had fallen upon hard times.

Terry's commitments to charitable causes stemmed very much from his generous nature which was movingly described by his friend and former employer, John Branch: 'He is the most generous, openhearted, kindest man ever to have been a boxer. He should have been a priest because he always thinks of others rather than himself. He would travel miles to do anyone a favour.'

Terry loved children, and early one morning asked a newspaper boy in the East End where he lived. 'That's a long way to come,' he replied when the boy told him. Later that day Spinks went and bought a bicycle which he gave to the boy the following morning. 'Here you are son, I think you deserve this,' he remarked with a smile.

One day after his illness, Terry accompanied Rosemary and a group of friends on a trip to the Isle of Wight. As they strolled along the seafront in the blazing sun, they came across a small group of children suffering from Downs syndrome. Without saying a word to anyone Terry walked up to one of their carers, thrust a five pound note into her hand and asked her to buy the children ice-creams.

Wherever he went, people took to Terry and wanted to talk to him. Over the years he only had to walk into a bar of a local pub and a host of customers wanted to shake his hand, pose for photographs or get an autograph. It didn't matter whether he signed a piece of paper or a beer mat because his signature meant the world to the recipient.

Although it had always been that way, there were occasions when intrusions became a hindrance. 'There were times when his popularity became a bit too much for both of us, particularly when we were engaged,' recalled his first wife Valerie. 'I remember several occasions when we were in restaurants and wanted to be on our own, but somebody would come up to our table and insist on starting a conversation. I'd got quite angry.'

Despite all the lows in his life, Terry remained as popular as ever. During recent years he received requests for signed photographs from fans in Norway, Germany, the Czech Republic, America and Australia, as well as countless numbers from all parts of the United Kingdom. Another measure of his immense popularity was the fact that almost 30 years since he first went there, he still received letters and Christmas cards from friends he made in South Korea.

* * *

The fact that Spinks was never honoured for his Olympic achievement had become a source of great annoyance to many people, particularly in the East End. One evening during 1995 while Terry was still a patient at Sutton Manor clinic, Eddie Johnson told Rosemary he thought it was a terrible injustice that he had been overlooked for an MBE.

Having lived in the East End all of his life Eddie knew a lot of people, so without further ado he started petitions in his pubs on Terry's behalf. He also wrote to the Nominations Committee at Downing Street, and his action became the start of a campaign which intensified as the years passed.

'I feel we must honour him while he is still with us,' Johnson told a local newspaper. 'So many of our heroes only get their dues when they are no longer here.'

After a delegation from Manchester Ex-Boxers Association visited London, they set about collecting signatures in the north of England to help the campaign. Terry's old mate, Terry Gill, also set up a petition, while former ABA flyweight champion and England international, Derek Lloyd, wrote to the Nominations Committee.

Meanwhile, Rosemary spoke to many people, and also wrote letters to the Princess Royal, herself a former Olympian, Tony Banks, the Sports Minister of the time, and the Nominations Committee. She even included photographs of Spinks with other boxing gold medal winners Dick McTaggatt and Chris Finnegan together in evening dress at a dinner. Chris and Dick, who had both been honoured, wholeheartedly supported the campaign and also wrote letters of nomination.

As the months and years passed by nothing happened. There was a growing feeling that the nominations were being ignored, but nobody could understand why. Some people thought Terry's link with the Kray twins could be the barrier, but this was sheer speculation. In reality, Terry was never regarded by the authorities as an associate, and was never investigated for any supposed wrong-doing. He was nothing more than one of a number of highprofile celebrities invited to attend charity functions organised by the twins. Their guest lists included plenty of prominent members in public office as well as sportsmen.

There was no denying that Spinks appeared in group photographs with the Krays, some of which were used in subsequent publications about them. Yet so did many other well known people both male and female, some of whom were subsequently honoured for their contributions to particular aspects of life. As far as Terry was concerned, the photographs he appeared in were innocent. He always maintained that he only knew the Krays as honest businessmen, and at no time was he ever asked to do anything illegal.

Reggie Kray in particular had great respect for Spinks, and in April 1965 invited him, Terry Allen and Ted 'Kid' Lewis to his wedding. Even when he was ill in prison many years later, Reggie often asked visitors from the East End how Terry Spinks was and that he be told he said 'Hello'.

As Terry continued to be overlooked, so the campaign gained momentum. People from all walks of life wrote letters and offered their support. Among them were Sir Henry Cooper and veteran boxing commentator and journalist, Reg Gutteridge, who in fact originally thought Spinks had already been honoured.

'My own award proves the Palace are not anti-boxing,' Sir Henry told the *Sunday Telegraph* in June 2000. 'Why Terry is still waiting for his gong after all these years is beyond me.'

Chris Finnegan added his weight to the campaign. 'I was awarded the MBE only a few months after I'd won my gold and the day I went to the Palace is one of the highlights of my life.' he remarked. 'It is diabolical that Terry has been left out, and I would do anything to help right this wrong. I can't understand why the authorities have insulted a great champion like this.'

Dick McTaggart, regarded by boxing enthusiasts as Britain's greatest amateur boxer of all time, was another person outraged by the situation. 'I think it is disgusting that he has been overlooked,' he remarked. 'He was just a wee lad of 18 when he won the gold medal. It was an incredible achievement, but it seems that the people who matter have taken no notice.'

A number of national newspapers also gave Spinks strong support, none more so than Colin Hart in the *Sun.* In a moving lengthy story in April 2000, he wrote:

> My inspiration to tell Spinks' story is The Sun's successful crusade to get film star Michael Caine his knighthood. I'm not asking for anything as lofty as a knighthood for Terry. Just the MBE he earned and didn't get nearly half a century ago.

The one glimmer of hope Colin gave Spinks and his army of supporters was that it took England's 1966 World Cup winning stars Nobby Stiles, Roger Hunt, Alan Ball, Ray Wilson and George Cohen 34 years before they got Royal recognition.

Although Spinks maintained a dignified silence, members of the London Ex-Boxers Association lobbied successive Prime Ministers and even members of the Royal Family. Labour MP for Ilford South, Mike Gapes, also took up Spinks case, while the publication *East End Life* advised readers to support him by writing to their MP or the Sports Minister.

Representations were also made to Kate Hoey who succeeded Tony Banks as Minister of Sport. She worked enthusiastically on Terry's behalf, continuing to do so even after losing her ministerial position. In an article in the *Guardian* on 5 November 2001, she raised questions over the selection system for the New Year's Honours List, making particular reference to the case of Terry Spinks:

> The system is riddled with inconsistencies and is biased towards personalities. The unsung heroes of sport are those least likely to be going to the Palace, while those who are paid large salaries in sporting quangos are almost guaranteed a gong.
>
> For years efforts have been made by many in sport and successive sports ministers (including myself) to get recognition for the boxer Terry Spinks. Olympic gold winner in 1956, now 63 and in poor health, Spinks is the only gold medallist still living who has not been called to the Palace. Despite years of unstinting work for charity in the East End of London, he continues to be overlooked.

Ms Hoey's article was an inspiration to Terry's supporters, not least stalwart campaigner, Ron Olver. Writing in *Boxing News* two weeks later, he commended her criticism of the system which had treated the former Olympic champion so unfairly for years:

> And so say all of us. It is indeed a disgrace Terry has been overlooked, and I have this to say to those responsible for the selection process - Terry's friends and fans will continue to press his claims for official recognition, and will never, never, never stop trying to obtain the award he so richly deserves.
>
> That's not a warning, it's a promise. So cheer up, Terry. We're all

> behind you, and with everyone's perseverance there can eventually only be one winner your good self.

Since the campaign began in 1995, the hopes of supporters rose as publication of each new list of New Year and Queen's Birthday Honours became due. With almost predictable regularity, however, those hopes were dashed. People regarded it as a terrible injustice that Terry continued to be overlooked, and not surprisingly many reflected the saying: 'One rule for the rich, another for the poor'.

Disappointment turned into anger, but the determination to obtain justice intensified. In an article entitled *'Terry Spinks: The Forgotten Olympian,'* published in October 2001, the writer concluded:

> In and out of the ring, Terry has always been a model professional. No bad mouthing of opponents or disputing decisions of referees. He is an honourable man, and even 40 years after retirement from boxing his popularity remains as high as ever. Sadly, his only enemies appear to be the individuals who award New Year and Birthday Honours.

Although the article was well-timed, as was that of Kate Hoey, it is unlikely that either had any impact on what was finally occurring. Behind the scenes, favourable consideration had already been given to Terry's nomination, and on Saturday 10 November 2001, the letter everyone had been waiting for, dropped through the letter box. He had been nominated to receive an MBE.

As Rosemary held power of attorney for Terry, and handled his mail, it was she who opened the letter. She was ecstatic, but there was just one problem. Nominees are notified several weeks in advance of the official announcement, and during the interim period confidentiality must be maintained. The letter stressed that should the information be leaked to a third party, the nomination could be cancelled.

Terry was typically composed when Rosemary read him the letter. 'Oh, that's nice,' he remarked

.'Terry, is that all you've got to say?' said Rosemary full of emotion and excitement

.'Well, I am very proud,' he replied. 'I shall be honoured to receive it.'

There were celebrations throughout the East End once the New Year Honours List was published. In the pubs and clubs the toast was *'Terry Spinks* '. When an announcement was made at Charlie Magri's pub on New Year's Eve, the place erupted. There was genuine excitement because true East End folk knew that justice had finally been done. Terry was the calmest person in the place as congratulations were heaped upon him. 'I don't know what all the fuss is about,' he said with typical modesty.

In the days following publication of his honour, Spinks was in tremendous demand. Photographers and reporters sought pictures and a story, and it was as though the clock had been turned back to December 1956 when he returned from Melbourne. In the street, people stopped to shake his hand, while at home it became a full-time job dealing with telephone calls and post.

On New Year's Eve alone, 80 telephone calls were received at Rosemary's house. Callers included George Cohen, a member of the 1966 England world cup winning team, former boxers Alan Minter, John H Stracey, Chris Finnegan and Dick McTaggatt, all of whom were delighted that Terry had finally been honoured. His close friend Terry Gill called from Tenerife.

By mid-afternoon the situation was so hectic that Terry suggested they left the 'phone off the hook. 'We can't do that,' said Rosemary, 'people are so happy for you they just want to offer their congratulations.'

'Well, if anyone else rings tell them I've gone to bed for a while,' said Spinks casually. It wasn't disrespect just the words of a quiet, modest man who hated fuss and attention.

When the London Ex-Boxers Association held their first meeting of 2002, the gathering of about 200 members and guests stood and clapped Terry all the way to his seat. There was genuine pride and happiness because the Association had been so solidly behind the campaign seeking to get him honoured.

16

TRIP TO THE PALACE

The trip to Buckingham Palace for Terry's investiture would be the most important event in the lives of the 1956 Olympic Gold medallist and the lady who had saved his life. Few people deserved it more and thanks to the relentless efforts of Rosemary, Spinks would be well enough to appreciate and enjoy every minute of it.

Although there had been no indication when the event would take place there was tremendous excitement and anticipation as they awaited further contact. In the meantime day-to-day life became extremely hectic as more and more people made contact, many of whom they had not heard from in years. National and local newspaper reporters clamoured for interviews as did writers from a variety of magazines and periodicals along with a host of photographers.

At the time Johnny Claydon was the licensee of The White Hart public house at Green Street just a few hundred yards from the West Ham United football ground. Because of his love and respect for the former Olympic champion he applied to the brewery, and was granted, permission to change the name of the premises to The Terry Spinks MBE.

During the evening of Saturday 23 February 2002 more than 200 people from all walks of life packed into the pub for the official opening. Five days later Claydon hosted the official launch of Terry's biography, *East End Idol*. It was Spinks' sixty-fourth birthday and also an anniversary for Johnny who, 24 years ago to the day, had fought Charlie Nash for the British lightweight championship.

Again the venue was packed with friends and admirers many of whom were past and present boxers. They included former world champions Alan Minter and Charlie Magri, former British featherweight champions Bobby Neill and Sammy McCarthy as well as former East End boxers Terry Murphy, Ron Richardson, Terry Gill, Ron Jones, Bernie Dillon, Terry Collins, Terry Brown, Stan McDermott and his son John who had recently turned professional, and Mickey O'Sullivan who did an outstanding job standing in at the last minute as the Master of Ceremonies.

There were a number of speeches, the highlight of which came from the late Reg Gutteridge OBE. He had the packed gathering in fits of laughter saying that the new Terry Spinks MBE was the first synagogue he had ever been in.

At one point Reg, whose talks often contained the occasional expletive, recognised the local mayor, a Sikh gentleman, in the audience. Holding up a hand as a gesture of apology he remarked: 'I'm sorry my lord, I don't normally swear like this. It's these bloody East Enders, they are a bad influence on me.'

The publication of the book was an added stimulus for Spinks because in the weeks and months that followed dozens of invitations were received for him to do book signings at pubs, clubs and other venues throughout London, particularly in the East End. Calls also came from further afield to attend similar events in Kent, Sussex, Norfolk, Suffolk, Essex, Oxfordshire, Devon and the West Midlands and included reunions with old customers at his pubs at Upchurch and Worthing.

Between book signings a variety of other events were attended. Former boxer Bernard Hart, chairman of the Lonsdale International Sporting Club, organised a sell-out black tie dinner in Terry's honour at the Marriott Hotel in London's west end.

When the Metropolitan Police boxed an American Select Team at their Chigwell Sports Club to raise money for the victims of the September 11 terrorist attacks, Spinks was invited as a guest and donated signed copies of his biography for auction. Another important event was when Brighton Police resurrected an old boxing club at Moulescombe for the purpose of getting troubled local youngsters off the streets. Their first choice as guest of honour at their opening show was Terry Spinks. On another occasion he was invited as a guest at the Barnardo's Classic Golf Day at Chigwell Golf Course.

Spinks was also extremely popular in Wales and was invited there on a number of occasions during the years to do book signings. He was guest of honour at a gentleman's evening at Newbridge Rugby Club and the following day visited The Royal Oak public house in Cardiff where he and Sammy McCarthy posed for photographs holding the Lonsdale belt won by Jim Driscoll in the early 1920's. The extremely valuable trophy had been collected from a bank vault especially for the occasion.

Later in the year Terry and Sammy were among invited guests at Merthyr for the unveiling of a statue in honour of former undefeated British, European and Commonwealth bantamweight champion, Johnny Owen. The main guest was former world champion, Lupe Pintor, who was Johnny's opponent in his fatal challenge for the world title at Los Angeles on 19th September 1980. The Welshman was knocked out in the 12th round and sadly died on 4 November the same year from injuries sustained during the fight.

The forty-seven years old Mexican travelled to Wales to be present at the event where he became an instant hit with the local people. Spinks was equally popular because of the friendship he established years earlier with Howard Winstone following their championship fight in 1961. Although Pintor spoke very little English, he communicated well enough to acknowledge that he knew of Terry's achievements in the ring. The two greeted each other and embraced as the great champions they were.

Despite the popular little East End idol being in huge demand, distance was no object. Keeping him in the spotlight again was essential for his health and well being. Whilst Rosemary ensured that he was always immaculately dressed for every occasion, her husband Terry did the bulk of the chauffeuring.

Spinks had always been an extremely popular man both in and out of the ring, but the awarding of the MBE and publishing of his biography brought people even closer to him. The difficulties he had encountered in the past were well known and at every event he was constantly the centre of attention. Yet it was this day-to-day contact with genuine people that motivated him. Consequently, he bore no resemblance to the tragic figure of ten years earlier when death looked imminent.

It was a moving situation because although older and less mobile, Terry was once again a bright, chirpy and contented individual. With his life-long friend, Sammy McCarthy, often at his side, he took everything in his stride. There was a warm smile and handshake for everyone as he signed books by the dozen and posed for photographs. Yet whilst it was an incredible recovery from the problems of the past, care was still essential. Consequently, whenever he showed signs of tiredness, the ever alert Rosemary was quick to call time.

* * *

Terry's investiture was eventually set for 2 May 2002 which amazingly also happened to be Rosemary's birthday. After all she had done for him with the constant care and campaigning, it was nothing less than she deserved and is best described as a fairy tale ending. The date had a further significance in that it was 41 years to the day that Spinks lost his British featherweight title to Howard Winstone.

Meanwhile a television company were conducting research for a programme entitled 'Secrets of the Honours System.' Having learned of the length of time it had been before Spinks was honoured, they were keen to feature him in the production. It was therefore agreed that members of the team would follow the former boxer and his guests to Buckingham Palace where they had been granted permission to film in specific areas of the grounds.

The Spinks household at Chadwell Heath came to life shortly after 5am on 2 May and preparations got into full swing for the big day ahead. One of Terry's chosen guests, Sammy McCarthy, arrived just before 7am followed shortly afterwards by the television crew. They filmed all of the former boxer's trophies and certificates and took close-up footage of him dressing in his top hat and tails. A blue chauffeur-driven Rolls Royce Phantom which had been hired for the journey also arrived in good time.

With the exception of Terry's son Jarvis who was to meet them at The Mall, the party set off for Buckingham Palace at 8am. They were due at their destination by 10am, but even allowing for the London rush hour traffic, they were confident of arriving in good time.

It was a bright sunny morning as they began what they believed would be an exciting journey. After all the years of frustration, campaigning and waiting for recognition it appeared that the gods were at last being kind. That was until they were about halfway to the Palace and traffic suddenly came to an abrupt halt. The area from Hackney Road to Shoreditch High Street was gridlocked due to roadworks and there was no escape route. Consequently more than an hour passed during which time they did little more than a mile.

Knowing they were due at their destination by 10.00am and that the gates closed by 10.30am at the latest the tension in the car was unbearable. Rosemary was devastated and convinced they wouldn't make it in time. 'We've waited and campaigned all these years for this,' she said to Sammy who sat nervously beside her, 'and now we're not even going to get there.'

They waited and waited for what seemed like an eternity, but eventually, thanks to a combination of luck and skilful driving by the chauffeur, they began making slow progress. They finally arrived at Buckingham Palace at exactly 10.30am just as the gates were closing. As they pulled up, the gate keepers, having identified a large sticker on the car windscreen issued by the Palace, went in to a panic and furiously waved them into the main parade area.

Once inside the grounds they were all subjected to a full security check during which a search was made beneath the car for hidden explosives. Then, closely followed by the film crew, they were directed to a courtyard where they met Ernie Hearn, a friend who was also to receive the MBE for services to the community. He had been due to receive his honour on an earlier date, but successfully applied for his ceremony to be changed in order that he could accompany Terry inside the Palace.

Inside the building, Rosemary, Sammy and Jarvis were directed to the guest area whilst Terry and Ernie were escorted to another area where they joined other award winners. A high ranking army officer then explained procedure and protocol and announced that Prince Charles would conduct the investiture. Although there was no prior indication of this it was, in some respects fortunate, because Spinks had met the Prince on a number of previous occasions.

Terry learned his lines well, bowing smartly at both his initial meeting with the Royal host and at the end of his investiture ceremony. They spoke for several minutes throughout which Prince Charles gently held Terry's right arm. Smiling warmly, the affection he had for the former Olympic champion was clear for all to see.

Outside the Palace dozens of friends and family members, among them George Carr, the Pearly King of Southwark, gathered to welcome Terry and his guests as they came out. They cheered and waved small Union Jack flags and Spinks responded magnificently. He repeatedly teased a uniformed policeman and made the crowds shriek with laughter as he flexed the muscles in his forehead to make his top hat pop up and down. Every lady in close proximity of him was kissed at least once.

After photographs had been taken the party were taken to Stratford where arrangements had been made for a grand party at the celebrity restaurant, Phoenix Apollo. A large crowd awaited their arrival amongst them former boxers Charlie Magri, Bobby Neill and Ronnie Cooper together with Reg Gutteridge OBE and *Sun* newspaper's boxing correspondent Colin Hart who had given great support to Terry's campaign.

As it was a double celebration party, more family members were there including Rosemary's mother Iris, to celebrate her daughter's birthday. A huge cake decorated with candles and sparklers was presented to her. It was a real East End occasion during the course of which Dick McTaggart telephoned from Scotland to congratulate his fellow Olympian. It had been an incredible day, without doubt the greatest in Terry's life since he won his gold medal 46 years earlier.

The awarding of the MBE brought more prestigious invitations. Nine days later, on Saturday 11 May, he was a guest at Upton Park for West Ham United's final home game of the season against Bolton Wanderers. It began with a conducted tour of the stadium, then at half time he was taken on to the pitch where he drew lucky raffle ticket numbers. His attendance was a particular honour because he was the first sporting personality to be invited to the ground since the Queen opened the new Bobby Moore Stand.

A few weeks later Channel 4 Television broadcast the documentary 'Secrets of the Honour System.' It featured the situation involving Spinks and included interviews with Kate Hoey, MP, Reg Gutteridge OBE and Colin Hart. All were highly critical of the delay in him being awarded his honour. The programme also showed clips of him setting off for Buckingham Palace, conversations during the journey and of him, Rosemary, Sammy and Jarvis leaving the Palace to cheering crowds.

* * *

Rosemary had always maintained that if Terry ever received an honour she would organise the biggest party the East End had ever known. True to her word, and assisted by her husband and a group of close friends, she successfully staged what was aptly advertised as 'An East Enders Night' at York Hall, Bethnal Green on 1 June 2002. The venue was chosen because for years it had been referred to as 'the home of boxing.'

It was a hugely popular event and long before the doors opened at 6.30pm, the queue stretched for several hundred yards. Apart from many people coming from throughout London and the Home Counties, coaches brought parties of others from Scotland, Wales and the Midlands. It was a thoroughly professional affair with an amazing buffet which included an assortment of seafood provided free of charge by Ernie Johnson who Terry knew from his boyhood and Lyceum Ballroom days. Former world welterweight champion, John H. Stracey, provided the music and a highly collectable souvenir brochure was produced to commemorate the occasion. There were also speeches, presentations, a raffle, auctions and a book signing session.

Master of Ceremonies was John McDonald who, for many years has introduced boxers at promotions staged by Barry Hearn and Matchroom. Guests included former boxing champions Charlie Magri, Alan Minter and Chris Finnegan, Reg Gutteridge OBE and Joan Turner once known as the world's strongest woman who, at her peak, tore telephone directories in half. Many members of the cast and production team of the film 'Shiner' in which Terry and Rosemary guested, were also present as were six Pearly Kings and Queens who sang a host of cockney songs during the evening.

The only minor setbacks were that, although it was always expected to be a huge event, the management of York Hall clearly didn't anticipate the size of the crowd which descended at opening time and made a beeline for the bar. Consequently the staff on duty couldn't cope. Obliged to wait long periods to get served many people left the building and went to nearby off-licences and a supermarket to purchase their supplies of booze. The door staff engaged by the hosts to ensure a trouble-free evening discretely turned a blind eye.

Earlier in the day, between setting up the hall and the doors opening, some disreputable individual stole a machine hired to select lucky raffle ticket numbers. Although this caused only minor inconvenience it left a nasty taste and had to be paid for.

The event was a complete success and the attendance, believed to be in excess of 1,100, was a fitting tribute to Terry. After all expenses were paid, £6,200 was left over which he suggested went to charity. At his request equal amounts were donated to West Ham Boxing Club, Arbour Youth Club, Angels with Dirty Faces and London Ex-Boxers Association. It was so typical of the generosity he had shown throughout his life and confirmed beyond doubt that the award of the MBE for services to boxing and charity was a worthy one.

17

FIGHTING FOR LIFE

With Terry continuing to maintain good health he was able to fulfil most engagements invited to. Apart from the succession of book signings around the country, he and Rosemary were guests at the Chelsea Flower Show the week after their party. They were chauffeured to and from the event courtesy of the charity Help the Aged. A feature of the day was the presenting of a well known actress and a sporting personality from the 1950's. Dora Bryan and Terry Spinks were chosen to fill these roles.

In April 2003, Terry and Rosemary were guests at a stage show featuring the popular comedian, Bobby Davro at the Wyllotts Centre, Potters Bar in Hertfordshire. Bobby was a good friend so before the show commenced Spinks and Sammy McCarthy visited his dressing room and presented him with a bottle of champagne. During his performance the comedian introduced them telling the audience they were two of the greatest British boxers of all time.

In June the same year East End bookmaker, Johnny Claridge, engaged Terry to officially open a new betting shop at Plaistow Road in East London. To ensure the former Olympian arrived in style Johnny hired a white stretch limousine to get him to the shop.

During the opening ceremony Spinks presented the bookmaker with a signed framed photograph to go on the shop wall. Johnny then offered his guest a free bet which he couldn't resist. After a cursory glance through *Sporting Life*, he picked Kuringal running in the first race at Brighton: "This one looks good," he said to Johnny. "How about letting me have a tenner on it?"

A couple of hours later at a small celebration at a nearby pub, Spinks met his first senior amateur opponent, George Rix, a fellow

East Ender whom he outpointed in December 1955. They had seen very little of each other for almost 50 years so it was a great reunion. A solid friendship developed and would last until George passed away in 2009.

A frequent visitor to the Spinks household, George often told a story about when he was in the army and posted to Singapore. At first he was extremely nervous but when an officer addressed his group and enquired if any of them were boxers, he immediately put up his hand. Asked if he had achieved anything in the sport George explained that he once boxed Terry Spinks who went on to win an Olympic gold medal. Shortly afterwards he was taken to a nearby military training centre. From that point onwards he received better quality food than those not involved in sport and claimed he never saw another riffle during the rest of his army service.

There was more good news for Terry early in the afternoon when someone walked in and told him that his horse had won: "That's nice," he replied modestly. "I wish a few more came in like that a few years ago." When Johnny Claridge re-appeared, Terry called out, "Hey John, you owe me a nice few quid on that horse I backed." As John reached for his hip pocket, Spinks laughed and said "Put it away, I was only joking. It's just nice to be able to pick a winner for a change."

* * *

Terry continued to lead a reasonably active life with very few health problems until the latter part of 2005 when he had a fall. He and Rosemary had been shopping and on returning home he got out of the car and lost his footing on a slight slope leading to their drive. He fell heavily backwards and although Rosemary was able to help him to his feet he was quite dazed and shaken. Despite him insisting that he was alright she was fearful that he had banged his head. Not prepared to take any chances she therefore took him straight to the local hospital, King George, at Goodmayes.

An X-ray confirmed that there was no injury to Terry's head, just bruising to his shoulders and back. Although he was allowed home and advised to rest for a few days it was the first indication of problems and within a few weeks his condition gave cause for concern. He did manage to attend an annual Ex-Boxers Association awards luncheon in London and made a presentation, but it was noticeable that he was not well.

By 20 February the following year Terry's health had deteriorated rapidly. Realising that he was very poorly Rosemary telephoned Roding private hospital at Redbridge, Essex a short distance from her home and was given an appointment for the following morning. Knowing how serious the situation was she contacted her friends, Mickey and Barbara O'Sullivan, who met her in the hospital car park with a wheelchair for Terry.

They were seen almost immediately by Dr John Jestico a neurologist who recognised Spinks the moment he was wheeled into the consulting room. After being helped from the wheelchair he was very unsteady on his feet, appeared distressed and confused and not fully aware of the surroundings. Dr Jestico explained to Rosemary at the outset that he wanted to establish the nature of Terry's illness before being told his personal history. At the completion of his initial examination he then had an in-depth discussion with Rosemary. She disclosed all of the difficulties Terry had experienced including emotional and depressing aspects over the years which had caused him to take to alcohol.

The neurologist confirmed that a lot of Terry's symptoms were attributed to the large amount of alcohol he had consumed over the years, and also his depression. When he was examined he had particular symptoms which led Dr Jestico to believe that he may have an obstruction to the flow of fluid which normally went around the brain.

The situation regarding this particular condition is that although in most patients there is no obvious cause, repeated head injury can be a cause of it. Dr Jestico therefore suspected that in Terry's case it was a long term situation in relation to boxing.

At the conclusion of his examination Dr Jestico advised Rosemary that Spinks was very unwell and needed to go into hospital immediately. He therefore telephoned staff at Dahlia, his own ward at King George Hospital, and explained the severity of the situation and told them to be prepared for Terry's arrival. Without any delay, Rosemary therefore put Terry into her car and took him straight to King George where staff were awaiting them. Terry was an inpatient at the hospital for exactly four weeks during which time he was confined to a wheelchair. Although he was described as being quite fit for his age, he was very unsteady on his feet and unable to take more than a few steps without falling or having to be given support. There was also some impairment of memory.

Rosemary attended the hospital every day from 11.00am until 2.00pm and only left Terry's side when he was required to sleep for an hour. She then returned and stayed with him until 8.00pm when it was time for him to be prepared for his night's sleep.

Terry always had a steady stream of visitors, but Rosemary was careful to limit them to just one or two at a time because he quickly became tired. The only time she relaxed her strict regime was on 28 February, his sixty-eighth birthday, when he received two cakes and visits from many close friends concerned about his predicament.

During the course of his confinement at King George Hospital, Spinks underwent a series of tests and was kept under observation. Dr Jestico, who carefully monitored his situation, did his rounds of Dahlia ward every Wednesday and family members needing to speak to him about particular patients were required to make an appointment. Rosemary, who kept a day-to-day diary throughout Terry's confinement, always had plenty of questions about his condition and welfare, so therefore made her appointments well in advance. Consequently, she was sitting outside his office each Wednesday morning when he arrived.

There were occasions when Dr Jestico didn't have time to stop and speak to her so she trotted along the corridors behind him firing questions all the way. She was determined to ensure that he understood all of her concerns. At one stage the doctor went on two weeks holiday, but went into his ward on the Saturday morning before he was due to return two days later. Rosemary happened to see him and waved. He briefly acknowledged her and she heard him say to the nurses: "Oh, she's seen me so I suppose I'd better go over to her. I knew I shouldn't have come in."

Not having seen Dr Jestico for almost two weeks Rosemary had become extremely concerned about Terry. She wanted to know the ins and outs of everything especially what would happen in the immediate future. With patience and understanding he was usually able to appease her and by doing so a strong trusting bond developed between them.

Following consultations between Dr Jestico and Mr Fary Afshar, a consultant neurosurgeon at Harley Street who practised at the Royal London Hospital at Whitechapel, Spinks was given lumbar punctures on two occasions in which spinal fluid was withdrawn from his lower back. He also underwent a number of scans which revealed that he had hydrocephalus, a condition in which fluid accumulates in the brain. Dr Jestico had suspected that this could be the problem during his initial examination of Terry at Roding Hospital. It meant that chambers inside the brain had become enlarged because the circulation of fluid wasn't functioning normally. It is known that people who develop hydrocephalus have involvement of memory concentration and balance.

Spinks was very ill and on 22 March 2006 he was transferred by ambulance to the Royal London Hospital where Mr Afshar and his team conducted a procedure to revert the hydrocephalus. This necessitated drilling a small hole in the skull and inserting a ventricular peritoneal shunt into the brain to withdraw the fluid. This was done through a connecting tube which passed under the skin and down to the abdomen.

Once the operation had been carried out Rosemary hoped it would all be over, but the following day she was told that the shunt had malfunctioned. Terry therefore had to undergo a further procedure to have another one fitted. Walking to the operating theatre with him again was extremely upsetting for her.

The second shunt was fitted at 11.00pm on 23 March, a Thursday, and Rosemary and her husband stayed at the hospital until Terry returned to the ward at 4.30am the following morning. They then went home, but at 7.30am received a telephone call from the hospital saying that the new shunt had also malfunctioned. Terry therefore needed to have a third operation in as many days to have a temporary drain attached. This would allow the unwanted fluid to drain from the brain into a bag attached to the outside of his head.

Rosemary was back at the Royal London Hospital by 9.30am and Terry was taken back to the operating theatre at 11.00am. As the hours slowly passed by Rosemary was beside herself with worry, convinced that he wasn't going to make it. It was the first time since his problems flared up that she became really negative. The news of Terry's plight had spread quickly and a number of close friends including Sammy McCarthy, Terry Bey, Don Dirs, Chris and Michelle Carr, and a close family friend Joan McFadyen, visited the hospital during the day to give her support.

Terry eventually returned to the ward at 3.30pm, but was extremely ill, so much so, that most people feared the worst. Rosemary became hysterical and insisted on staying at the hospital throughout the period that his condition remained critical. She had built up good relationships with staff of all levels and was given a room near to the hospital which had been designed especially for family members in such circumstances.

Although Terry's condition stabilised to some extent more bad news was not far away. On the Sunday night less than three days after his last operation, he pulled the tube out of the shunt that was in his brain. He was again extremely poorly and on 27 March had an emergency brain scan. Rosemary had been contacted by the hospital and asked to attend as soon as possible. She arrived just as Spinks was being taken to the theatre.

Mr Afshar fitted the shunt again two days later and over the next few days Terry's condition improved. The fluid was draining from his brain effectively and by 1 April he was well enough to be transferred by ambulance back to King George Hospital. He spent almost three weeks there during which time he had constant physiotherapy.

Although he was allowed home on 19 April, Terry needed constant 24 hours-a-day care. It was like looking after a newborn baby, but with Rosemary on hand throughout, strongly supported by her husband, he slowly made improvement. He gradually learned to walk again and to the surprise of Mr Afshar and his team the most recent operation produced a significant improvement. Within a month or two he was able to walk independently, his speech improved and his overall condition was generally far better than at any time since investigations into his problems were first made some months earlier.

Terry's courage and durability were incredible because despite what were serious setbacks he always bounced back as in his younger days when he was a fighter. After surgery he had been very unwell needing help with dressing, feeding, bathroom and general day-to-day movements. At his worst he was completely chair-bound and could rarely speak coherently, but as soon as the shunt was functioning correctly he began to make a slow but steady recovery.

Over the ensuing years the shunt and tube had to be revised as a matter of course. This meant visits to the hospital, but these were necessary to aid Terry's continued improvement. Rosemary was an absolute tower of strength and her care, patience and love were crucial throughout this stage of his life and pivotal to him gradually being able to do more for himself.

With the continued support of Rosemary, her husband and a small group of close friends, Terry was eventually able to go on holiday and attend a number of important functions. Unfortunately nothing lasts forever and in 2011 his health again deteriorated considerably. He became confused, couldn't walk properly and when he was unable to get up the stairs at home, a stairlift had to be installed.

Rosemary had by this time established strong friendships with Dr Jestico and Mr Afshar whereby she was able to telephone them at any time there was a concern over Terry's health. As soon as the new problems arose she therefore had further consultations with them and also Dr Cafelli who had taken over from Dr Jestico at King George Hospital. Although all three were of the opinion that Terry's shunt was working she was not convinced and kept telling them so.

Extremely concerned about Terry's condition Rosemary took him to Harley Street to see Mr Afshar taking with her new scans in order that he could compare them with previous ones. Unfortunately, a difficulty arose in that the computer he used to view them malfunctioned. He immediately called for an engineer and while they were waiting she had plenty of time to talk to him. During an in-depth one-to-one discussion she explained why she was convinced that the shunt was not working.

Respecting her opinion and determination to get the best possible treatment for Terry, Mr Afshar called a radiologist to look at the new scans with him. A few days later he telephoned Rosemary and said that he didn't think the shunt was working. Terry was therefore admitted to the London Clinic, a private hospital at Devonshire Place, Marylebone, on 13 May and underwent a further operation. At about 10.30pm that evening Mr Afshar explained to Rosemary that the shunt had not been functioning because the tube attached to it had become disconnected. This had caused the fluid to build up in Terry's brain again.

During the course of the operation Mr Afshar renewed the whole system, fitting what is known as a non-programmable shunt which is set to a low pressure and cannot be adjusted. The previous one was adjustable and had enabled Terry to be seen at the neurosurgeon's practice at Harley Street to have the pressure adjusted.

Terry was kept in hospital for three nights and in order that she could be beside him another bed was set up for Rosemary. During that short period he improved immensely, walking and talking well and was generally more alert. He was therefore allowed home, but about four weeks later started deteriorating again. Rosemary immediately contacted Mr Afshar and explained the situation. "I must have been like a bad dream to that poor man," she explained on recalling the events.

When Terry returned to the London Clinic a series of tests revealed that the shunt had become blocked and yet another operation was necessary. With Rosemary constantly at his side, he remained at the hospital for four nights, but did not respond as well as previously. All the operations were taking their toll on him, but there was no alternative because without the shunt he couldn't function at all. Nevertheless, he improved slowly and an indication of this was the volume of affection he showed towards the nurses. Kisses were at a premium!

In view of the improvement in Terry's health it had been hoped to take him to Florida for a holiday during October, but on 27 September he was suddenly taken ill again. He hadn't been well earlier in the day causing Rosemary to take him to their local doctor who diagnosed a chest infection and prescribed a course of antibiotics. On returning home he was given one dose and then had a short sleep. Later, while sitting at a table having a bowl of soup, his eyes became glazed and it was obvious that he was unaware of where he was or what was happening around him.

Rosemary had no alternative but to call an ambulance and on their arrival the paramedics quickly concluded that he needed to go to hospital. Being reluctant to allow this to happen again Rosemary called Dr Jestico on his mobile phone, but found he was on holiday in Spain. Despite this he was incredible and telephoned her back and spoke to the paramedics who explained that Terry's blood pressure was very low and he clearly had a serious problem.

Dr Jestico then explained to Rosemary that there was absolutely no alternative but to get Terry to hospital quickly. When told he would be going to Queen's at Romford, however, she complained bitterly. A few years earlier her mother had died there and she had made a formal complaint about unsatisfactory medical service. She pleaded with the paramedics to take Terry to King George, but was told there was no neurology department there. He had to go to Queen's.

Rosemary went in the ambulance with Terry. Shortly after arriving at the hospital he was transferred to the acute assessment ward because on examination it was thought he had an infection in his brain. Later the same night a sample of fluid was taken from the brain for testing. Being extremely concerned at this procedure Rosemary telephoned Mr Afshar who, on hearing what she told him, was of the opinion that it was not necessary. Medical staff at the hospital, however, insisted that it was done.

Desperate for support, Rosemary telephoned Don Dirs one of Terry's oldest and closest friends. He immediately joined her at the hospital and stayed for most of the first night.

Although the brain fluid tests proved negative, Terry's condition deteriorated to such an extent that he was transferred to intensive care where he remained for two days. He was so poorly that Rosemary contacted his son Jarvis who visited the hospital as did Sammy McCarthy. Another close friend, Chris Carr, on seeing Terry lying in bed wearing an oxygen mask, was so upset that he immediately turned and walked out of the ward. He stood outside for a short while in tears because he thought the former boxer was dying.

When Terry's condition improved slightly he was transferred to another ward, but after just two days was so ill that he was returned to intensive care. Again he improved sufficiently to return to a general ward where it was decided to do a lumber puncture because the doctors still believed there might be an infection in his brain. This was extremely painful and Rosemary had to help hold Terry down while it was done. Again the results were negative.

The neurosurgeon monitoring Spinks was Mr Bobby Arvin who was confident the shunt was functioning correctly. He knew Mr Afshar and during telephone conversations they agreed that it should remain in place. A further look at the shunt confirmed their belief. Both came to the conclusion that Terry had a chest infection which had developed into pneumonia. With constant medical care and a further course of antibiotics he slowly improved. The nurses all loved him and he was soon back to his normal romantic self.

News of his recovery spread and a regular stream of visitors called at the hospital each day and staff made special efforts to accommodate them. One person who has since become a good family friend is Jimmy Deneen, a porter at Queen's. A real boxing fan, he knew everything about Spinks' ring career. Whenever it was known that he had to have a scan or x-ray, Jimmy made sure he was on hand with a trolley to take him to the relevant department. He even ensured that he was the man to take his idol back to the ward.

Terry was eventually discharged from Queen's Hospital on 28 October 2011. Although he had missed the planned holiday in Florida and a grand Olympics Ball at Earl's Court three weeks earlier, he had survived yet another serious illness. Many people hadn't expected him to recover, but yet again he had defied all the odds.

18

LIFE GOES ON

Although Terry's shunt was first fitted in 2006, he was eventually able to lead a reasonable albeit restricted life. Again, Rosemary's persistence and determination were the driving factors. Having battled relentlessly throughout the traumatic times of some years earlier she was determined to ensure that he overcame the latest difficulties.

A very strong-minded woman, Rosemary knew everything there was to know about Terry's health and conditions and frequently challenged medical opinion when she felt the need to do so. The care and attention she gave him were first class and couldn't have been bettered by any trained professionals. She rarely left her house without him and whether it was on shopping trips or visits to friends or family, Terry was at her side.

Relaxed, happy and motivated, Spinks' health continued to improve to such an extent that he was even well enough to travel abroad for holidays. With the help of her family and a small group of close friends Rosemary took him to warm sunny resorts in Cyprus, Florida (three times), Tenerife and Lanzarote. Before each trip she took him to Mr Afshar for precautionary check-ups and every time he was given a clean bill of health. An indication of how much he had improved was born out by the fact that whilst in Florida he was able to go to large amusement parks and enjoy rides on the big roller coasters without a care in the world. Wherever they were he went swimming regularly and generally enjoyed himself.

On the home front Terry was kept active attending social events connected mainly with boxing and the Olympic Games. On 19 October 2006 he was an invited guest at a Sport England Olympics night in London. Then three days later, a Sunday, he attended a special Golden Boys Celebration Luncheon at the Hospitality Suite of West Ham United Football Club to mark the 50th anniversary of him and Dick McTaggart winning gold medals at the 1956 Olympics at Melbourne. Other medal winning boxers of the successful British team present were Tommy Nicholls (silver) and John 'Cowboy' McCormack (bronze). Nicky Gargano, who also won bronze, was also invited, but unable to attend.

The silver service event which featured music throughout lunch, and a comedian, was attended by a crowd of 350 which included top boxers John Conteh, Charlie Magri, Dave 'Boy' Green and Chris Finnegan. Master of Ceremonies, Steve Holdsworth, introduced the Olympians as a parade of champions - McCormack followed by Nicholls and McTaggart. Being on home ground Spinks was the last to appear, walking smartly into the suite accompanied by Mr Fary Afshar and Dr John Jestico who Rosemary maintained had saved his life. There was hardly a dry eye in the place and he was given a standing ovation as he made his way to his table.

A short but moving tribute speech was made to Terry by his close friend Chris Carr after which the four boxers received large framed montages of the 1956 Olympics, Terry's being presented to him by Reg Gutteridge OBE. A fifth was accepted on behalf of Nicky Gargano.

As they stood on the stage Reg joked about all the things that Terry had been presented with over the years. Looking at the montage he remarked: 'I hope you've got somewhere to put this bloody great thing whatever it is.'

Spinks smiled and said: 'I'll put it up for auction.'

Gutteridge, a natural comedian who adored Terry, responded quickly. 'I didn't know you were Jewish,' he quipped, but them in all seriousness added, 'We can't be all be gold medal winners and champions, but we can be a nice person.' Looking out to the packed audience he said with emphasis, 'And this kid is.'

Everything was done to ensure the event was special, the little extras making it something to remember. A banner containing photos of Terry and Dick was created and during proceedings it was signed by every boxer present and later auctioned for charity.

A souvenir brochure was produced and contained a moving message by Lord Sebastian Coe, Leader of the 2012 Olympic Organising Committee, which read:

> It gives me enormous pleasure to pay personal tribute to my fellow Olympians Terry Spinks and Dick McTaggart. Though I wasn't born when they won their gold medals in Melbourne, as an avid boxing fan I

learned at an early age about their magnificent victories. Their triumph has meant so much to amateur boxing and to the people of the country. It certainly ensured the names of Spinks and McTaggart became part of the folklore of the British Olympic Movement. How heart-warming it is to know their achievements 12,000 miles away in Australia half a century ago has not been forgotten. I know exactly what kind of dedication it takes to win Olympic medals. Terry and Dick thoroughly deserve this 50th anniversary celebration lunch in their honour because they embody the true spirit of the Olympics. Not only were they team mates in 1956 but also they have remained friends ever since. It is gratifying the other three medallists from that brilliant boxing squad, Tommy Nicholls (silver), Nicky Gargano (bronze) and John " Cowboy" McCormack (bronze) are able to share in today's festivities. As leader of the London Olympic Organising Committee, I will be an extremely happy man if we can find the youngsters good enough to emulate Terry, Dick and co in 2012.
My best wishes to everyone attending this function.

Seb Coe

With Terry continuing to maintain good health, Rosemary and her friends organised a special luncheon on 16 March 2008 to celebrate his seventieth birthday. Again the Hospitality Suite of West Ham United football club was the venue and the fact that over 300 people were in attendance demonstrated the immense popularity of the man. It had been just the same with the Golden Boys event 18 months earlier with the organisers claiming that had there been sufficient space twice that number would have purchased tickets.

Once everyone was seated, Master of Ceremonies, Steve Holdsworth, introduced Terry who proudly walked into the room to the accompaniment of the famous West Ham song 'I'm for ever blowing bubbles.' Once he reached his table everyone stood and sang 'Happy Birthday.'

Music played throughout lunch after which came the highlight of the event, an extremely original and professional version of 'This is Your Life.' It was researched and presented by close family friend Richard Barber who, for many years, has been an inspector for the British Boxing Board of Control and at the time wrote the Old Timers column in *Boxing News*.

Complete with red book, Richard skilfully took the attentive audience through the highs and lows of Terry's life and, at the appropriate moments, called particular guests to the stage. In order, they were Danny Enifer, Tony Rawlinson, George Rix, Bernie Dillon, Dick McTaggart, Tommy Nicholls, Reg Gutteridge OBE, Sammy McCarthy, Bobby Neill, Jarvis Spinks (Terry's son), Johnny Claydon and finally Dr John Jestico and Mr Fary Afshar.

Terry then presented glass plaques to Dr Jestico and Mr Afshar and thanked them for everything they had done for him. He also made presentations to Richard Barber and to Brian and Dawn Jones who had videoed the whole event which was subsequently reproduced on DVD.

A huge cake to celebrate Terry's birthday was cut up and distributed to all tables. A large banner had been created bearing two photographs, one of him as a young boxer with his Lonsdale belt and another of him in modern times. As with the Golden Boys event, this was signed by all the boxers present and later auctioned with other items. There was also a raffle.

The event was a resounding success and at the end former Southern Area featherweight champion, Phil Lungdren who, at the time was chairman of the Southern Area Council of the British Boxing Board of Control, told Rosemary he couldn't wait until Spinks was seventy-five so they could have another party.

A few weeks later Terry had what was a historic and extremely emotional meeting with former Pakistani boxer, Sammy Harris, his first opponent at the Melbourne Olympics. They had not met since then, but Sammy, who settled in Britain during 1963 and lived at Burnt Oak in North West London, was seriously ill with the lung condition pulmonary fibrosis. Knowing that he was dying he told his daughter he would love to meet Spinks again. She telephoned Rosemary and a meeting was arranged at Sammy's home where his family laid on a fantastic buffet lunch.

Despite their respective health problems the two former Olympians thoroughly enjoyed the reunion. They were in good form as they sat next to each other chatting about old times in the presence of a reporter and photographer from a local newspaper who had been invited along to record the event. Smartly dressed in his Olympic blazer, Spinks took along his gold medal to show his former opponent who was equally smart in a two piece suit.

'It was good to see Sam,' said Terry. 'It was a long time ago, but I can still recall the match – he was a strong fighter.'

Harris was equally delighted to meet his old opponent after almost 52 years. 'I remember looking at him in the ring and thinking he looks so young,' he recalled. 'It was pretty close. I was going for the knockout, but he was going for tactical points. My God! he was fast; he just didn't give me the chance to get close.'

It was crucial that the reunion took place when it did because just several weeks later Sammy's daughter telephoned Rosemary to say that he had passed away. Like Spinks he had dedicated a lot of time to boxing, coaching youngsters at Finchley Boxing Club for 10 years. Meeting Terry again was his dying wish.

* * *

Over the next two years or so, Rosemary continued to keep Terry active, taking him everywhere with her. Although he was slower in both mind and body, he was generally happy and this showed in his personality and attitude towards other people. He had always maintained close contact with Dick McTaggart and in November 2009 they were special guests at an England versus Scotland amateur boxing international dinner at the Royal Lancaster Hotel in London. Before the boxing commenced Terry, headed by a drummer, led the English team into the ring while Dick did likewise with the Scottish boxers headed by bagpipes.

Despite almost 50 years elapsing since he won his gold medal, Spinks continued to attract media attention even for mundane events. One such occasion was at Easter 2010 when Terry, Rosemary and her husband, younger son Graham, his wife Penny and their three children took a short break at Bath. It was a trip down memory lane because many years earlier Rosemary's parents owned Ashgrove Guest House at Bathwick Street. She and Terry spent many happy times there when they were much younger and as her mother had recently passed away she wanted to stay at the guest house again to relive old memories.

During their two-day stay they visited the abbey, Roman Baths and all the places they knew before. News of Terry's presence in Bath was relayed to a local newspaper office and a reporter soon tracked him down. A meeting took place in a local cafe and photographs were taken and used to illustrate a short story in the *Bath Chronicle* on 8 April.

For many years Rosemary and her husband took Spinks to Ex-Boxers Association events in various parts of the country. In particular a special welcome was always afforded them at Brighton, Home Counties and more recently the newly formed Hastings group where a seat and parking place was reserved for Terry. Members of the association were honoured to have him as a member and always offered to pay his expenses which were of course refused.

When Brighton held their monthly meeting just a few days after Terry's seventy-fourth birthday special efforts were made to celebrate the occasion. He was presented with a large cake, films of his fights were shown and in a speech about it being Olympic year it was stated members were privileged to have him in their presence.

Three weeks earlier Terry had attended a Home Counties monthly meeting, the highlight of which was the presentation of a cheque for £1,600 to the organisers of Headley Court, the British Army Rehabilitation Centre in Surrey. The amount was raised as a result of painstaking efforts by Dave Porter, a former amateur boxer and for many years a British Boxing Board of Control inspector.

Dave had acquired a pair of boxing gloves which, over a period of years, he was able to get signed by Henry Cooper (before he became Sir Henry), Joe Bugner and referee Harry Gibbs. The much sought after gloves were raffled and at the meeting the winning ticket was drawn by former Southern Area bantamweight champion, Mark Goult who, like Spinks also suffers from a serious disability. He and Terry jointly presented the cheque to an officer from Headley Court.

Spinks had visited the rehabilitation centre the previous year at an event also organised by Dave Porter. Along with Sammy McCarthy, Mark Goult, former British and European Super-Middleweight champion, James Cook, actor/singer Jess Conrad and members of the British Boxing Board of Control, he was introduced from the stage. Smartly dressed in his Olympic blazer and proudly displaying his gold medal, he received the biggest ovation of the night.

* * *

As arrangements for the 2012 London Olympic Games got into full swing, Terry again became much sought after by members of the media. Having been born at Canning Town just a short distance from the new Olympic Stadium at Stratford, he was very much a local gold medallist who had never been forgotten and over a period of several months Rosemary was contacted by journalists from newspapers and magazines. In December 2011 a BBC television crew visited her home to interview her, Terry and their close friends regarding his achievement in 1956.

The following month photographers commissioned to take photographs of particular British gold medallists visited the Chadwell Heath address. Their works were subsequently exhibited at a John Lewis store at the new Westfield Shopping Centre adjacent to the Olympic Stadium. The feature of the exhibition, which was launched on 9 March 2012, was a group photograph which included Terry wearing his Olympic blazer and tie. There was also a large individual picture of him.

In April Rosemary received correspondence from the British Olympic Association Torch Relay organisers, stating that if Terry wanted to be considered for the London 2012 Torch Relay evening celebrations, an application form should be completed. Unfortunately his medical condition was such that he could never be fit enough, but the situation was reassurance that he was still very much in the minds of the organisers. Had fitness permitted there would have been no more popular torch bearer.

During the past decade the name of Terry Spinks regularly featured with the big names of the Olympics. In March 2005 he was a guest at a reception given at Buckingham Palace by the Queen and the Duke of Edinburgh to celebrate the Centenary of the British Olympic Association.

EIIR

The Master of the Household
has received Her Majesty's command to invite

Mr. Terry Spinks

to a Reception to be given at Buckingham Palace by
The Queen and The Duke of Edinburgh
on Wednesday, 23rd March, 2005 at 6.00 p.m.
to celebrate the Centenary of the British Olympic Association

A reply is requested to:
The Master of the Household,
Buckingham Palace,
London SW1A 1AA.

Dress: Lounge Suit / Day Dress
or Team Suit / Blazer

Guests are asked to arrive between 5.15 and 5.50 p.m.

Even before the 2008 event at Beijing, he whetted media appetite and together with other gold medallists from past decades, Tessa Sanderson (Javelin 1984), Rodney Pattison (Sailing 1968 and '72) and David Hemery (Athletics 1968) he was a guest at a Saga Magazine photo shoot in London. A four-page article was subsequently published in the August edition of the magazine with photographs and stories recalling their respective moments of triumph.

When considering all the medical setbacks it was amazing that Terry was so firmly in the minds of the organisers of the 2012 London Olympics. As far as they were concerned it was hoped that, as far as was humanly possible, he would be able to feature in one form or another. Although the continued care Rosemary had given him over the years had brought him to this place, many people were, however, realistic enough to know that anything could happen.

With his health having deteriorated rapidly over a period of weeks, fate duly played its hand and deprived Spinks from witnessing the huge sporting event. It had been much the same some weeks earlier when the great former Welsh rugby union captain, Mervyn Davis, who had bravely battled serious illness for several years, was deprived by just two days from witnessing the Welsh team's grand slam triumph in March 2012.

19

THE FINAL ROUND

The effects from years of ill health and a series of major operations finally took their toll on Terry and he passed away at his Chadwell Heath home at 6.30pm on Thursday 26 April 2012. It was quick and peaceful, and most importantly Rosemary was with him at the crucial moment. After all they had been through together it was an ending they both deserved.

Terry had not been well since the previous weekend and Rosemary was so concerned that she telephoned Dr Jestico and described his condition and symptoms. Believing he had possibly got another chest infection the doctor advised that Terry be put back on antibiotics to see how he responded. If he showed no improvement Dr Jestico would call and see him later in the day which is exactly what happened. He was shocked at the amount of weight Spinks had lost and how frail he was. He warned Rosemary that he could just pass away peacefully, but added that knowing his powers of recuperation he might get over it.

On Dr Jestico's advice Terry was seen by his family doctor the following day. He confirmed that there was a recurrence of a chest infection, but was of the opinion that he would get over it. This raised Rosemary's hopes because Spinks had recovered from serious bouts of ill health many times before, but when the doctor advised that he was admitted to hospital she flatly rejected it. Several weeks earlier agreement had been reached with Terry's son, Jarvis, that whatever condition he developed the former boxer would not be going into hospital again. When his time was up he would spend his final days at home.

By the Wednesday, Spinks had shown no signs of improvement. He was very poorly and getting progressively weaker, not being able to get from his bedroom to the bathroom unaided. The stairlift had to be used to convey him up and down the stairs, and a wheelchair was used in the house for the first time. Another major problem was that Rosemary was having great difficulty feeding Terry because he could not swallow properly.

Early that evening she telephoned a distant relative who was a district nurse and explained that she was extremely worried about Terry. They had met a few weeks earlier and Rosemary was told that if she ever needed her help she only had to ask. At about 9pm, the nurse arrived at the house with Rosemary's daughter-in-law, Andrea. Terry was sitting on the sofa and on seeing him she immediately said: 'He should be in bed.' After a brief examination he was wheeled into the hall, put on the stairlift and taken to his room and put to bed.

Rosemary gave him antibiotics and did everything she could to ensure he was comfortable. Only then did she leave his side and went downstairs where they had a monitor which would detect the slightest sound. Even after she went to bed she made frequent checks. When she heard him cough at about 4am, she jumped out of bed, went to his room and spent the rest of the night sitting on a stool at his bedside. Although she spoke to him Terry was unable to respond.

Early that morning, Rosemary telephoned family friend, Chris Carr, who lived a short distance away and asked him to come over as soon as possible. She wanted to move Terry into her bed because it was larger and would be more comfortable for him. The room was much bigger which would make it easier to look after him. As soon as Chris arrived he and Rosemary's husband carried Spinks into the larger room and put him to bed.

Later that day Terry's son, Jarvis, arrived on a pre-arranged visit, but found his father in extreme difficulty. He was gurgling frequently and unable to swallow. Something needed to be done quickly so while Jarvis, Chris and Rosemary's son, Graham, remained at the house, she and her husband went to the doctor's surgery to try and get somebody to return with them. Nobody was immediately available, but later in the afternoon the practice nurse and a GP attended and examined Terry. Although they agreed that he was very poorly, they did not think he would die that day. His condition was, however of such concern that they attempted to contact nurses to visit and care for him, but were unable to locate anybody.

At that point Rosemary, out of sheer desperation, telephoned her nurse friend who went straight to the house. On arrival she told Rosemary's husband to go to the surgery and persuade a doctor to return to the house and give Terry an injection to try and address the persistent gurgling in his throat. It was a matter of urgency.

Meanwhile, the gurgling worsened. Rosemary was terrified and cuddled Terry for a short time, but while doing so he passed away peacefully in her arms. The nurse, who was beside her, leaned over, examined him briefly before turning to Rosemary and saying: 'He's gone.'

Rosemary's daughter-in-law, Andrea, was downstairs and at the nurse's request, telephoned Terry Ellmore and told him to forget the original request, but to bring the doctor back because Spinks had passed away. The doctor who attended certified the cause of death as bronchopneumonia and dementia.

Although Rosemary was devastated she would receive an abundance of support from family and close friends. It had been that way throughout the time she had cared for Terry, not least from neighbours Sylvia and Charlie Andrews who had been towers of strength. Sylvia had been in and out of the house all day and only returned to her own home ten minutes before Spinks passed away. When Rosemary's husband gave them the bad news they returned immediately and stayed for the whole evening.

As arrangements were being made to remove Terry's body from the house, the nurse remarked that he had never gone out looking scruffy and wasn't going to now. After being given a bowl of warm water with shower gel in it, she washed him all over. At her request, Rosemary and her husband then got an entire set of clean clothes - shirt, cardigan, trousers and socks which she then dressed Terry in before putting on his slippers. The final act was to brush his hair and shave him with an electric razor.

Knowing that news of Terry's death would circulate rapidly, Rosemary's younger son, Graham, remained at the house that night and throughout the next day to deal with telephone calls and associated matters. A total of 206 calls were received, and over the next few days hundreds of cards were delivered.

The funeral arrangements were conducted by the highly respected East End undertakers, T. Cribb & Sons, who were family friends of Terry's father. Mr Cribb, senior, came out of retirement to handle it personally. This situation was of considerable help to Rosemary who was having great difficulty coping with the loss of Terry. Because of the long relationship with the family the funeral directors afforded her the opportunity to visit the Chapel of Rest to see him every day.

At one point a few days after Terry's death members of the family were at the undertaker's office and were told by a member of staff that an ITV crew were making a film about the workings of the company. Asked if they could film Terry's funeral, the general opinion was that as he had spent most of his life in the spotlight why not let him go out in it.

* * *

Following Terry's death obituaries appeared in most local and national newspapers. At boxing promotions over the next few days tributes were paid by the traditional sounding of '10-bells', including at the Royal Albert Hall where, in September 1960, Spinks beat Bobby Neill to claim the British featherweight title.

Other tributes came from far and wide. Former training partner at the West Ham Boxing Club gym, Paul Warwick, contacted the *Newham Recorder* from Canada saying: 'Terry Spinks was one of the true gentlemen of the sport of boxing. I still have fond memories of our days at the gym.'

West Ham club secretary, Lianne Jameson, contacted the same newspaper and said: 'Apart from Terry's magnificent achievements in the ring he was a true gentleman. He put West Ham ABC on the map and without him we probably would not be the club we are today.'

They were fitting comments and very much in line with a phrase Rosemary had used for years to describe Terry. Whenever the opportunity arose she would say: 'If the world was full of Terry Spinks' what a wonderful world it would be.'

* * *

The funeral of Terry Spinks MBE took place on 9 May 2012 starting with a service at The Convent, Bethell Avenue, Plaistow, E16. He was given a wonderful send off, his coffin being conveyed aboard a glass-sided carriage and drawn in style by two magnificently groomed black horses.

The carriage was heavily decorated with flowers including a stunning wreath from West Ham Boxing Club. Olympic rings were attached to one side while Terry's Olympic gold medal and MBE were displayed on a red cushion inside the carriage facing out of the rear window along with a photograph of him. Earlier that morning dozens of other floral tributes arrived including one in the shape of a crown sent by the residents of Upchurch where Terry had his first public house.

About 30 family members and close friends arrived at Terry's house at Chadwell Heath shortly before 1pm and followed as the horse drawn carriage made its way slowly and steadily towards its destination. It passed through Goodmayes and along the Barking Road before stopping for a few moments at the top of Cumberland Road where Terry had lived with his father until Rosemary started to care for him. It then went slowly past the local conservative club where the former boxer went with his father most days before his first major illness.

The next stop for the procession was the Black Horse public house behind which West Ham Boxing Club had been situated for many years. Police stopped both lanes of the traffic outside the club where veteran trainer Mickey May, club secretary Lianne Jameson and a contingent of young boxers, all smartly dressed in their club tracksuits, lined both sides of the road.

Bethell Avenue was crammed with hundreds of mourners who broke into respectful clapping as the horse-drawn carriage approached The Convent. Many more were packed inside for the service conducted by Monseigneur John Armitage. The Convent was chosen because it was the only venue in the locality big enough to hold the anticipated attendance believed to be the biggest in the East End since the passing of the Kray twins. It was good forethought because dozens who attended to pay their final respects had to stand at the back and sides of the building.

As Terry was not a Catholic special permission had to be applied for to use The Convent, but this was quickly bestowed upon him as a tribute to his recognition in the East End. It was yet another example of the esteem in which he was held.

The event was a real boxing occasion as fighters past and present turned up to pay their respects to arguably one of Britain's most popular ringmen. They had travelled from all parts of the country and included a number of former champions. Alan Minter, Alec Johnson, Terry Murphy, Terry Downes, Dave 'Boy' Green, Sammy McCarthy, Bobby Neill, Prince Rodney, Vernon Sollas and Kevin Mitchell headed the list. They were joined by Billy Walker, Tony Hudson, Terry Waller, Johnny Claydon, Vinnie Mitchell, Mark Goult, Ron Cooper, Billy Aird, Mickey Pye, Johnny Kramer, Johnny McKenna, Danny Wells, Phil Lungdren, Jimmy Tibbs, Barry Price, Jarvis Astaire, Harry Holland, Kenny Lynch and former Board of

Control steward, Judge Alan Simpson, who had travelled all the way from Leeds. There was a particularly large contingent of members from Brighton Ex-Boxers Association who were joined by representatives from similar organisations.

Spinks was taken into The Convent to the accompaniment of Nat 'King' Cole's recording of 'Smile'. During a period of quiet refection midway through the service, a recording of Matt Monroe's version of 'If I Never Sing Another Song' was played. This had been selected because the words were considered so relevant to Terry. A huge boxing fan, Matt had been at most of the former Olympians fights. After the service, during which a number of glowing tributes were paid, Spinks was carried out to the fitting Tina Turner song 'Simply the Best'.

The service was followed by burial at the nearby East London Cemetery and despite pouring rain, a cortege of about 200 mourners adhered to an old East End custom of walking to the grave behind the coffin. The procession was headed by West Ham Amateur boxing club captain, Charlie Driscoll, carrying the club flag while other young members walked either side of the horse-drawn carriage.

The day was concluded with a wake at East Ham Working Mens Club, but although the organisers catered for 200, the food ran out within a short time. It continued for several hours with very few in a hurry to leave, a further indication of the respect people had for Spinks.

It had always been expected that donations would be made following his death and a notice was therefore contained in the order of service leaflet that such were made payable to West Ham Boxing Club. Terry never forgot those who helped him reach Olympic champion level and it was therefore appropriate that the club be the beneficiary. It would have been his wish. An amount of £1,100 was collected by way of single personal donations and subsequent local events, one of which was Allsorts Day Nursery Sports Day. In the programme it was stated that all proceeds of the sale of programmes and raffle tickets, would be donated to Rosemary for her chosen charity in memory of Terry.

20

REFLECTIONS

Having battled so bravely for so long it was, in many respects, a happy release when Terry passed away. He was very poorly and nobody wanted to see him in a vegetative state. After all he achieved in life and did for others he deserved to pass with dignity.

As life gradually settled down, those close to Terry were able to reflect on his life with clearer minds. Everyone knew it had been like a roller-coaster, full of ups and downs, but living the good life without any thought for the possible consequences. Although the downs were usually self-inflicted, he never blamed anyone but himself, frequently remarking 'I've had a wonderful life'.

During the ensuing weeks tributes continued to pour in, one of the most moving being on 6 May 2012 at the monthly meeting of Brighton Ex-Boxers Association. Beforehand, a chair, displaying a West Ham United Football shirt, a lighted candle and a photograph of Spinks was placed where he always sat whenever he attended the gatherings. A one minute silence was followed by a heartfelt tribute by chairman, Ernie Price.

It was fitting that within months of his passing both Brighton Ex-Boxers Association and West Ham Amateur Boxing Club saw fit to donate trophies in memory of Terry. Brighton EBA decided that their trophy would be awarded annually to a local person who had done outstanding work for charity. Consequently, at the association's annual convention on 11 August, Jarvis Spinks presented it to the former British and Commonwealth heavyweight champion, Scott Welch.

On 15 September, West Ham ABC's Terry Spinks Memorial Trophy was presented to 18-years-old club captain, Charlie Driscoll, who had been with the club since he was 11, during which time he won numerous national titles.

Carrying the club flag he had led a procession of members from outside their headquarters to The Convent on the day of Terry's funeral. After leading them into and out of the building, he headed the procession to East London Cemetery.

* * *

When Terry announced his retirement from boxing just before Christmas 1962, it was a wise decision as far as his close friends were concerned. By this stage he was taking punches which in his prime he would have avoided. He showed great courage throughout his career, but the terrible accident suffered by Bobby Neill was always on people's minds. Nobody wanted his career to finish like that.

Spinks never let anyone down, and whenever he climbed through the ropes the fans knew he would provide plenty of excitement and an abundance of skill. As an amateur he was never stopped in 200 contests. In the professional ring, Billy Davis was the only Englishman to beat him. His other defeats were inflicted by four Scotsmen, Billy Rafferty, Bobby Neill, John O'Brien and Bobby Fisher, an Irishman and a Welshman, Derry Treanor and Howard Winstone.

When Terry turned professional, many fans believed that if he could maintain the form shown at Melbourne, he could progress to a world title. The professional ring, however, is a very different battleground and only the most dedicated fighters reach the top. Whilst Spinks had tremendous natural talent, his liking for the good life and the wrong food probably destroyed any chance he ever had of becoming a world champion.

For much of his professional career, his body was weakened by weight reducing measures, yet he still pushed himself to the limit. Whenever he was hurt his great fighting heart made him punch back, but if the truth were known his physical strength did not match his spirit. Consequently there were a number of occasions when his stamina ran out while he was still battling hard.

When Spinks was at his peak the world featherweight title was held by Davey Moore of America, against whom he would have had little chance. A fighter of exceptional class and power, Moore took the title from Hogan Bassey in 1959 and held it until March 1963 when he was beaten by Sugar Ramos with such tragic consequences. British fans briefly saw his class in October 1959 when he travelled to London and beat Bobby Neill in two minutes 55 seconds of the opening round. Four months earlier Bobby had knocked Spinks out in nine rounds.

Although boxing had changed dramatically since those days, Terry still loved it and would not have a word said against it. Over the years he was frequently asked if he had any regrets about having been a boxer. His answer was usually the same: 'Definitely not. It gave me the opportunity to earn money and do things I wouldn't have had any chance of doing otherwise.'

He insisted that he owed everything to boxing and would have done it all over again. 'It was the only way to get out of the East End and earn big money,' he remarked. Yet he did have sound advice for any youngster contemplating taking up the sport. 'You must learn to box properly and serve your apprenticeship in the amateur ranks. Then if you like it try being a professional. Give it a go for 18 months or so, but if you can't see a future then my advice is give it up.'

Despite the serious nature of the illnesses he suffered, Terry still had a wonderful long-term memory. Recalling the latter part of his career he confessed that when he was boxing well he always believed his best form would return. 'But I was just kidding myself,' he admitted, 'Just as all the other boxers who think the same are kidding themselves. One of the differences between a good boxer and a bad boxer is that one knows when to quit, the other doesn't.'

Spinks never made any secret of the fact that he always enjoyed the limelight. 'In many ways I missed the excitement and publicity of my boxing days,' he confessed. In fact, throughout his life he talked with great pride about his career whether it was to journalists, on radio and television, or with fans in pubs or at dinner functions.

'I can still feel the thrill I experienced when Mr Onslow Fane, President of the Board of Control, fastened the cold metal of the Lonsdale belt around my sweating waist after taking the featherweight title from Bobby Neill;' he remarked with tremendous pride one day many years after retiring from the ring.

The best fighter he ever saw was Carlos Ortiz. The fight which impressed him most was when Ortiz beat Dave Charnley in London in 1958 before Carlos became world lightweight champion. 'For me, Charnley was Britain's best pound for pound fighter of the post war years,' insisted Spinks. 'But for every three punches he landed,

Ortiz found a way to score with four or five. To do that makes him the greatest in my book.'

Although Terry never lost his desire for a bet it became much more controlled in later life when he was more addicted to the flashing lights of a fruit machine than dogs and horses. 'Lend us a quid,' he often said as his eyes focused on a one-arm bandit in a pub bar. 'I've got a feeling I'm going to win the jackpot.' Given the chance, however, he would never refuse a trip down memory lane to Newmarket racecourse or an evening at an East End dog track.

'I've always been a bit partial to a flutter,' he admitted with a grin. 'My biggest bet? I once put £1000 to win on a horse at Hamilton. It came up, but plenty of others didn't and a lot of my ring earnings went that way.'

Terry was a fighter all of his life, not just in the boxing ring. Having been born in the East End as war threatened, it had to be that way, and his experiences as a child undoubtedly hardened him for the physical and emotional difficulties which lay ahead.

Although he had many successes in the ring, some of his most significant battles involved his personal life in the later years. He conquered his addiction to gambling but his greatest victory was surely when he beat the bottle. Following his original illness in 1993 he did not touch alcohol and whenever he attended an official function or visited pubs he was content drinking non-alcoholic beer, fruit juice or even water.

Despite the tremendous help he received from Rosemary, Terry showed amazing determination and will-power. As a result, he regained all his pride and self-respect. When she first started caring for him he weighed less than seven stones. With no desire to live, he was dirty and unkempt, and had no decent clothes to wear. Gradually, however, he became a chirpy, smiling 12 stoner, clean and immaculately dressed and enjoyed life again.

Although he never made a full recovery from his illness, his progress was incredible. He loved to go out with his mates, particularly Sammy McCarthy and Ron Cooper, who were of tremendous support for Rosemary. For much of the time they talked about the old times, their lives in boxing and the people they've known.

* * *

Terry's life was indeed a huge roller-coaster ride, but despite the agonies he suffered from gambling and drink, he had no regrets and apportioned no blame for his personal set-backs. He accepted life for what it was. Even the serious money problems and broken marriages failed to disillusion him. Apart from the early stages of his original illness when he was not in control of himself, he was rarely dispirited. He considered that he had a wonderful life and would have done the same all over again. As a life-long fan of Frank Sinatra with a sharp sense of humour, he was quick to remark, 'I did it my way.'

The Terry Spinks story represents a real slice of East End folklore. Like his friend Billy Walker a few years later, he had what the public needed and loved. He was hero material - the local boy made good, and was a true professional in every sense of the word. Every time he climbed into the ring, whether it be at a small hall or large arena, the place was packed. He was an Olympic hero and East End character rolled into one. He had a huge following because he gave the fans what they wanted - true value for money.

A typical example of the esteem in which Spinks was held occurred during the summer of 2003. The press officer for Sports Network telephoned Rosemary asking if he would attend an event at the Sheraton Park Tower Hotel, Knightsbridge, to promote the professional signing of promising featherweight boxer Kevin Mitchell. Like Terry he was a gifted amateur with West Ham ABC and during his junior and senior amateur career had been presented with many trophies at annual club awards nights by the former Olympian.

Spinks was taken to the event by his trusted 'minder', Chris Carr, and sat on the top table with Mitchell and promoter, Frank Warren. When asked what he thought of Kevin as a boxer Terry said that he was very gifted and with proper dedication had the natural talent to become a champion.

Mitchell also spoke highly of Terry and in front of the Sky Sports Television cameras told the interviewer that he was one of his boxing idols.

On 17 July 2003 Spinks was a ringside guest of Frank Warren at the Goresbrook Leisure Centre, Dagenham, and was impressed by Mitchell's professional debut which he won by a first round knockout.

Apart from his skills in the boxing ring, Spinks always possessed charm and charisma which earned him respect and admiration throughout his life. He made and lost a lot of money, had countless friends and a host of memories. What people liked about him was that he was always a down-to-earth East End lad. He never changed, and despite the fame he achieved, was just as comfortable among working class folk in an East End pub as mixing with the rich and famous at a West End dinner. He treated everyone alike, and whatever the circumstances was always relaxed and receptive. Even when in poor health he still made tremendous efforts to sign autographs and photographs because he hated letting anyone down.

Despite the serious illnesses he suffered during the later years of his life, Spinks knew only too well the massive part Rosemary played in keeping him alive. For 19 years her life revolved around him and there were times when he was so seriously ill that many people didn't expect him to survive.

Yet she never gave up and was determined to give him every chance to recover. Only the best possible medical treatment was good enough no matter what the cost. By obtaining the services of such skilled and caring professionals as Mr Fary Afshar and Dr John Jestico she certainly ensured that he got it.

Rosemary was afforded the freedom to call either man, day or night, whenever a serious problem occurred with Terry. Before going abroad Mr Afshar would give him a check-up and always told her that if difficulties arose she should call his mobile phone and he would make arrangements with medics in the foreign country. In particular when they were due to go to Cyprus he advised her that if Terry experienced problems she should try to get him to a particular hospital in Nicosia where he had worked and still knew senior staff.

With the passing of time the professional relationship developed into a personal friendship whereby there were occasions when both Mr Afshar and Dr Jestico were invited by Rosemary to private family events. Also in December 2009, when a surprise party was held at a private hall at Chadwell Heath to celebrate the retirement of Dr Jestico from King George's Hospital, Terry, Rosemary and her husband were all invited.

Apart from Mr Afshar and Dr Jestico, Rosemary and her family also received great support from their local GP, Dr Kana and his staff at their surgery. Whenever there were concerns regarding Terry's health they always addressed them as a matter of urgency.

* * *

Terry Spinks was one of the loveliest men anyone could wish to meet. He remains the only British boxer ever to have won Schoolboys, ABA, Olympic and British professional championships and the youngest British boxer to win an Olympic gold medal. To be awarded the MBE after so long was nothing less than he deserved and the trip to Buckingham Palace was the climax of his incredible life. An ambassador for boxing, and sport in general, he will always be remembered as a genuine idol in the East End. The poem engraved on his gravestone so accurately describes Spinks:

Happy, smiling, always content,

Loved and respected wherever he went,

Always so thoughtful, loving and kind

A beautiful memory left behind.

Long may he rest in peace.

BIBLIOGRAPHY

Books

Prior, David, *Ringside with the Amateurs*, Private publication, 1995.

Whiting, George, *Great Fights of the Sixties*, Leslie Frewin, 1967.

Newspapers

Boxing News

Boxing Weekly

Daily Express

Daily Mirror

East London Advertiser

Evening News

Evening Standard

Newmarket Journal

Sporting Life

Stratford Express

The Guardian

The People

The Star

APPENDIX

Terry Spinks Senior Amateur Fighting Record 1955-1957

Date	*Opponent*	*Result*	*Venue*
1955			
Dec 9	G. Rix (Barking)	W Pts 3	Dagenham
1956			
Jan 19	P. Pestaille (St Pancras)	W RSC 1	Romford
Mar 1	John Holt (Repton)	W Pts 3	York Hall
Mar 15	Bernie Dillon (Stepney Inst) (N.E. Div. Semi-Final)	W Disq 2	York Hall
Mar 16	John Holt (Repton) (N.E. Div. Final)	W Pts 3	York Hall
April 9	Ron Rice (Downham) (London ABA Semi-Final)	W RSC 2	Albert Hall
April 9	Eric Secombe (St Pancras) (London ABA Final)	W Pts 3	Albert Hall
April 27	Alex Ambrose (Army) (ABA Flyweight Semi-Final)	W Pts 3	Wembley
April 27	Peter Walsh (Royal Northern) (ABA Flyweight Final)	W Pts 3	Wembley
May 6	Henryk Kukier (ABA v Poland)	L Pts 3	Warsaw
May 8	Janusz Litke (ABA v Poland)	W Pts 3	Gdansk
June 20	Vladimir Stolnikov (ABA v Russia)	L Pts 3	Moscow
June 23	Viktor Bystrov (ABA v Russia)	L Pts 3	Moscow
June 28	Ossi Pavalin (ABA v Finland)	W Pts 3	Helsinki
Aug 31	Waldemar Stephanie (London v Berlin)	W Pts 3	Berlin
Sept 2	Rudolph Waletzko (London v Hanover)	W Pts 3	Hanover
Sept 14	R. Haas (West Ham v Swiss and German Select Team)	W Pts 3	Basle

Oct 6	Frank Spenser (Cannock St Lukes)	W Pts	4	Birmingham
Oct 16	Salvatore Manca (London v Rome)	L Pts	3	Albert Hall
Oct 22	Eric Secombe (Times)	W Pts	4	Manor Place Baths
Nov 24	Sammy Harris (Pakistan) (Olympic First Series)	W Pts	3	Melbourne
Nov 26	Abel Landonio (Argentina) (Olympic Second Series)	W Pts	3	Melbourne
Nov 28	Vladimir Stolnikov (USSR) (Olympic Quarter-Finals)	W Pts	3	Melbourne
Nov 30	Rene Libeer (France) (Olympic Semi-Finals)	W Pts	3	Melbourne
Dec 1	Mircia Dobrescu (Rumania) (Olympic Flyweight Final)	W Pts	3	Melbourne
1957				
Feb 28	Laurie McKay (Scotland)	W Pts	4	West Ham Baths

(Announced that he was turning professional)

Senior Amateur Summary

Bouts Taken	26
Won	22
Lost	4

Terry Spinks Professional Fighting Record 1957-1963

Date	*Opponent*	*Result*	*Venue*
1957			
April 9	Jim Loughrey	W RSC 4	Harringay
April 30	Jerry Parker	W Pts 6	Manor Place Baths
May 14	Billy Kane	W RSC 2	Shoreditch
June 4	Jerry Parker	W Pts 6	Harringay
July 16	Pat Clancy	W Ret 3	Shoreditch
Aug 12	Jerry Parker	W Pts 6	Southampton
Aug 27	George McDade	W Ret 3	Canning Town
Sept 10	Ivan McCready	W Pts 8	Shoreditch
Oct 8	Pancho Bhatachaji	W Pts 8	Royal Albert Hall
Dec 2	Stanislas Sobolak	W RSC 6	Leyton Baths
Dec 10	Malcolm McLeod	W Pts 8	Harringay
1958			
Jan 14	Malcolm McLeod	W Ret 3	Empress Hall
Feb 6	George McDade	W Pts 8	Liverpool
Mar 11	Attia Ben Aissa	W KO 7	Streatham
Mar 31	Alex Bollaert	W Pts 8	Leyton Baths
April 15	Eric Brett	W Pts 8	Harringay
April 29	Henry Schmidt	W Pts 8	Shoreditch
May 20	Pierre Cossemyns	W Pts 8	Empress Hall
July 15	Terry Toole	W RSC 7	Streatham
Aug 28	Billy Rafferty	L RSC 5	Paisley Ice Rink
Oct 7	Eddie O'Connor	W Pts 8	Shoreditch
Nov 27	Mohammad Zarzi	W Pts 8	Seymour Hall
Dec 5	Pat Supple	W Pts 10	Wembley
1959			
Jan 12	Sugar Ray	W KO 7	Earls Court
Jan 26	Eddie Burns	W RSC 5	Leyton Baths
Feb 26	Con Mount Bassie	W Pts 8	Leyton Baths
Mar 24	Pierre Cossemyns	W Pts 10	Streatham
Apr 13	Eric Brett	W Pts 8	Nottingham
June 2	Bobby Neill	L KO 9	Wembley
Sept 1	Derry Treanor	L Pts 8	Streatham
Sept 15	John O'Brien	L Pts 12	Wembley
	(British featherweight championship eliminator)		
Dec 7	George Dormer	W Pts 8	Leyton Baths
1960			
Jan 18	Junior Cassidy	W Pts 8	Leyton Baths

Jan 26	Johnny Kidd	W Pts 12	Olympia
	(British featherweight championship eliminator)		
May 31	Roy Jacobs	Drew 10	Wembley
June 13	Dave Croll	W Pts 8	Walthamstow
Sept 27	Bobby Neill	W RSC 7	Royal Albert Hall
	(won British featherweight championship)		
Nov 22	Bobby Neill	W KO 14	Wembley
	(retained British featherweight championship)		
1961			
Mar 7	Dave Hilton	W Disq 7	Wembley
May 2	Howard Winstone	L Ret 10	Wembley
	(lost British featherweight championship)		
Oct 3	Kimpo Amarfio	W Pts 8	N.S.C.
Oct 25	Con Mount Bassie	W Pts 8	Cardiff
1962			
Feb 7	Eugene Lecozannet	W Pts 8	Seymour Hall
Feb 15	Ron Jones	W Pts 8	West Ham Baths
Mar 6	Jean Biosca	W Pts 8	Seymour Hall
Mar 27	Billy Davis	W Pts 8	Wembley
May 22	Billy Davis	L Pts 10	Wembley
July 17	Bobby Fisher	L RSC 7	Finsbury Park
Dec 11	Johnny Mantle	W RSC 8	Royal Albert Hall

Career Summary

Bouts Taken	49
Won	41
Drawn	1
Lost	7